American Sexual Histories

BLACKWELL READERS IN AMERICAN SOCIAL AND CULTURAL HISTORY

Series Editor: Jacqueline Jones, Brandeis University

The *Blackwell Readers in American Social and Cultural History* series introduces students to well-defined topics in American history from a socio-cultural perspective. Using primary and secondary sources, the volumes present the most important works available on a particular topic in a succinct and accessible format designed to fit easily into courses offered in American history or American studies.

1   *POPULAR CULTURE IN AMERICAN HISTORY*
edited by Jim Cullen

2   *AMERICAN INDIANS*
edited by Nancy Shoemaker

3   *THE CIVIL RIGHTS MOVEMENT*
edited by Jack E. Davis

4   *THE OLD SOUTH*
edited by Mark M. Smith

5   *AMERICAN RADICALISM*
edited by Daniel Pope

6   *AMERICAN SEXUAL HISTORIES*
edited by Elizabeth Reis

7   *AMERICAN TECHNOLOGY*
edited by Carroll Pursell

American Sexual Histories

Edited by

Elizabeth Reis

Copyright © Blackwell Publishers Ltd 2001; editorial matter and
organization copyright © Elizabeth Reis 2001

First published 2001

2 4 6 8 10 9 7 5 3 1

Blackwell Publishers Inc.
350 Main Street
Malden, Massachusetts 02148
USA

Blackwell Publishers Ltd
108 Cowley Road
Oxford OX4 1JF
UK

Library of Congress Cataloging-in-Publication Data

American sexual histories / edited by Elizabeth Reis.
p. cm.—(Blackwell readers in American social and cultural history; 6)
Includes bibliographical references and index.
ISBN 0–631–22080–1 (alk. paper)—ISBN 0–631–22081–X (pb)
1. Sex customs—United States—History. 2. Sex customs—United
States—History—Sources. I. Reis, Elizabeth, 1958– II. Series.

HQ18.U5 A458 2001
306.7'0973—dc21   00–060796

British Library Cataloguing in Publication Data
A CIP catalogue record for this book is available from the British Library.

Typeset in 10 on 12 Pt Plantin
by Kolam Information Services Pvt. Ltd., Pondicherry, India
Printed in Great Britain by TJ International, Padstow, Cornwall

This book is printed on acid-free paper.

Contents

Series Editor's Preface   x

Acknowledgments   xii

About the Contributors   xiii

Introduction   I

PART I   EARLY AMERICA

I   **THINGS FEARFUL TO NAME**   13
     Introduction

     "Things Fearful to Name": Bestiality in Early America   14
     John Murrin

     Document A: Of Plymouth Plantation: the Pilgrims   35
     in America   *William Bradford*

     Document B: Records of the Colony and Plantation of New   37
     Haven, from 1638 to 1649   *Charles J. Hoadly*

     Further Reading   44

2   **EROTICIZING THE MIDDLE GROUND**   45
     Introduction

     Eroticizing the Middle Ground: Anglo-Indian   46
     Relations along the Eighteenth-century Frontier
     Richard Godbeer

Document A: John Rolfe to Sir Thomas Dale, April 1614   64

Document B: A New Voyage to Carolina   68
John Lawson

Document C: Quebec to Carolina in 1785–1786   70
Robert Hunter, Jr

Further Reading   71

3   **GIRLING OF IT**   **72**
    Introduction

"Girling of It" in Eighteenth-century New Hampshire   73
Laurel Thatcher Ulrich and Lois K. Stabler

Document A: Bundling: Its Origins,   85
Progress, and Decline in America   *Henry Reed Stiles*

Document B: The Ladies Library   87

Document C: Female Policy Detected, or the Arts   89
of a Designing Woman Laid Open   *Edward Ward*

Further Reading   90

PART II   NINETEENTH CENTURY

4   **THE PSYCHOLOGY OF FREE LOVE**   **93**
    Introduction

The Psychology of Free Love: Sexuality   94
in the Oneida Community   *Lawrence Foster*

Document A: History of American Socialisms   109
John Humphrey Noyes

Document B: Male Continence   110
John Humphrey Noyes

Further Reading   114

5   **MINISTERIAL MISDEEDS**   **116**
    Introduction

Ministerial Misdeeds: the Onderdonk Trial and Sexual   117
Harassment in the 1840s   *Patricia Cline Cohen*

Document A: Trial of the Right Rev. Benjamin   134
T. Onderdonk, D.D., Bishop of New York

Document B: De Darkie's Comic Al-Me-Nig   144

Further Reading   144

6   WHITE WOMEN, BLACK MEN, AND ADULTERY   145
      IN THE ANTEBELLUM SOUTH
      Introduction

      Adultery: Dorothea Bourne and Edmond   146
      Martha Hodes

      Document A: Lewis Bourne Divorce Petition   165

      Further Reading   168

PART III   EARLY TWENTIETH CENTURY

7   HYSTERIA   171
      Introduction

      Hysteria: the Revolt of the "Good Girl"   172
      Elizabeth Lunbeck

      Document A: The Case of Miss A   *L. E. Emerson*   190

      Further Reading   196

8   CHRISTIAN BROTHERHOOD OR SEXUAL   198
      PERVERSION?
      Introduction

      Christian Brotherhood or Sexual Perversion?   199
      Homosexual Identities and the Construction
      of Sexual Boundaries in the World War I Era
      George Chauncey, Jr

      Document A: Alleged Immoral Conditions and   217
      Practices at the Naval Training Station, Newport,
      Rhode Island

      Document B: The Intersexes: a History of   221
      Similisexualism   *Edward Irenaeus Prime Stevenson*

      Document C: Sexual Perversion, Satyriasis, and   224
      Nymphomania   *G. Frank Lydston*

      Further Reading   226

9   ABOUT TO MEET HER MAKER   227
      Introduction

      "About to Meet Her Maker": Women, Doctors,   228
      Dying Declarations, and the State's Investigation of
      Abortion, Chicago, 1867–1940   *Leslie J. Reagan*

      Document A: A Maryland Abortionist Gets No Pardon   246

Document B: Dying Declarations Obtained in Abortion Case as Condition to Rendering Aid 247

Document C: Comments of "Esther E." 248

Further Reading 249

10 CONTRACEPTIVE CONSUMERS 250
Introduction

Contraceptive Consumers: Gender and the Political Economy of Birth Control in the 1930s *Andrea Tone* 251

Document A: Advertisements for Lysol 269

Document B: Facts and Frauds in Women's Hygiene *Rachel Lynn Palmer and Sarah K. Greenberg* 271

Document C: What Do the American Women Think about Birth Control? *Henry F. Pringle* 273

Document D: The Accident of Birth 278

Further Reading 279

PART IV MODERN AMERICA

11 MIXING BODIES AND CULTURES 283
Introduction

Mixing Bodies and Cultures: the Meaning of America's Fascination with Sex between "Orientals" and "Whites" *Henry Yu* 284

Document A: A Stanford Girl Weds a Chinese 299

Document B: My Oriental Husbands *Mrs Emma Fong Kuno* 301

Document C: Why Japanese and Americans Should Not Intermarry 304

Document D: Intermarriage: Standpoint and Tentative Questionnaire – Confidential 306

Further Reading 309

12 THE SEXUALIZED WOMAN 310
Introduction

The Sexualized Woman: the Lesbian, the Prostitute, and the Containment of Female Sexuality in Postwar America *Donna Penn* 311

Document A: Variations in Sexual Behavior: a   327
Psychodynamic Study of Deviations in Various
Expressions of Sexual Behavior   *Frank Caprio*

Document B: I Am a Homosexual Woman   330
Jane McKinnon

Document C: The Detective   *James Mills*   334

Document D: Beebo Brinker   *Ann Bannon*   339

Further Reading   341

**13   THE POPULATION BOMB AND THE SEXUAL   342
       REVOLUTION**
Introduction

The Population Bomb and the Sexual Revolution: 343
Toward Choice   *Rickie Solinger*

Document A: The Slavery of Sex Freedom: 365
America's Moral Crisis   *Howard Whitman*

Document B: Are We Still Stereotyping the Unmarried   368
Mother?   *Rose Bernstein*

Document C: Population Crisis: Hearings before the   371
Subcommittee on Foreign Aid Expenditures of the
Committee on Government Operations

Further Reading   374

14   SEX CHANGE AND THE POPULAR PRESS   376
Introduction

Sex Change and the Popular Press: 377
Historical Notes on Transsexuality in the
United States, 1930–1955   *Joanne Meyerowitz*

Document A: Girl Changes into Man   398

Document B: Psychopathia Transexualis   401
Dr D. O. Cauldwell

Document C: New Sex Switches: 406
Behind the Sensational Headlines Loom
Unpleasant Medical Facts

Document D: I Want to Become a Woman   408

Further Reading   409

Index   **410**

Series Editor's Preface

The purpose of the Blackwell Readers in American Social and Cultural History is to introduce students to cutting-edge historical scholarship that draws upon a variety of disciplines, and to encourage students to "do" history themselves by examining some of the primary texts upon which that scholarship is based.

Each of us lives life with a wholeness that is at odds with the way scholars often dissect the human experience. Anthropologists, psychologists, literary critics, and political scientists (to name just a few) study only discrete parts of our existence. The result is a rather arbitrary collection of disciplinary boundaries enshrined not only in specialized publications but also in university academic departments and in professional organizations.

As a scholarly enterprise, the study of history necessarily crosses these boundaries of knowledge in order to provide a comprehensive view of the past. Over the last few years, social and cultural historians have reached across the disciplines to understand the history of the British North American colonies and the United States in all its fullness. Unfortunately, much of that scholarship, published in specialized monographs and journals, remains inaccessible to undergraduates. Consequently, instructors often face choices that are not very appealing – to ignore the recent scholarship altogether, assign bulky readers that are too detailed for an undergraduate audience, or cobble together packages of recent articles that lack an overall contextual framework. The individual volumes of this series each focus on a significant topic in American history, and bring new, exciting scholarship to students in a compact, accessible format.

The series is designed to complement textbooks and other general readings assigned in undergraduate courses. Each editor has culled particularly innovative and provocative scholarly essays from widely scattered books and journals, and provided an introduction summarizing the major themes of the essays and documents that follow. The essays reproduced here were chosen because of the authors' innovative (and often interdisciplinary) methodology and their ability to reconceptualize historical issues in fresh and insightful ways. Thus students can appreciate the rich complexity of an historical topic and the way that scholars have explored the topic from different perspectives, and in the process transcend the highly artificial disciplinary boundaries that have served to compartmentalize knowledge about the past in the United States.

Also included in each volume are primary texts, at least some of which have been drawn from the essays themselves. By linking primary and secondary material, the editors are able to introduce students to the historian's craft, allowing them to explore this material in depth, and draw additional insights – or interpretations contrary to those of the scholars under discussion – from it. Suggestions for further reading offer depth to the analysis.

Jacqueline Jones
Brandeis University

Acknowledgments

I would like to thank the contributors to this book for their help and encouragement. All of them gave me good advice as to which documents to include here, and some went beyond the call of duty and dug out primary sources from their own file cabinet archives. Their insightful scholarship has informed my thinking on the issues of sex and sexuality, and I value their friendship and collegiality.

I am grateful to Jacqueline Jones, Susan Rabinowitz, Ken Provencher, and the anonymous readers at Blackwell for their guidance. I also appreciate the suggestions offered by Diane Baxter, Howard Brick, Cynthia Eller, Ellen Herman, Peggy Pascoe, Judith Raiskin, Pamela Tamarkin Reis, Sharon Ullman, and Mary Wood. As usual, my husband, Matthew Dennis, devoted himself to me, putting aside his own research and writing to help with every aspect of this project. With love, I dedicate this book to him and to our children, Sam and Leah.

About the Contributors

George Chauncey Jr is Professor of History and Director of the Lesbian and Gay Studies Project of the Center for Gender Studies at the University of Chicago. He is the author of *Gay New York: Gender, Urban Culture, and the Making of the Gay Male World* (1994) and the coeditor of *Hidden from History* (1989) and *Thinking Sexuality Transnationally* (1999), and is currently finishing *The Strange Career of the Closet: Gay Culture, Consciousness, and Politics from the Second World War to the Gay Liberation Era*.

Patricia Cline Cohen is a professor of history at the University of California at Santa Barbara. Her most recent book is *The Murder of Helen Jewett: The Life and Death of a Prostitute in Nineteenth-century New York* (1998). Her current research is on gender and travel in the era of the transportation revolution, 1790 to 1860.

Lawrence Foster is an American social historian at Georgia Institute of Technology in Atlanta. His first book, *Religion and Sexuality* (1981) uses comparative anthropological perspectives to analyze the introduction of new forms of marriage, family life, and sex roles in the celibate Shakers, "free love" Oneida, and polygamous Mormon communities in nineteenth-century America. His second book, *Women, Family, and Utopia* (1991), further explores the impact of these groups on the lives of women. He is currently editing a third book on the origin of the Oneida Community, entitled *The Turbulence of Free Love*.

Richard Godbeer is Associate Professor of History at University of California, Riverside. He is the author of *The Devil's Dominion: Magic* *and Religion in Early New England* (1992) and he is completing a book on attitudes toward sex in early America.

Martha Hodes is Assistant Professor of History at New York University. She is the author of the prize-winning *White Women, Black Men: Illicit Sex in the Nineteenth-century South* (1997), and the editor of *Sex, Love, Race: Crossing Boundaries in North American History* (1999). She is the recipient of fellowships from the National Endowment for the Humanities, the American Council of Learned Societies, and the Schomburg Center for Research in Black Culture of the New York Public Library.

Elizabeth Lunbeck is Associate Professor of History at Princeton University. She is the author of the prize-winning *The Psychiatric Persuasion: Knowledge, Gender, and Power in Modern America* (1994), and is currently working on a history of the borderline personality.

Joanne Meyerowitz teaches history at Indiana University and edits the *Journal of American History*. She is the author of *Women Adrift: Independent Wage Earners in Chicago, 1880–1930* (1988) and the editor of *Not June Cleaver: Women and Gender in Postwar America, 1945–1960* (1994). She is currently writing a history of transsexuality in the USA.

Donna Penn has published several articles on the social construction of lesbianism in the postwar USA. Her work has appeared in several publications, including *Radical History Review, Gender and History,* and *Gender and American History since 1890,* ed. Barbara Melosh.

Leslie J. Reagan is Associate Professor at the University of Illinois, with a joint appointment in the Department of History and the College of Medicine's Medical Humanities and Social Sciences Program. She is the author of the prize-winning *When Abortion Was a Crime: Women, Medicine, and Law in the United States, 1867–1973* (1997) and "Crossing the Border for Abortions: California Activists, Mexican Clinics, and the Creation of a Feminist Health Agency in the 1960s," in *Feminist Studies,* Summer 2000. She is currently working on several projects, including histories of miscarriage, breast cancer, and the cultural practice of examining the body for evidence of disease and crime.

Elizabeth Reis teaches history and women's studies at the University of Oregon. She is the author of *Damned Women: Sinners and Witches in Puritan New England* (1997) and the editor of *Spellbound: Women and Witchcraft in America* (1998). She is currently researching the history of angel belief in America.

Rickie Solinger is the author of *Wake up Little Susie: Single Pregnancy and Race before Roe v. Wade* (2nd edn 2000); *The Abortionist: a Woman* *against the Law* (1994); and a number of articles about reproductive politics in the USA. Her new book, *Beggars and Choosers: How the Politics of Choice Shapes Abortion, Adoption, and Welfare in the United States*, will be published in 2001. Solinger is the editor of *Abortion Wars: a Half-century of Struggle, 1950–2000* (1998).

Lois K. Stabler is a retired high school teacher and the editor of *Very Poor and of Lo Make: the Journal of Abner Sanger* (1986).

Andrea Tone teaches history at the Georgia Institute of Technology. She is the author of *The Business of Benevolence: Industrial Paternalism in Progressive America* and the editor of *Controlling Reproduction: an American History* (1997). She is finishing *Devices and Desires*, a book on the social history of the American birth control industry, and starting a project on women, tranquilizers, and Cold War technology.

Laurel Thatcher Ulrich is Phillips Professor of Early American History at Harvard University and the author of a number of articles and books in women's history, including *A Midwife's Tale: the Life of Martha Ballard Based on Her Diary, 1785–1812*, which won the Pulitzer Prize for History in 1991. She is completing a book on textiles in early America.

Henry Yu teaches US history and Asian American studies at UCLA. He is the author of *Thinking Orientals: Migration, Contact and Exoticism in Modern America* (2001), and is currently working on a book entitled *How Tiger Woods Lost His Stripes*.

Introduction

Elizabeth Reis

Sex has a history. Sex and sexuality are "historical," not merely because – obviously – humans have engaged in sexual relations from the beginning of time, but because history itself is not merely the past but what people have made of it. History is representation and interpretation of past events and processes; it is narrative and analysis of earlier times, persons, and situations. If the past is settled and cannot now change, historical depictions certainly can and must as humanity itself changes, embraces new assumptions, and asks new questions of its ancestors and their times. Given the fact that sexual practices, related in various ways to reproduction and to bodily pleasure, have always been with us, and given our historically informed sense that our world evolves and changes, it is understandable that ideas and behaviors regarding sexuality have changed as well. In short, though universal, sexuality is not immutable. We do not need Sigmund Freud to tell us that humans have been concerned – even obsessed – with sex, but we would do well to make such attention to sex a focus of historical analysis, as did the historians represented in this book. Moreover, as their essays illustrate, sexuality has an *American* history, a story of great importance and complexity.

Historians concern themselves fundamentally with tracing and analyzing change over time. How have sexual behaviors and attitudes toward these behaviors changed throughout American history? People have continually engaged in forms of heterosexual sex, homosexual sex, and masturbation; they have used birth control, been raped, and had abortions. But how the frequency and nature, the acceptance or disapproval, of such practices have varied over time is not always clear. As interpretations and applications of moral values shift, the sexual matters to which they are applied take on new meanings and implications. The material nature of life in colonial America and the United States – how people make a living, where and how they live, the things they make, buy, and use – itself has changed dramatically, affecting all aspects of existence, including sexual mores and sexual behaviors. This volume explores the changing history of sexuality in America as a product of a dialogue between such values and shifting material circumstances.

Frank discussion of sexuality has often been veiled by a cloak of reticence. Most historical actors left little trace of their sexual practices and of how they felt about their behavior, making it impossible to uncover the full range of sexual behavior in the past. Nor can we hope to recover fully its meanings to participants. Words left behind from earlier eras do not always carry the same meanings they do today, and sexual partners most likely related to each other in ways not always comparable to those of our own era. Even when there are traces, historians face the challenge of reading the tracks carefully and critically, in a way that speaks to us yet respects specific historical contexts. Intimate relations have shown continuity but also dramatic change over time in America, and it is our challenge (whether as students or as professional historians) to analyze these significant but elusive matters with care and imagination.

There have always been clashes between moral prescriptions, scientific pronouncements, governmental policies, economic conditions, and individuals' actual practice. In fact, in these public dissonances historians can sometimes discover a good deal about the competing ideals as well as the imperfect realities of human life. Through communally constructed sexual categories (which change and are not always clearly articulated or defined), we classify people and make assumptions about how we should understand and treat them. Indeed we use the categories we find in our social worlds to define ourselves. Such categories are often understood as basic, even biological, but in fact they are specific to particular cultural worlds, which vary over place and time. Sexual markers – male and female, married and unmarried, or gay and straight, for example – help to set social boundaries, order communal life, and establish or protect political power. Often we see normality defined in sexual terms, and often its nature is articulated only negatively, in opposition to people and behaviors accused of (and punished for their alleged) deviance or perversity. Thus the perceived margins define the supposed mainstream; that which is somehow considered indecent establishes what is "moral." For this reason, historians of sexuality have studied the exceptional and transgressive, not simply to confront the full range of American experiences, but to contribute to our understanding of "normal," "mainstream," everyday life. By studying the supposedly abnormal, we learn how the shifting boundaries of normality have been differentiated, maintained, and policed.

Attitudes toward sex play a significant role in setting and maintaining the frontiers of gender, ethnicity, race, class, and religion, even the threshold that separates childhood from adulthood. Sexual definitions of persons, associated with particular genders, ethnic groups, racial categories, classes, or religions, serve selective interests, enhancing some parties while denigrating others.[1] For example, it was widely believed in seventeenth-century New England that women, like the biblical Eve, were easily beguiled. As historian Laurel Thatcher Ulrich has shown, Puritan writers represented women as weak and unstable by nature, susceptible to suggestion and temptation. Women were understood to be physically and sexually vulnerable, easily aroused and quick to succumb. Yet by the mid-eighteenth century, in New England and throughout the Anglo-American world, the sexual system of expectations and prescriptions for male and female sexual comportment had altered to the point that women were increasingly reckoned as forces for purity in society. Like the character in Samuel Richardson's novel *Pamela*, women represented chastity, innocence, and virtue, bridling the sensuality and carnality of men.[2] Americans' sexualized sense of the natures of women and men would continue to shift through the nineteenth and twentieth centuries.

Similarly, race as a concept and category employed by Americans has always been infused with sexual implications. Here we see notions of sex in symbiosis with race used to define otherness, often to demonize it, and to subordinate entire groups of people. That Native American men virtually never raped female captives (common practice among Europeans), for example, was initially understood providentially, as a direct intervention of God to save colonial women. Soon, however, the restraint of Indian men was interpreted by whites as a mark against their virility. Thomas Jefferson, in his *Notes on the State of Virginia* (1785), leapt to the defense of native inhabitants of America against the theories of George Louis Leclerc, Comte de Buffon. The French scholar had declared that "the savage is feeble, and has small organs of generation; he has neither hair nor beard, and no ardor whatever for his female.... Physical love constitutes their only morality; their heart is icy, their society cold, and their rule harsh. ... They are indifferent because they have little sexual capacity, and this indifference to the other sex is the fundamental defect which weakens their nature, prevents its development, and ... uproots society at the same time." Though

Jefferson disputed Buffon's charges, he nonetheless wrote of African Americans in similarly derisive sexual terms: "They are more ardent [than whites] after their female: but love seems with them to be more an eager desire, than a tender delicate mixture of sentiment and sensation." In both racial descriptions, sexuality is implicated and deployed as a weapon to demean and subordinate. By defining the extremes of men's ardor – too little or too much among red and black "savages" – scholars like Buffon and Jefferson located normality precisely in terms of white, male, Western civilization.[3]

Sexual labeling and sexualized evaluations used to distinguish members of society, ordering, ranking, and controlling people in the process, can be observed in the realm of religion as well. Building on ancient tropes, anti-Catholic writers impugn Catholic priests' celibacy and charge priests with lechery indulged with nuns or with homosexual acts with boys or fellow priests. Anti-Semitic myths of Jewish male effeminacy and weakness similarly used sexualized allegations to attack Jews as morally and physically inferior. Perhaps the greatest perceived offense against civilized Christian order in nineteenth-century America emerged with the rise of Mormonism, particularly its polygamous marriage practices. Religious persecution, like those attacks inspired by misogynous, ethnocentric, or racist feelings (or by class-based prejudices, which could easily be illustrated as well), employed sexualized language and operated in a polemic infused with sexual meaning.

The language and discourse of sex, and its variations throughout American history, is a topic of some importance, giving the lie to the children's adage "Sticks and stones can break my bones, but words can never hurt me." Words can hurt. Words and labels can also be used to liberate, and the absence of words can sometimes conceal and protect. In the nineteenth century it was considered improper for women to talk about sex, and this reticence, reflected in the sources, has led historians to debate for years whether or not Victorian women were actively sexual. Did they embody prescribed middle-class prudishness towards sex, or did they disregard such strictures in private and allow themselves to enjoy their bodies sexually? It is hard to imagine that nineteenth-century women did not appreciate sexual relations or masturbation, even if they did not talk openly about their sexual experiences. Does an altered sexual grammar and lexicon actually effect, enable, or curtail sexual expression and experience? Did historical actors do those things which lacked a name or words to describe them? Does language and discourse merely reflect, or does it actually construct behavior? Many tend to attribute sexual liberation to a more frank, open atmosphere surrounding discussion of these issues. Today, books, videos, magazines, television, film, every venue of popular culture display a veritable how-to manual for enjoying our sex lives. Yet, despite this candor, not everyone lives a life of sexual satisfaction. Similarly, we must not assume that in periods of public sexual reserve everyone led lives of sexual restriction and inhibition. As the French theorist Michel Foucault has suggested, sex talk does not equal sexual freedom or pleasure. As historians, we should assess the impact of public discussion and display, but we must not make unwarranted assumptions regarding private sexual philosophy and practice.

We can see the changing understanding of sexual orientation, and perhaps transformations in sexual practices as well, in the emergence of an increasingly public homosexual presence in modern America. It has become possible for women and men to live their lives as homosexuals, to reject conventional marriage and remake domestic and public life. The shift to a more liberal attitude concerning sexual expression characteristic of the twentieth century parallels another shift: the evolution of identity politics in America. Collectively, through political action, homosexuality has become less a complex of specific sexual acts and more an identity. By their perceived ability to vote as a block, homosexuals have gained political clout and, with it, increased legitimacy and respectability, even though gays and lesbians continue to be reviled in many corners of contemporary America.

Lately scholars and transgender activists have questioned the core of identity politics. What does it mean "to be" male or female, woman or man, straight or gay? Until recently we have assumed that to be male or female (our biological sex) was fixed and that becoming girls, boys, men, and women just happened "naturally." This paradigm has been challenged, and a consensus is emerging (amid continued debate) that the process of "becoming" a gender is, in part, culturally constructed and performative. Today, transgendered people – those who seek to alter their bodies' physical shapes and their gender expressions as well as those who are born intersexed, with indeterminate genitalia – are proving that even what we think of as "givens" – our bodies – are just as malleable and open to interpretation as our behavior. Transgendered identities, just like gay, lesbian, or bisexual identities, require a language that is just now developing. In a politically charged act, some scholars and activists have embraced and rehabilitated the label "queer" to express some of the ambiguities and possibilities of this fluid sexual world.

Throughout American history, values and assumptions about sex became manifest in the execution of policy and legislation that sought to regulate sexual expression. We are not surprised to learn of colonial courts in Connecticut or Massachusetts prosecuting subjects for fornication, adultery, or sodomy. But given our sense of the ways that American society liberalized in the nineteenth and twentieth centuries, when it has become possible for some to step out of the closet, even into public life, we might not expect to find anti-sodomy legislation – that is, prohibition of same-sex acts between consenting adults – still on the books as late as 1998 in places as disparate as Georgia and Rhode Island. It would be a mistake, therefore, to see the history of sexuality simply as a steady progression from a harsh, rigidly enforced puritanical regime of yesteryear to a liberal, enlightened, free, and tolerant milieu of today.

Nor can we conclude that intervention of the state into the intimate matters of sexuality has necessarily abated, that greater sexual freedom has been a result of increased sexual privacy, as such a liberalizing trend might suggest. In the colonial period, for example, women practiced both abortion and birth control with no fear of legal hindrance because neither was illegal; abortion was practiced without shame before "quickening," the moment when a woman felt the fetus move inside the uterus. Governmental intervention escalated only in the nineteenth century. In 1873, the Comstock Law prohibited both birth control and abortion, making it illegal to have in one's possession any "obscene" articles, including instruments, visual images, printed material, and drugs relating to contraception and abortion. By 1900 abortion was illegal in every state, except when employed under special therapeutic circumstances. Times have changed. Yet even today the progress that women have made in controlling their own reproductive lives is clouded by continuing challenges to the legality of abortion ensured by the 1973 Supreme Court decision in *Roe* v. *Wade*.

Just as we cannot claim the progressive disinvestment of the state in private matters of sexuality, neither can we deduce that new reproductive or contraceptive options for women have been introduced or employed purely for their benefit. Certainly technological innovations have allowed women to distinguish their sexual and reproductive lives. The vulcanization of rubber that permitted the mass production of condoms, for example, or the invention of the birth control pill in 1960, potentially offered women (and men) a freedom of action they had not previously enjoyed. But new sexual technologies were not necessarily used to liberate women. Eugenicists and other birth control advocates in the 1920s and 1930s worried about the decline in the birth rate among the white middle class, for example, calling the phenomenon "race suicide." They advocated sterilization of women of color and indigent women and promoted birth control for limiting the birth of "defectives." Even today, black women's reproductive lives can be affected by racism. The coercive prescription of Norplant (a long-acting contraceptive implanted in the arm) to black women on welfare is just one example of how public policy confronts sexuality in highly problematic ways. Such social engineering defines black women's birth rates as a social problem, by implication the result of their supposedly uncontrollable sexuality and greed for entitlements, and intervenes to control them. Trends in state involvement in sexual matters remain unclear, however, as the contemporary United States witnesses shifting campaigns for and against abortion rights and contraception, new regulations and approaches toward sexual harassment, and changing frontiers in the debates over free speech and pornography. It will be left to future historians of sexuality to sort out these and other matters, like the impact of the Internet on America's sexual history.

The history of sexuality in America provides strong arguments that our contemporary ideas about sex are culturally constructed, as they are elsewhere. If the essays and documents collected here prove one point about that history, it is that at various times Americans have had strikingly different ideas about what constituted "normal" sexual interactions. Rather than seeing sexuality as a constant, transcending the boundaries of time and place, contemporary scholars consider it the product of specific material, historical, political, and cultural circumstances. The topics covered here reflect scholars' commitments to expansive and inclusive inquiry. The articles and documents chosen incorporate a broad range of subjects, including the histories and meanings of marital sex, birth control, abortion, homosexuality, sexual harassment, transgender identities, constructions of race and sex, and intermarriage. They survey the history of consensual sex between adults, both heterosexual and same-sex couples, and they address the history of forced sex, of unwanted sexual advances. Unfortunately, there are a number of subjects – for example, the history of masturbation and pornography – that this collection cannot include, not for reasons of lesser importance but for exigencies of space. Among the greatest challenges facing an editor of a volume like this is what to leave out.

While the essays in this work are diverse in their treatment of the history of sexuality in America, they nonetheless agree in several areas. If sexuality is a historical phenomenon, not a timeless, unchanging force, it is also a public matter. Though we typically consider sexual acts to be private, they have public implications which make them the subject of discussion, debate, and deliberations by courts and congresses. Moreover, communal standards of what is "normal" and "right" may shape private expression of sexuality, whether or not such prescriptions and restrictions are written into legal codes. Throughout American history women and men have had to confront personal and public representations and opinions of sexuality, and how they have done so is a chief subject of this anthology.

The essays included necessarily stress conflict, focusing on those times and places in which people's sexual desires or identities have challenged prevailing behavioral norms or in which social boundaries and proscriptions have attempted to dictate individual sexual practices. It is precisely during these contested moments that rules and practices are often defined or redefined. The collected essays locate specific historical moments when issues of sexuality took prominence and cultural constructions were questioned or contradicted. Some topics, like the relationship between sexuality and Christianization of Indians during the colonial period, or the emergence of new homosexual identities in the twentieth century, are specific to certain historical times; others, like the relationship between marriage and sexuality, are themes that persist throughout American history. As a matter of convenience or to highlight the origins of continuing debates, however, I have had to make difficult choices and divide the book into sections, placing consideration of some topics in particular chronological periods.

Paired with each essay are primary source documents, in most cases some of the same documents analyzed by the essays' authors. Reading such material connects students directly to the historical situations studied and exposes them to the methodological problems of assessing and interpreting evidence. Instructors may wish to utilize the source documents as an opportunity to explore the process of historical detection and appraisal. Thus, while surveying a range of historical literature analyzing the meanings and practices of sex among American women and men from the colonial period to the present, students should also be able to glimpse how historians work. Reading these primary sources may prod some students to challenge the particular interpretations offered here and to venture alternative conclusions. Above all, students should grasp that our understanding of sexuality has been an important foundation for the social construction of gender and race, of cultural identity and difference, that beliefs and standards have varied over time, and that sexual matters have been the focus of significant concern, debate, and conflict throughout American history.

Notes

1 See, for example, Keith Thomas, "The double standard," *Journal of the History of Ideas*, 20 (1959), 195–216, which argues that the double sexual standard in early modern European society was basic to a hierarchical system which subordinated women to men.
2 See Laurel Thatcher Ulrich, *Good Wives: Images and Realities in the Lives of Women in Northern New England, 1650–1750* (New York, 1982), ch. 5, "The

serpent beguiled me," 89–105, esp. 97, 104–5. See also Cornelia Hughes Dayton, *Women before the Bar: Gender, Law, and Society in Connecticut, 1639–1789* (Chapel Hill, NC, 1995).
3 Quoted by Jefferson in *Notes on the State of Virginia* (1785), ed. William Peden (Chapel Hill, NC, 1954), Query VI, 58–9; Query XIV, 139. Perhaps the best example of Jefferson's racist, sexualized derision of Africans is his claim that blacks themselves favored whites as sexual partners, "declared by their preference for them, as uniformly as is the preference of the Oran-ootan for the black women over those of his own species" (138).

Further Reading

Clinton, Catherine and Michele Gillespie, eds. *The Devil's Lane: Sex and Race in the Early South*. New York: Oxford University Press, 1997.
D'Emilio, John and Estelle B. Freedman. *Intimate Matters: a History of Sexuality in America*. New York: Harper & Row, 1988.
Ericksen, Julia A. with Sally A. Steffen. *Kiss and Tell: Surveying Sex in the Twentieth Century*. Cambridge, MA: Harvard University Press, 1999.
Hodes, Martha. *Love, Sex, Race: Crossing Boundaries in North American History*. New York: New York University Press, 1998.
McCall, Laura, and Donald Yacovone, eds. *A Shared Experience: Men, Women, and the History of Gender*. New York: New York University Press, 1998.
Michel, Sonya and Robyn Muncy, eds. *Engendering America: a Documentary History 1865 to the Present*. New York: McGraw-Hill College, 1999.
Peiss, Kathy, and Christina Simmons, with Robert A. Padgug, eds. *Passion and Power: Sexuality in History*. Philadelphia: Temple University Press, 1989.
Smith, Merril D., ed. *Sex and Sexuality in Early America*. New York: New York University Press, 1998.

Part I
Early America

1

Things Fearful to Name

Introduction

Bestiality and sodomy have long been seen as "unnatural," following biblical proscriptions, but as John Murrin points out in this article, the way in which these "crimes" have been prosecuted has varied tremendously, even in the North American colonies. Since evidence of penetration was required for prosecution, both bestiality and sodomy have been seen as male crimes; in the American colonies, only two cases involving women and homosexual sex have been discovered, and these were treated as lascivious behavior rather than crimes against nature. Similarly, women appear in only two cases concerning bestiality. Murrin suggests that the crimes of witchcraft and bestiality were closely related in both the dramatic ways that each challenged the social order and community efforts to suppress the crimes. Women, in the eyes of the colonists, manifested their evil inclination by bonding to the devil and becoming witches; men served Satan by blurring the otherwise clear division between humans and beasts.

In the following extended excerpt from his essay examining all of colonial Anglo-America, Murrin treats New England. Neither in colonial America generally, nor in New England specifically, were bestiality or sodomy cases common. Nonetheless, through a meticulous search of the court records and private sources, Murrin is able to analyze court and community attitudes toward both offenses as well as toward the alleged offender. Bestiality seems to have horrified colonists generally, though sources suggest that often the charges were not taken seriously. Sodomy, on the other hand, seems to have been tolerated, though it remained a criminal act in most colonies, and those accused were subject to prosecution and punishment.

"Things Fearful to Name": Bestiality in Early America

John Murrin

In the Old Testament, the Lord has no tolerance for either sodomy or bestiality.[1] He destroyed Sodom and Gomorrah with fire and brimstone and later empowered the people of Israel to slaughter the Benjaminites because of the sodomitical activities of the people of Gibeah.[2] His command was unequivocal:

> If a man also lie with mankind as he lieth with a woman, both of them have committed an abomination: they shall surely be put to death. . . . And if a man lie with a beast, he shall surely be put to death; and ye shall slay the beast. And if a woman approach unto any beast, and lie down thereto, thou shalt kill the woman and the beast; they shall surely be put to death; their blood *shall be* upon them. (Leviticus 20: 13, 15–16)

In the New Testament, Paul shared the same revulsion:

> For this cause God gave them up unto vile affections: for even their women did change the natural use into that which is against nature: And likewise also the men, leaving the natural use of the women, burned in their lust one toward another, men with men working that which is unseemly. (Romans 1: 26–7)

By the early modern era, virtually all Christian theologians shared Paul's condemnation of "unnatural" sexual acts, a category that became so widely used that it is still deeply embedded in the criminal codes of American state governments. And yet, despite these shared beliefs, Christian societies differed dramatically in the kinds of unnatural sexual acts that they chose to prosecute. . . .

Excerpted from John Murrin, " 'Things Fearful to Name': Bestiality in Early America," *Explorations in Early American Culture Pennsylvania History: a Journal of Mid-Atlantic Studies*, 65 (1998), 8–43.

Although one woman and her dog were hanged at Tyburn in 1679,[3] women were almost never tried for homosexual actions or for bestiality, largely because the requirement of penetration almost defined the offense as a male act. Protestant clergymen sometimes agitated for a broader definition of the crime, something more in keeping with the biblical mandates. But, for reasons that remain unclear, the law courts continued to insist on penetration.[4]

In the American colonies, only two cases have emerged, both in New England, that involved women engaged in sexual play with one another. They were treated as lewd and lascivious behavior, not as potential crimes against nature, even though one of the principal offenders, the servant Elizabeth Johnson, was also punished for the highly provocative offense of "stopping her ears with her hands when the Word of God was read."[5] Only two cases of female bestiality have come to light in the colonies. In 1702 the grand jury refused to indict one woman in Boston. But in Monmouth County, New Jersey, Hannah Corkin was indicted for buggery in 1757 but convicted only of attempted buggery. Her offense must have been flagrant, however, for she received an exceptionally severe sentence – four whippings, each of twenty lashes, in four different towns in consecutive weeks.[6]

Trials for deviant sex reversed the patterns that prevailed in trials for witchcraft. According to both the Bible and early modern theology, men and women could commit either crime, but only men were actively suspected of sodomy or bestiality, while women were always the prime targets of witchcraft accusations. Men who fell under suspicion of witchcraft were usually related to a woman who was the chief suspect. But in any sexual relation with an animal, as Scandinavian bestiality trials reveal, a man was seen doing the devil's work in a way that went beyond conventional sins. God had created an orderly nature with clear boundaries between humans and beasts. Satan, and the buggerers who served him, were challenging those boundaries and threatening to reduce everything to confusion. Swedish sources are rich in this imagery, but it also appears in New England. In New Haven Colony, when one man interrupted another buggering a cow, the accused claimed that he was merely milking her. "Yet it is the Devills Milking and would bring him to the gallows," his accuser replied.[7] People still believed, as we shall see in several dramatic North American cases, that sexual unions between humans and animals, and between different species of animals, could produce offspring.[8] In Sweden, the Swiss Canton of Fribourg, the Republic of Geneva, and New England, the active prosecution of witchcraft and bestiality rose and fell together. For both clergy and magistrates, at least in regimes strongly dedicated to godliness, the two crimes seemed closely related. In the Netherlands, by contrast, the magistrates rejected clerical advice about both crimes. Bestiality was almost ignored. The last conviction for witchcraft occurred in 1595, and the last trial in 1610.[9]

Bestiality lowered a man to the level of a beast, but it also left something human in the animal. To eat a defiled animal thus involved the danger of cannibalism. The fear of human debasement ran deep enough to prevent men from milking cows. Women performed that chore. Any Swedish man who entered a barn that housed milk cows needed a superb excuse, or he would attract suspicion of bestial motives.[10] So strong was the sense of defilement from any copulation with animals that in Sweden it overrode the double standard of sexual behavior. Men would turn in other men for this offense, even though conviction usually meant death. The lack of sodomy trials in Sweden suggests that, for 150 years after 1630, bestiality seemed uniquely odious among crimes that men were likely to commit. In Sweden, as in New England, the active suppression of bestiality was accompanied by a major witch hunt aimed mostly at women, but in New England the campaign against bestiality lost its energy far sooner than in Sweden. . . .

Sodomy and bestiality in colonial New England have come under considerable scrutiny in the last two decades. Robert F. Oaks argued that homosexual relations must have been far more common than surviving legal records indicate and that, measured against the punishments meted out for buggery, the region was fairly tolerant of sodomy. Roger Thompson has replied that the region was a bastion of homophobic sentiment and that deviant sexual behavior was extremely rare. John Canup has also stressed the distinctive Puritan preoccupation with "the beast within" to account for the region's extraordinary horror of buggery.[11]

All of these scholars are making valid and important points. As in any society, many incidents of proscribed behavior never came to the attention of the authorities. But even if we multiply the known sodomy incidents by, shall we say, a factor of fifty, the number of participants would still be a tiny fraction of the total population, though probably not a trivial proportion of teenage boys. The ferocity of the rhetoric denouncing sodomy was indeed distinctive, and as Thompson points out, we have to wonder why the clergy and the magistrates worried so much about things that seldom happened. But then we have very little rhetoric at all from other colonies on this subject. New Englanders published sermons and even a few ponderous tomes of divinity or religious history. Other colonies did not. And yet if we set this rhetoric aside for a moment, the region's actual treatment of men or boys accused of sodomy was quite similar to what we have seen in other parts of colonial North America. Even the Puritans nearly always found a way to avoid executing the accused. The only two exceptions occurred in New Haven Colony, which was also the only colony to abolish jury trials.

In 1646 New Haven hanged William Plaine of Guilford, a married man who had committed sodomy with two men in England. In New England, "he had corrupted a great parte of the youth of Gilford by masturbation, which he had committed & provoked others to the like, above 100 tymes," reported John Winthrop; "& to some who questioned the lawfullnesse of suche a filthy practice, he did insinuate seedes of Atheism, questioning whither there were a God & c." Theophilus Eaton, the governor of New Haven, wrote to Winthrop on how to proceed in this case. The issue, no doubt was whether masturbation could be a capital crime. Winthrop agreed that this "monster in humaine shape . . . exceedinge all humane Rules, & examples that ever had been heard off" deserved to die but remained vague about the biblical basis for executing him. Winthrop noted only his "frustratinge of the Ordinance of marriage & the hindringe the generation of mankinde." After the fact, New Haven adopted a law to cover the case. It declared that public masturbation, by "corrupting or tempting others to doe the like, . . . tends to the sin of Sodomy, if it be not one kind of it"; and "if the case considered with the aggravating circumstances, shall according to the mind of God revealed in his word require it, he shall be put to death, as the court of magistrates shall determine." In short, Plaine's crime was inciting others to sodomy.[12]

Unfortunately the New Haven Colony records do not survive for this case, or we would have a much fuller account of how many boys were involved with Plaine. But if these encounters happened more than a hundred times, they had been going on for months before any lad notified the authorities or some respectable resident interrupted one of the frolics. In the town of Guilford, many youths had sexual experiences for an extended period of time that godly adults knew nothing about.

Nine years later Thomas and Peter Richards interrupted John Knight and Peter Vincon, a servant boy, "Acting filthyness together," which the two brothers described in lurid detail. Vincon's testimony suggested that he had sometimes been a willing partner and on other occasions had resisted. On the day in question, Knight had said "shall we play" and Vincon had replied, "no play," but Knight "came to him" anyway. Partly because Knight had also tried to rape young Mary Clark several times, the court condemned him to death. Nothing in the record indicates that Vincon was punished, although he is described as "the age of fourteene yeares or somewhat more." This case is the only example of conventional sodomy that led to an execution in colonial New England, although Mingo, a slave in Charlestown, Massachusetts, was hanged for "forcible buggery" (i.e., homosexual rape) in 1712. In 1755 at Lake

George, a Massachusetts soldier named Bickerstaff received the then unprecedented sentence of 100 lashes for "Profane swearing and a Sodomitical attempt." He was then drummed out of camp with a noose around his neck, a dramatic way of telling him that he deserved to die, and was kept in confinement for the rest of the campaign. But he was not executed.[13]

Puritan New England's first known encounter with the problem of sodomy occurred aboard the *Talbot* on its way to Salem in 1629. According to Rev. Francis Higginson, "This day we examined 5 beastly Sodomiticall boys, which confessed their wickedness not to bee named. The fact was so fowl we reserved them to bee punished by the governor when we came to New England, who afterward sent them backe to the [Massachusetts Bay] company to bee punished in ould England, as the crime deserved." Those over fourteen could have been hanged, but since five executions would almost have doubled the known total executed for sodomy in seventeenth-century England, we can be reasonably certain that they suffered some lesser punishment.[14]

Even New Haven Colony, the world's most severely Puritan society, learned to cope with youthful sex play among boys without resorting to the halter. At "a meeting of ye court extraordinary" in March 1653, the magistrates examined six "youthes" who "had committed much wickedness in a filthy corrupting way one wth another." Their confessions "were of such a filthy nature as is not fitt to be made known in a publique way," but all six were publicly whipped. John Clarke, a servant who was probably older than the "youthes," was "charged by one of them for some filthy cariag," which he denied. When one of the other boys "in some measure cleered him" of that accusation, the court left his punishment to his master but warned Clarke "that if ever any such cariag came forth against him hereafter, the Court would call these miscariages upon him to minde againe." The court feared, no doubt, that it might have another William Plaine on its hands. As this judgment indicates, hardly anyone in New Haven Colony ever received a complete acquittal.[15]

The most remarkable New England case was the whole adult life of Nicholas Sension of Wethersfield, Connecticut. He settled there around 1640, married a woman who then became a church member (he did not), and prospered. Quite often, he solicited sexual relations with other men. Once he even tried to seduce an unwilling bedmate while members of the Connecticut General Court were sleeping in the same room. The whole town seems to have known about his inclinations. He was reprimanded once in the 1640s and again in the 1660s, but people also liked him. Even a servant who resented and refused his sexual advances asked to remain in his service. Sension apparently established a long-term relationship with Nathaniel Pond, but after Pond was killed in Metacom's (King Philip's) War in 1675, Sension began once more to solicit sex from several young men. He was finally tried for sodomy in 1677, but the jury convicted him only of attempted sodomy. The court, dominated by magistrates from other communities who probably did not know Sension at all well, disfranchised him, ordered him to stand on the gallows with a noose around his neck, had him severely whipped, committed him to prison at the court's pleasure, and bound him to good behavior for a year. Had Sension lived about thirty miles southwest of Wethersfield in New Haven Colony, where there were no juries, he almost certainly would have been hanged, probably in the 1640s. The sentence, even though it could not be capital because of the jury verdict, reflects how one would expect a Puritan magistrate to respond to the foul crime of "going after strange flesh" (Jude: v. 7). Far more remarkable is the community's toleration of Sension's behavior for nearly forty years. Two centuries before the category of "homosexual" was invented, many ordinary residents of Wethersfield were willing, historian Richard Godbeer has argued, "to treat sodomy as a condition rather than as an act; it became in their minds a habitual course of action that characterized some men throughout their lives."[16]

Like New Jersey, eighteenth-century New England had its own example of a clergyman, often accused of sodomy, yet accepted by most of his congregation. Stephen Gorton, minister to the Baptist congregation in New London, Connecticut, drew criticism for his homosexual inclinations from the 1720s into the 1750s. Several flagrant infractions prompted some church members to withdraw from the congregation, and in 1757 Gorton was suspended. Yet after he repented publicly for his sin, the congregation voted two to one to restore him to his pulpit. The women favored him by a margin of three to one, while the men split about evenly. But clearly these serious Christians believed that sodomy was a forgivable offense.[17]

In New England for most of the seventeenth century, men who committed bestiality received no mercy. Those convicted of the act, as distinct from the attempt, were hanged. The court always allowed a fair amount of time between the trial and the execution so that the condemned man could have an opportunity to repent. God could forgive him. Humans dared not even try. "It is a *Crying* sin," explained Samuel Danforth; "it makes a clamorous noise in the ears of the holy God: it will not suffer God to rest in Heaven. . . . It defiles the Land; the Earth groans under the burthen of such Wickedness."[18]

The region experienced something close to a bestiality panic between 1640 and 1643. When the Great Migration finally ceased in 1641, New England probably had a higher percentage of young unmarried men than at any other point in the century. This group was much smaller than in colonies farther south. In Massachusetts the sex ratio (the number of men per one hundred women) was about 132 in 1641 at a time when it may still have exceeded 400 in Virginia. Yet young unmarried men, usually without known family attachments, provoked most of the cases of bestiality in the 1640s.[19]

In July 1640 Aaron Starke of Windsor was accused of buggering a heifer. A year earlier he had been whipped and fined, and the letter R was burned upon his cheek (for attempted rape?), for "the wrong done to Mary Holt . . . and when both are fit for that Condition to marry her." Instead, a month or two later she was whipped and banished for "vncleane practises" with John Bennett. Starke was still single when accused of bestiality. He "confesseth that he leaned crosse over the heifers Flanke, though at the first he denied that he came neere her, lastly he acknowledgeth that he had twice committed the acte wth the heifer but that shee was to narrowe." The court ordered a constable to keep him "wth locke and Chaine and hold him to hard labour & course diet" until summoned to trial. Nicholas Sension, the lifelong homosexual, was fined for not appearing to testify at this trial. One has to wonder how intimate the relationship was between these two men. The records of the next several courts have not survived, but Stark was not executed. Connecticut had not yet declared bestiality a capital crime, and the court may also have concluded that his confession amounted to no more than admission of the attempt, not the act. At any rate, Starke survived to be whipped for some other, unstated offense in 1643. He was also condemned to serve Capt. John Mason during the pleasure of the court.[20]

Masschusetts began to experience similar trouble in the winter 1640–41. "A wicked fellow, given up to bestiality, fearing to be taken by the hand of justice, fled to Long Island, and there was drowned," noted John Winthrop with equal measure of disgust and satisfaction. "He had confessed to some, that he was so given up to that abomination, that he never saw any beast go before him but he lusted after it." In December 1641 The General Court (the whole legislature) sentenced William Hatchet, an eighteen or twenty-year-old servant in Salem, to be hanged for buggering a cow on the Lord's day. He had always been "a very stupid, idle, and ill-disposed boy, and would never regard the means of instruction, either in the church or family," claimed Winthrop. He was seen by a woman too ill to attend public worship that day who, "looking out at her window, espied him in the very act; but being affrighted at it, and dwelling alone, she durst not call to him, but at night made it known" to a magistrate. Hatchet then "confessed the attempt and some entrance, but denied the completing of the fact." During the trial, "much scruple there was with many, because there was but one witness," whereas the Bible requires two for conviction of a capital crime. A majority voted to convict him on the strength of the woman's testimony and Hatchet's admission of some penetration, but when Governor Richard Bellingham could not overcome his own doubts and pronounce the sentence of death, the deputy governor, John Endicott, performed that function. The cow, of course, was condemned "to bee slayne & burnt or buried."

Only then did Hatchet confess "the full completing this foul fact, and attempting the like before." He became so penitent that his execution was postponed an extra week to let the grace of the Lord complete its work. "There is no doubt to be made but the Lord hath received his soul to his mercy," Winthrop affirmed. In March 1643 the Court of Assistants sentenced an Irish servant, Teagu Ocrimi, to stand at the place of execution with a halter around his neck and to be severely whipped "for a foule, & divilish attempt to bugger a cow of M^r. Makepeaces." The moral was sobering. "As people increased, so sin abounded, and especially the sin of uncleanness," concluded Winthrop, "and still the providence of God found them out."[21]

In neighboring Plymouth Colony, not long after Hatchet had been hanged in Massachusetts, someone saw Thomas Granger buggering a mare. His parents lived in Scituate, but this sixteen- or seventeen-year-old lad was a servant in a respectable household in Duxbury. During his examination, he confessed to having sex with "a mare, a cow, two goats, five sheep, two calves and a turkey." A large part of some poor farmer's flock of sheep had to be paraded before him so that he could identify which ones he had buggered and which could be spared. All of the defiled animals were slaughtered before his face on September 8, 1642, and then he was hanged. The animal carcasses were "cast into a great and large pit that was digged of purpose for them, and no use made of any part of them." Governor William Bradford wondered why "even sodomy and buggery (things fearful to name) have broke forth in this land oftener than once." The vigilance of churches and magistrates provided one answer. In populous old countries, such deeds "lie hid, as it were, in a wood or thicket and many horrible evils by that means are never seen nor known; whereas here they are, as it were, brought into the light and set in the plain field, or rather on a hill, made conspicuous to the view of all" – surely a less than inspirational application of John Winthrop's ideal of a city upon a hill![22]

In New Haven Colony, the exposure of abomination took an even more dramatic form when the Lord intervened directly to reveal the unspeakable wickedness of a lewd and irreverent servant. George Spencer, an ugly balding man with one "pearle" or false eye, had probably been whipped in Boston for receiving stolen goods, and had also been punished in New Haven for botching an attempt to escape to Virginia. He admitted that he had gained no spiritual benefit from the ministry of the famed John Davenport, that he had not said a single prayer during his five years in New England, and that he read the Bible only when ordered to do so by his master. In February, 1642, Spencer's life took a cruel turn when a sow gave birth to a dead deformed piglet. The "monster" was completely bald and had "butt one eye in the midle of the face, and thatt large and open, like some blemished eye of a man." Out of its forehead "a thing of flesh grew forth and hung downe, itt was hollow, and like a mans instrum^t of gen^{r}ation."

The magistrates arrested Spencer and put him in prison. New Haven had not yet tried a capital crime. Spencer had seen enough of the colony's system of justice to know that the magistrates expected offenders to confess and repent. He had recently seen a man merely whipped for molesting a child, and as Spencer made clear, he thought that child molestation was a more disgusting crime than bestiality. Yet he denied his guilt until one magistrate "remembered him of that place of scripture, he that hideth his sin shall not prosper, butt he y^t confesseth and forsaketh his sins shall finde mercie." Spencer then "answered he was sory and confessed he had done itt," only to learn that his confession would get him hanged and that mercy would come only from the Lord, not the Colony of New Haven. He retracted and repeated his confession several times in a desperate attempt to find a formula that would save his life. But on April 8, 1642, two months after the birth of the monster, the sow was put to the sword in front of the unrepentant Spencer, and he was hanged, "a terrible example of divine justice and wrath."[23]

The bestiality panic of 1641–43 passed, but the precedents remained. In late 1645 another New Haven sow gave birth to two deformed piglets that reminded observers of another servant whose name was, incredibly, Thomas Hogg. Although imprisoned for two or three months – longer than anyone else in the colony's history – Hogg refused to confess. The magistrates clearly believed he was guilty. They even brought him to the sow, made him fondle her, and noted that "immedyatly there appeared a working of lust in the sow" but not in another one that they also made him "scratch," and then asked him "what he thought of it, he said he saw a hand of God in it." Hogg wore a steel truss for his hernia, and because it kept cutting open his britches, his private parts had become rather too public. Apparently the deformed eyes of one piglet reminded observers of the hang of his scrotum, which far too many people had seen. But he never confessed, and without a second witness, the court did not hang him. It whipped him instead for general lewdness, which included at least one incident of masturbation.[24]

In 1647 a Connecticut jury found John Nubery, the seventeen-year-old son of a respectable settler, guilty of bestiality. Out "of horror of Conscience &c: to gloryfie God," he went before a magistrate and voluntarily confessed to several such attempts, "once to penetration but not to effution of seed." Connecticut hanged him, but as the elder Winthrop noted, "his Repentance & godly ende" were "very observable." This case, more clearly than any other, displays the Puritan hope that God would pardon an offence that humans could not forgive.[25]

By 1647 Massachusetts, Plymouth, New Haven, and Connecticut had each convicted and hanged one young man for bestiality. But then the pace fell off. New Haven hanged two more men. Walter Robinson, a fifteen-year-old boy who was seen by a sailor buggering a bitch in Milford, ran away when the sailor called to him that "he would be hanged," and finally admitted slight penetration of the animal, which was enough for the court to hang him in 1655.[26] Far more spectacular was the case of William Potter, one of the original founders of New Haven Colony, a member of John Davenport's church (it had the strictest admission procedures in all of New England), and a family man. A "weake infirme man," he was about sixty years old and had recently been exempted from the military watch because of his poor health. But his ailments did not impede his unusual sex life. In 1662, his teen-aged son saw him buggering one of their sows and went to get his mother, who confirmed what father was doing. In what was clearly a lethal decision that they both understood, mother and son informed a magistrate. Confronted with two witnesses, Potter confessed. He admitted to a lifelong fondness for this activity beginning in England at about age ten. His wife had caught him some years earlier copulating with his bitch. He had persuaded her not to tell the authorities and had even hanged the dog, apparently in a fit of remorse. This time he was, of course, condemned to die. In what remains the most awkward moment in any early American court record that I have read, Potter led his wife through his flocks, pointing out to her every animal that had been a sexual partner. On the day of his execution, a cow, two heifers, three sheep, and two sows all died with him. The case was so scandalous that Cotton Mather was still casting anathemas upon it thirty-seven years later.[27]

New Haven even detected an abomination when animals of different species grew amorous with one another. In 1655 Nicholas Bayley's dog tried to copulate with a sow. When a neighbor admonished Bayley to execute the dog, Bayley's wife retorted, "what would you have the poore creature doe, if he had not a bitch, he must have some thing." The court found this remark so shocking that it banished the depraved couple. It may be no coincidence that the Bayleys had also fallen under suspicion of witchcraft.[28]

Bestiality seemed so loathsome that even jokes about it were punishable. Young Jeremiah Johnson, the only person whose sense of humor emerges from the voluminous court records of New Haven colony and town, once overheard Edmund Dorman praying loudly in a swamp for a wife: "Lord thou knowest my necessity & canst supply it, Lord bend & bow her will & make her sensible of my condition." When someone later asked him for whom Dorman was praying, Johnson replied, "it may be his mare that God would make her seruiseable." Dorman, who married Hannah Hull three months later, sued Johnson for slander in September 1662. After several witnesses recounted other irreverent remarks that Johnson had made, the court warned him "that it was a fearefull thing to come to that height of sinning as to sit in ye seat of ye scorner," put off its decision for several months, and then imposed a good-behavior bond of £10 on him, the only one I can recall seeing that had no time limit.[29]

Puritan missionaries even tried to impose their standards on the Indians. In January 1647 the first group of "praying Indians" agreed to abide by a set of laws that punished both adultery and bestiality with death. New England's priorities emerged quite clearly here. The code said nothing about sodomy, an offense that did occur among Indians, but instead prohibited bestiality among a people who had no large domesticated animals before the Europeans arrived and who had never shared the Christian prohibition of premarital sexual relations between men and women. The offense may have been unknown among the Indians.[30]

They did not remain ignorant for long. In 1656 two Indians informed Roger Williams, the founder of Rhode Island and at that time the president of the colony's Court of Trials, that they had seen Richard Chasmore of Pawtuxet, known locally as "Long Dick," buggering a heifer. One had seen him in the winter, the other in the spring. Williams tried to arrest Chasmore, but some men of Pawtuxet were able to protect him until he could flee to New Netherland. Pawtuxet was then on territory disputed between Rhode Island and Massachusetts. One measure of Williams's outrage at this abomination is that he wrote to Governor Bellingham of Massachusetts and urged him to arrest Chasmore when he returned to Pawtuxet and bring him to trial in Boston. Chasmore's friends seemed willing to subject him to trial in Rhode Island. "I guesse ye bottome of ye Councell js," Williams explained, that the Chasmore faction expected "an easier doome with us where Indian Testimonie will not easily passe," although Williams had also heard that some men of Pawtuxet were beginning to believe the allegations against Chasmore "from his owne expressions."

Massachusetts did arrest Chasmore. But while the party was passing through Providence on its way to Boston, a group of local men, supported by an emergency Providence town meeting, liberated Chasmore who, however, agreed to stand trial in Newport in March 1657. Williams not only stepped down from the bench to prosecute Chasmore, but he also accused Chasmore's liberators and even threatened to send them to England for punishment by Oliver Cromwell's government. When no one was willing to testify for the prosecution in any of these cases, everyone went free. The Puritan horror of bestiality had finally encountered a stronger force in New England, the determination not to let the testimony of Indians condemn a white man to death. Williams understood those odds, which is no doubt why he tried Chasmore "upon a Comon fame of Buggarie" and not for the act itself, but the jury acquitted him anyway. No Indians testified in the case, but for the first time in New England records there is more than a hint that in at least one town, bestiality did not destroy a man's standing in his community.[31]

In the same year, 1657, the Massachusetts Court of Assistants not only dismissed the charge of bestiality that Ruben Cuppie made against Richard Pitfold but also whipped Cuppie for an irresponsible allegation that could have threatened the life of another. But in 1674 Massachusetts hanged Benjamin Goad of Roxbury, the seventeen-year-old son of godly parents, who was caught buggering a mare in an open field in the early afternoon of a sunny day. Goad did not fit the profile of an irresponsible and unattached servant, and the jury hesitated before convicting him, asking the bench to decide whether an initial admission and only one witness provided sufficient evidence to hang him. Others must also have thought that the penalty was too severe. "You pity his Youth and tender years," replied Samuel Danforth in the only published New England sermon that focused specifically on bestiality, "but I pray pity the holy Law of God, which is shamefully violated; pity the glorious name of God, which is horribly profaned; pity the Land, which is fearfully polluted and defiled." Goad, he added, "was extremely addicted to Sloth and Idleness" and "lived in Disobedience to his Parents; in Lying, Stealing, Sabbath breaking, and was wont to flee away from Catechism." Yet the critics made their point in a quieter way. Goad became the last New England colonist to hang for bestiality.[32]

Between 1642 and 1662 New England executed six men for bestiality. During nearly the same years, these colonies hanged thirteen women and two men for witchcraft. The bestiality trials began when the population of single servants was at its peak, but the witchcraft trials started a few years later, only when the region finally had enough post-menopausal women, who were always the prime suspects in New England, to attract a significant number of accusations. Nine of the executions (seven women and two of their husbands) were in Connecticut, four in Massachusetts, and two in New Haven. Hartford had a severe witch panic in 1662–63 when eleven people were tried, of whom four were executed and two escaped. The willingness of the courts to execute witches faltered when some people were convicted who simply did not match the stereotype of what a witch should be. In Massachusetts the deputies outvoted the magistrates to insist on the execution of Ann Hibben, a magistrate's widow, in 1656. The Hartford trials placed Judith Varlet, the niece of Peter Stuyvesant, in peril of her life, although she did survive. Between 1663 and the Salem outbreak in 1692, only one person was executed for witchcraft in New England – Goody Glover in Boston in 1688. During the same three decades, Benjamin Goad was the only man executed for bestiality.

On the eve of the Salem trials, the totals stood at about two to one: sixteen executions for witchcraft (fourteen women and two men), and seven men for bestiality. The Salem outbreak was truly bizarre. There the testimony of lowly orphan girls acquired more credibility than that of respected churchmembers, such as Rebecca Nurse and Mary Easty. No one who confessed was ever hanged, but all of those who were hanged insisted they were innocent. Had the Salem frenzy not occurred, the parallels between the earlier witch and bestiality prosecutions probably would have emerged long ago. Salem has diminished the significance of all of the early witch trials. But after Salem, no one else was executed for witchcraft in New England.

After Benjamin Goad, no one else was executed for bestiality in colonial New England. Plymouth convicted Thomas Saddeler in 1681 but only had him whipped. In Maine, Benjamin Preble "utterly disownes" what the court called "a scandelous report areiseing from some publique fame of Buggery." But "severall evidences have been taken, although the treuth lyes darke & undiscovered, relating either to the Accusers or accused." The court let the matter drop. In Massachusetts, when John Barrett of Chelmsford was accused in 1674, the Middlesex County Court merely admonished him and never sent him to Boston for trial. Petty juries refused to convict Jack, a black "servant" in 1676, or John Lawrence of Sudbury a year later. Grand juries refused to indict Samuel Bayley of Weymouth in 1683 and Jonathan Gardiner of Roxbury in 1685. As Judge Samuel Sewall noted, there was only one witness against Gardiner. Thirty years later when a cow "brought forth a calf, which had so much of a human visage as to make the attentive spectators apprehensive that the poor animal had been impregnated by a beastly Negro," Cotton Mather did not launch a grim hunt for the human perpetrator. Instead he wrote up a description of the "monster" for the enlightenment of the Royal Society in London.[33]

In Connecticut a petty jury tried Simon Drake for sodomizing a cow in 1674 but found the accusation not "legally proved" although there was "great Ground of Suspition." The court released him. A year later a grand jury refused to indict John Sherwood of "some sodimeticall practices." Three later cases show that things had changed decisively. In 1697 John Arnoll (or Arnold) of Fairfield was caught in the act of buggering a mare by Phillip Lewis. Lewis reprimanded him and then returned with a friend, to whom Arnoll confessed that he was "very sorrowfull" for what he had done. Thirty years earlier this testimony would have satisfied the two-witness rule, and Arnoll would have hanged. But he was not even brought to trial.[34]

In 1713 two interlocking Connecticut trials showed some of the ways that settlers linked bestiality and witchcraft in their own minds. While walking into the woods in Colchester, Connecticut one July day, Bethiah Taylor came upon Joseph Chapman copulating with a cow, "but she being afraid for her own Life dare not call to him but went immediatly... to Deacon Samuel Loomis" and asked his advice. He had little to offer, and when Chapman also showed up, she went home. Two or three weeks later Chapman came to her house, told her that he had been expecting a court summons upon her complaint, and threatened to sue her to protect his name if he was not brought to trial. One suspects that Taylor, having got nowhere talking with the deacon, had consulted her own friends. The story was spreading, probably among local women, and Chapman hoped he could intimidate her into silence. But instead the authorities came to arrest him, and he fled and had to be pursued and captured.

Then, in a pretrial deposition, eighteen-year-old John Brown testified that two years earlier he had heard Goodwife Taylor call the wife of Thomas Brown (probably a relative of John) a witch who had turned herself into a cat to torment the Taylor children. Brown, no doubt, hoped to discredit Taylor's testimony. Someone who cried "Witch" might also accuse a man of buggery. But Jonathan Lisburn, a fifty-year-old man, testified that three years earlier, in 1710, he had come upon Brown, then fifteen years old, buggering a mare. The "Sight being So amazing i did not Know what do doe wharfore i whent unto naibor pumry for advise," he reported. Pomeroy hesitated and then advised him to consult with a clergyman and "to discors with John to See if he colde no waiy Be made Senciable of his Sin." Bestiality was becoming for-givable. Lisburn took this advice and talked with the local minister and with Brown. When he asked Brown why he did such a thing, Brown replied "that he did not Know what was the mater he thought that he was Beweched. . . . " In other words Chapman's defender was himself a buggerer willing to accuse others of witchcraft. Brown also escaped for a time, but the court clamped both men in irons, convicted them, and had them shamed on the gallows and whipped, but not hanged. Goody Taylor's testimony held up. In a Puritan society that offered no legal protection for personal confessions to a clergymen, even the minister was forced to testify in court about what Lisburn and Brown had told him.

In 1710 Brown had been detected in the act by a man, who kept the matter private among the two of them, a trusted neighbor, and a minister. Nobody alerted the legal authorities. In 1713 Chapman was interrupted by a woman, who also went first to a prominent member of the local church, but then the news got out, probably through the female gossip network, as in Virginia a year earlier. At a distance of nearly three centuries, we have to wonder how much Chapman and Brown knew about each other's buggery. Had it become, as in parts of England a century before, something that older boys showed to younger ones?

By 1713 the double standard of sexual behavior had reasserted itself throughout the region. It had been in some jeopardy in the Puritan era, when courts had sometimes punished men more severely than women for the same act of fornication, and when quite a few men had pleaded guilty to sexual offenses and accepted their punishment. After 1700, almost without exception, men would not plead guilty to any sexual offense except making love to their own wives before their wedding day. Some husbands, just to avoid a small fine, pleaded not guilty to that charge as well, even though that plea left their pregnant wives open to acute embarrassment. Juries nearly always sided with the men, not the women. As the 1713 bestiality convictions indicate, the double standard now extended to that crime as well. Brown and Chapman tried to protect each other.

Benjamin Goad was hanged in 1674. Metacom's (King Philip's) War broke out in 1675, and New England spent most of the next four decades at war with neighboring Indians and New France. The massive mobilization of men for these wars created an ethic of male bonding powerful enough to overcome the disgust and loathing that the previous generation had felt for bestiality. When men live together for a long time without women, some of them will turn to one another for sexual gratification.

No doubt some will also turn to the animal population. After 1713 occasional accusations of bestiality turn up in the court records of the New England colonies, but they simply reinforce the pattern already in place by 1713. When James Warren saw Gershom Thomas having sex with a heifer on a Sunday morning in 1746, Thomas's friends urged Warren to keep the matter private and even offered to pay him. When Mary Corey awoke one morning in 1743 and heard her husband Seth copulating with his bitch, she fled to a neighbor's house, while Seth sought out his brother as a mediator and, perhaps in contrition, executed the dog. Confronted by Joseph Hebard, who was probably Mary's father, Seth confessed that "I am a Deavl." Hebard "advised him to go Into some hole or Corner and Cast himself on ye Earth Before God and Beg of God that he would Brake his hart and humble him." The case went before a magistrate but never came to trial. Between 1713 and the Revolution, only one case that I know of was actually tried. It ended in acquittal when three jurors outlasted the nine who favored conviction. In this area, as in so many others, New England looked a lot more like old England in the eighteenth century than it still resembled the city upon a hill once envisioned by John Winthrop.

Bestiality discredited men in the way that witchcraft discredited women. At least in New England, both began as unforgivable crimes that were becoming forgivable by the end of the seventeenth century. No one was executed for bestiality after Benjamin Goad in 1674. During the Salem witch trials, no one who confessed was executed. All nineteen of those hanged insisted they were innocent. In the eyes of the court, they remained unrepentant. But when Mary Lacey, Jr., confessed in court in July 1692 that she had actually worshipped Satan, a magistrate reassured her that "you may yet be delivered if god give you repentance." "I hope he will," she replied. She survived.[35] In all likelihood, acts of sodomy and bestiality were much rarer in New England than in other mainland colonies. Yet New England prosecuted both offenses, and witchcraft, far more vigorously than the other colonies except New Netherland with its singular horror for male sodomy.

Within New England, bestiality stigmatized young men, mostly teenagers, with the spectacular exception of sixty-year-old William Potter in New Haven. The panic of the early 1640s involved mostly male servants who had no relatives in New England. (The exception was Thomas Granger in Plymouth Colony, and even he was living in someone else's household.) After the mid-1640s, the accused were much more likely to come from respectable households, and the passion for executing them began to diminish. The offense usually involved an actual transgression against a real animal, except in the New Haven pig cases when deformed piglets provided the only tangible evidence.

Witchcraft, by contrast, stigmatized mostly older women, often grandmothers. When men were the accusers, the typical offender was a woman past menopause who had acquired title to property and had no male heirs. When women were the primary accusers, as at Hartford in 1662–63 and Salem in 1692, elderly women remained the primary suspects, but more of them were churchmembers with no lack of male

heirs. And more men were accused, some of whom, such as Rev. George
Burroughs, had acquired a reputation for abusing their wives and children. An accusation of witchcraft, unlike one for bestiality, usually did
not involve a specific act. The crime was more in the imagination of the
victim than in the deeds of the accused. Once spectral evidence became
sufficient for conviction, the accused were left with no effective defense.
Nobody could prove that her spectre had *not* tormented somebody.

In the early American bestiality cases, women – who seldom spent
time in the fields or forests – appear quite disproportionately as accusers.
This pattern suggests that the double standard of sexual propriety probably protected most men from accusations by other men most of the
time. Men must have witnessed this offense far more often than women,
but they hardly ever pursued the matter into a court of law. Harrie
Negro's accusers in West Jersey were all women. At least one woman
was involved in the Virginia cases of 1644 and 1712. A South Carolina
woman testified against John Dixon. Even though Francis Oldfield
finally brought Dixon before a magistrate, he agonized for months before
taking that step. In New England the record does not indicate who
denounced Thomas Granger in Plymouth, Benjamin Goad in Massachusetts, or Aaron Starke in Connecticut. God, or the piglets,
denounced George Spencer and put Thomas Hogg's life in peril, while
John Nubery denounced himself. But in the cases that have left adequate
information about the accusers, women played an outsized role in New
England as well. Only Walter Robinson of New Haven, denounced by a
sailor, and John Arnoll of Connecticut were prosecuted by men. William
Hatchet of Massachusetts, William Potter of New Haven, and Joseph
Chapman of Connecticut were all turned in by women. The Chapman
case, by exposing John Brown's earlier act of buggery, gives us a clear
glimpse of men shielding other men from the law while also trying to
reform the malefactor. Quite possibly, even in New England, the double
standard operated effectively most of the time for most men when the
offense involved sodomy or bestiality. Rather more slowly, men began to
apply it once again to fornication as well.

The legal system offers indirect evidence for this hypothesis. Magistrates belonged to the social and cultural elite. Jurors were often ordinary
farmers. All six men sentenced to death for sodomy in the seventeenth
century – one in Virginia in 1624, three in New Netherland, and two in
New Haven – were condemned without a jury trial. The only colonial
jury known to have condemned anyone to die for this offense gave its
verdicts in Pennsylvania in 1748. By contrast, New England juries were
willing to convict young men of bestiality at least until 1674. After 1674
no one was executed for bestiality in New England before the Revolution
and only two men in New Jersey. If male sodomy was indeed more

common than bestiality, this pattern suggests that ordinary men in New England found buggery a much more loathsome offense – until the accused turned out to be the son of a friend or acquaintance.

Another striking pattern was the inability of contemporaries to see animals as victims in bestiality cases. In insisting on penetration as a defining element of the crime, the courts allowed legal custom to override Scripture. But in destroying the animals involved in this offense, they allowed Scripture to override their own better sensibilities. In 1641 the Massachusetts Body of Liberties explicitly prohibited "any Tirranny or Crueltie towards any bruite Creature which are usuallie kept for mans use," and Quaker West New Jersey exempted animals from judicial forfeiture after a crime unless they were inherently dangerous. Yet courts in both colonies condemned animals to death after someone had buggered them. No one in the colonies took the initiative to intercede on behalf of such a victim the way a French convent and parish priest did in 1750 to prevent a court at Vanvres from condemning a she-ass to death. They bore "witness that she is in word and deed and in all her habits of life a most honest creature" who must have been an unwilling participant in the crime. The court agreed and set the animal free.[36]

In August 1799, a century and a quarter after the execution of Benjamin Goad, the Connecticut Superior Court condemned Gideon Washburn of Litchfield to hang for acts of bestiality committed over a five-year period with two cows, two mares, and a heifer. In October Washburn petitioned the legislature for a pardon or a postponement of the execution, which was scheduled to take place on his eighty-third birthday. He protested his innocence but also complained that the jury had violated the Puritan two-witness rule. Of the four witnesses against him, "*three* of them [had testified] each to *one* fact, and the other to *three* several facts, that no *two* witnesses testified of any *one* fact." Washburn's memory, but not his morals, harkened back to the Puritan era when the biblical two-witness rule had been enforced. But under English common law, which was already beginning to prevail at the time of his birth, one witness became sufficient to convict even a capital offender if the jury found the testimony credible. Washburn's petition provoked what must have been a furious debate. The original manuscript has orders and counter-orders written all over the reverse side. The lower house voted to comply with his request for a pardon, but the upper house would agree to no more than a postponement. The legislature finally ordered him hanged on the third Friday in January 1800.[37] [In all likelihood, he was the last person formally executed for this offense in what is now the United States.] ...

Occasional bestiality trials have occurred in the United States since then. In Reconstruction Virginia a black teenager, Austin Robertson, was sentenced to a year in the penitentiary for buggering a heifer, but that conviction was overturned on the grounds that penetration had not been proved and was probably impossible because Robertson was too short. As late as the 1950s, an Indiana man was convicted of bestiality with a chicken. He appealed on the grounds that a chicken was not a beast under Indiana law. The court agreed with him but upheld his conviction for sodomy. Bestiality has never again become the abomination and obsession that it was, briefly, for seventeenth-century New Englanders.[38]

Notes

1 This paper was prepared for a joint meeting of the Shelby Cullom Davis Center and the Philadelphia (now McNeil) Center for Early American Studies, held at Princeton University, January 16, 1998. The author wishes to thank William Chester Jordan for his persistent encouragement of the project, Mary Fissell for her thoughtful formal commentary, and the numerous participants for their many helpful suggestions.

2 All biblical citations are to the "Authorized" or King James version. In this paper I use sodomy to indicate sexual relations between men, and buggery to mean relations between men and animals, even though actual usage, then and now, was and is much looser.

3 Keith Thomas, *Man and the Natural World. Changing Attitudes in England 1500–1800* (London: Allen Lane, 1983).

4 See, for example, the opinion of Rev. Charles Chauncy, 1642, in William Bradford, *Of Plymouth Plantation, 1620–1647*, ed. Samuel Eliot Morison (New York: Alfred A. Knopf, 1959), 410.

5 George Francis Dow, ed., *Records and Files of the Quarterly Courts of Essex County* [Massachusetts], vol. 1: *1636–1656* (Salem, Mass.: The Essex Institute, 1911), 44 (the quotation is from Dow's summary of the case); Nathaniel B. Shurtleff and David Pulsifer, eds., *Records of the Colony of New Plymouth in New England*, 12 vols. (Boston: William White, 1855–61), II, 137 (hereafter, *Plym. Recs.*).

6 Henry Clay Reed, "Chapters in a History of Crime and Punishment in New Jersey" (PhD dissertation: Princeton University, 1939), 462.

7 Jonas Liliequist, "Peasants against Nature: Crossing the Boundaries between Man and Animal in Seventeenth- and Eighteenth-Century Sweden," *Focaal*, No. 13 (1990), esp. pp. 33–39; Trial of John Ferris, June 30, 1657, Records of New Haven Colony: General Court, May 1653 to Dec. 1664, pp. 145–46 (Connecticut State Library, Hartford).

8 See Winthrop D. Jordan, *White over Black: American Attitudes toward the Negro, 1550–1812* (Chapel Hill: University of North Carolina Press, 1968), 28–32.

9 J. H. Huizinga, *Dutch Civilisation in the Seventeenth Century and Other Essays* (New York: Harper and Row, 1969), 59–60.

10 Liliequist, "Peasants against Nature," esp. pp. 39–40, 45–46.

11   Robert F. Oaks, "'Things Fearful to Name': Sodomy and Buggery in Seven-
     teenth-Century New England," *Journal of Social History*, 12 (1978–79), 268–
     81; Roger Thompson, *Sex in Middlesex: Popular Mores in a Massachusetts
     County, 1649–1699* (Amherst: The University of Massachusetts Press,
     1986), esp. 71–82; Thompson, "Attitudes Towards Homosexuality in the
     Seventeenth-Century New England Colonies," *Journal of American Studies*,
     23 (1989), 27–40; John Canup, "'The Cry of Sodom Enquired Into': Bes-
     tiality and the Wilderness of Human Nature in Seventeenth-Century New
     England," American Antiquarian Society, *Proceedings*, 98 (1988), 113–34.

12   Richard S. Dunn, James Savage, and Laetitia Yeandle, eds., *The Journal of
     John Winthrop, 1630–1649* (Cambridge: The Belknap Press of Harvard
     University Press, 1996), 629; J. Hammond Trumbull, ed., *The True-Blue
     Laws of Connecticut and New-Haven* (Hartford: American Publishing Co.,
     1879), 201.

13   Records of New Haven Colony: General Court, May 1653 to Dec. 1664,
     pp. 89–91; M. Halsey Thomas, ed., *The Diary of Samuel Sewall, 1674–1729*
     (New York: Farrar, Straus and Giroux, 1973), II, 677, 678; Louis Effing-
     ham de Forest, ed., *The Journals and Papers of Seth Pomeroy, Sometime
     General in the Colonial Service* (New York: Society of Colonial Wars in the
     State of New York, 1926), 106.

14   "Francis Higgeson's Journal," in Stewart Mitchell, ed., *The Founding of
     Massachusetts* (Boston: Massachusetts Historical Society, 1930), 71.

15   Franklin Bowditch Dexter, ed., *New Haven Town Records, 1649–1662* (New
     Haven: New Haven Colony Historical Society, 1917), 178–79.

16   Richard Godbeer, "'The Cry of Sodom': Discourse, Intercourse, and
     Desire in Colonial New England," *William and Mary Quarterly*, 3rd ser.,
     52 (1995), 259–86, esp. p. 283 (quotation).

17   Godbeer, "'The Cry of Sodom,'" 277–79.

18   Samuel Danforth, *The Cry of Sodom Enquired into; Upon Occasion of the
     Arraignment and Condemnation of Benjamin Goad, for his Prodigious Villany.
     Together with a Solemn Exhortation to Tremble at Gods Judgements, and to
     Abandon Youthful Lusts* (Cambridge, Mass.: Marmaduke Johnson, 1674), 8.

19   Virginia DeJohn Anderson, *New England's Generation: The Great Migration
     and the Formation of Society and Culture in the Seventeenth Century* (New
     York: Cambridge University Press, 1991), 223.

20   *Records of the Particular Court of Connecticut, 1639–1663* (Hartford: Con-
     necticut Historical Society, 1928), 3, 4, 13, 20; J. Hammond Trumbull, *The
     Public Records of the Colony of Connecticut*, 15 vols. (Hartford: Brown &
     Parsons, 1850–90), I, 77.

21   Winthrop, *Journal*, ed. Dunn, 342–43, 374–76; Nathaniel B. Shurtleff, ed.,
     *Records of the Governor and Company of the Massachusetts Bay in New Eng-
     land, 1628–1686* 5 vols. in 6 (Boston: William White, 1853–54), I, 344
     (hereafter cited as *Recs. Mass. Bay Co.*); John Noble and John F. Cronin,
     eds., *Records of the Court of Assistants of the Colony of the Massachusetts Bay,
     1630–1692* (Boston: Suffolk County, 1901–28), II, 121 (hereafter cited as
     Recs. Mass. Ct. Assts.).

22 Bradford, *Of Plymouth Plantation, 1620–1647*, ed. Morison, 320–22, 316–17.

23 Charles J. Hoadly, ed., *Records of the Colony and Plantation of New Haven, from 1638 to 1649* (Hartford: Case, Tiffany, and Company, 1857), 62–73.

24 *Ibid.*, 295–96. Hogg was successfully reabsorbed into the community. He was standing watch for the colony by 1648, took the standard oath of submission to the colony in 1654, and died insolvent, a ward of the town, sometime before the March 12, 1686 session of the New Haven County Court. *Ibid.*, 378, 140; New Haven County Court Records, 1666–1698, p. 159 (Connecticut State Library, Hartford). In 1655 when a third monster piglet was born, the whole town of New Haven filed past to see if it resembled anyone in particular. It did not, and no one was accused. Dexter, ed., *New Haven Town Records, 1649–1662*, 245–46.

25 *Recs. Partic. Ct.*, 48, 49; Winthrop, *Journal*, ed. Dunn, 771.

26 Records of New Haven Colony: General Court, May 1653 to Dec. 1654, pp. 85–87 (Connecticut State Library, Hartford).

27 Charles J. Hoadly, ed., *Records of the Colony or Jurisdiction of New Haven, from May 1653 to the Union. Together with the New Haven Code of 1656* (Hartford: Case, Tiffany, and Company, 1858), 180, 440–43; Cotton Mather, *Pillars of Salt. An History of Some Criminals Executed in this Land; for Capital Crimes. With some of their Dying Speeches; Collected and Published, For the Warning of such as Live in Destructive Courses of Ungodliness....* (Boston: B. Green and J. Allen, 1699), reprinted in Daniel E. Williams, ed., *Pillars of Salt: An Anthology of Early American Criminal Narratives* (Madison, Wis.: Madison House, 1993), 65–93, at pp. 67–69.

28 Dexter, ed. *New Haven Town Recs., 1649–1662*, 245–46; John Putnam Demos, *Entertaining Satan: Witchcraft and the Culture of Early New England* (New York: Oxford University Press, 1982), 403.

29 Franklin B. Dexter, ed., *New Haven Town Records, 1662–1684* (New Haven: New Haven Colony Historical Society, 1919), 7–8, 22–23.

30 Thomas Shepard, *The Clear Sun-shine of the Gospel Breaking Forth upon the Indians in New England*... (London: R. Cotes for John Bellamy, 1648), in Massachusetts Historical Society, *Collections*, 3d ser., 4 (1834), 40. See Virginia DeJohn Anderson, "King Philip's Herds: Indians, Colonists, and the Problem of Livestock in Early New England," *William and Mary Quarterly*, 3d ser., 51 (1994), 601–24.

31 All of the documents in this case are assembled in Bradford Fuller Swan, *The Case of Richard Chasmore alias Long Dick* (Providence: Society of Colonial Wars in the State of Rhode Island and Providence Plantations, 1944).

32 Noble, ed., *Recs. Mass. Ct. Assts.*, III, 66–67; I, 10, 14; Thomas, ed., *Diary of Samuel Sewall*, I, 4; Danforth, *Cry of Sodom*, esp. p. 8.

33 Pulsifer, ed., *Plym. Recs.*, VI, 74; Robert E. Moody, ed., *Province and Court Records of Maine*, Vol. III: *Province of Maine Records, 1680–1692* (Portland: Maine Historical Society, 1947), 199; Thompson, *Sex in Middlesex*, 73; Noble, ed., *Recs. Mass. Ct. Assts.*, I, 74, 87–88, 251, 273, 281; Thomas, ed. *Diary of Samuel Sewall*, I, 64; Cotton Mather to the Royal Society, July

3, 1716, in Kenneth Silverman, ed., *Selected Letters of Cotton Mather* (Baton Rouge: Louisiana State University Press, 1971), 209–10.

34   Lacy, ed., Recs. Conn. Ct. Assts., I, 52–53, 60; Connecticut State Archives, Crimes and Misdemeanors, 1662–1789, Ist ser., I, 216 (Connecticut State Library, Hartford).

35   Paul Boyer and Stephen Nissenbaum, eds., *The Salem Witchcraft Papers: Verbatim Transcripts of the Legal Documents of the Salem Witchcraft Outbreak of 1692* (New York: Da Capo Press, 1977), II, 520.

36   Edmund S. Morgan, ed., *Puritan Political Ideas, 1558–1794* (Indianapolis: The Bobbs-Merrill Company, Inc., 1965), 197; Aaron Leaming and Jacob Spicer, eds, *The Grants, Concessions, and Original Constitutions of New Jersey* (1752), 2nd edn (Somerville, NJ: Honeyman & Co., 1881), 404; E. P. Evans, *The Criminal Prosecution and Capital Punishment of Animals* (New York: E. P. Dutton and Company, 1906), 150–51.

37   Connecticut State Archives, Crimes and Misdemeanors, 2nd ser., II, 87a, 87b, 87c, 88a (Connecticut State Library, Hartford – emphasis in original); Albert E. Van Dusen, ed., *The Public Records of the State of Connecticut*, IX (Hartford: Connecticut State Library, 1953), 437–38.

38   Secretary of the Commonwealth, Executive Papers, Box 16, Dec. 16–31, 1870, Dec. 29 packet (Library of Virginia, Richmond).

Documents

In the first document William Bradford describes the early years of Plymouth colony. The excerpt includes an account of Thomas Granger's alleged crime of buggery committed in 1642 with several farm animals, including a turkey. Surprisingly, as John Murrin explains, the animal "victims" as well as the defendants required punishment in the eyes of authorities. Why?

Of Plymouth Plantation: the Pilgrims in America
William Bradford

Besids the occation before mentioned in these writings concerning the abuse of those 2. children, they had aboute the same time a case of

Excerpted from William Bradford, *Of Plymouth Plantation: the Pilgrims in America*, ed. Harvey Wish (New York: Capricorn Books, 1952), pp. 202–4.

buggerie fell out amongst them, which occasioned these questions, to which these answers have been made.

And after the time of the writing of these things befell a very sadd accidente of the like foule nature in this govermente, this very year, which I shall now relate. Ther was a youth whose name was Thomas Granger; he was servant to an honest man of Duxbery, being aboute 16. or 17. years of age. (His father & mother lived at the same time at Sityate.) He was this year detected of buggery (and indicted for the same) with a mare, a cowe, tow goats, five sheep, 2. calves, and a turkey. Horrible it is to mention, but the truth of the historie requires it. He was first discovered by one that accidentally saw his lewd practise towards the mare. (I forbear perticulers.) Being upon it examined and committed, in the end he not only confest the fact with that beast at that time, but sundrie times before, and at severall times with all the rest of the forenamed in his indictmente; and this his free-confession was not only in private to the magistrats, (though at first he strived to deney it,) but to sundrie, both ministers & others, and afterwards, upon his indictmente, to the whole court & jury; and confirmed it at his execution. And wheras some of the sheep could not so well be knowne by his description of them, others with them were brought before him, and he declared which were they, and which were not. And accordingly he was cast by the jury, and condemned, and after executed about the 8. of September, 1642. A very sade spectakle it was; for first the mare, and then the cowe, and the rest of the lesser catle, were kild before his face, according to the law, Levit: 20. 15. and then he him selfe was executed. The catle were all cast into a great & large pitte that was digged of purpose for them, and no use made of any part of them.

Upon the examenation of this person, and also of a former that had made some sodomiticall attempts upon another, it being demanded of them how they came first to the knowledge and practice of such wickednes, the one confessed he had long used it in old England; and this youth last spoaken of said he was taught it by an other that had heard of such things from some in England when he was ther, and they kept catle togeather. By which it appears how one wicked person may infecte many; and what care all ought to have what servants they bring into their families.

But it may be demanded how came it to pass that so many wicked persons and profane people should so quickly come over into this land, & mixe them selves amongst them? seeing it was religious men that begane the work, and they came for religions sake. I confess this may be marveilled at, at least in time to come, when the reasons therof should not be knowne; and the more because here was so many hardships and wants mett withall. I shall therefore indeavor to give some answer hereunto. And first, according to that in the gospell, it is ever to be remembred that where the Lord begins to sow good seed, ther the envious man will endeavore to sow tares. 2. Men being to come over into a wildernes, in which much labour & servise was to be done aboute building & planting, &c., such as wanted help in that respecte, when they could not have such as they would, were glad to take such as they could; and so, many untoward servants, sundry of them proved, that were thus brought over, both men & women kind; who, when their times were expired, became families of them selves, which gave increase hereunto. 3. An other and a maine reason hearof was, that men, finding so many godly disposed persons willing to come into these parts, some begane to make a trade of it, to transeport passengers & their goods, and hired ships for that end; and then, to make up their fraight and advance their profite, cared not who the persons were, so they had money to pay them. And by this means the cuntrie became pestered with many unworthy persons, who, being come over, crept into one place or other. 4. Again, the Lords blesing usually following his people, as well in outward as spirituall things, (though afflictions be mixed withall,) doe make many to adhear to the people of God, as many followed Christ, for the loaves sake, Iohn 6. 26. and a mixed multitud came into the willdernes with the people of God out of Eagipte of old, Exod. 12. 38; so allso ther were sente by their freinds some under hope that they would be made better; others that they might be eased of such burthens, and they kept from shame at home that would necessarily follow their dissolute courses. And thus, by one means or other, in 20. years time, it is a question whether the greater part be not growne the worser. . . .

Records of the Colony and Plantation of New Haven, from 1638 to 1649

Charles J. Hoadly

The next set of documents concerns two cases of bestiality in New Haven. The first involved George Spencer, a one-eyed man, who in 1641 first denied then later admitted the crime, before he ultimately recanted his confession. Authorities scoffed at his retraction, assuming he "acted by a lying speritt in his denyalls" because other compelling evidence indicted him: a sow, presumably

Excerpted from Charles J. Hoadly (ed.), *Records of the Colony and Plantation of New Haven, from 1638 to 1649* (Hartford, CT: Case, Tiffany, and Company, 1857), pp. 62–73, 295–6.

one of his prey, gave birth to a deformed piglet that looked just like Spencer. The "monster" also had "butt one eye in the midle of the face." Read carefully for the way in which the sin of bestiality was linked to other sins of which Spencer was also found guilty: lying, stubbornness, and ridiculing the Lord's Day. Why do you think Spencer's confession was so important to obtain?

This section's final document from 1646 focuses on another New Haven man, Thomas Hogg, who would not confess to bestiality, though the court punished him for other sins, including public masturbation, lying, and stealing. What evidence did the court attempt to procure in this case?

A Gen^rll Court Held at Newhaven the 2^d of the 1^t Moneth, 1641, about Geor: Spencer

Francis Browne admitted member of the Court and received the charge.

The 14th of February, 1641, John Wakeman a planter and member of this church acquainted the magistrates thatt a sow of his wch he had lately bought of Hen: Browning, then wth pigge, had now brought among divers liveing and rightly shaped pigs, one pdigious monster, wch he then brought wth him to be veiwed and considered. The monster was come to the full growth as the other piggs for ought could be discerned, butt brought forth dead. Itt had no haire on the whole body, the skin was very tender, and of a reddish white collour like a childs; the head most straing, itt had butt one eye in the midle of the face, and thatt large and open, like some blemished eye of a man; over the eye, in the bottome of the foreheade wch was like a childes, a thing of flesh grew forth and hung downe, itt was hollow, and like a mans instrum^t of gen^ration. A nose, mouth and chinne deformed, butt nott much vnlike a childs, the neck and eares had allso such resemblance. This monster being after opened and compared wth a pig of the same farrow, there was an aparant difference in all the inwards. Some hand of God appeared in an imp^rssion upon Goodwife Wakemans speritt, sadly expecting, though she knew nott why, some strange accedent in thatt sows pigging, and a strange imp^rssion was allso upon many thatt saw the monster, (therein guided by the neare resemblance of the eye,) that one George Spencer, late servant to the said Henry Browning, had beene actor in unnatureall and abominable filthynes wth the sow, thus divers upon the first sight, expressed their apprehensions w^thout any know-ledge whatt conjecture others had made. The foremenconed George Spencer so suspected hath butt one eye for vse, the other hath (as itt is called) a pearle in itt, is whitish & deformed, and his deformed eye being beheld and compard together wth the eye of the monster, seamed to be as like as the eye in the glass to the eye in the face; the man had beene form^rly notorious in the plantatiō for a prophane, lying, scoffing and lewd speritt, as was testfyed to his face, butt being examined concerning this abominatiō, att first he said he had nott done itt thatt he knew off, then denyed itt, butt being comitted to prison, partly on strong probabilities of this fact, and ptly for other miscarriages, the same evening, being the 24th of February as above, Mr. Goodyeare, one of the magistrates, went to the prison, found Sam: Martin and another yong man talking w^{t}h the said Georg Spencer, he asked him if he had nott comitted thatt abominable filthynes w^{t}h the sow, the prison^{r} att first denyed itt. Mr. Goodyeare asked him whatt he thought of the monster w^{c}h had beene shewed him, whether he did not take notice of something in itt like him, the prison^{r} after a little pause asked the magistrate whose sow itt was, who replyed, he knew best himselfe, att w^{c}h the prison^{r} was againe silent, the magistrate apprehending in the prisoner some relenting, as a preparatiō to confession, remembred him of thatt place of scripture, he thatt hideth his sin shall not prosper, butt he y^{t} confesseth and forsaketh his sins shall finde mercie, and asked him if he were nott sory he had denyed the fact w^{c}h seemed to be witnessed frō heaven agst him. The p^{r}son^{r} answered he was sory and confessed he had done itt, butt as Mr. Goodyeare was going away, the p^{r}son^{r} tolde Sam: Martin what he had confessed to Mr. Goodyeare was for fauo^{r}, thereupon Sam: Martin called Mr. Goodyeare back. Mr. Goodyeare retourning, asked the prison^{r} if he said soe, who said no, affirīng y^{t} Sam: Martin mistook him, Mr. Goodyeare demaunded of him whether had comitted the fact yea or no, he answered he had done itt, and so Mr. Goodyeare departed.

The 25th of Febr. 1641, both the magistrates w^{t}h divers others went to the prison to speake w^{t}h the prisoner, wished him to give glory to God, in a free confessiō of his sin, he againe confest the bestiality before meñconed, said he had comitted itt while he was in Mr. Brownings service, and in a hogstie of his; yett Mr. Goodyeare after going to him, he att first denyed the fact, but Robt Seely the marshall thereupon minding him of w^{t} he had confest to him, he againe freely confessed the fact, butt said he had nott done itt in the stye w^{c}h Mr. Goodyeare spake off, butt in a stye w^{t}hin a stable belonging to Mr. Browning. And thatt he, the said Geo: Spencer being there att worke, the sow came into the stable, and then the temptatiō and his corruptiō did worke, and he drove the sow into the stye, and then comitted thatt filthynes.

The 26th of Feb: Mr. Eaton and Mr. Davenport going to speake w^{t}h the prisoner, Mr. Goodyeare came to them and in the presence of Goodman Mansfield, Will Newmā, Tho: Yale, Theophilus Higginson, Joh: Brocktt and others, questioned him more perticularly concerīng the beastiality, namely how long the temptatiō had beene upon his speritt before he comitted itt; he answered itt had beene upon his speritt 2 or 3 dayes before; being asked w^{t} workings he had w^{t}hin him att thatt time, he said he found some workings against itt, both frō the haynousnes of the sin and the loathsomenes of the creature; being asked whether he did nott in thatt time seeke help frō God against the temptatiō, he said no, if he had he thought God would have helped him; being asked whether he did nott vse to pray to God, he answered he had not since he came to New England wᶜh was betweene 4 or 5 yeares agoe, in Engl[and] he did vse to pray, butt itt was onely in his bed; being asked in wᵗ manner, he answered [he] said (Our Father &c); being asked whether he did nott read the scriptures he answere[d] his maʳ putt him upon itt else nott, being asked whether he found nott some workinge [*upon him*] in the publique ministry, he answered sometimes he had some workings, butt they did nott abide wᵗh him, being asked how long he was in the stye wᵗh the sow, he said about 2 howers; being asked about wᵗ time, he said about 6 a clock in the evening, when the sun was sett, and the day light almost shutt in; being asked wᵗ itt was in the monster thatt did affect him, he answered the whitnes in the eye; being charged frō the testimony wᶜh had beene given by sundry person who had conversed wᵗh him, wᵗh a prophaiñe, atheisticall carryag, in unfaithfullnes and stubornes to his maʳ, a course of notorious lying, filthnes, scoffing att the ordinances, wayes and people of God, he confest miscarryages to his maʳ, and lying, and thatt he had scoffed att the Lords day, calling itt the Ladyes day, butt denyed other scoffing, wicked and bitter speeches witnessed against him, and other formʳ acts of filthynes, either with Indians or English, wᶜh out of his owne mouth were charged upon him. On the Lords day, being the 27ᵗʰ of Feb: he caused a bill to be putt up, intreating the prayers of the church to God on his behalfe, for the pardon of the sinns he had committed, and confessed, professing he was sory he had greived the magistrates in denying itt, acknowledging thatt Satan had hardened his hart both comitt and denye it.

Att a Genʳˡˡ Court held att Newhaven the 2ᵈ of March 1641

George Spencer being brought to the Barr and charged as wᵗh other crimes so wᵗh the foremenconed beastiality, and the monster shewed, upon wᶜh God from heaven seamed both to stamp out the sin, and as wᵗh his finger to single out the actor; being wisht therefore, as he had done before many wittnesses formerly, so againe, by confessiō to give glory to God; butt he impudently and wᵗh desperate imprecatiōˢ against himselfe denyed all thatt he had formerly confessed, whereupon the formʳ perticulars were fully testified in open Court to the prisonʳˢ face by the persons before menčoned respectively, and other testimonyes was added, namely, Robᵗ Seely the Marshall affirmed thatt the prisonʳ did dictate to him the foremenčoned bill by wᶜh he desired the prayers of the church for the pardon of thatt beastiality, professing therein thatt Satan had sometimes hardened his hart to deny itt, and y^t on the Lords day att night after he had heard himselfe prayed for in the congregatiō, he againe confessed the fact to him, and seamed to be greived for the sinne, and some teares fell from the prison^{rs} eyes greiving as he said thatt he had denyed itt. . . .

The Court, weighing the premises did finde and conclude the prisoner to be guilty of this unnatureall and abominable fact of beastiality, and thatt he was acted by a lying speritt in his denyalls. And according to the fundamentall agreem^t, made and published by full and gen^{rll} consent, when the plantatiō began and government was settled, that the judiciall law of God given by Moses and expounded in other parts of scripture, so far as itt is a hedg and a fence to the morrall law, and neither ceremoniall nor tipicall, nor had any referrence to Canaan, hath an everlasting equity in itt, and should be the rule of their proceedings. They judged the crime cappitall, and thatt the prisoner and the sow, according to Levit. 20 and 15, should be put to death, butt the time of executiō, and the kinde of death were respited till the next Gen^{rll} Court. . . .

Being hereupon demaunded in Court whether he would yett give glory to God in a free acknowledgm^t of his sinfull and abominable filthynes in the beastiality before named, he answered he would leave itt to God, adding thatt he had condemned himselfe by his former confessions.

The Court seriously considering the clearnes of the testimonyes together w^{t}h his answers, were aboundantly satisfied and confirmed, both concerning his guilt, and their form^r sentence against him, and now proceeded to determine whatt time, and what kinde of death he should dye. Itt was therefore by gen^{rll} consent concluded and adjudged, thatt on the 6th day next, being the 8 of Aprill, he the said Georg Spencer shall be hanged upon a gallows till he be dead, the place to be the farthest part of the feild called the Oyster-shell field, by the sea side, butt thatt first, the foremencõned sow att the said place of executiō shall be slaine in his sight, being run through w^{t}h a sworde.

The 8th of Aprill, 1642

The day of executiō being come, Georg Spencer the prisoner was brought to the place apoynted by the Court for executiō, in a cart; upon sight of the gallowes he seemed to be much amazed and trembled, after some pause he began to speake to the youths about him, exorting them all to take warning by his example how they neglect and dispise the meanes of Grace, and their soules good as he had done, in the educatiō he had from his parents, the goverm^t of his religious ma^r, and the publique ministry he had lived vnder, by all w^{c}h he might have gott much sperituall good, butt thatt his hart was hardened. In perticular he directed and pressed his exhort.

upon Anthony Stevens, servant to Mr. Malbon, then present, who being discontented wth his condicō, as the prisoner had heard, purposed to be gone from this place. He tolde him if he went from the ordinances he went from Christ, as he had heard itt delivered in publique, and many other wordes he vsed to the same purpose; wch being finished, he was advised to improve the small remainder of his time in the acknowledgm^t of his owne form^r sinfull miscarriages, together wth the abominable lewdnes he had committed wth the sow there present, and his desperate obstinacie in such fearefull denyalls after such cleare and full confession as he had oft made before sundry witnesses. Att first wth the acknowledgment of sundry evills, both in his yonger yeares, and in his late service, he joyned a denyall of his fact, butt the halter being fastened to the gallowes, and fitted to his neck, and being tolde it was an ill time now to pvoke God when he was falling into his hands, as a righteous and seveere judge who had vengeanc att hand for all his other sins, so for his impudency and atheisme, he justified the sentence as righteous, and fully confessed the beastiality in all the scircumstances, according to the evidence in Court, and called for one Will Harding, a sawyer there present, who coming neare, the prisoner charged upon him the murder of his soule, affirming thatt the said William Harding coming into the prison to him, had given him councell to deny the fact, and had tolde him thatt the Court could nott proceed against him, butt by his owne confession, wch pernicious councell had stopped his eare against all wholsome councell and advice thatt had, from time to time, beene given him, both by Mr. Davenport and others, for his speri-tuall good, and had hardened his hart to such a peremtory denyall in Court, though he had so often confessed the fact more privately, and though executiō had beene respited betwixt 5 and 6 weeks after the first sentence, and his life so long spared, yett the councell of the said Harding had beene a meanes to hinder his repentance, and now he was ready to dye, and knew no other butt he must goe presently to hell.

Thomas Hogg

Thomas Hogg haveing bin imprisoned vpon suspition of bestyality wth a sow of his mistreses, for about 2 or 3 monthes agoe, there was a discovery of that wch is conceived bestyalitye, a sow of Mrs. Lambertons pigging two monsters, one of them had a faire & white skinne & head, as Thomas Hoggs is. It being considred of, Mr. Pell was sent for, and afterward was fownd another wth a head lik a childs & one eye lik his, the bigger on the right side, as if God would discrib the party, wth the discription of the instrument of bestyalytie. This examinant being sent for & examjned about it, he fetched a deepe sight, fell in his counten-ance, but denyed it; but information was made of sundry loathsome passadges concerning him, as discovereing his nakednesse in more places then one, seemeing therby to indeauo^r the corrupting others, and being told of it, he said his breeches were rent, when indead his sperit was rent.

Thomas Hogg said his belly was broake, & his breeches were streight, & he wore a steele trusse, & soe it might happen his members might be seene.

Goodie Camp informed the court, that for all she could say to him, yet he did goe so as his filthy nakednesse did appeare; she has given him a needle & thridd to mend his breeches, but soone it was out againe, & he would tell her his breeches were tore & burnt.

The faults for w^{c}h he was imprisoned were two. For that of bestyalytie, guilt did appeare in his carryadge, although he denyed he was at farme when the sow took bore, & would not have gon to fetch home the swyne about their pigging time, & being sent once & agayne, he went, but brought them not home, but one of bro. Thompsons famyly fownd them in lesse then halfe a day.

Afterward the governo^r & deputy, intending to examyne him, caused him to be hadd downe vnto his M^{rs} yard, where the swyne were, & they bid him scratt the sow that had the monsters, & immedyatly there appeared a working of lust in the sow, insomuch that she powred out seede before them, & then, being asked what he thought of it, he said he saw a hand of God in it. Afterwards hee was bid to scratt another sow as he did the former, but that was not moved at all, which Thomas Hogg acknowledged to be true, but said he never had to doe w^{t}h the other sow. The court was informed that he seeing his m^{rs} swyne, & this sow that had the monsters, yet he would not bring them home.

Nicholas Elsie said he knoweth that Thomas Hogg did question whether that sow was his mistrises or noe, & shewed an vnwillingnesse to have them home.

Mary, servant vnto Mrs. Lamberton, informed the court that the neagar was the first in the famyly that observed his discovereing his nakednesse, & told him she would flying fier in his breeches if he continued thus; and divers times herself saw it, & told him of it, but he would deny it.

He had discovered himselfe to be an impudent lyar, and forward in stealing. Lucretia, the governo^{r}s neagar weoman, informed the court that while she was in the famyly w^{t}h h^m, she saw him act filthjnesse w^{t}h his hands by the fier side, & the next day the child & Hannah told her of it, & she asked whether hee was not ashamed. And she hath seene him take his hand out of the pott & a dumpling with it. Mary, aforementioned, added she saw him take cheese out of the buttrey, & speaking to him about it he denyed it presently.

The centence of the court was, (leaveing that about beastyalytye to be further considred on,) that for his filthynesse, lyeing & pilfering, he should be sevearly whipped, & for the future time during his imprisonement, that he be kept wth a meane dyet & hard labour, that his lusts may not bee fedd.

Further Reading

Brown, Kathleen M. "'Changed...into the fashion of man': the politics of sexual difference in a seventeenth-century Anglo-American settlement." *Journal of the History of Sexuality*, 6 (1995), 171–93.

Cannup, John. "'The cry of Sodom enquired into': bestiality and the wilderness of human nature in seventeenth-century New England." *American Antiquarian Society Proceedings*, 98 (1988), 113–34.

Godbeer, Richard. "'The cry of Sodom': discourse, intercourse, and desire in colonial New England." *William and Mary Quarterly*, 3rd series, 52 (1995), 259–86.

Oaks, Robert F. "'Things fearful to name': sodomy and buggery in seventeenth-century New England." *Journal of Social History*, 12 (1978–9), 268–81.

Reis, Elizabeth. Damned Women: Sinners and Witches in Puritan New England. Ithaca, NY: Cornell University Press, 1997.

Thompson, Roger. *Sex in Middlesex: Popular Mores in a Massachusetts County, 1649–1699*. Amherst: University of Massachusetts Press, 1986.

Thompson, Roger. "Attitudes towards homosexuality in the seventeenth-century New England colonies." *Journal of American Studies*, 23 (1989), 27–40.

Warner, Michael, "New English Sodom." *American Literature*, 64 (March 1992), 19–47.

2
Eroticizing the Middle Ground

Introduction

Richard Godbeer's article examines the nature of sexual contact between European men and Indian women. Though European men reluctantly married Indian women, they were not averse to having sex with them. Accounts describe sexual relationships ranging from rape to casual sex to lasting romantic unions. Colonial male traders and travelers commented extensively on what they saw as the loose sexual morality of Indian women; and they seem to have taken every opportunity to take advantage of this perceived cultural difference. Godbeer wisely cautions us against assuming that the traders understood Indian women's motivations. Whether the nature of the coupling was short-lived or a more lasting relationship, Indian women were not simply promiscuous or victims of male desire. Sources indicate that while some Native women entered into intimate, emotional relationships with European men, others used their bodies as a medium of either commercial or diplomatic exchange. Regardless of its motivation, sex across the cultural divide had significant consequences, including the birth of Anglo-Indian babies and the spread of sexually transmitted diseases.

Eroticizing the Middle Ground: Anglo-Indian Sexual Relations along the Eighteenth-century Frontier

Richard Godbeer

John Lawson, English explorer and naturalist, traveled extensively through the Carolinas in 1700–1701, following a horsehoe-shaped course that took him deep into the backcountry. Several years later, after settling in North Carolina, Lawson published a vividly detailed journal of his experiences and observations during the expedition. A recurrent topic in his account was sexual contact between colonists and Indians. English traders who lived among the Indians, he observed, usually had "Indian wives," women who provided sexual companionship and domestic services for the duration of the traders' residence in the community. One trader pointed out to Lawson a "cabin" that belonged to his "father-in-law": "he called him so by reason the old man had given him a young Indian girl, that was his daughter, to lie with him, make bread, and to be necessary in what she was capable to assist him in, during his abode among them." Although traders generally envisaged that such relationships would last only until they moved on, some Englishmen who became "accustomed to the conversation of these savage women, and their way of living" were "so allured with that careless sort of life, as to be constant to their Indian wife," never returning to live "amongst the English." Alongside these relationships, temporary and lasting, casual sex between Englishmen and Indian women was also common, Lawson wrote. Some of these encounters he construed as involving sexual commerce: like many other eighteenth-century Europeans, Lawson characterized as prostitution exchanges that functioned for native Americans as a component of diplomatic, social, and economic reciprocity. Lawson lamented that promiscuous sex between Indians and Englishmen had led to the rampant circulation of venereal disease, another common theme in European writings about

Excerpted from Richard Godbeer, "Eroticizing the Middle Ground: Anglo-Indian Relations along the Eighteenth-century Frontier," in Martha Hodes (ed.), Sex, Race, Love: Crossing Boundaries in North American History (New York: New York University Press, 1999), pp. 91–111.

sexual contact with native Americans. Fortunately, he observed, Indians were well versed in a range of cures.[1]

Lawson's comments on Anglo-Indian sexual relations were not anomalous. Other eighteenth-century travelers in the southern backcountry noted the prevalence of both casual sex and domestic relationships between native Americans and Englishmen. This essay uses travel journals in conjuction with letters written by traders, colonial officials, and itinerant missionaries, as well as official records, to examine Anglo-Indian sexual relations along the southern frontier. The writers whose journals, letters, and reports provide the basis for what follows had their own preoccupations, biases, and ulterior motives in writing about Anglo-Indian relations. Their remarks about indigenous culture are most suspect, often revealing more of the authors' fantasies and fears than of the societies they purported to describe. Yet these accounts are remarkably consistent in asserting that Anglo-Indian sexual relations were common along the frontier, and their different perspectives on the subject are instructive when placed in counterpoint to one another. If read with great caution and in conjuction, they reveal not only the English male attitudes that they were designed to express, but also the cultural negotiations and compromises into which such men were drawn, often unwittingly; these accounts provide a valuable, albeit incomplete, body of information about the complex dynamics involved in erotic and romantic concourse across the racial divide.

What follows does not challenge the conventional wisdom that early colonists, and later those who lived within the established parameters of colonial society, were generally unwilling to countenance intermarriage with native Americans. It contends, however, that sex had an important role to play in Anglo-Indian relations along and beyond the edges of colonial settlement. As travelers, traders, soldiers, and diplomats dealt with native Americans on what one historian has called "the middle ground,"[2] their interactions, accommodations, cultural misunderstandings, and conflicts were as much sexual as they were economic, diplomatic, and military. That sexual middle ground bore witness to the many possibilities of intercultural contact: it embodied not only the violence of colonial appropriation but also the mutual and successful accommodation of different peoples.

Despite a shortage of women in the early English settlements, especially in the Chesapeake, male colonists were reluctant to take Indian women as wives. The settlers' aversion to Anglo-Indian marriage was based on a range of concerns, some ideological and others pragmatic. Most fundamental were biblical injunctions against marriage to non-Christians and English disdain for the Indians' "barbaric" way of life. Forced to rely on

Indian food supplies and advice as they struggled to survive in a new environment, the colonists sought to shore up their battered sense of superiority by maintaining a self-conscious boundary between the "savage" natives and their "civilized" selves; Anglo-Indian marriage threatened that strategy both physically and symbolically. On a more practical level, colonists harbored suspicions that the Indians might use intermarriage as a way to infiltrate colonial settlements. They were also concerned that Anglo-Indian unions might give rise to native male jealousy. Those settlers who valued premarital chastity were shocked by the Indians' apparently permissive attitude toward sexual experimentation before marriage, while even those without such scruples worried about the alleged prevalence of syphillis among the Indians. Marriage to native women, then, endangered the colonists' sense of cultural supremacy as well as their mores, safety, and health.[3]

Perhaps the most eloquent expression of colonial discomfort with the idea of Anglo-Indian union was contained, ironically, within a marriage proposal. When John Rolfe petitioned to marry Pocahontas in 1614, he dwelt at length on possible objections to their marriage and his own ambivalence toward the union.[4] Aware that his "settled and long continued affection" for Pocahontas might be mistaken for sexual desperation, Rolfe insisted that he could, if he wanted, find English women to satisfy his "carnall" needs (albeit at the price of "a seared conscience") and that he did not lack marital prospects back in England. He was driven by love, "not any hungry appetite, to gorge myself with incontinency." But Rolfe's petition expressed profound anxiety about cultural and spiritual contamination through union with a "strange" and "barbarous" woman. In a "private controversy," Rolfe had sought to justify his "affection" to himself as well as to others. He had recalled "the heavie displeasure which almightie God conceived against the sonnes of Levie and Israel for marrying strange wives," and had weighed the "inconveniences" of uniting "in love with one whose education hath bin rude, her manners barbarous, her generation accursed," and "discrepant in all nurtriture" from himself. Scriptural injuctions, a fear of the "barbarous," and anxieties about sexual degeneration combined with his suspicion that Satan himself had "hatched" his love for Pocahontas to form a lurid nightmare of self-destruction. Rolfe had finally convinced himself that dedicating his marriage to the spiritual redemption of Pocahontas would enable a triumph over "transitory pleasures and worldly vanities," a sanctification of the flesh. Their union would justify itself not only as a political alliance, "for the good of this plantation, for the honour of our country," but also and, indeed, primarily as an evangelical enterprise, "for the converting to the true knowledge of God and Jesus Christ an unbelieving creature, namely Pocahontas."

Rolfe's "private controversy" may have been partly, or even wholly, concocted as a way to assure critics that he understood and even shared their objections to his marriage proposal; but even if a tactical ploy, it remains helpful in conveying the kind of nightmarish image that Rolfe believed intermarriage would provoke in his fellow colonists. His more positive view of intermarriage as a happy and high-minded conjuction of spiritual duty and romantic fulfilment was not widely shared by his contemporaries. During the first decade of settlement in the Chesapeake, English males had been drawn away to Indian communities by sheer hunger and an equally desperate appetite for female companionship, but the union between Rolfe and Pocahontas in 1614 did not lead to a spate of Anglo-Indian marriages. Not only did English prejudice against such unions remain firmly in place, but Indian women had little reason to choose as husbands men who were generally much less adept at hunting, fishing, and other pertinent skills than prospective mates in their own communities.[5] The greater availability of English women by the end of the seventeenth century removed any practical justification for intermarriage, while the growing population of slaves provided an outlet for planters' extramarital sexual appetites. Throughout the colonial period, Anglo-Americans living in eastern settlements occasionally formed sexual and domestic relationships with Indians, but most of those who did so seem to have been marginal figures. [Much more common were marriages between Indians and African Americans.] Any English man or woman who became sexually intimate with an Indian was liable to stigmatization as "debased" or "defiled." For many members of colonial society, Anglo-Indian sexual relations or marriages remained fundamentally problematic in their cultural implications.[6]

There were individuals who saw the colonists' repudiation of intermarriage as a lost opportunity. Writing in the early eighteenth century, the Virginia planter William Byrd lamented the settlers' "squeamish" and "unreasonable" opposition to Anglo-Indian marriage, caused according to him by their "aversion to the copper complexion of the natives." Intermarriage, as John Rolfe had clearly understood, could be used as a tool of conversion: "a sprightly lover," Byrd wrote, "is the most prevailing missionary that can be sent amongst these or any other infidels." Furthermore, Anglo-Indian marriage could have prevented bloodshed by allowing the colonists to expand onto land deeded to them through dowry agreements: "the poor Indians would have had less reason to complain that the English took away their land if they had received it by way of a portion with their daughters." And finally, Byrd wrote, the predominantly male colonial population in the seventeenth-century Chesapeake would have grown much more rapidly had the men been willing to marry Indians. Native women, he wrote, would have proven "altogether as honest wives for the first planters" as the English "damsels" who crossed the Atlantic, many of whom were reputed to have shady pasts.

Byrd pointed out that the issue of color would have faded as the progeny of interracial marriages became paler with each passing generation: "if a Moor may be washed white in three generations, surely an Indian might have been blanched in two." By the early eighteenth century, there would have been no "reproach" attached to such a union because the physical signs of intermarriage would have disappeared. Besides, Byrd argued, the early colonists should have ignored superficial distinctions, focusing instead on underlying similarities and the Indians' potential for "improvement." Like James Harriot and John White, Byrd portrayed Indians as underdeveloped rather than intrinsically primitive: "All nations of men have the same natural dignity, and we all know that very bright talents may be lodged under a very dark skin. The principal difference between one people and another proceeds only from the different opportunities of improvement." Byrd's self-conscious magnanimity in no way compromised his sense of cultural superiority: like their land, the native inhabitants' "complexion" and "talents" could be "improved" by becoming anglicized.[7] . . .

Yet Byrd's straightforward claim that Virginia colonists were physically repelled by the Indians' "copper complexion" belied the more complex attitude toward Indians as aesthetic and sexual objects that emerges from early American writings, including Byrd's own. English culture did invest light-colored skin with connotations of virtue, cleanliness, and civilized beauty; migrants to North America proved themselves true Englishmen by expressing disdain for Indian (and, of course, African) complexions.[8] But cultural imperatives did not prevent English colonists from finding Indians with whom they interacted attractive and desirable: experience often conflicted with preconceptions. . . .

Explorers and early colonists had often commented on native beauty and provided those who followed with a tantalizing portrait of Indian sexual culture as uninhibited and permissive.[9] Eighteenth-century settlers and Europeans traveling in North America also commented on the beauty of Indian women, although usually framing their remarks with defensive caveats about the natives' dark color or lack of hygiene. Such remarks came overwhelmingly from genteel travelers and reflected a preoccupation with cleanliness and fashionable, leisured pallor (dark skin indicating the need to labor outside) that colonists outside the elite would most likely not have shared. Diron D'Artaguiette, a French official in Louisiana, wrote in the 1720s that the Natchez women's habit of blackening their teeth, "together with their tawney color," made them "rather disagreeable to those who are not prejudiced in their favor";

nevertheless, he conceded, they had "rather regular features" and were "fairly passable." Robert Hunter, a young merchant who traveled in North America during 1785–86 to collect debts owed to his father's firm in London, described Indian women as "handsome ... notwithstanding their color." According to Luigi Castiglioni, a Milanese botanist traveling through the United States in 1785–87, Indian women were "very dirty and ill-smelling," but some "combine[d] a pretty figure with a vivacious face." Lawson declared much less grudgingly that Indian women were "as fine-shaped creatures (take them generally) as any in the universe ... not so uncouth or unlikely, as we suppose them."[10]

Descriptions of Indian women were often at least implicitly pornographic, incorporating fantasies about scantily clad, innocent yet alluring, and apparently available women into narratives of sexual aggression....

William Bartram, a Philadelphia naturalist who traveled through the Carolinas, Georgia, and Florida in 1773–77, provided a particularly redolent description of native beauty in a passage that used idyllic motifs to frame, and partly camouflage, an account of thwarted sexual assault. Bartram conjured for his readers an enticing image of "primitive innocence," discovered in "a vast expanse of green meadows and strawberry fields" by Bartram and his companions as they traveled through the South Carolina backcountry:

> companies of young, innocent Cherokee virgins, some busily gathering the rich fragrant fruit, others having already filled their baskets, lay reclined under the shade of floriferous and fragrant native bowers of Magnolia, Azalea, Philadelphus, perfumed Calycanthus, sweet Yellow Jessamine and cerulian Glycine frutescens, disclosing their beauties to the fluttering breeze, and bathing their limbs in the cool fleeting streams; while other parties, more gay and libertine, were yet collecting strawberries or wantonly chasing their companions, tantalising them, staining their lips and cheeks with the rich fruit.

The strangers' arrival threatened to transform this charming and sensual scene into one of sexual violence. The prospect of "sylvan nymphs," Bartram wrote, was "perhaps too enticing for hearty young men to continue idle speculators," and so they crept down toward the young women, determined "to have a more active part in their delicious sports." Bartram admitted that their interest in the "Cherokee virgins" was at least potentially sexual and predatory:

> although we meant no other than an innocent frolic with this gay assembly of hamadryades, we shall leave it to the person of feeling and sensibility to form an idea to what lengths our passions might have hurried us, thus

warmed and excited, had it not been for the vigilance and care of some
envious matrons who lay in ambush, and espying us gave the alarm, time
enough for the nymphs to rally and assemble together.

The defensive maneuvers executed by the "matrons" and perhaps also
a sudden realization that Indian men might be close at hand jolted
the travelers into a more circumspect and gentlemanly comportment.
Once Bartram and his companions convinced the "matrons" that
they were willing to restrain themselves, tension dissipated and the
strangers were invited to join them in eating some fruit, "encircled by
the whole assembly of the innocently jocose sylvan nymphs." Bartram's
account allowed readers to delight in visions of Edenic innocence while
participating vicariously in the travelers' voyeurism as well as their barely
contained lust for the native women. In doing so, he invited them to
appropriate his own experiences and fantasies into a pornographic gaze
upon the New World.[11]

Other eighteenth-century authors admitted that those who came into
contact with native inhabitants were eager to sample "their favors,"
although they usually emphasized the Indian women's eagerness to
oblige, given their allegedly permissive sexual mores.[12] Early observers
of the Indians had sometimes reminded their readers that the indigenous
peoples' apparently relaxed attitude toward sex should be understood as
"rather a horrible licentiousness than a liberty," but travelers throughout
the colonial period not infrequently welcomed the opportunity to enjoy a
little sexual "liberty," or even "licentiousness."[13] In October 1711, for
example, when Byrd took part in militia exercises just outside the Indian
settlement at Nottoway Town, he noted in his dairy that he and other
militiamen entertained themselves by cavorting with native women. One
morning, they "rose about 6 o'clock and then took a walk about the
town to see some Indian girls, with which [they] played the wag." In the
evening of the following day, he wrote, "some of my troop went with me
into the town to see the girls and kissed them without proceeding any
further." The following night, "Jenny, an Indian girl, had got drunk and
made us good sport." (It is not clear from Byrd's laconic entry how far
the "sport" went and to what extent Jenny was a willing participant.)[14] ...

Although, as we will see, sexual interest in native women sometimes
took the form of violent assault, it would be wrong to assume that
English advances were always unwelcome or that the advances always
came from the English. Eighteenth-century observers noted with prurient fascination that young women in many Indian tribes were free to
experiment sexually prior to marriage and eager to do so with white as
well as native men. Some narratives made sweeping generalizations on

this as on many aspects of Indian mores. "The 'Flos Virginis,'" wrote Lawson, "so much coveted by the Europeans, is never valued by these savages."[15] But other writers recognized that not all Indian nations had the same attitude and noted carefully for the benefit of prospective travelers which ones seemed to be sexually permissive. D'Artaguiette informed readers that young Illinois women were "the mistresses of their own bodies (to use their own expression)" and welcomed the attentions of European visitors, whereas Arkansas women were not available (their menfolk had convinced them, "if one cares to believe the interpreters," that they would die if they had sex with Europeans).[16] Thomas Nairne, a soldier and diplomat in South Carolina during the early eighteenth century, noted that Chickasaw mores forbade the sexual license allowed youngsters elsewhere: "[y]ou shall not see them ogle and splite glances as the other savages['] ladies usually do." Under the guise of praising such nations for preventing "scandalous liberties," such passages warned which Indian women the travelers could not approach without risking native anger and retribution.[17]

Europeans and colonists found that native women generally expected some kind of gift in exchange for a sexual encounter. Byrd wrote that Indian women were "a little mercenary in their amours and seldom bestow[ed] their favors out of stark love and kindness." When four Saponi women offered themselves to Byrd and his companions, "the price they set upon their charms" was "a pair of red stockings."[18] Travelers and writers assumed that such women were prostituting themselves, an interpretation that conveniently conflated native women with, and reduced them to, vendible goods, but Indians themselves would have perceived such encounters very differently. The notion of exchange lay at the very heart of native American culture, providing a funda-mental structure with accompanying rituals of civility for any interaction, including courtship. Young women who asked for goods in exchange for sexual intimacy were insisting upon a social etiquette that Europeans frequently misinterpreted, blind as they were to the underlying cultural logic.

In some cases, native women may have used their bodies to procure goods of value to their kin network, cannily exploiting travelers' hunger for female companionship. Such goods as women were likely to demand in return for use of their bodies were also precious as commodities of exchange for food and other essentials. A "pretty young girl" whom one of Lawson's companions had procured for the night persuaded her pro-spective bedfellow to show her "all the treasure he was possessed of, as beads, red cadis [cheap serge], etc., which she liked very well, and per-mitted him to put them into his pocket again." Before morning, she disappeared with the entire contents of his pocket, and also his shoes.

The travelers had intended to use some of these "treasures" to pay for their "victuals."[19]

Among the native peoples encountered by Lawson in the Carolinas, sexual commerce was highly organized, or so he perceived. Certain young women were "set apart" to be "trading girls." They had "a particular tonsure" by which they were distinguished from those women available for marriage. Most of their income went to "the king's purse." Lawson characterized the "king" as "the chief bawd, exercising his prerogative over all the stews of his nation, and his own cabin (very often) being the chiefest brothel-house." The "trading girls" apparently "led that course of life for several years," using abortive medicine to end any incidental conceptions; their marital prospects were not, so far as Lawson could discern, damaged by their "having been common to so many."[20]

From the Indians' perspective, "trading girls" may well have functioned not only as a commercial proposition but also as a component of diplomatic ritual. Since diplomacy and commerce were bound together in Indian exchange culture, it would not be surprising if sex as diplomatic courtesy and sex as trade were sometimes conflated. Lawson noted that when another of his companions refused a trading girl offered to him by a sachem, "his majesty flew into a violent passion, to be thus slighted, telling the Englishmen, they were good for nothing."[21] The sachem may well have been frustrated by his failure to extract goods from the traveler in return for the woman's services, but he may also have been enraged by the white man's lack of manners in rejecting a gesture of welcome. Byrd's reference to "the compliment of bedfellows" as customary Indian "hospitality" certainly points in that direction.[22]

English forts offered ample opportunities for Indians to deploy female bodies as a medium of exchange. Some women functioned as temporary companions to officers with the means to support them. Visiting Fort Niagara in 1785, Robert Hunter observed an "abundance of squaws" who were "mostly kept by the gentlemen who reside there." These "kept" women were "dressed remarkably well" and "living in the height of luxury." Nonetheless, Hunter noted disapprovingly, they would "immediately leave their keeper" if "any little quarrel" occurred and take up with someone else. Even while being "kept" they would, "before their keeper's face, go with anybody else who will offer them some rum, which they are extravagantly fond of." The women were willing to partner irrespective of English racial distinctions: "[e]verybody is alike indifferent to them, black, white, or Indian." The picture that emerges from Hunter's account is of a fluid and multiracial sexual marketplace in which native women provided services, apparently on their own terms, to the troops in residence, either in the form of brief encounters or as part of a temporary domestic relationship. Whether the initial decision to engage sexually with the fort's inhabitants had been made by the women themselves or by relatives is unclear (this presumably varied from nation to nation), but Hunter's description of the women's behavior at the fort suggests that they considered themselves free of English control and indeed empowered by demand for their services. The goods that they procured as a result of these sojourns would presumably make their way back to kin networks. Such women, then, acted as conduits for the acquisition of wealth and status.[23] . . .

Traders, who spent most of their time traveling beyond the frontier and who often lived in native communities for prolonged periods, had by far the most sustained and intimate contact with Indians. Those among them who succeeded in establishing a cordial, trusting rapport with their hosts became valuable diplomatic as well as economic intermediaries between native and colonial societies. It was not unusual for traders to enter relationships with Indian women, which not only satisfied personal needs but also eased their acceptance into the local community. However, while some traders settled into at least temporarily stable relationships, others were notoriously promiscuous – thus Lawson's attribution of responsibility for the spread of veneral disease in many Indian communities. The traders who attracted most attention from colonial officials were those who treated the Indians with least respect. Their abusive and violent behavior, which often manifested itself in sexual form, could poison Indian attitudes not only toward the individual concerned but also toward Englishmen in general, undermining decades of patient diplomacy. Although it is clear that many traders dealt peaceably and respectfully with the native peoples among whom they lived, the outrages perpetrated by their colleagues often overshadowed the more constructive results of trading activity in both Indian and colonial minds.

Maverick and abusive sexual behavior toward neighboring Indians disturbed colonial officials and clerics for moral and practical reasons. Anglican missionaries touring the backcountry claimed that many of the traders were "utter strangers to the virtues of temperance and chastity."[24] Appalled by the traders' "notoriously lewd and immoral practices," they feared that the Indians would be discouraged from converting by the image of English Christianity that the traders presented.[25] Such concerns were not without foundation: in 1725 a Cherokee "priest" in conversation with the trader and interpreter Alexander Long expressed (presumably ironic) amazement that men with "such good priests and such knowledge as they have" could be so "debauched" and "wicked."[26] Those involved in colonial government lamented "the evil impressions which those savages are liable to receive from the rudest of mortals," and worried about the disruption of peaceful relations by the abusive and insulting behavior of the traders, some of whom were "more savage than them."[27] In letters of instruction that captured effectively the blend of ethical and pragmatic concerns that motivated colonial officials, the commissioners for Indian trade in South Carolina enjoined agents "to regulate the lives of the traders, so that they give not the Indians offence and scandal, against the Christian religion, and to bring them within the bounds of morality at least."[28]

The negative impact of the traders' "immoral practices" on diplomatic relations caused colonial officials grave concern. Informants in the back-country kept members of the governing elite appraised of traders' sexual depredations. David Crawley, himself involved in trade along the frontier, devoted part of a 1715 letter to a forceful denunciation of South Carolina traders and, specifically, their behavior toward the Indians with whom they were staying: "when they had sent the [Indian] men away about their business or they were gone ahunting [I] have heard them brag to each other of debauching their [the Indians'] wives sumtime forc[ing] them and once s[aw] it myself in the day time."[29] William Byrd, to whom Crawley's letter was addressed, claimed that the misconduct of Carolina traders toward the Indians, "abusing their women and evil entreating their men," was "the true reason of the fatal war which the nations round about made upon Carolina in the year 1713."[30] ...

The Indians themselves were not reticent in expressing outrage when traders preyed on their women. In 1752 leaders of the Lower Creek nation met with the governor's agent and "complained very heavily of the white people in general for debauching their wives and mentioned several in particular that were found guilty, and said if his Excellency would not punish them for it, the injured persons would certainly put their own laws in execution."[31] At a 1765 meeting with representatives of the new English government in Louisiana, Choctaw chiefs protested "the behaviour of the traders towards our women," claiming that "often when the traders sent for a basket of bread and the generous Indian sent his own wife to supply their wants, instead of taking the bread out of the basket they put their hands upon the breast of their wives." The chiefs warned that such "indecent freedom" threatened to produce "very great disturbances."[32] ...

Yet while government officials focused their attention on the political damage wrought by "debauched" traders who moved beyond the frontier, eighteenth-century travelers often encountered traders whose dealings with native peoples were peaceful and constructive. Those who lived in Indian communities for extended periods often established domestic relationships with native women for the duration of their stay. This kind of arrangement was compatible with the Indian view that marriage did not necessarily constitute a permanent bond. In addition to functioning as "she-bed-fellow[s]," "dressing their victuals," and performing other domestic chores, native wives could help traders develop a closer "friendship with the savages," learn the local language more quickly, and become acquainted with "the affairs and customs of the country."[33] They could prove invaluable as intermediaries, sources of information about Indian movements, and fronts for illegal trade.[34]

Traders who became involved with Indian women were given privileges otherwise unavailable to outsiders. Bartram, for example, mentioned a man who, "being married to a Cherokee woman of family, was indulged to keep a stock of cattle." Indian women, Bartram wrote, were usually loyal and energetic in promoting the interests of "their temporary husbands": "they labour and watch constantly to promote their private interests, and detect and prevent any plots or evil designs which may threaten their persons, or operate against their trade or business." Should conflict arise between a trader and members of the community in which he was living, the kin associations he had acquired through his marriage could offer some measure of protection.[35] But traders did not take Indian wives simply because white women were unavailable and doing so benefited them commercially. Their attitude toward such relationships was clearly pragmatic but not necessarily cynical: as Bartram put it, although "fully sensible" of the advantages offered by such "affections and friendship in matters of trade and commerce," in many cases "their love and esteem" for each other were quite "sincere." As we will see, some Anglo-Indian unions developed into lasting and devoted marriages, causing Englishmen to settle permanently in native communities.[36]

From the perspective of Indian wives and their kinfolk, marriage to an English trader, whether temporary or lasting, had much to offer as they drew the Englishman, along with his goods, into the kinship orbit. Eighteenth-century observers paid little attention to the practical advantages that native women derived from such relationships, claiming that they were "prone to European attachments" because their own menfolk were "not so vigorous or impatient in their love as we are."[37] Like John Rolfe in his discussion of Pocahontas, later writers tended to gloss the complex political and economic considerations that underlay Indian attitudes toward intermarriage as a straightforward "love" for the English. Yet we may surmise that Indian women were drawn to traders as much by the attendant benefits as by English sexual enthusiasm. Such relationships conferred considerable status, given the important economic and diplomatic roles played by trader-husbands, and enabled women to gain access to valuable goods that they then passed on to their kin. This did not always sit well with other Indians interested in acquiring goods. In 1753 representatives of the Lower Creek nation complained that traders had inflated their prices in order to compensate for the expense of "giv[ing] away such quantities to their wives."[38] The emergence of substantial female majorities in many eighteenth-century Indian nations, resulting from an upsurge in warfare brought on by the increased Euro-American presence, may have softened objections to marriage with whites and highlighted the advantages. While a straight-forward demographic explanation for Indian interest in intermarriage would be reductive, it may well have been part of the picture for at least some native peoples....

Although partnerships between traders and Indian women were often intended to last only for the duration of the Englishman's residence, some developed into lasting marriages. As Lawson acknowledged, it was not unusual for traders to settle permanently in native communities, drawn by their personal attachments to native women, as well as by the Indians' way of life:

> we often find that Englishmen, and other Europeans that have been accustomed to the conversation of these savage women, and their way of living, have been so allured with that careless sort of life, as to be constant to their Indian wife, and her relations, as long as they lived, without ever desiring to return again amongst the English, although they had very fair opportunities of advantages amongst their countrymen; of which sort I have known several.[39]

Other colonists whose business took them westward sometimes found personal happiness and material opportunities among native peoples. At Pittsburgh the actor-manager John Bernard met a land surveyor named Wools, whose surveying "had led him among the Indians near the Mississippi, where he had married a king's daughter" and received "a tract of land which he soon contrived to convert into a handsome independence." Wools had married his wife in an Indian ceremony.[40] Englishmen who settled with Indian partners in Indian territory on Indian terms struck observers as bizarre and unsettling curiosities. Like Indian captives who refused to return to colonial society[41] and settlers in the backcountry who dressed and behaved "as Indians,"[42] they brought into question the resilience and superiority of English culture.[43]

The issue of cultural allegiance became most pressing when English-men had children with Indian women. Regardless of whether the context was a casual sexual liaison, a temporary relationship, or a lasting mar-riage, decisions had to be made about the children's upbringing. Lawson considered it a "great misfortune" that such children went to the mother by "rule and custom amongst all the savages of America," and so were raised "in a state of infidelity."[44] But this was clearly an unwarranted generalization. Nathaniel Osborne, an Anglican missionary, mentioned in a 1715 report that he had recently baptized five "mulatto children," the offspring of "our Indian traders, by Indian women during their abode amongst them."[45] Alexander Cameron, a British agent among the Cherokee from 1764 to 1781, married an Indian woman who resided with him at his plantation, Lochaber, and bore him three children, all of whom were later sent to England.[46] On a recruiting expedition in 1775, Bernard Elliott stayed as a houseguest with the trader George Galphin, whose daughters by an Indian woman were "politely enough educated with music, etc."[47] But most traders lacked the resources of Cameron or Galphin and were themselves no longer fully committed to an English way of life. Their children often built lives that straddled the physical and cultural frontier: by the middle of the eighteenth century, many of the traders were themselves offspring of Anglo-Indian relationships.[48]

The ritual through which a mixed couple formalized their marriage had far-reaching implications for cultural power in the relationship and could be fraught with anxieties for those involved. The trader James Adair mentioned an Englishman who married an Indian, Dark-Lanthorn, "according to the manner of the Cherokee," but then took her to an English settlement in order to remarry in an English ceremony, which involved having Dark-Lanthorn baptized. According to a Frenchman who traveled through North America in 1795–97, marrying according to Indian custom appealed to some European men because they could treat the ceremony as binding them no longer than they themselves chose.[49] But in this case the Englishman worried about the apparent transience of native marriages and the implications of the matriarchal system within which they were contracted:

> observing that marriages were commonly of a short duration in that wanton female government, he flattered himself of ingrossing her affections, could he be so happy as to get her sanctified by one of our own beloved men with a large quantity of holy water in baptism – and be taught the conjugal duty, by virtue of her new Christian name, when they were married anew.

The personal negotiations and educative process involved in preparing for a marriage of this sort must have been challenging, regardless of which culture predominated. Dark-Lanthorn became increasingly impatient as a minister subjected her to a detailed examination prior to the marriage ceremony. Her husband, acting as interpreter, "recommended to her a very strict chastity in the married state," the importance of which he clearly feared she did not appreciate. "Very well," Dark-Lanthorn replied, "that's a good speech, and fit for every woman alike, unless she is very old – But what says he now?" When the cleric continued to question her about religious doctrine and lectured her on the need for "a proper care in domestic life," she called him an "Evil Spirit" and instructed her husband to "[t]ell him his speech [was] troublesome and light."

Adair finished his account by noting sardonically that the minister later had to erase Dark-Lanthorn's name from his book of converts "on account of her adulteries." Adair gave no clue as to the circumstances under which these alleged "adulteries" took place. If, for example, Dark-Lanthorn left her husband without a formal divorce and then initiated a sexual relationship with another man, this would have counted as adultery from an English legal perspective, but not necessarily from an Indian perspective. Whatever the actual train of events, Adair saw the collapse of their marriage as a warning to those contemplating alliances to women from cultures not only "savage" but also subject to "wanton female government." Such marriages involved the risk that one's spouse might not prove susceptible to patriarchal structures, a particularly horrifying testimony to the backcountry's inversion of "civilized" norms and the potential cost of embracing the middle ground.[50]

Compromise, accommodation, confusion, tension, and fracture: all of these figured in the relationship between Dark-Lanthorn and her unnamed English husband. They also encapsulate more generally the range of dynamics produced by Anglo-Indian erotic and romantic relations. The surviving evidence suggests that sexual contact between Indians and Englishmen created a broad spectrum of intercultural scenarios, with violent coercion at one extreme and respectful coexistence at the other. Along and beyond the frontier, as Indians and Englishmen eroticized the middle ground between their cultures, they bore testimony together to the possibilities of their meeting as well as to its dangers and ultimate tragedy. Rape was doubtless more common and relations in general more contested than the extant sources, with all their biases, suggest; but we should not ignore evidence for more positive interactions. Indians and Englishmen could and sometimes did enjoy each other, love each other, and live together in peace.

Eighteenth-century commentators on Anglo-Indian relations reacted to interracial sex along the frontier with prurient ambivalence. Most of these writers adopted a tone that combined to varying degrees incomprehension, condescending humor, and disapproval, even as they reveled in the voyeuristic possibilities afforded by such interactions. Genteel travelers, including those who partook of Indian women, sought to distance themselves, at least rhetorically, from interracial familiarities. Their determination to sustain a sense of cultural difference and superiority demanded no less. Members of the southern elite invested heavily, both psychologically and economically, in their own gentility and worried about humiliating comparisons with their counterparts across the Atlantic.[51] The adoption by backcountry inhabitants of Indian customs and their occasional absorption into native communities, despite "fair opportunities of advantages amongst their countrymen," raised the specter of cultural degeneration and must have deepened the self-doubts of those who aspired to gentility.... [The colonial elite] and their European guests clearly saw the eroticization of contact with Indians as alluring yet dangerous: those attracted sexually to Indians might be "beguiled and vanquished" in more ways than one.

Notes

1 John Lawson, *A New Voyage to Carolina*, ed. Hugh Talmage Lefler (1708; reprint, Chapel Hill: University of North Carolina Press, 1967), 25–26, 29–30, 35–36, 41, 190–92, 194.

2 Richard White, *The Middle Ground: Indians, Empires, and Republics in the Great Lakes Region, 1650–1815* (New York: Cambridge University Press, 1991).

3 David D. Smits provides the most thorough examination of English attitudes toward intermarriage with native Americans in "'Abominable Mixture': Toward the Repudiation of Anglo-Indian Intermarriage in Seventeenth-Century Virginia," *Virginia Magazine of History and Biography* 95 (1987): 157–92.

4 John Rolfe to Sir Thomas Dale, April 1614, in *The Old Dominion in the Seventeenth Century: A Documentary History of Virginia, 1606–1689*, ed. Warren M. Billings (Chapel Hill: University of North Carolina Press, 1975), 216–19.

5 Smits, "'Abominable Mixture,'" 168, 176.

6 Smits, "'Abominable Mixture,'" 188–89.

7 William Byrd, "History of the Dividing Line," in *The Prose Works of William Byrd of Westover*, ed. Louis B. Wright (Cambridge: Harvard University Press, 1966), 160–61, 221–22.

8 See Winthrop D. Jordan, *White over Black: American Attitudes toward the Negro, 1550–1812* (Chapel Hill: University of North Carolina Press, 1968), pt. I.

9 Smits, "'Abominable Mixture,'" esp. 158–60; Kathleen M. Brown, *Good Wives, Nasty Wenches, and Anxious Patriarchs: Gender, Race, and Power in Colonial Virginia* (Chapel Hill: University of North Carolina Press, 1996), 58–61.

10 Bernard Diron D'Artaguiette, "Journal of Diron D'Artaguiette," in *Travels in the American Colonies*, ed. Newton D. Mereness (New York: Antiquarian Press, 1961), 48; Robert Hunter, Jr., *Quebec to Carolina in 1785–1786, Being the Travel Diary and Observations of Robert Hunter, Jr., A Young Merchant of London*, ed. Louis B. Wright and Marion Tinling (San Marino: Huntington

Library, 1943), 55; Luigi Castiglioni, *Luigi Castiglioni's "Viaggio": Travels in the United States of North America, 1785–87*, ed. and trans. Antonio Pace (1790; reprint, Syracuse: Syracuse University Press, 1983), 39; Lawson, *New Voyage to Carolina*, 189.

11 William Bartram, *The Travels of William Bartram*, ed. Francis Harper (1791; reprint, New Haven: Yale University Press, 1958), 225–26; see also 306–07.
12 Diron D'Artaguiette, "Journal," 48.
13 Richard Eden, preface to *The Decades of the New World* (London, 1555).
14 William Byrd, *The Secret Diary of William Byrd of Westover*, 1709–12, ed. Louis B. Wright and Marion Tinling (Richmond, Va.: Dietz Press, 1941), 423–25.
15 Lawson, *New Voyage to Carolina*, 41.
16 Diron D'Artaguiette, "Journal," 58, 73.
17 Thomas Nairne, *Nairne's Muskhogean Journals: The 1708 Expedition to the Mississippi River*, ed. Alexander Moore (Jackson: University Press of Mississippi, 1988), 44.
18 Byrd, "History of the Dividing Line," 218, 314. See also Castiglioni, *"Viaggio,"* 101.
19 Lawson, *New Voyage to Carolina*, 46–47.
20 Ibid., 41, 194.
21 Ibid., 50.
22 Byrd, "History of the Dividing Line," 218.
23 Hunter, *Quebec to Carolina*, 110–11.
24 William Tredwell Bull to Secretary of Society for Propagation of Gospel, Aug. 10, 1715, *South Carolina Historical Magazine* 63 (1962): 25.
25 Robert Maule to Secretary of Society for Propagation of Gospel, Aug. 2, 1711, *South Carolina Historical Magazine* 61 (1960): 8–9. See also Commissary Gideon Johnston to Secretary of Society for Propagation of Gospel, July 5, 1710, in *Carolina Chronicle: The Papers of Commissary Gideon Johnston, 1707–1716*, ed. Frank J. Klingberg (Chapel Hill: University of North Carolina Press, 1946), 53.
26 Alexander Long, "A Small Postscript of the Ways and Manners of the Indians Called Cherokees" (1725), *Southern Indian Studies* 21 (1969): 20.
27 Governor Johnstone to Don Antonio D'Ullua, May 3, 1766, in *Mississippi Provincial Archives, 1763–1766: English Dominion*, ed. Dunbar Rowland (Nashville: Brandon, 1911), 312–13.
28 W. L. McDowell, ed., *Colonial Records of South Carolina: Journals of the Commissioners of the Indian Trade, 1710–1718* (Columbia: South Carolina Archives Department, 1955), 30, 34. See also idem, ed., *Colonial Records of South Carolina: Documents Relating to Indian Affairs, 1750–1754* (Columbia: South Carolina Archives Department, 1958), 81, 87–88, 135–36; and idem, ed., *Colonial Records of South Carolina: Documents Relating to Indian Affairs, 1754–1765* (Columbia: University of South Carolina Press, 1970), 560.
29 David Crawley to William Byrd, July 30, 1715, in *The Correspondence of the Three William Byrds of Westover, Virginia, 1684–1776*, ed. Marion Tinling (Charlottesville: Virginia Historical Society, 1977), 1:289.

30   Byrd, "History of the Dividing Line," 311.

31   McDowell, *Documents Relating to Indian Affairs*, 1750–1754, 306.

32   Rowland, *Mississippi Provincial Archives*, 238–39, 241.

33   Lawson, *New Voyage to Carolina*, 29–30, 190–92.

34   "Journal of Colonel George Chicken's Mission from Charleston, South Carolina, to the Cherokees, 1726," in *Travels in the American Colonies*, ed. Mereness, 104; "David Taitt's Journal of a Journey through the Creek Country, 1772," in ibid., 512; McDowell, *Journal of the Commissioners of the Indian Trade, 1710–1718*, 17; idem, *Documents Relating to Indian Affairs, 1750–1754*, 70, 117; idem, *Documents Relating to Indian Affairs, 1754–1765*, 243–44, 247.

35   See, for example, the case of T——y, discussed below.

36   Bartram, *Travels*, 124, 221. See also Sylvia Van Kirk, *"Many Tender Ties": Women in Fur-Trade Society in Western Canada, 1670–1870* (Norman: University of Oklahoma Press, 1983), esp. 33.

37   Alexander Kellet, *A Pocket of Prose and Verse* (1778; reprint, New York: Garland, 1975), 20–21; Lawson, *New Voyage to Carolina*, 193. According to Lawson, "those Indian girls that have conversed with the English and other Europeans, never care for the conversation of their own countrymen afterwards."

38   McDowell, *Documents Relating to Indian Affairs, 1750–1754*, 407.

39   Lawson, *New Voyage to Carolina*, 192. See also Castiglioni, *"Viaggio,"* 83.

40   John Bernard, *Retrospections of America, 1797–1811* (New York: Harper and Brothers, 1887), 182.

41   See James Axtell, *The Invasion Within: The Contest of Cultures in Colonial North America* (New York: Oxford University Press, 1985), chap. 13; June Namias, *White Captives: Gender and Ethnicity on the American Frontier* (Chapel Hill: University of North Carolina Press, 1993); and John Demos, *The Unredeemed Captive: A Family Story from Early America* (New York: Vintage, 1994).

42   See Richard J. Hooker, ed., *The Carolina Backcountry on the Eve of the Revolution: The Journal and Other Writings of Charles Woodmason, Anglican Itinerant* (Chapel Hill: University of North Carolina Press, 1953), 121; and Tom Hatley, *The Dividing Paths: Cherokees and South Carolinians through the Revolutionary Era* (New York: Oxford University Press, 1995), 181–82.

43   See *South Carolina Gazette*, Aug. 15, 1743; "Journal of Antoine Bonnefoy's Captivity among the Cherokee Indians, 1741–1742," in *Travels in the American Colonies*, ed. Mereness, 249; "Historical Relation of Facts Delivered by Ludovick Grant, Indian Trader, to His Excellency the Governor of South Carolina, 1756," *South Carolina Historical and Genealogical Magazine* 10 (1909): 59; Knox Mellon, Jr., "Christian Priber and the Jesuit Myth," *South Carolina Historical Magazine* 61 (1960): 75–81.

44   Lawson, *New Voyage to Carolina*, 192.

45   Nathaniel Osborne to Secretary of Society for Propagation of Gospel, March 1, 1715, *South Carolina Historical and Genealogical Magazine* 50 (1949): 175.

46   John L. Nichols, "Alexander Cameron, British Agent among the Cherokee, 1764–1781," *South Carolina Historical Magazine* 97 (1996): esp. 100.

47   "Bernard Elliott's Recruiting Journal, 1775," *South Carolina Historical and Genealogical Magazine* 17 (1916): 98–99.

48   Hatley, *Dividing Paths*, 60–62, 85.

49   Duc de la Rochefoucault-Liancourt, *Travels through the United States of North America, the Country of the Iroquois, and Upper Canada* (London, 1799), 1:167.

50   James Adair, *The History of the American Indians* (1775; reprint, New York: Promontory Press, 1973), 133–35.

51   See Kenneth Lockridge, *The Diary, and Life, of William Byrd II of Virginia, 1674–1744* (Chapel Hill: University of North Carolina Press, 1987).

Documents

Our first document presents John Rolfe's marriage proposal to Pocahontas. In this petition of 1614, Rolfe expresses extreme ambivalence about the proposed union. He characterizes Indian women as "strange" and "barbarous," yet his declaration of love for Pocahontas seems sincere. Might his objections have been simply what he thought his contemporaries wanted to hear? How do you think he was able to balance his conflicting sentiments?

John Rolfe to Sir Thomas Dale, April 1614

John Rolfe Requests Permission to Marry Pocahontas, 1614

> Ra[l]ph Hamor, *A True Discourse of the Present Estate of Virginia, and the successe of the affaires there till the 18 of June. 1614*... (London, 1615), 61–68.

The coppie of the Gentle-mans letters to Sir Thomas Dale,
that after maried Powhatans daughter,
containing the reasons moving him thereunto.

Honourable Sir, and most worthy Governor:

Excerpted from *The Old Dominion in the Seventeenth Century: a Documentary History of Virginia, 1606–1689*, ed. Warren M. Billings (Chapel Hill: University of California Press, 1975), pp. 216–19.

When your leasure shall best serve you to peruse these lines, I trust in God, the beginning will not strike you into a greater admiration, then the end will give you good content. It is a matter of no small moment, concerning my own particular, which here I impart unto you, and which toucheth mee so neerely, as the tendernesse of my salvation. Howbeit I freely subject my selfe to your grave and mature judgement, deliberation, approbation and determination; assuring my selfe of your zealous admonitions, and godly comforts, either perswading me to desist, or incouraging me to persist therein, with a religious feare and godly care, for which (from the very instant, that this began to roote it selfe within the secret bosome of my brest) my daily and earnest praiers have bin, still are, and ever shall be produced forth with as sincere a godly zeale as I possibly may to be directed, aided and governed in all my thoughts, words and deedes, to the glory of God, and for my eternal consolation. To persevere wherein I never had more neede, nor (till now) could ever imagine to have bin moved with the like occasion.

But (my case standing as it doth) what better worldly refuge can I here seeke, then to shelter my selfe under the safety of your favourable protection? And did not my ease proceede from an unspotted conscience, I should not dare to offer to your view and approved judgement, these passions of my troubled soule, so full of feare and trembling is hypocrisie and dissimulation. But knowing my owne innocency and godly fervor, in the whole prosecution hereof, I doubt not of your benigne acceptance, and clement construction. As for malicious depravers, and turbulent spirits, to whom nothing is tastful, but what pleaseth their unsavory pallat, I passe not for them being well assured in my perswasion (by the often triall and proving of my selfe, in my holiest meditations and praiers) that I am called hereunto by the spirit of God; and it shall be sufficient for me to be protected by your selfe in all vertuous and pious indevours. And for my more happie proceeding herein, my daily oblations shall ever be addressed to bring to passe so good effects, that your selfe, and all the world may truely say: This is the worke of God, and it is marvelous in our eies.

But to avoid tedious preambles, and to come neerer the matter: first suffer me with your patence, to sweepe and make cleane the way wherein I walke, from all suspicions and doubts, which may be covered therein, and faithfully to reveale unto you what should move me hereunto.

Let therefore this my well advised protestation, which here I make betweene God and my own conscience, be a sufficient witnesse, at the dreadfull day of judgement (when the secret of all mens harts shall be opened) to condemne me herein, if my chiefest intent and purpose be not, to strive with all my power of body and minde, in the undertaking of so mightie a matter, no way led (so farre forth as mans weakenesse may permit) with the unbridled desire of carnall affection: but for the good of this plantation, for the honour of our countrie, for the glory of God, for my owne salvation, and for the converting to the true knowledge of God and Jesus Christ, an unbeleeving creature, namely Pokahuntas. To whom my hartie and best thoughts are, and have a long time bin so intangled, and inthralled in so intricate a laborinth, that I was even awearied to unwinde my selfe thereout. But almighty God, who never faileth his, that truely invocate his holy name hath opened the gate, and led me by the hand that I might plainely see and discerne the safe paths wherein to treade.

To you therefore (most noble Sir) the patron and Father of us in this countrey doe I utter the effects of this my setled and long continued affection (which hath made a mightie warre in my meditations) and here I doe truely relate, to what issue this dangerous combate is come unto, wherein I have not onely examined, but throughly [i.e., thoroughly] tried and pared my thoughts even to the quicke, before I could finde any fit wholesome and apt applications to cure so daungerous an ulcer. I never failed to offer my daily and faithfull praiers to God, for his sacred and holy assistance. I forgot not to set before mine eies the frailty of man-kinde, his prones [i.e., proneness] to evil, his indulgencie of wicked thoughts, with many other imperfections wherein man is daily insnared, and oftentimes overthrowne, and them compared to my present estate. Nor was I ignorant of the heavie displeasure which almightie God conceived against the sonnes of Levie and Israel for marrying strange wives, nor of the inconveniences which may thereby arise, with other the like good motions which made me looke about warily and with good circumspection, into the grounds and principall agitations, which thus should provoke me to be in love with one whose education hath bin rude, her manners barbarous, her generation accursed, and so discrep-ant in all nurtriture from my selfe, that oftentimes with feare and trem-bling, I have ended my private controversie with this: surely these are wicked instigations, hatched by him who seeketh and delighteth in mans destruction; and so with fervant praiers to be ever preserved from such diabolical assaults (as I tooke those to be) I have taken some rest.

Thus when I had thought I had obtained my peace and quietnesse, beholde another, but more gracious tentation [i.e., temptation] hath made breaches into my holiest and strongest meditations; with which I have bin put to a new triall, in a straighter manner then the former: for besides the many passions and sufferings which I have daily, hourely, yea and in my sleepe indured, even awaking mee to astonishment, taxing mee with remisnesse, and carelesnesse, refusing and neglecting to performe the duetie of a good Christian, pulling me by the eare, and crying: why dost not thou indevour to make her a Christian? And these have happened to my greater wonder, even when she hath bin furthest seperated from me, which in common reason (were it not an undoubted worke of God) might breede forgetfulnesse of a farre more worthie creature. Besides, I say the holy spirit of God hath often demaunded of me, why I was created? If not for transitory pleasures and worldly vanities, but to labour in the Lords vineyard, there to sow and plant, to nourish and increase the fruites thereof, daily adding with the good husband in the Gospell, somewhat to the tallent, that in the end the fruites may be reaped, to the comfort of the laborer in this life, and his salvation in the world to come? And if this be, as undoubtedly this is, the service Jesus Christ requireth of his best servant: wo unto him that hath these instruments of pietie put into his hands, and wilfully despiseth to worke with them. Likewise, adding hereunto her great apparance of love to me, her desire to be taught and instructed in the knowledge of God, her capableness of understanding, her aptnesse and willingnesse to receive anie good impression, and also the spirituall, besides her owne incitements stirring me up hereunto.

What should I doe? shall I be of so untoward a disposition, as to refuse to leade the blind into the right way? Shall I be so unnaturall, as not to give bread to the hungrie? or uncharitable, as not to cover the naked? Shall I despise to actuate these pious dueties of a Christian? Shall the base feare of displeasing the world, overpower and with holde mee from revealing unto man these spirituall workes of the Lord, which in my meditations and praiers, I have daily made knowne unto him? God forbid. I assuredly trust hee hath thus delt with me for my eternall felicitie, and for his glorie: and I hope so to be guided by his heavenly graice, that in the end by my faithfull paines, and christianlike labour, I shall attaine to that blessed promise, Pronounced by that holy Prophet Daniell unto the righteous that bring many unto the knowledge of God. Namely, that they shall shine like the starres forever and ever. A sweeter comfort cannot be to a true Christian, nor a greater incouragement for him to labour all the daies of his life, in the performance thereof, nor a greater gaine of consolation, to be desired at the hower of death, and in the day of judgement.

Againe by my reading, and conference with honest and religious persons, have I received no small encouragement, besides *serena mea conscientia* [i.e., "at peace with myself"], the cleerenesse of my conscience, clean from the filth of impurity, *quae est instar muri ahenei*, which is unto me, as a brasen wall. If I should set down at large, the perturbations and godly motions, which have striven within mee, I should but make a tedious and unnecessary volume. But I doubt not these shall be sufficient both to certifie you of my tru intents, in discharging of my dutie to God, and to your selfe, to whose gracious providence I humbly submit my selfe, for his glory, your honour, our Countreys good, the benefit of this Plantation, and for the converting of one unregenerate, to regeneration; which I beseech God to graunt, for his deere Sonne Christ Jesus his sake.

Now if the vulgar sort, who square all mens actions by the base rule of their own filthinesse, shall taxe or taunt me in this my godly labour: let them know, it is not any hungry appetite, to gorge my selfe with incontinency; sure (if I would, and were so sensually inclined) I might satisfie such desire, though not without a seared conscience, yet with Christians more pleasing to the eie, and lesse fearefull in the offence unlawfully committed. Nor am I in so desperate an estate, that I regard not what becommeth of mee; nor am I out of hope but one day to see my Country, nor so void of friends, nor mean in birth, but there to obtain a mach [i.e., match] to my great content: nor have I ignorantly passed over my hopes there, or regardlesly seek to loose the love of my friends, by taking this course: I know them all, and have not rashly overslipped any.

But shal it please God thus to dispose of me (which I earnestly desire to fulfill my ends before sette down) I will heartely accept of it as a godly taxe appointed me, and I will never cease, (God assisting me) until I have accomplished, and brought to perfection so holy a worke, in which I will daily pray God to blesse me, to mine, and her eternall happiness. And thus desiring no longer to live, to enjoy the blessings of God, then [i.e., than] this my resolution doth tend to such godly ends, as are by me before declared: not doubting of your favourable acceptance, I take my leave, beseeching Almighty God to raine downe upon you, such plentitude of his heavenly graces, as your heart can wish and desire, and so I rest,

At your commaund most willing to be disposed off

JOHN ROLFE.

A New Voyage to Carolina
John Lawson

John Lawson's account of his travels in the Carolinas in the early eighteenth century speaks of the usefulness as well as the drawbacks of Indian marriage partners to European traders. Lawson is particularly concerned with the children of such unions. What are his assumptions about the ways in which these children will be raised? How was this model different from the European one?

Excerpted from John Lawson, *A New Voyage to Carolina*, ed. Hugh Talmage Lefler (1708; reprint, Chapel Hill: University of North Carolina Press, 1967), pp. 191–2.

How does he acknowledge that some Englishmen might have preferred Indian ways of life?

The *Indian* Traders are those which travel and abide amongst the *Indians* for a long space of time; sometimes for a Year, two, or three. These Men have commonly their *Indian* Wives, whereby they soon learn the *Indian* Tongue, keep a Friendship with the Savages; and, besides the Satisfaction of a She-Bed-Fellow, they find these *Indian* Girls very serviceable to them, on Account of dressing their Victuals, and instructing 'em in the Affairs and Customs of the Country. Moreover, such a Man gets a great Trade with the Savages; for when a Person that lives amongst them, is reserv'd from the Conversation of their Women, 'tis impossible for him ever to accomplish his Designs amongst that People.

But one great Misfortune which oftentimes attends those that converse with these Savage Women, is, that they get Children by them, which are seldom educated any otherwise than in a State of Infidelity; for it is a certain Rule and Custom, amongst all the savages of *America*, that I was ever acquainted withal, to let the Children always fall to the Woman's Lot; for it often happens, that two *Indians* that have liv'd together, as Man and Wife, in which Time they have had several Children; if they part, and another Man possesses her, all the Children go along with the Mother, and none with the Father. And therefore, on this Score, it ever seems impossible for the Christians to get their Children (which they have by these *Indian* Women) away from them; whereby they might bring them up in the Knowledge of the Christian Principles. Nevertheless, we often find, that *English* Men, and other *Europeans* that have been accustom'd to the Conversation of these savage Women, and their Way of Living, have been so allur'd with that careless sort of Life, as to be constant to their *Indian* Wife, and her Relations, so long as they liv'd, without ever desiring to return again amongst the *English*, although they had very fair Opportunities of Advantages amongst their Countrymen; of which sort I have known several.

Quebec to Carolina in 1785–1786

Robert Hunter, Jr

The last document, a journal entry written by Robert Hunter, Jr, in the late eighteenth century, exemplifies European suspicion toward Native American women. How did Hunter characterize the Seneca and Mohawk women of Fort Niagra as potential marriage partners?

Catarogui, Monday, July 18

Fort Niagara was built by the French and taken by Sir William Johnson in 1759. To appearance it's not so strong as Fort Carlton, but commands a most noble view of the lake and river. In case it's given up to the Americans, there is a place on the British side where the English may build a fort that will command this. Four companies of the Twenty-ninth are there, the officers most agreeable men. They told us that many of the Seneca and Mohawk Indians were settling very fast, under the British government, upon the Grand River. The air of Niagara is reckoned unwholesome and the inhabitants are subject to the ague and fever, owing to a large swamp on the other side of the river. A few females would make this place more agreeable – I mean white ones, for there are abundance of squaws. Some of them have very fine features and in general they are dressed remarkably well, being mostly kept by the gentlemen who reside there. I am told they are not constant or faithful, but if any little quarrel happens they will immediately leave their keeper (though living in the height of luxury), who perhaps the next day will see them in the arms of a Negro. They have very little passion and scarcely know what love means. Everybody is alike indifferent to them, black, white, or Indian, and they will, before their keeper's face, go with anybody else that will offer them some rum, which they are extravagantly fond of. When they have been brought up with a man from their infancy no woman can be more faithful or love with greater ardor. One squaw is much more expensive than three or four white women, for you are sure to have the whole family to maintain, and they are very expensive in their dress here. As near as I can remember, the young ones wear a kind of English riding hat, ornamented with feathers and ribbons of different

Excerpted from Robert Hunter, Jr, *Quebec to Carolina in 1785–1786, Being the Travel Diary and Observations of Robert Hunter, Jr, a Young Merchant of London*, ed. Louis B. Wright and Marion Tinling (San Marino: Huntington Library, 1943), pp. 110–11.

colors, a blanket over their shoulders, which is covered with spangles and different-colored silk – so many blue ribbons curiously sewed upon it half way down their back, and so many red ones to the rest of the blanket, which reaches to the calf of their leg. They wear a petticoat, down to their knees, of a yellow color, and leggings perhaps of another, so as to have as much variety in their dress as possible.

Further Reading

Brooks, James F. "'This evil extends especially... to the feminine sex': negotiating captivity in the New Mexico borderlands." *Feminist Studies* (Summer 1996), 279–309.

Brown, Kathleen M. *Good Wives, Nasty Wenches, and Anxious Patriarchs: Gender, Race, and Power in Colonial Virginia.* Chapel Hill: University of North Carolina Press, 1996.

Dennis, Matthew. *Cultivating a Landscape of Peace: Iroquois – European Encounters in the Seventeenth Century.* Ithaca, NY: Cornell University Press, 1993.

Morgan, Edmund S. *American Slavery, American Freedom: the Ordeal of Colonial Virginia.* New York: W. W. Norton, 1975.

Sayre, Gordon, "Native American sexuality in the eyes of the beholders: 1535–1710." In Merril D. Smith (ed.), *Sex and Sexuality in Early America.* New York: New York University Press, 1998, pp. 35–54.

Smits, David D. "'Abominable mixture': toward the repudiation of Anglo-Indian intermarriage in seventeenth-century Virginia." *Virginia Magazine of History and Biography*, 95 (1987), 157–92.

Smits, David D. "'We are not to grow wild': seventeenth-century New England's repudiation of Anglo-Indian intermarriage." *American Indian Culture and Research Journal*, 11 (1987), 1–31.

3

Girling of It

Introduction

Scholars have recently dispelled the tenaciously held but inaccurate belief that colonial New Englanders were "puritanical" when it came to sex. Laurel Thatcher Ulrich and Lois K. Stabler remind us in this article that 30–40 percent of brides in the revolutionary era were already pregnant when they took their wedding vows. Clearly, waiting for the sanctity of marriage to consummate a physical relationship was not a high priority. Ulrich and Stabler's study of young women and men in Keene, New Hampshire, indicates a social world that included premarital sex and blurred boundaries between competing norms of sexual behavior.

The difficulty of travel between distant homes often required friends and relatives staying overnight at houses other than their own. Sometimes couples shared the same bed with one another, a custom known as "bundling." Surviving sources do not tell us enough about the nature of this intimacy. Did unmarried bedmates stay fully clothed and merely cuddle under the blankets? Or did one thing lead to another, culminating perhaps in the pre-marital pregnancies we can deduce from the social historical record? By examining the rich diary of one eighteenth-century man, Ulrich and Stabler analyze the broad range of courtship behavior in this essay.

"Girling of It" in Eighteenth-century New Hampshire

Laurel Thatcher Ulrich and Lois K. Stabler

On a clear, bright day late in July of 1780 a group of men were working in a corn field in Keene, New Hampshire, when three young women came to pick currants in a patch nearby. It was an ordinary day, an ordinary encounter, and, if we can believe the diary of Abner Sanger, an ordinary arrangement that followed. "Joseph Reed and Zadock Dodge don't finish plowing among corn," he wrote. "Said Reed and Dodge go to Major Willard's at night. Said Reed stays with Grate Willard and said Dodge stays with Hephzibah Crossfield." Both men were back in the field the next day, but one was "dumpish," Sanger wrote, and the other "asleep." "Said Joseph gives me an account of his and Dodge's girling of it at Major Willard's and of Dodge's being overcome by the fatigue of the last night with Hephzibah," he reported.[1]

Abner Sanger's diary is a rare document among eighteenth-century sources. It combines the work-a-day entries typical of farmers with the social and sexual commentary usually associated with urban sophisticates. Sanger was, in fact, a farmer, and not a very prosperous one at that. But he was also an avid reader and something of an iconoclast. A stubborn Loyalist, he had twice been arrested and imprisoned for refusing to sign the Association test.[2] After his second detention he was allowed (perhaps forced) to move with his mother and unmarried sister from their farm on the outskirts of town to what is now Main Street in Keene where he worked for his neighbors as a common laborer. In 1780 he was 41 years old and still unmarried.

Although he referred to the new nation as "The Divided States of America" or the "United States of Rebellion," the epithets he gave his neighbors, "Old Mother Damnable," "Dr. Num-Nose," and "Dirty Buttocks," had nothing to do with the war. Courtship, legitimate and illegitimate, is a recurring theme in the diary. He himself gave serious attention to at least four women between 1777 and 1782, all of whom rejected him. For his rivals he had sarcastic nicknames like "Unction" or "Lord Bugger." Probably some of what he imagined went on in his

Excerpted from Laurel Thatcher Ulrich and Lois K. Stabler, " 'Girling of It' in Eighteenth-century New Hampshire," in Peter Benes, ed., *Families and Children* (Cambridge, MA: Boston University, 1987), pp. 24–36.

neighbors' houses was a projection of his own thwarted hopes, but where
the diary can be checked against other sources it has proved accurate,
and in general the picture it provides conforms well with what else we
know about the time and place.

Abner Sanger's revelations are particularly interesting in light of recent
studies of premarital pregnancy in New England. Whereas premarital
conception had been relatively rare in the seventeenth century, in
the revolutionary era 30–40 percent of brides in many New England
towns were pregnant at marriage.[3] Our own study has confirmed that
pattern for Keene. Fourteen of thirty-one couples married between 1774
and 1782 had a child less than nine months after marriage, usually a great
deal less. For the pregnant brides, the average interval between marriage
and delivery was five months; one woman presumably gave birth on her
wedding day. During the same period there were four illegitimate births.

Such information has given new currency to Henry Stiles's antiquarian study of "bundling," a form of courtship in which a young man and
woman spent the night in bed together, presumably fully clothed. Historians disagree on the meaning and nature of bundling. Did it represent
a repressed and "innocent" sexuality characteristic of pre-modern societies? Or a more expressive, less guilt-ridden acknowledgment of physical attraction than would be possible in later generations? Was bundling
part of a general subversion of parental authority by the young? Or an
arrangement in which parents cooperated by allowing their children
greater autonomy in selecting a marriage partner?[4]

Abner Sanger's diary suggests that some form of bundling (he called it
"staying with") was indeed common, though he distinguished between
that practice and what he called "buggery." There were standards of
acceptable behavior in eighteenth-century Keene, though they were
neither "Puritan" nor "Victorian." In fact, the biographies of the three
women who came to the currant patch suggest a surprising tolerance for
what most historians would consider deviant behavior. Grate Willard
was a very young teenager, probably not yet fifteen; her partner, Joseph
Reed, was two years older. For them the all-night meeting seems to have
been a casual affair; each would marry someone else within three years.
Hephzibah Crossfield Bragg, on the other hand, was legally married,
though her husband had deserted her. Still in her twenties, she worked as
a housekeeper in the Willard house, and entertained a number of men,
including Abner Sanger. The third woman who came to the currant
patch, Susanna Wyman, was five months pregnant, a fact that may
explain her absence from the all-night affair at the Willards.[5] (She, too,
was closely associated with the Willard family; in 1785 she became the
Major's third wife.)

Although there was gossip about Hephzibah's exploits and Susanna's bastard, neither the women nor their families were generally disreputable. Major Willard, a prosperous landowner and mild Tory, had been Keene's first representative to the General Court. Susanna Wyman's father was a magistrate and had served as a colonel at Bunker Hill. Yet there were tensions between the casual and sometimes raucous behavior of families like the Willards and the more controlled sociability encouraged not only by the church but by English behavior books that had made their way to Keene. What we see in the Sanger diary is a society caught between competing norms of sexual behavior. A hundred years earlier Hephzibah Crossfield Bragg would have been brought to court for "lascivious behavior," if not for adultery. In eighteenth-century Keene there was sympathy for her plight, if not total approval of her conduct. Nor was it easy to define the misbehavior at the Willard house since what went on there was so difficult to distinguish from general patterns of sociability in the town.

Most interaction between men and women, like the initial encounter in the currant patch, was informal, seemingly accidental, an ordinary consequence of daily work. Abner Sanger frequently recorded encounters with young women in their own or their employers' houses. He arrived on an errand or to cut wood – then tarried. Going to Major Willard's house, for example, "to see about a team to sled," he stayed and played cards with the girls. There were no doubt subtle cues in the way young women responded to such a visit. "I stop at Washburn's to get cloth for a pocket," he wrote on 21 January 1779. "Her girls want me to go up chamber." There was probably nothing sacrosanct about a chamber (the girls were perhaps spinning or weaving there), but the invitation to prolong the visit (perhaps he talked with the girls while they continued to work) signaled some interest on the part of the women. Abner was so entranced with Abigail or "Nab" Washburn that on one visit he simply forgot his errand: "I go to Washburn's to grind my axe but don't," he wrote. "I spend until ten o'clock with Washburn's girls."[6]

In such a community the boundaries of work and play, of family and neighborhood were permeable. Large gatherings, sometimes but not always organized around work, provided additional opportunities for courting. Sanger mentioned "election frolics," "quilting frolics," just plain "frolics," and "drunken frolics," the latter sometimes including a "hurliburly of gaming." He noted huskings, house raisings, sleigh rides, shooting matches, and snow ball fights, and on one memorable summer afternoon he reported having "a cow-tord frolic with Polly Washburn and Abiel French."[7]

"Staying with" or "girling of it" also grew out of common patterns of neighborly interaction. Work that began very early or ended very late, a lame horse or a broken cart, a summons to nurse or watch with the sick, a session of the country court or a town meeting, simple visiting, and all-night "frolics" all provided opportunities for sleeping away from home. On 8 May 1775 Sanger wrote, "I go to old Gideon Ellis' and eat supper and lodge. Veize come and lodged with Sally Blood." For Sanger staying at the Ellis's house was a simple convenience; for the other man it was a chance to get better acquainted with Sally.

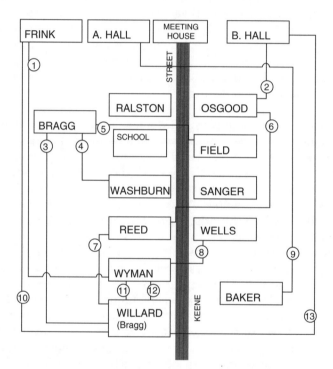

Figure I   Schematic location of households related by marriage in the central part of Keene, New Hampshire, ca. 1780. Not to scale: approximate distance of Frink household to meeting house is two-tenths of a mile; Willard household to meeting house, seven-tenths of a mile. Key to numbers: 1. Willard Frink and Susan Wyman; 2. Hananiah Hall and Mary Osgood; 3. Henry Bragg and Hephzibah Crossfield; 4. Ebenezer Bragg and Abigail Washburn; 5. Thomas Field and Mary Bragg; 6. Joseph Reed and Mary Osgood; 7. Lockhart Willard and Salome Reed; 8. Isaac Wyman and Sarah Wells; 9. Rev. Aaron Hall and Sarah Baker; 10. Thomas Frink and Abigail Willard; 11. Joseph Willard and Susanna Wyman; 12. Joshua Wyman and Hannah Willard; 13. Ziba Hall and Grate Willard.

Keene men and women worked for, borrowed from, lodged with – and married – their neighbors (Figure 1). Casual encounters were confirmed by gifts (a silk handkerchief, a thimble or ring, money wrapped up in a note), as well as by more formal visits. Sanger paid a great deal of attention to the way his rival, Henry Bragg, was dressed when he visited Nab Washburn. Being "some fixed up" signaled courtship rather than an errand. So did frequent coming and going from a single house. "Captain Benjamin Ellis passes twice to Ash Swamp and back again," Sanger reported. "He coddles Rachel Morse as he goes backward and forward as is storied at Bailey's."[8]

The most detailed picture of courtship in the diary is of Ebenezer Bragg's pursuit of Abigail Washburn. Sanger's own affection for "Nab" explains his willingness to get up at dawn to keep a close watch on his rival, whom he called "Unction." The picture of Unction that emerges from the diary is wonderfully flamboyant and quite literally colorful. "Unction comes up from Connecticut . . . ," Sanger wrote on 22 October 1779. "He is fire red in an old red, threadbare coat, a shining ribbon and loop on his hat, boots and etc., a new horse for William Bragg. He goes and shows himself to Nab Washburn, gets insisted with old 'Mother Damnable' and stays with Nab Washburn all night." Sanger's account of the courtship could be titled "I Spy Unction."

8 February 1779: "I spy Unction before sunrise coming from Old Mr. Washburn's very gaily dressed."

26 February: "I spy lights in Washburn's chamber, suppose Unction to be there."

2 March: "I spy Unction dressing himself in Thomas Field's bedroom to go and see Abigail Washburn. After he went off I soon discover a light [in] Washburn's chamber."

The next morning: "I get up before sunrise and watch to see if Unction comes from Washburn's. I spy him coming away a little after sunrise in his roast meat" (presumably a reference to the color of his coat).

And so on through the spring and summer. There is no reason to doubt Sanger's observations. Unction "stayed with" Abigail Washburn frequently between February 1779 and October 1780 when they were finally married. Nor were these visits the result of a formal engagement; their marriage was not published until 14 May 1780, more than a year after the all-night visits began. What we do not know, of course, is what "stayed with" actually meant. Presumably it involved some sort of intimacy. "This night Unk and Nab solace themselves and their selves in great delight," Sanger wrote on 2 April 1779.

Yet in common usage, "staying with" certainly meant less than our "sleeping with." Whether it implied an all-night conversation with a few

furtive kisses or a prolonged period of non-coital sexual play, we do not
know. In 1782 Sanger was himself "staying with" two different girls,
evidence in itself that bundling, if that is what it was, did not imply a
long-term commitment. On 20 August he reported "Esther Scovill and I
have some jaw. She is mad because I stay with Poll Bailey and Rachel
Morse." Was Esther jealous? Angry about the behavior itself? Or concerned about Sanger's simultaneous interest in two women?

The form of the diary entries is consistent. Unction "stayed with"
Nab. Abner "stayed with" Rachel and Poll. Joseph Reed and Zadock
Dodge "stayed with" Grate Willard and Hephzibah Crossfield. The
designation, if not the actual behavior, was the same in all these cases.
"Girling of it" might lead to sexual intercourse, as all those early births
attest, but then again it might not. Nab Washburn was not pregnant at
marriage, nor as far as we know were any of the other girls Sanger or his
friends "stayed with," a fact that tends to confirm the view of the old
bundling song,

> Cate, Nance and Sue proved just and true,
> Tho' bundling did practise;
> But Ruth beguil'd and proved with child,
> Who bundling did despise.[9]

Statistically at least, Nab, Grate, Polly, Rachel, and Hephzibah
"proved just and true," though as the Sanger diary so convincingly
shows, statistics don't tell all.

Measured by the standards of their Puritan ancestors or their Victorian descendants, eighteenth-century New Englanders were permissive.
By the mid-eighteenth century courts had virtually stopped enforcing the
old laws against fornication, and while ministers might preach reforma-
tion they had little power to enforce it. Yet community surveillance of
private behavior continued. The kind of gossip reported in the Sanger
diary inhibited privacy, but it also encouraged conformity. In Keene,
marriage usually followed, if it did not always precede, pregnancy.
Probably most sexual intercourse occurred within a context of commitment – that is, if not an absolute promise to marry, at least an implicit
agreement to marry if pregnancy resulted.

Some historians have suggested that pregnant brides may have
belonged to a deviant subgroup. We have not found that to be so. In
fact, in our sample, pregnant brides were just as likely as other women to
be daughters of church members. Bridal pregnancy was probably a very
familiar pattern by this time; a number of town leaders, including two
magistrates as well as several selectmen, had welcomed their first children within eight months of marriage. Nor can we find evidence that a

formal engagement preceded intimacy; the timing of the marriages suggests the opposite, that engagements followed sure evidence of pregnancy.

"Girling of it," then, was a sport as well as a method of courtship. It developed in a world where young persons were largely responsible for their own behavior, moving across fields and in and out of each other's households with little restraint from parents, employers, the church, or the courts. Young folks socialized in berry patches, across looms, and around woodpiles, developing attractions and alliances at husking bees and barnraisings that might lead to all-night encounters. Though men as well as women accepted the possibility of pregnancy and the ultimate necessity of marriage, young adulthood was characterized less by restraint than by freedom – freedom to visit, to party, to tarry, and to choose one's mate. Hence the recurring ritual of the annual town meeting, the election of newly married men to the office of hog reeve. Among all the lesser offices to which a young man might ascend, this one was reserved for bridegrooms. Even a man who had once been a town clerk or selectman might serve out a term in this homely, and perhaps increasingly nonfunctional, office during the year following his marriage.[10] The symbolism and rough humor of the custom is clear. A freely wandering male, like a wandering hog, must eventually be ringed or yoked – for the good of the town.

This is not to say that everyone approved of all-night courting – or of the cardplaying, frolicking, and drinking Sanger described. Keene's new minister, Aaron Hall, moved rapidly after his ordination in 1778 to establish alternate forms of entertainment for young people. He not only preached on the necessity of "family government" and on the evils of "drunkenness," he added "social meetings" to the "singing meetings" that already existed. In the diary the church events often appear side by side with the more traditional frolics, perhaps as a kind of comment on their success. On 22 February 1779, for example, Sanger reported, "We hear much bow-woohing and joy goes at Field's shop by reason of their having much of homo to drink," adding, "This night is the last social meeting of the Rev. Mr. Hall."[11]

The young Yale graduate faced some serious challenges – a church that had been without a minister for six years, a town that appeared to be divided both spiritually and politically, and an economy straining under the continued needs of the Revolution. Aaron Hall proved both firm and popular. (He served as Keene's minister until his death in 1814.) As a condition of settlement he had insisted on the abandonment of the half-way covenant, and was successful in moving nine of the twenty half-way members into full membership. He signaled his commitment to the parish by marrying, on Christmas Day 1782, a local girl, Sarah Baker. By the spring a new home for the couple was under construction, land and labor donated by the town. Even Abner Sanger, who was sometimes skeptical about the activities of "Priest Hall," showed up to work on the house.

Aaron Hall's social meetings reinforced traditional Christian values among young people. At the same time English literature which passed among the town's readers helped to encourage ladylike and gentlemanly behavior. Abner Sanger sometimes chose literature over sermons. In 1774, for example, he spent two consecutive sabbaths reading "Milton's admirable poems called *Paradise Lost*."[12] He was even more impressed with a three-volume set called *The Ladies Library* that Sally Baker, Hall's future bride, seems to have borrowed from a visiting minister. Between March and September of 1780 Sanger made no fewer than thirty-three references to the book in his diary. "I go to Baker's," he wrote on 11 March. "Miss Sally shows me the *Ladies Library* books belonging to Reverend Mr. Ripley and [his] lady."

By the end of the summer Mrs. Ripley's books were in high demand among Keene's readers.[13] It is hard to evaluate the books' appeal in a town like Keene. Certainly reading material was scarce; it may simply have been a welcome relief from sermons and almanacs. Yet its combination of conservatism and innovation may have offered security to men like Abner Sanger and women like Sally Baker in this era of social change. First published in London in 1714, the book simultaneously promoted the traditional feminine virtues of modesty, meekness, and charity and the newer values of improved education for women and free choice of marriage partners.[14] If the authors' insistence that women were capable of learning grammar and math, of reading Greek and Roman histories, and of studying moral philosophy had little practical application in Keene, it could certainly be used to justify reading *something*, if only *The Ladies Library*.

The less idealistic side of courtship in Keene is better reflected in another English book Sanger read, Edward Ward's *Female Policy Detected, or the Arts of a Designing Woman Laid Open*. While giving a nod in a closing poem to an ideal state in which the "Sexes would join as Angels do above,/ Not to fulfill their lust, but deal their love," it devoted most of its brisk advice to helping a young man negotiate the pitfalls of sexual attraction. Women were fickle. They were dangerous. They were greedy. Success in love therefore required both art and strenuous effort. Even when a man was assured he was "the favourite of a lady," he must still be "industrious to oblige her, and as watchful to preserve her from the efforts of rivals," for a mistress often behaved "like a pop-gun, the last pellet she receives, will drive out the former."[15] Sanger could give testimony of that.

All of these currents – the concerns of the new minister, the introduction of genteel values, and the realities of sexual intrigue – come together in Sanger's account of his own pursuit of Hephzibah Crossfield Bragg. On 18 August 1780, about a month after Hephzibah's encounter with Zadock Dodge in the currant patch, Sanger wrote, "I spy Joshua Reed going to Major Willard's, walking very stately and I do suppose it fix an intention to spend the night with Hepzibah Bragg and etc. I spy lights in Major Willard's north room in the evening." Later that fall Sanger learned from another man that Seth Putnam "stays with" Hephzibah the "whole night" at her father's house.[16] By that time Sanger was himself sending poems to her and looking for every opportunity to share her company. "I go to Major Willard's old barn with Hephzibah Crossfield to milking," he wrote on 4 December 1780, adding "Moonlight and pleasant, warm, cloudy."

Although Hephizibah was married and the mother of at least two children, she behaved as though she were single. Perhaps Sanger and her other friends considered her as good as divorced; there is in fact evidence in this period for local acceptance of a kind of "common law" divorce. In 1783 the Keene Congregational Church questioned accepting the membership of Michael Metcalf whose wife Mercy had been married earlier to David Fisher (who was still alive). But when the pastor of Mercy's church in Upton, Massachusetts, wrote to assure them that Fisher had deserted Mercy and fathered a child by another woman, her story was accepted "as equal to a bill of divorcement from her former husband."[17] Hephzy was not as well-behaved as Mercy – she had failed to transform her half-way covenant into full church membership – but for a time at least no one seemed to question her behavior.

In the fall of 1780 Grate Willard became the wife of Ziba Hall, a man twice her age. That winter Sanger composed a bit of verse, "a dialogue, 'Hephzy and Grate and Old Lads,'" and sent it to Hephzibah. He apparently hoped she would follow the example of her friend; he was thirteen years older than she.[18] Nor was his admiration dampened when Aaron Hall began to show concern about affairs at Major Willard's. "Hephzy Crossfield is not at meeting because Priest Hall had stamped at her last Sunday," Sanger wrote on 29 July 1781. The "stamping" had only a temporary effect. Soon Hephzy was back in church. "This day Hephzy Crossfield is at Meeting dressed airy without a bonnet," Sanger wrote on 2 September.

Through the summer and fall Sanger expressed both caution and captivation, on one day reporting a long talk about Hephzy with one of Major Willard's hands ("He informs me considerable"), on another writing happily about a morning spent with Hephzy conversing "on themes of marriage." He was charmed to find her and two other young women at Major Willard's "with sparrowgrass and other flowers on their heads," but disturbed by persistent rumors from the Willard house. On 16 September 1781 he wrote "a letter to Hephzy Crossfield on Buggery and etc." A few days later he reported meeting "young Josiah Willard in street. He tells me that he hears that I am going to be married and etc." Unfortunately the details behind those *et ceteras* are lost.[19]

On 27 September, Sanger sent Hephzy another letter. Her window was open the next day, as he thought in answer, but he did not respond. At meeting that Sunday Aaron Hall preached on family government. "Hephzy Crossfield looks as if she had been whipped. Prent also," Sanger wrote. "Prent" was Prentice Willard, the Major's younger brother and by this time Sanger's rival. Like Hephzibah, Prentice was married but separated; his wife lived ten miles away in Chesterfield. Perhaps it was the presence of the two wandering spouses in one house that disturbed Aaron Hall. On 19 October Hephzy sent word that she wanted to see Abner, but when he went to the house two days later, "Lord Bugger, Prent Williard, gets authority to turn me out of or at the door." Authority from whom? Had the Major decided at long last to "govern" his family, or had Hephzibah told Prentice to send her would-be suitor away?

From this time forward Prentice Willard was "Lord Bugger" or "Lord Debauche" to Sanger. The gossip grew more insistent. "I go up to John or cooper White's in evening," Sanger wrote on 5 December 1781. "Said White tells me about Lord Bugger, Prentice Willard, giving him an account of his keeping a whore in his quarters, of rendezvous, and that all means had been tried to carry off Susa Wyman's bastard." Was the "whore" Hephzy? Or Susa, the Willards' next-door neighbor? The allusion to the baby, who was then over a year old, is unclear. Was the man talking about an effort to place the baby elsewhere now that it was weaned, or was he implying an earlier and darker effort to "carry off" or abort the unborn child? By February Moses Goodridge was informing Sanger of the "probability that buggering goes on in the kitchen between Lord Bugger and Hepzibah Crossfield."[20]

Despite the gossip Hephzibah and Prentice turned up regularly at meeting, she in a "sky-blue cloak." Having lost the lady, Sanger turned to the pleasures of talk. He reported conversations with Thomas Fisher "about fucksters and some about Lord High Bugger and Hephzibah Crossfield." He talked to Dr. Perring and to Ruth Lawrence about the pair and in August spent a full hour "in telling Mrs. Ralston of Lord Bugger's maneuvers."[21] On 27 March 1782 he wrote, "This night the whore curtains are put up at Major Willard's chamber windows anew or first after old lady sickens, whether Free Masons occasioned it or not."

The reference is puzzling. The term "whore curtain" is as idiosyncratic – and probably as unrecoverable – as Sanger's earlier references to

Unction's "roast meat." The context suggests two possible interpretations. One is that "whore curtains" were not curtains at all, but eggs, or
rotten pumpkins, or excrement smeared on Major Willard's windows to
shame him for the "buggering" that supposedly went on in his house.
Such extralegal efforts to enforce moral codes were common in an earlier
period in England and still not unheard of in revolutionary America. Yet
the suggestion that the "curtains" had appeared before – though not since
Mrs. Willard's illness – suggests a more prosaic interpretation, that some
sort of curtain had indeed been put up in the Major's windows in pre-
paration for a Masonic meeting. That Abner Sanger called the unfamiliar
coverings "whore curtains" suggests his own mistrust of Masonic secrecy,
his own dismay at an effort to shield a house from the sort of neighborly
watching that was so much a part of town life in Keene. It suggests he may
also have read or heard antimasonic arguments linking Freemasonry with
the scarlet woman, "the Mother of Harlots," in the Book of Revelation.[22]
That Keene's most prominent Mason, Josiah Willard, may have had a real
"scarlet woman" in his house only strengthened the image.

Despite the rumors, no one in Keene in 1781 was willing to press a legal
accusation of adultery against either Hephzibah Bragg or Prentice Willard. In the autumn of 1783, a year after Abner Sanger's diary closed,
Hephzibah moved to Windsor, Connecticut, where she sued for a divorce.
Sally Baker's father, the local justice of the peace, certified depositions
from Josiah Willard and his son Lockhart that Hephzibah had lived with
their family "as a housekeeper" for the past four years and during that
entire time Henry Bragg had "wilfully neglected to provide for her and
intirely deserted her" and that it was "generally known and commonly
reported in this Town that he did wilfully desert, and totally neglect his
Duty to her for several years previous." She got her divorce. Whether she
remarried we do not know. She seems simply to have disappeared from
the historical record, sparrow grass, sky blue cloak, and all.[23]

If Abner Sanger kept a diary after 1782 it has not survived, though
there is a brief "Memorandum Book" for the early 1790s, after he
moved to Dublin, New Hampshire. In 1784 he had married Elizabeth
Johnson, a widow with three children. In the next ten years they had
seven children of their own, five of whom survived. The first daughter
was named Hepzibah; the second Abigail, though Elizabeth Sanger may
never have known why.

Notes

1   *Very Poor and of Lo Make: the Journal of Abner Sanger*, ed. Lois K. Stabler
    (Portsmouth, NH: Peter Randall for the Historical Society of Cheshire

County, New Hampshire, 1986). Sanger's journal, the original of which is held by the Library of Congress, covers daily life in Keene, New Hampshire, from 1774 to 1782 and Dublin, New Hampshire, from 1791 to 1794. Son of an original proprietor of Keene, Abner Sanger (1739–1822) grew up in Keene as the town was settled; he served in the French and Indian war and in 1775 accompanied the local militia to answer the call from Lexington and Concord.

2 *New Hampshire State Papers*, VII, pp. 596–7, VIII, p. 627.
3 Daniel Scott Smith and Michael Hindus, "Premarital Pregnancy in America, 1640–1971: An Overview and Interpretation," *Journal of Interdisciplinary History*, 4 (1975): 538; Robert Gross, *The Minutemen and Their World* (New York: Hill and Wang, 1976), p. 235; and Christopher Jedrey, *The World of John Cleaveland: Family and Community in Eighteenth-Century New England* (New York: Norton, 1979), p. 152.
4 Henry Stiles, *Bundling, Its Origins, Progress and Decline in America* (n.p., 1871); Smith and Hindus, pp. 537–70; Laurel Thatcher Ulrich, *Good Wives: Image and Reality in the Lives of Women in Northern New England, 1650–1750* (New York: Alfred A. Knopf, 1982), pp. 122–3.
5 Lois Stabler compiled these figures from Frank W. Whitcomb, *Vital Statistics of Keene, New Hampshire* (City of Keene, 1905), cross-checked with the original records in the City Clerk's Office, and Records of The Church of Christ in Keene, microfilm, Keene Public Library. Laurel Ulrich has found almost identical figures for Hallowell, Maine, in the same period.
6 Sanger Diary, 22 March, 21 January, 23 February 1779.
7 Election frolic, 27 May 1779; quilting frolics, 21 May 1778, 18 June 1778; frolics, 7 December 1780, 9 February 1780, 28 November 1782; drunken frolic, 28 December 1779; huskings, 13 October 1781, 26 September 1782; raising, 25 July 1781; snowballing, 9 February 1779; sleigh riding, 8 December 1780, 20 December 1778, 30 December 1778, 31 December 1778, 28–29 January 1780, 1 January 1781.
8 Sanger Diary, 10 March 1779, 24 August 1782.
9 Stiles, *Bundling*, p. 66.
10 Lois Stabler compiled these figures from the town records.
11 Sanger Diary, 22 February 1779. "Homo" may have been an alcoholic beverage made from "humbo," a New Hampshire term for maple sugar.
12 Sanger Diary, 6, 13 November 1774.
13 Sanger Diary, 7, 8, 9, 10, 11, 13, 14, 15, 16, 17 September 1780.
14 *The Ladies Library*, 7th ed. (London: Richard Steele, 1772), e.g. I:12, II:13.
15 Ward's book was first published in London in 1695 and frequently reprinted thereafter. The quotations given here are from the first American edition, [Edward Ward], *Female Policy Detected* (Boston, 1786), pp. 23, 12.
16 Sanger Diary, 3, 5 October 1780.
17 Records of the Church of Christ, pp. 43, 51.
18 Sanger Diary, 23, 25, 26 February 1781.
19 Sanger Diary, 21, 28 August, 3 September 1781.

20 Sanger Diary, 16 February 1782.
21 Sanger Diary, 10, 24 March, 17 April, 18 June, 5 August 1782.
22 On the nineteenth-century image, see Dorothy Ann Lipson, *Freemasonry in Federalist Connecticut* (Princeton: Princeton University Press, 1977), p. 319.
23 Divorce Records, Boxes 97–99, Connecticut Superior Court File Papers, Hartford District, MS, Connecticut State Library, Hartford.

Documents

In the first document we have an excerpt from Henry Reed Stiles's bundling book. Written in the nineteenth century, after the practice was no longer common, Stiles's book is a major source of our information on this dating custom, though much of what he writes is secondhand and difficult to verify. Stiles includes a letter written by a young woman to her aunt describing the former's first reaction to the concept of bundling. This letter had first appeared in a newspaper apparently as a rebuttal to criticism of bundling. We might consider, however, the meaning or implications of such a fact: the publication of an aunt's letter from her niece on courtship, a personal, private matter. This surely suggests the possibility that the letter falls into the genre of public, and likely fictional, epistolary didacticism, the practice of teaching moral lessons through purposeful letters, offered widely through print. Based on his inclusion of the letter, do you think that Stiles believes in bundling's innocence?

Bundling: Its Origins, Progress, and Decline in America

Henry Reed Stiles

That which is called bundling here, though bad enough, is not a twentieth part so bad. Here it is only a mode of courtship. The parties instead of sitting up together, go to bed together; but go to bed with their clothes on. This would appear to be a perilous fashion; but I have been assured

Excerpted from Henry Reed Stiles, *Bundling: Its Origins, Progress, and Decline in America* (Albany, NY: Joel Munsell, 1871), pp. 117–23.

by the individual above, that he had proof to the contrary; for in the particular case alluded to, the only case I ever heard of on good authority, although he was invited by the parents of a pretty girl who stood near him, to bundle with her, and although he *did* bundle with her, he had every reason to believe, that if he had been very free, or more free than he might have been at a country frolick after they had invited him to escort her, to sit up with her, to dance with her, he would have been treated as a traitor by all parties. He had a fair opportunity of knowing the truth, and he spoke of the matter as if he would prefer the etiquette of sitting up to the etiquette of going to bed with a girl who had been so brought up. He complained of her as a prude. The following communication appears, however, to be one that may be depended on: . . .

You remember how you told me, before I left home, that I was so well looking that if I went so far back in the country I should be very much admired and flattered, and have as many lovers as I could wish for. I find it all true. The people here are remarkably kind and attentive to me; they seem to think that I must be something more than common because I have always lived so near Portland.

But I must tell you that since I have been here I have had a beau. You must know that the young men, *in particular*, are very attentive to me. Well, among these is *one* who is considered the finest young man in the place, and well he may be – he owns a good farm, which has a large barn upon it, and a neat two story house, all finished. These are the fruits of his own industry; besides he is remarkably good looking, is very large but well proportioned, and has a good share of what I call real manly beauty. . . .

If you go to walk with a young man here, instead of offering you his arm as the young men do up our way, he either takes your hand in his, or passes one arm around your waist; and this he does with such a provoking, careless honesty, that you cannot for your life be offended with him. Well, I had walked with my Jonathan several times in this kind of style. I confess there was something in him I could not but like – he does not lack for wit, and has a good share of common sense; his language is never studied – he always seems to speak from the heart. So when he asked what sort of a companion he would make, I very candidly answered, that I thought he would make a very agreeable one. "I think just so of you," said he, "and it shall not be my fault," he continued, "if we are not companions for life." "We shall surely make a bargain," said he, after sitting silent a few moments, "so we'll *bundle* tonight." "*Bundle* what?" I asked. "*We* will bundle together," said he; "you surely know what I mean." "I know that our farmers bundle *wheat, cornstalks* and *hay*; do you mean that you want me to help you bundle any of these?" enquired I. "I mean that I want you to stay with me to-night! It is the custom in this place, when a man stays with a girl, if it is warm weather, for them to throw themselves on the bed, outside the bed clothes; if the weather is cold, they crawl under the clothes, then if they have anything to *say*, they say it – when they get tired of talking they go to sleep; this is what we call bundling – now what do you call it in your part of the world?" "We have no such works," answered I; "not amongst respectable people, nor do I think that any people would, that either thought themselves respectable, or wished to be thought so."

"Don't be too severe upon us Miss —, I have always observed that those who *make believe* so much modesty, have in reality but little. I always act as I feel, and speak as I think. I wish you to do the same, but have none of your make-believes with me – you smile – you begin to think you have been a little too scrupulous – you have no objection to bundling *now*, have you?" "Indeed I have." "I am not to be trifled with; so, if you refuse, I have done with you forever." "Then be done as quick as you please, for I'll not bundle with you nor with any other man." "Then farewell proud girl," said he. "Farewell honest man," said I, and off he went sure enough.

I have since made enquiries about *bundling*, and find that it is *really* the custom here, and that they think no more harm of it, than we do our way of a young couple sitting up together. I have known an instance, since I have been here, of a girl's taking her sweetheart to a neighbor's house and asking for a bed or two to lodge in, or rather to *bundle* in. They had company at her father's, so that their beds were occupied; she thought no harm of it. She and her family are respectable.

The Ladies Library

The second document is an excerpt from *The Ladies Library*, a three-volume book first published in 1714, which Abner Sanger read and commented on frequently in his diary. Although the title page claims that the book was "Written by a Lady," modern readers might question that assertion. The selections here concern dress and modesty. What are the author's expectations of women? Can you imagine why Sanger would have enjoyed reading this book?

If dress, as we are told in Scripture, was to cover Nakedness, it seems in our Days not to answer the End of it, especially with the ladies; who, one

Excerpted from *The Ladies Library* (London: J. T., 1714), I, pp. 67–9, 188–90.

would imagine by their Dress, are so far from reckoning themselves obliged to their mother *Eve*, for dressing them, that they are for throwing away the very Fig-Leaves; they have already uncover'd their Shoulders and Breasts, and as they have gone so far in a few Months, what may they not do in Years? They should consider that Cloaths were not the Effect of Pride but of Sin, and that instead of making them vain, it should humble and mortifie them, as having lost that Innocence which was a much greater Ornament to them than the most glorious Apparel can be. Since Shame was the Original of Cloathing, it ought to be modest, and all the Fashions which are not so are sinful; arguing the Wantonness of the Wearer, and provoking that of the Spectator; both which carry Sin in them.

The defending the Body from Cold, seems to be, to many, not a principal but an accidental End of Apparel. Naked Breasts and naked Bosoms, in both Sexes, shew us that Health, as desirable as it is, is not consider'd by Youth, when any strong Passion is in the way. Those Ladies that would catch Cold at the fanning of a Summer-Evening's Breeze, bear the rudest Winter-Blasts, to lay open their Breasts and Shoulders; the most delicate of 'em are insensible of Wind or Weather. Would one not believe they are so warm'd from within, that they are insensible of Cold from without? And what must men think of such Women, who will endure so much to be so much seen? Nothing in the world is so easily communicated as Desire; and instead of mortifying it, the very Churches are the Places that help now to enflame it; People dress for them as want only as for the *Play-House*: And a Woman has not any Beauty which she will not take Care to expose there to Advantage. Hence it is, that Divine Service, instead of raising Men and Women's Souls in Devotion to the great *Creator*, is often made use of to convey wanton Glances to each other; and when they pretend to be delivered from Temptation, they with Pleasure give themselves up to it. God, who will not be mock'd, knows the Heart, and will at the last Day call them to a dreadful Account for this wicked Abuse of Holy Ordinances.

Another End of *Apparel* is the distinguishing of *Sexes* and *Qualities*, which, like the other two Ends of it, *Modesty* and *Health*, is neglected and despis'd. Women, without blushing, assume the *Coat*, *Periwig*, *Hat* and *Feather*, and ride as furiously as if there was really nothing in Sex, or they desired there should be no Difference. . . . God himself expressly commanded the Jews that the *Man* should not wear the *Apparel* of the *Woman*, nor the *Woman* that of the *Man*: But our Ladies, like our Politicians, think the Jewish Laws do not extend to Christians, and resolving at any rate to please, will wear a *Hat* or a *Head*, as it sets them off best.

Female Policy Detected, or the Arts of a Designing Woman Laid Open

Edward Ward

The final document is from another book in Sanger's library, *Female Policy Detected, or the Arts of a Designing Woman Laid Open*. How do you think the author's negative attitude toward women might have influenced the way Sanger and other young men treated the women they courted? How might young women who read this book have responded to these prescriptions of female behavior?

Expect no good Quality in a Woman more than what she shows; for it is a Maxim in their Politicks, to put the best Side outwards.

If you love a Woman, be careful how you show it; for your nibling at the Bait, may too early discover a willingness to be caught.

Waste not your Strength in the Enjoyments of Beauty, neither your Time or Money, in corrupting Virtue; but marry a chaste Wife, of a good Family, with a moderate Fortune, and you need not question being happy.

Of the Inconstancy of WOMEN

Whosoever resigns her Virtue to gratify another's Will, will not scruple the same Freedom with another, to pleasure her own; for few Women love so well as to love a Gallant better than themselves.

She who will lose her Reputation to oblige you, will hazard your Love to gratify herself; and she that will do both, can never be Constant.

Put no Confidence in a Woman that has lost her Honour; for she who is without Reputation, hath nothing to engage her to be Faithful.

Constancy is maintain'd by Virtue; and she that hath lost her Virtue, hath nothing left to oblige her to be constant.

She that prefers Pleasure before Virtue will be constant to her Lust, but not to you.

Nothing engages a Man's Affection so much to a Woman, as a Belief of her Constancy; but 'tis better to believe her otherwise, for then she can never deceive you. Women are sensible that Constancy is more priz'd

Excerpted from Edward Ward, *Female Policy Detected, or the Arts of a Designing Woman Laid Open* (Boston, 1786), pp. 10–12.

than Beauty; but it is a Maxim among their Sex, to deceive us most in what we most value.

Nothing is more ridiculous than to keep a Miss; for she that you keep, will keep another if she can; there being the same Ambition in her to be Mistress of another, as there is in you to be Master of her; and he that thinks a Woman constant, because he keeps her, proves a Knave to himself, and a Fool to his Madam.

Put not Faith in a Woman who is Wife to another; for she who is not constant to her Husband, will never be so to you.

Further Reading

Dayton, Cornelia Hughes. "Taking the trade: abortion and gender relations in an eighteenth-century New England village." *William and Mary Quarterly*, 3rd series, 48 (1991), 19–49.

Dayton, Cornelia Hughes. *Women Before the Bar: Gender, Law, and Society in Connecticut, 1639–1789*. Chapel Hill: University of North Carolina Press, 1995.

Godbeer, Richard. " 'Love raptures': marital, romantic, and erotic images of Jesus Christ in Puritan New England, 1670–1730." *New England Quarterly*, 68 (1995), 355–85.

Hambleton, Else L. "The regulation of sex in seventeenth- century Massachusetts: the Quarterly Court vs. Priscilla Willson and Mr Samuel Appleton." In Merril D. Smith (ed.), *Sex and Sexuality in Early America*. New York: New York University Press, 1998, pp. 89–115.

Ulrich, Laurel Thatcher. *Good Wives: Image and Reality in the Lives of Women in Northern New England, 1650–1750*, 2nd edn. New York: Vintage Books, 1991.

Verduin, Kathleen. " 'Our cursed natures': sexuality and the Puritan conscience." *New England Quarterly*, 56 (1983), 220–37.

Wilson, Lisa. *Ye Heart of a Man: the Domestic Life of Men in Colonial New England*. New Haven, CT: Yale University Press, 1999.

Part II
Nineteenth Century

4

The Psychology of Free Love

Introduction

Radical religious and sexual experiments in communal living became popular in nineteenth-century America. In this essay Lawrence Foster focuses on Oneidans, one of the utopian communities that lasted longer than most; it began in 1846 in upstate New York and disbanded in 1879. Headed by John Humphrey Noyes, the Oneidans could be considered Christian communists, sharing property and placing sexuality and reproduction under communal control. The Oneidans struggled with ways to balance three needs: their quest for religious perfectionism, the reality of individual sexual desire, and the wish to prevent conception.

Like other utopians, the Oneidans created elaborate alternatives to the nuclear family and monogamous marital sexuality. They grappled with what they saw as the troubling potential of the erotic by demanding extreme self-control for male partners. Unlike the Shakers who advocated celibacy as a solution for both women and men, Noyes promoted male continence, or coitus reservatus, a system whereby men restrained from ejaculation while encouraging their female partners to reach orgasm. Community surveillance of sexuality characterized Oneidans, as it did most utopian groups. Oneidans created a system of complex marriage; each male member of the group was technically "married" to each female, thus countenancing sexual relations with a wide range of partners but discouraging exclusive romantic attachments.

The Psychology of Free Love: Sexuality in the Oneida Community

Lawrence Foster

Few communal experiments in America have attracted more attention than the Oneida Community, founded in nineteenth-century New York State by the eccentric Vermont-born genius John Humphrey Noyes. Historians, sociologists, psychologists, literary scholars, and popular writers alike have continued to be intrigued by the "complex marriage" system at Oneida, which both Noyes and his critics somewhat misleadingly referred to as "free love."[1] Virtually every treatment of utopian communities or alternative marriage and sexual patterns in America includes the obligatory chapter on the Oneida "free love" colony.

Despite this widespread interest, most analyses of Oneida have been superficial or sensational, simply retelling once again the external arrangements of complex marriage, male continence, mutual criticism, stirpiculture, and other distinctive community practices. Writers have found in the Oneida Community a mirror that reflects their own concerns and preoccupations. John Humphrey Noyes has been variously described as a "Yankee saint," whose sexual attitudes and practices can serve as a model for "liberated" present-day life styles, as a "Vermont Casanova," with sick and exploitative attitudes toward women, and even as a prototype for Hitler, because Noyes's stirpiculture or eugenics experiment could be seen as prefiguring some of the most repressive and threatening human-engineering experiments of the twentieth century.[2] Seldom have scholars or the general public attempted to understand Noyes and his experiments in communal living on their own terms, considering both their strengths and weaknesses.

Studies of the psychology of Oneida sexuality have been particularly biased and idiosyncratic, suggesting little more than a Rorschach test might. This is true in part because of the enormous complexity of Noyes's ideas and practices. If presented selectively, they can be analyzed convincingly using almost any psychological framework, from classic Freudian, Jungian, or behaviorist approaches to more modern

Excerpted from Lawrence Foster, "The Psychology of Free Love: Sexuality in the Oneida Community," in *Women, Family, and Utopia: Communal Experiments of the Shakers, the Oneida Community, and the Mormons* (Syracuse, NY: Syracuse University Press, 1991), pp. 75–90 perspectives found in gestalt psychology, transactional analysis, or ego psychology. With rare exceptions, writers who have attempted to analyze Noyes's psychology have failed to read more than a handful of the many books and pamphlets published by the community before confidently asserting that he perfectly exemplifies their pet psychological theories. Virtually no use has been made of the revealing newspapers that Noyes and his associates published (eventually on a daily basis) between 1834 and 1879, of the interviews with leading Oneida members after the community's breakup, which are now held at the Kinsey Institute, or of the community diaries and records that were not burned in the late 1940s and are now held at the Syracuse University Library in Syracuse, New York.

This chapter is a preliminary attempt to reconstruct, more thoroughly than has heretofore been possible, the sexual ideology and attitudes that underlay the Oneida experiment and the way in which sexual expression occurred and was channeled at Oneida. After focusing on the complex sexual ideology and practices introduced by John Humphrey Noyes, the chapter also will briefly consider the backgrounds and experiences of the approximately two hundred adults who joined the community in the 1840s and 1850s and the factors that led to the breakup of the community in 1879–81.

Before launching into this ambitious analysis, let me emphasize three points. First is the enormous complexity of human sexuality, by which I mean not simply coitus itself but also the broader interrelationships between men and women that occur both between individuals and in society. Oneida tested the outer limits of human behavior in this area during more than thirty years of the community's existence. Even sexually sophisticated individuals today can learn much about the range of possible sexual expression by paying close attention to the Oneida experiment. A second, closely related point is that no single psychological theory alone convincingly explains the Oneida Community. Noyes formulated, both in theory and in practice, a distinctive approach to understanding and revitalizing relations between men and women. Although insights from various psychological theories inform this analysis, I shall be trying to understand the Oneida Community on its own terms rather than forcing its experience into the procrustean bed of any single theory. A final caveat, lest anyone be disappointed, is that when I speak of "free love" in this essay, I am referring to the system used at Oneida, not to what anyone else may have fantasized free love to be like. Oneida free love was in many ways anything but free. Although the range of adult heterosexual contacts within the community was greatly extended, any exclusive romantic attachments were rigorously broken up as a threat to community stability. In this as in other respects, a convincing analysis of Oneida must first see the community on its own terms.

I

To understand the Oneida Community, both its theoretical underpinnings and its practice, one must first understand its founder, John Humphrey Noyes. To a large extent, Oneida is best understood as the lengthened shadow of this one extraordinary man, reflecting his complex personality and concerns. Noyes struggled with unusual intensity to overcome his religious and sexual problems. Unlike most individuals, who simply seek to reach an accommodation with the larger world, Noyes adopted a prophetic stance, arguing that his insights provided a universally valid model for setting the world straight. Possessed by this extraordinary and compelling idea, unable or unwilling to work within what he considered to be an unstable and inconsistent value framework, Noyes sought "to initiate, both in himself as well as in others, a process of moral regeneration."[3] He projected his ego strengths and weaknesses onto the world. He was one of those individuals about whom William James wrote in whom a "superior intellect" and a "psychopathic temperament" coalesce, thereby creating "the best possible condition for the kind of effective genius that gets into biographical dictionaries. Such figures do not remain mere critics and understanders with their intellect. Their ideas possess them, they inflict them, for better or worse, upon their companions or their age."[4]

The world into which John Humphrey Noyes was born in southern Vermont in 1811 was one which was undergoing disquieting social, political, and religious changes as the young American republic gradually left behind elements of its more cohesive colonial past and moved into the rough-and-tumble world of nineteenth-century capitalist individualism. Like many of the people who would later join his communities, Noyes grew up in a family of higher than average intellectual and social attainments. His father, John, was a successful businessman who served in the United States House of Representatives, while his strong-willed and deeply religious mother, Polly Hayes, was a second cousin to Rutherford B. Hayes, who later became the nineteenth president of the United States.

The close-knit family environment in which young John grew up on the family holdings in Putney, Vermont, would later be reflected in many of the features of the organizational life of the Putney and Oneida communities. The family was emotionally ingrown yet strongly aware of its distinctive talents and capabilities. All four of Noyes's father's brothers had, apparently because of shyness, married close cousins. The elder John Noyes himself had married Polly Hayes only after a long and desultory courtship when he was forty. Throughout his life young John shared his father's intense shyness around women, as well as the related tendency to intellectualize relations with the opposite sex. The complex marriage system that John Humphrey Noyes would eventually institute among his followers at Putney and Oneida would reflect the curious combination of intimacy and distance he had first experienced in his own family.[5]

Young John Noyes first began to move out into the world on his own as a result of his conversion in a religious revival in 1831. That conversion sent him off to Andover and then to Yale theological seminaries to study to become a minister. Noyes was an intense and driven young man who seemed to expect absolute perfection of himself. He compulsively read his Bible as much as twelve to sixteen hours a day, trying to discover God's will for his life. Finally, after an intellectual breakthrough in 1834, he realized that God could not expect the impossible of him. The total perfection that God demanded of all true Christians must be achieved through a right attitude and an inner sense of salvation from sin, not by any outward acts per se. When Noyes publicly announced that he was "perfect" in this sense, he was viewed as crazy by his colleagues, and he lost his license to preach. For three emotionally tumultuous years until 1837, he wandered quixotically throughout New England and New York State trying to convert the world to his highly idiosyncratic, perfectionist religious beliefs. He was determined to establish "right relations with God," a common value framework for the world, but instead he found his message either ignored or ridiculed. On several occasions, he experienced such intense psychic turmoil that his family and close associates feared he was temporarily deranged.[6]

During this difficult period, when all religious and social truth seemed uncertain, Noyes also began to question and rethink the basis for relations between the sexes. He struggled to understand his sexual impulses and to determine why so many of the perfectionists with whom he was associated were engaged in such erratic and often self-destructive sexual experimentation. Eventually Noyes applied the same principles to sexual relations that he had to understanding religious truth. He concluded that if one had the right attitude, sexual relations, like other activities in life, would be expressed in an outward manner that would be pleasing to God. The sexual impulse was basically a good one, but it needed to be expressed through proper channels. Noyes rejected the extremes of Shaker celibacy, on the one hand, or spiritualist promiscuity, on the other. In his words,

> The Shaker and the licentious spiritualist are alike in their fundamental error, which is an over-emphasis of the importance of the outward act of sexual union. The Shaker, with a prurient swollen imagination of the

importance of the act, pronounces it a damnable abomination prohibited to the saints. The licentious spiritualist, with the same morbid imagination, thinks it right and necessary in the face of all human regulations, to perform it at the bidding of impulse.

Noyes declared that neither the act of sexual union nor abstinence from it had any importance in itself. The goal, rather, was "a healthy development and faithful subordination of the sexual susceptibility."[7] As early as 1837, he argued that eventually in the holy community of Christians, love, including sexual love, would be expressed freely among all God's saints.

Public announcement of the latter views temporarily lost Noyes virtually all of his remaining supporters. In attempting to justify himself and rehabilitate his reputation, he began during the late 1830s to settle down and establish the organizational forms that would eventually allow his principles to be realized in functioning community life. After returning home to Putney, Vermont, Noyes started first a Bible School, then a Society of Inquiry, and finally the full-scale Putney Community, which ultimately, after its relocation to Oneida, New York in 1848, would become the Oneida Community and last for more than thirty additional years. The process of development was a gradual one, part of an attempt to find the best way of expressing the group's religious convictions in practice.[8]

At the core of Noyes's religious beliefs was a millenarian expectation that the ideal patterns of the kingdom of heaven could literally be realized on earth in his communal experiments. Noyes argued that he and his followers were returning to the ideals of early Christianity, the "primitive Christian church." Following his hero St. Paul, Noyes argued that the spirit not the letter of the law was what really mattered. Noyes and his followers did not slavishly seek to follow the *forms* of early Christianity but instead attempted to realize the *spirit* of early Christianity in their particular nineteenth-century setting. Perfection, not in externals but in internal attitudes and a sense of salvation from sin, was required by God of all true Christians on earth.

The complex and highly unorthodox religious beliefs around which Noyes's perfectionists eventually organized their communities at Oneida and its smaller branches were most fully presented and elaborated in Noyes's articles in the community newspapers and in the compendium of those articles published in 1847 as *The Berean: A Manual for the Help of Those Who Seek the Faith of the Primitive Church*. Theologically, the core of Noyes's heresies was his belief that the Second Coming of Christ had occurred in 70 AD when the Temple in Jerusalem was destroyed and the great Diaspora began. Noyes argued that at that time there was a primary resurrection and judgment in the spiritual world which marked the beginning of the Kingdom of God in the heavens. A second and final resurrection judgment was now approaching: "The church on earth is now rising to meet the approaching kingdom in the heavens, and to become its duplicate and representative on earth."[9]

Associated with Noyes's millenarian conviction that the kingdom of heaven could literally be realized on earth was his intense desire to overcome the disruptive individualism of nineteenth-century America by instituting among his followers a new set of religious and social values. Those values stressed the subordination of individuals and their private, selfish interests to the good of the larger community, as interpreted by Noyes. The goal, most briefly stated, was to move beyond the "egotism for two" implicit in monogamous family life to create "an enlarged family" in which all loyalties, including sexual loyalties, would eventually be raised to the level of the entire community.[10] These new values were introduced and internalized during the decade at Putney through the practice of male continence, mutual criticism, and complex marriage.

Male continence, the extraordinary method of birth control used at Putney and Oneida, was developed initially in response to the problems of Noyes's wife, Harriet. During the first six years of their married life, Harriet was traumatized by five difficult childbirths, four of which resulted in the death of the child. Noyes's attempt to spare Harriet such agony in the future led him to develop the distinction between sexual intercourse for "amative" and "propagative" purposes. The primary concern of sexual intercourse was social or "amative" – to allow the sexes to communicate and express affection for each other. Noyes argued that such intercourse could be separated from propagative intercourse in practice, and without artificial aids, by "male continence," the practice that is technically known as *coitus reservatus*. Under male continence, a couple would engage in sexual congress without the man ever ejaculating, either during intercourse or after withdrawal. Noyes saw this practice, which required substantial male self-control, as a logical outgrowth of his principles. In his view, regular intercourse is wasteful, sowing the seed where one does not want or expect it to grow. "Yet it is equally manifest that the natural instinct of our nature demands frequent congress of the sexes, not for propagative, but for social and spiritual purposes. It results from this that simple congress of the sexes, without the propagative crisis, is the order of nature for the gratification of ordinary amative instincts."[11]

Recognizing the controversial nature of male continence, Noyes used several intriguing analogies to explain and defend his unorthodox method of birth control. He denied that male continence was "unnatural." If it was, then "cooking, wearing clothes, living in houses, and almost everything else done by civilized man, is unnatural in the same sense. . . . Every instance of self-denial is an interruption of some natural act. The man who virtuously contents himself with a look at a beautiful woman is conscious of such an interruption. The lover who stops at a kiss denies himself a natural progression." Noyes was merely drawing the line further along than a group such as the Shakers, which had only resorted to "the most imposing of human contrivances for avoiding the woes of undesired propagation."[12]

To describe the process of male continence, Noyes used a striking analogy:

> The situation may be compared to a stream in three conditions, viz., 1, a fall; 2, a course of rapids above the fall; and 3, still water above the rapids. The skillful boatman may choose whether he will remain in the still water, or venture more or less down the rapids, or run his boat over the fall. But there is a point on the verge of the fall where he has no control over his course; and just above that there is a point where he will have to struggle with the current in a way which will give his nerves a severe trial, even though he may escape the fall. If he is willing to learn, experience will teach him the wisdom of confining his excursions to the region of easy rowing, unless he has an object in view that is worth the cost of going over the falls.[13]

How well did such an unusual system work? Initial experimentation by Noyes and his followers at Putney in the early 1840s suggested that the procedure was effective in curtailing pregnancies. And during the twenty years between 1848 and 1868, when male continence was almost the sole sanctioned method of sexual intercourse at Oneida, community records show only twelve unplanned births in a group numbering approximately two hundred adults, equally balanced between the sexes and having frequent sexual congress with a variety of partners during that time.[14] Undoubtedly that low birth rate can be traced in part to the practice of having women past the menopause induct young men into male continence and having older, more experienced men induct young women. But the effectiveness of male continence as a means of birth control in a regulated community setting is incontestable.

The psychological effects of the system are more ambiguous. Unfortunately, approximately forty years ago an extensive body of diaries, journals, and other personal papers of community members which might have shed light on this matter was destroyed. And the items that were fortuitously saved are only now in the process of becoming available to outside scholarship at Syracuse University Library, under various restrictions. As a result, the analysis that follows is based primarily on other sources, including a close reading of the first twenty-one years of the newspapers published by Noyes and his associates and of every book and pamphlet published by the Oneida Community throughout its existence, as well as on the interviews with the community members after the breakup, now held at the Kinsey Institute.[15] These sources are often remarkably candid in discussing ideals and problems of all sorts.

These sources suggest that there were indeed serious problems associated with both the introduction and dissolution of community life, but that at other times throughout most of the community's existence male continence and other forms of community control do not appear to have been perceived as especially burdensome. Even during the troubled late stages of Oneida's history, a careful medical study of the health of the community by Noyes's son Theodore showed less incidence of "nervous disorders" than in the society at large, although the relationship of such disorders to male continence is not clear.[16] Noyes himself felt that a slightly higher than average level of sexual tension was not necessarily harmful.[17] His son Pierrepont dimly recalled a quality of restrained romantic excitement pervading and invigorating community life, an atmosphere that Abel Easton described as a sort of "continuous courtship."[18] Finally, the practice of male continence for many years evidently did not lead to impotence. When Noyes instituted his experiment in "scientific propagation" in 1868, many men who had long practiced male continence deliberately sired children.

Despite the disclaimers, it is difficult to believe that there were no significant problems associated with male continence. Probably even with unusually strong religious commitment, proper training, and stringent enforcement procedures, few men could have found the technique "easy," as Noyes declared it was for "spiritual men." Hints in Noyes's writings, for instance, suggest that masturbation, and associated anti-social withdrawal from community life, may have been a problem at times, but the record is inconclusive. Whatever the difficulties associated with male continence, most Oneida men evidently preferred it to celibacy, the only other option, which seems to have been practiced by a few men of the community.[19]

However men may have reacted, women at Oneida evidently found the practice an improvement. In describing his early experimentation with male continence, Noyes observed, "My wife's experience was very satisfactory, as it had never been before."[20] The medical historian Norman Himes opined "that the Oneida Community stands out historically as perhaps the only group experiment, at least in the Western World, placing great emphasis on the full satisfaction of the woman, and this in a culture dominated by male attitudes."[21] And the sex researcher Havelock Ellis concluded that some women did reach orgasm when male continence was practiced.[22]

Male continence can be viewed as an accentuation and synthesis of certain characteristic Victorian sexual attitudes that sought internalized control of sexual expression.[23] The primary importance of the technique was practical, however. Noyes declared that the "Oneida Community in an important sense owed its existence to the discovery of Male Continence" and that the principle underlying its practice "has been the very soul of its working constitution."[24] Male continence undercut the emotional and physical exclusiveness of couples. It prevented the complications having children would have posed to establishing the primary loyalty to the community in all things. And it allowed a degree of sexual pleasure, coupled with stringent self-control and self-denial, not found in artificial methods of birth control. Few would be tempted simply to make a "hobby" of the practice and withdraw from the normal round of community life into exclusive emotional and sexual attachments.

The second form of social control that helped to prepare the way for complex marriage and the close community life associated with it was the practice of "mutual criticism." Under this special form of group feedback and control, which has parallels with a variety of modern techniques, from gestalt therapy to Chinese thought control, the person to receive criticism would be openly and honestly evaluated by other members of the group to encourage his or her character development. Usually criticism sessions at Oneida were conducted by groups of ten to fifteen members, with an approximately equal balance between the sexes. The person to receive criticism would remain silent while other members of the group, in turn, discussed his or her strengths and weaknesses. The process brought faults and irritating personality characteristics into the open, rather than letting the problems fester in secret. Topics brought up in the sessions could range from ideological issues to the most private personal and sexual matters. In the absence of a formal governmental structure at Oneida, mutual criticism served as the chief means of informally establishing and sustaining community cohesion and norms.

Institutionalization of male continence and mutual criticism among Noyes's followers preceded his further action at Putney in 1846 to move out from traditional monogamous marriage into a new group form called complex marriage. The details of this difficult transition, which was not completed until the early 1850s at Oneida, are not important to this analysis.[25] Suffice it to note that the essence of the complex marriage system Noyes eventually introduced among his followers was the elimination of "selfishness" – the subordination of individual self-interest to the interests of the community, which in turn was dedicated to achieving God's will. Even individual sexual loyalties had to be given up, raised instead to the level of the community, to the "enlarged family."

Noyes argued that the resulting ties were at least as binding and as demanding as those of ordinary marriage. In the words of the community handbook, "The honor and faithfulness that constitutes an ideal marriage, may exist between two hundred as well as two; while the guarantees for women and children are much greater in the Community than they can be in any private family."[26] To sustain such larger ties, any tendencies toward "special love" (exclusive romantic attachments) were rigorously discouraged. Special individual attachments to offspring or close friendships between members of the same sex were similarly broken up. The enlarged family at Oneida eventually all lived under one roof in a large Mansion House, ate together, worked together, gathered daily for religious-and-business meetings of the whole group, and shared all but the most basic personal property in common.[27]

It is interesting to speculate about the psychological motives that led Noyes to set up a community in which intense loyalty to the group was required, but all exclusive sexual and social attachments were discouraged. The sociologist Maren Lockwood Carden makes the acute, if only partially correct, observation that Noyes was never able "to commit himself fully to any idea, action, or person."[28] A more accurate statement might be, instead, that Noyes always was firmly committed to his own sense of mission and core ideas, but he was never willing to open himself up to close personal relationships, either with men or with women. Until Noyes was able to find followers willing to acknowledge his unique, God-given leadership, he remained intensely shy and insecure. Once his supreme authority was accepted, however, he was able to relax somewhat and benevolently delegate authority to his loyal subordinates who, in turn, showed great flexibility in putting his ideas into practice.[29] As Robert David Thomas has suggested in *The Man Who Would Be Perfect*, Noyes was a man whose great ego strengths and weaknesses were reflected in a sharp ambivalence about his competing drives for autonomy and for dependence. In effect, Noyes skillfully used his communities, with their institutionalized combination of emotional distance and closeness, to overcome his inner divisions and establish a sense of worth and power.

II

John Humphrey Noyes was far more than an isolated individual propounding idiosyncratic, if very interesting, social and sexual theories. He was also the founder of a community that at its peak numbered some three hundred members at Oneida and its branch communities and successfully put his theories into practice for more than thirty years. One wonders, therefore, what kinds of people were attracted to Oneida and why. Did individuals who joined the group, as Maren Lockwood Carden suggests, have an unusual "psychological makeup" that led them to want to participate in the complex system at Oneida?[30] And, whatever their backgrounds, how did Oneida members adapt successfully to the social and sexual system there that broke up all exclusive personal relationships to focus primary attention on larger communal goals?

Fortunately, extensive primary and secondary records help us to begin to answer these questions. Robert Fogarty's analysis of the Oneida Community as an experiment in "conservative Christian utopianism" provides a particularly valuable starting point for such an analysis.[31] Fogarty uses the Oneida Family Register, a manuscript giving names and personal data on the first 111 people who joined the community, as well as US census data from 1850 to 1880 and annual reports and newspapers printed at Oneida, to reconstruct backgrounds and histories of the members. From his work and from other sources, it becomes apparent that individuals were not attracted to the group because of any narrow social or psychological factors.

The most striking features of Oneida Community members were the careful process by which selection occurred and the extraordinarily high rate of retention. Although a few accessions to the group and a few defections from it would occur throughout the community's existence, 84 of the 109 adults who joined during the first two years at Oneida either died in the community or lived there until its breakup.[32] This impressive degree of membership stability was connected with the carefully selected character of the group. Members were deliberately chosen on the basis of complete loyalty to Noyes's leadership and to his perfectionist ideals. Members represented a wide range of occupational backgrounds, personality types, and special interests that could contribute to the success of the community. They came from most of the areas of New York and New England where sizable pockets of Noyes's perfectionist followers lived, and many of them were relatively affluent. By 1857, for example, the members had invested almost $108,000 in the Oneida Community and its branches. Only such a large capital backing allowed the community to continue to function despite a loss of $40,000 during the initial decade before Oneida finally began to achieve financial stability.[33]

The psychological attraction of Oneida to new members can be briefly summarized. Most individuals for whom we have data were in an emotionally unsettled state when they joined the community. Usually they had been religious "seekers," distressed at repeatedly experiencing the emotional ups and downs of revivalistic religion. They yearned for release from this emotional roller coaster and thus were attracted by Noyes's promise to provide "salvation from sin" within a stable, supportive, and authoritative communal structure.[34] Interestingly, Oneida's sexual system does not appear to have been the major attraction for new members; indeed, in some cases it proved a deterrent to joining the group.[35] Despite the emotionally unsettled state of individuals when they entered Oneida, they do not appear to have had any special "character structure" that could differentiate them from the generality of Americans of their day. The detailed psychological critiques of Oneida Community members that were given in mutual criticism sessions and reported in the community newspaper from 1850 onward show the full range of human types, with almost every conceivable character strength and weakness. Oneidans, like converts to any religious or secular ideology which attempts a radical restructuring of the lives of its adherents, found Noyes's system appealing because it helped them to overcome the disorder they experienced and to become resocialized to a more secure and satisfying way of life.

How well did individuals at Oneida adjust to the constriants of the group's social and sexual system, especially the deliberate breaking up of all exclusive emotional relationships? Available evidence does suggest that the initial transition to complex marriage was turbulent. Once the initial transition was completed, however, individuals generally appear to have adapted well to communal living. Tendencies to return to "worldly" patterns were countered by the control mechanisms of male continence, mutual criticism, and ascending and descending fellowship. Even with its constraints, the community was anything but dour, gloomy, and ascetic. A wide variety of expressions of cultural and intellectual life were encouraged. Special activities ranged from spirited dancing to community-produced plays, musical events, and skits that helped to vary the normal routine and keep the community lively.[36] Noyes's son Pierrepont recalled: "The grown folks seemed almost as bent on being happy as they did on being good. Everyone worked; almost everyone seemed to have time for play, or perhaps I should say recreation."[37] For more than two decades, life at Oneida would continue to follow a basically tranquil course.

III

Despite its many strengths, the Oneida Community eventually experienced sufficient internal and external tension that it terminated both its complex marriage and its communistic economic systems by the early 1880s. What were the chief factors contributing to the end of complex marriage and the breakup of the community? This complicated but fascinating question is analyzed more fully elsewhere, so here I shall present only the briefest possible summary before discussing the larger significance of the Oneida experiment.

The Oneida Community can in many ways be considered as the length-ened shadow of one man – John Humphrey Noyes. So long as Noyes retained his ability to lead, the community prospered. By the late 1870s, however, Noyes's leadership was faltering, and no other individuals were able to pull together an increasingly divided community. Thus, when an external campaign against the community was launched in the mid-1870s, the Oneida Community was no longer confident of its mission and the loyalty of its members. Rather than risk an externally induced breakdown of the community, leaders of the group acted skillfully in August 1879 to terminate their distinctive sexual arrangements while they could still be counted a success. Little more than a year later, on January 1, 1881, the community formally ended its communal economic system, reorganizing as a joint-stock corporation in which former community members held shares. Thus ended the communal phase of one of the most remarkable religious and economic experiments in American history . . .

Ultimately, Noyes sought to achieve a balance between opposing tendencies of his time. He attempted to develop a wholesome and unified form of communal life that would demonstrate the validity of his views in practice. By gathering a loyal following and setting up a community that put his new synthesis of truth into practice, Noyes was able to overcome his personal insecurities and project onto the world a creative vision of human potentialities that still deserves attention today.

Notes

1   This chapter was originally published under the title "The Psychology of Free Love in the Oneida Community," *Australasian Journal of American Studies* 5 (Dec. 1986): 14–26.

2   The characterization of Noyes as a "Yankee Saint" is found in Robert Allerton Parker, *A Yankee Saint: John Humphrey Noyes and the Oneida Com-munty* (New York: Putnam's 1935). For the comment that Noyes has been treated as a "Vermont Casanova," see Robert Davis Thomas, *The Man Who Would Be Perfect: John Humphrey Noyes and the Utopian Impulse* (Philadelphia: University of Pennsylvania Press, 1997). The comparison of Noyes and Hitler appears in Erik Achorn, "Mary Cragin: Perfectionist Saint," *New England Quarterly* 28 (1955): 490–518.

3   Kenelm Burridge, *New Heaven, New Earth: a Study of Millenarian Activities* (New York: Schocken Books, 1969), 163.

4   William James, *The Varieties of Religious Experience* (Cambridge, MA: Harvard University Press, 1985), 36–7.

5   On Noyes's early life, see Parker, *Yankee Saint*; Thomas, *Man Who Would Be Perfect*; and George Wallingford Noyes, *Religious Experience of John Humphrey Noyes, Founder of the Oneida Community* (Freeport, NY: Books for Libraries Press, 1971).

6   See John Humphrey Noyes, *Confessions of John H. Noyes, Part I: Confession of Religious Experience, Including a History of Modern Perfectionism* (Oneida Reserve, NY: Leonard, 1849); G. W. Noyes, ed., *Religious Experience*; and Lawrence Foster, *Religion and Sexuality: Three American Communal Experiments of the Nineteenth Century* (New York: Oxford University Press, 1981), 75–9.

7   "A Word of Warning," *Perfectionist and Theocratic Watchman* 5 (July 12, 1845): 34.

8   In 1838 Noyes married Harriet Holton, in part influenced by the social and financial resources she could devote to his cause. "Financial Romance: How the O.C. Got Its Capital," *Circular* 2, n.s. (Jan. 8, 1866): 366.

9   *First Annual Report of the Oneida Association*, 11–12. Also see Noyes's *Confessions*; his *The Berean: A Manual for the Help of Those Who Seek the Faith of the Primitive Church* (Putney, Vt.: Office of the *Spiritual Magazine*, 1847); and G. W. Noyes, ed., *Religious Experience*.

10 Foster, *Religion and Sexuality*, 90–3.

11 Noyes, "Bible Argument Defining the Relations of the Sexes in the Kingdom of Heaven," in *First Annual Report of the Oneida Association*, 32.

12 John Humphrey Noyes, *The Berean. Male Continence: Essay on Scientific Propagation* (New York: Arno Press, 1969), 7, 9.

13 Ibid., 8.

14 Maren Lockwood Carden, *Oneida: Utopian Community to Modern Corporation* (New York: Harper & Row, 1971), 51, finds evidence that thirty-one births occurred at Oneida between 1848 and 1868, but some of these births were planned. The R. L. Dickinson Papers at the Kinsey Institute indicate that only twelve unplanned births occurred during that period. Whatever the true number, the figure for accidental births was remarkably low.

15 For a summary of the major printed sources on Oneida, see Lester G. Wells, *The Oneida Community Collection in the Syracuse University Library* (Syracuse, NY: Syracuse University, 1961).

16 Theodore R. Noyes, M.D., "Report on Nervous Diseases in the Oneida Community," as printed in John Humphrey Noyes, *Essay on Scientific Propagation* (Oneida, NY: Oneida Community, 1872), 25–32. Also see Ely van de Warker, "Gynecological Study of the Oneida Community," *American Journal of Obstetrics and Diseases of Women and Children* 17 (Aug. 1884): 755–810. Note that the contemporary analysis of male sexual behavior by Alfred Kinsey and his associates argues that men practicing *coitus reservatus* can indeed achieve orgasm without ejaculation and describes how this can occur. Kinsey et al., *Sexual Behavior in the Human Male*, 158–61.

17 Noyes, *Male Continence*, 20.

18 Pierrepont B. Noyes, *My Father's House: An Oneida Boyhood* (New York: Farrar & Reinhart, 1937), 131; Allan Estlake, *The Oneida Community: a Record of an Attempt to Carry out the Principles of Christian Unselfishness and Scientific Race Improvement* (New York: AMS Press, 1973), 26.

19 Celibacy was a theoretical alternative to complex marriage and was practiced by some of the men. See P. B. Noyes, *My Father's House*, 150 and passim.

20   Noyes, *Male Continence*, 20.
21   Norman Himes, *Medical History of Contraception* (1936; reprint New York: Schocken, 1970), 271.
22   Havelock Ellis, *Studies in the Psychology of Sex* (Philadelphia: F. A. Davis, 1911), 553.
23   See Barker-Benfield, "Spermatic Economy," as well as other essays collected in Thomas L. Altherr, ed., *Procreation or Pleasure: Sexual Attitudes in American History* (Malabar, Fla.: Krieger, 1983).
24   Noyes, *Male Continence*, 21.
25   Foster, *Religion and Sexuality*, 100–116.
26   *Handbook of the Oneida Community, Containing a Brief Sketch of Its Present Condition, Internal Economy and Leading Principles*, no. 2 (Oneida, NY: Oneida Community, 1871), 56.
27   Foster, *Religion and Sexuality*, 116–18.
28   Carden, *Oneida*, 30.
29   Foster, *Religion and Sexuality*, 85–86, 105–6.
30   Carden, *Oneida*, 107.
31   Robert S. Fogarty, *Daily Journal of Oneida Community* (Philadelphia: Porcupine Press, 1975).
32   Carden, *Oneida*, 77.
33   *Handbook of the Oneida Community, 1875* (Oneida, NY: Office of the *Oneida Circular*, 1875), 15.
34   Fogarty, "Oneida Community"; and Persons, "Christian Communitarianism."
35   Foster, *Religion and Sexuality*, 110.
36   Ibid., 116–18.
37   P. B. Noyes, *My Father's House*, 138.

Documents

The first document, an excerpt from the 1870 *Hand-Book* of the Oneida Community, defends the concept of free love. The *Hand-Book* contends that, contrary to popular opinion, free love does not mean promiscuous sexual behavior but is rather a means toward building a controlled community, one with property and sexuality shared among committed members. Why might this prospect have been appealing for the women and men who decided to live in Oneida? Does it seem designed to promote sexual liberation or sexual control of its members?

History of American Socialisms

John Humphrey Noyes

Free Love

[From the *Hand-Book* of the Oneida Community.]

This terrible combination of two very good ideas – freedom and love – was first used by the writers of the Oneida Community about twenty-one years ago, and probably originated with them. It was however soon taken up by a very different class of speculators scattered about the country, and has come to be the name of a form of socialism with which we have but little affinity. Still it is sometimes applied to our Communities; and as we are certainly responsible for starting it into circulation, it seems to be our duty to tell what meaning we attach to it, and in what sense we are willing to accept it as a designation of our social system.

The obvious and essential difference between marriage and licentious connections may be stated thus:

Marriage is permanent union. Licentiousness deals in temporary flirtations.

In marriage, Communism of property goes with Communism of persons. In licentiousness, love is paid for as hired labor.

Marriage makes a man responsible for the consequences of his acts of love to a woman. In licentiousness, a man imposes on a woman the heavy burdens of maternity, ruining perhaps her reputation and her health, and then goes his way without responsibility.

Marriage provides for the maintenance and education of children. Licentiousness ignores children as nuisances, and leaves them to chance.

Now in respect to every one of these points of difference between marriage and licentiousness, *we stand with marriage*. Free Love with us does *not* mean freedom to love to-day and leave to-morrow; nor freedom to take a woman's person and keep our property to ourselves; nor freedom to freight a woman with our offspring and send her down stream without care or help; nor freedom to beget children and leave them to the street and the poor-house. Our Communities are *families*, as distinctly bounded and separated from promiscuous society as ordinary households. The tie that binds us together is as permanent and sacred, to say

Excerpted from John Humphrey Noyes, *History of American Socialisms* (Philadelphia: J. B. Lippincott, 1870), pp. 638–40.

the least, as that of marriage, for it is our religion. We receive no members (except by deception or mistake), who do not give heart and hand to the family interest for life and forever. Community of property extends just as far as freedom of love. Every man's care and every dollar of the common property is pledged for the maintenance and protection of the women, and the education of the children of the Community. Bastardy, in any disastrous sense of the word, is simply impossible in such a social state. Whoever will take the trouble to follow our track from the beginning, will find no forsaken women or children by the way. In this respect we claim to be in advance of marriage and common civilization.

We are not sure how far the class of socialists called "Free Lovers" would claim for themselves any thing like the above defense from the charge of reckless and cruel freedom; but our impression is that their position, scattered as they are, without organization or definite separation from surrounding society, makes it impossible for them to follow and care for the consequences of their freedom, and thus exposes them to the just charge of licentiousness. At all events their platform is entirely different from ours, and they must answer for themselves. *We* are not "Free Lovers" in any sense that makes love less binding or responsible than it is in marriage.

Male Continence

John Humphrey Noyes

The second document, written by Oneida leader and founder John Humphrey Noyes, expains the rationale behind male continence as well as its practical application. Noyes was convinced that the sexual practice of withdrawing without emission made sense on a spiritual as well as a physical level. Contrary to other extreme methods of birth control, such as celibacy, *coitus reservatus* promoted at least some male sexual pleasure. Noyes understood the self-discipline required for the method's effectiveness, yet he contended nonetheless that male continence was the most "natural" of the options. How did Noyes justify and defend this sexual practice?

Excerpted from John Humphrey Noyes, *Male Continence* (Oneida, NY: Office of Oneida Circular, 1872), pp. 5–10.

New York, *July* 26, 1866

The first question, or rather, perhaps I should say, the *previous* question in regard to Male Continence is, whether it is desirable or proper that men and women should establish intelligent voluntary control over the propagative function. Is it not better (it may be asked), to leave "nature" to take its course (subject to the general rules of legal chastity), and let children come as chance or the unknown powers may direct, without putting any restraint on sexual intercourse after it is once licensed by marriage, or on the freedom of all to take out such license? If you assent to this latter view, or have any inclination toward it, I would recommend to you the study of *Malthus on Population*; not that I think he has pointed out anything like the true *method* of voluntary control over propagation, but because he has demonstrated beyond debate the absolute *necessity* of such control in some way, unless we consent and expect that the human race, like the lower animals, shall be forever kept down to its necessary limits, by the ghastly agencies of war, pestilence and famine.

For my part, I have no doubt that it is perfectly proper that we should endeavour to rise above "nature" and the destiny of the brutes in this matter. There is no reason why we should not seek and hope for discovery in this direction, as freely as in the development of steam power or the art of printing; and we may rationally expect that He who has promised the "good time" when vice and misery shall be abolished, will at last give us sure light on this darkest of all problems – how to subject human propagation to the control of science.

But whether study and invention in this direction are proper or not, they are actually at work in all quarters, reputable and disreputable. Let us see how many different ways have already been proposed for limiting human increase.

In the first place, the practice of child-killing, either by exposure or violence, is almost as old as the world, and as extensive as barbarism. Even Plato recommended something of this kind, as a waste-gate for vicious increase, in his scheme of a model republic.

Then we have the practice of abortion reduced in modern times to a science, and almost to a distinct profession. A large part of this business is carried on by means of medicines advertized in obscure but intelligible terms as embryo-destroyers or preventives of conception. Every large city has its professional abortionist. Many ordinary physicians destroy embryos to order; and the skill to do this terrible deed has even descended among the common people.

Then what a variety of artificial tricks there are for frustrating the natural effects of the propagative act. You allude to several of these contrivances, in terms of condemnation from which I should not dissent. The least objectionable of them (if there is any difference), seems to be that recommended many years ago by Robert Dale Owen, in a book entitled Moral Physiology; viz., the simple device of withdrawing immediately before emission.

Besides all these disreputable methods, we have several more respectable schemes for attaining the great object of limiting propagation. Malthus proposes and urges that all men, and especially the poor, shall be taught their responsibilities in the light of science, and so be put under inducements *not to marry*. This prudential check on population – the discouragement of marriage – undoubtedly operates to a considerable extent in all civilized society, and to the greatest extent on the classes most enlightened. It seems to have been favored by Saint Paul; (see 1st Cor. 7); and probably would not be condemned generally by people who claim to be considerate. And yet its advocates have to confess that it increases the danger of licentiousness; and on the whole the teaching that is most popular, in spite of Malthus and Paul, is that marriage, with all its liabilities, is a moral and patriotic duty.

Finally, Shakerism, which actually prohibits marriage on religious grounds, is only the most stringent and imposing of human contrivances for avoiding the woes of undesired propagation.

All these experimenters in the art of controlling propagation may be reduced in principle to three classes, viz.:

1. Those that seek to prevent the intercourse of the sexes, such as Malthus and the Shakers.
2. Those that seek to prevent the natural effects of the propagative act, viz., the French inventors and Owen.
3. Those that seek to destroy the living results of the propagative act, viz., the abortionists and child-killers.

Now it may seem to you that any new scheme of control over propagation must inevitably fall to one of these three classes; but I assure you that we have a method that does not fairly belong to any of them. I will try to show you our fourth way.

We begin by *analyzing* the act of sexual intercourse. It has a beginning, a middle, and an end. Its beginning and most elementary form is the simple *presence* of the male organ in the female. Then usually follows a series of reciprocal *motions*. Finally this exercise brings on a nervous action or ejaculatory *crisis* which expels the seed. Now we insist that this whole process, up to the very moment of emission, is *voluntary*, entirely under the control of the moral faculty, and *can be stopped at any point*. In other words, the *presence* and the *motions* can be continued or stopped at will, and it is only the final *crisis* of emission that is automatic or uncontrollable.

Suppose, then, that a man, in lawful intercourse with woman, choosing for good reasons not to beget a child or to disable himself, should stop at the primary stage and content himself with simple *presence* continued as long as agreeable? Would there be any harm? It cannot be injurious to refrain from voluntary excitement. Would there be no *good?* I appeal to the memory of every man who has had good sexual experience to say whether, on the whole, the sweetest and noblest period of intercourse with woman is not that *first* moment of simple presence and spiritual effusion, before the muscular exercise begins.

But we may go farther. Suppose the man chooses for good reasons, as before, to enjoy not only the simple *presence*, but also the *reciprocal motion*, and yet to stop short of the final *crisis*. Again I ask, Would there be any harm? Or would it do no good? I suppose physiologists might say, and I would acknowledge, that the excitement by motion *might* be carried so far that a voluntary suppression of the commencing crisis would be injurious. But what if a man, knowing his own power and limits, should not even *approach* the crisis, and yet be able to enjoy the presence and the motion *ad libitum*? If you say that this is impossible, I answer that I *know* it is possible – nay, that it is easy.

I will admit, however, that it may be impossible to some, while it is possible to others. Paul intimates that some cannot "contain." Men of certain temperaments and conditions are afflicted with involuntary emissions on very trivial excitement and in their sleep. But I insist that these are exceptional morbid cases that should be disciplined and improved; and that, in the normal condition, men are entirely competent to choose in sexual intercourse whether they will stop at any point in the voluntary stages of it, and so make it simply an act of communion, or go through to the involuntary stage, and make it an act of propagation.

The situation may be compared to a stream in the three conditions of a fall, a course of rapids above the fall, and still water above the rapids. The skillful boatman may choose whether he will remain in the still water, or venture more or less down the rapids, or run his boat over the fall. But there is a point on the verge of the fall where he has no control over his course; and just above that there is a point where he will have to struggle with the current in a way which will give his nerves a severe trial, even though he may escape the fall. If he is willing to learn, experience will teach him the wisdom of confining his excursions to the region of easy rowing, unless he has an object in view that is worth the cost of going over the falls.

You have now our whole theory of "Male Continence." It consists in analyzing sexual intercourse, recognizing in it two distinct acts, the social and the propagative, which can be separated practically, and affirming that it is best, not only with reference to remote prudential considerations, but for immediate pleasure, that a man should content himself with the social act, except when he intends procreation. . . .

The wholesale and ever ready objection to this method is that it is *unnatural, and unauthorized by the example of other animals*. I may answer in a wholesale way, that cooking, wearing clothes, living in houses, and almost everything else done by civilized man, is unnatural in the same sense, and that a close adherence to the example of the brutes would require us to forego speech and go on "all fours!" But on the other hand, if it is natural in the best sense, as I believe it is, for rational beings to forsake the example of the brutes and improve nature by invention and discovery in all directions, then truly the argument turns the other way, and we shall have to confess that until men and women find a way to elevate their sexual performances above those of the brutes, by introducing into them moral culture, they are living in *unnatural* degradation.

But I will come closer to this objection. The real meaning of it is, that Male Continence in sexual intercourse is a difficult and injurious interruption of a natural act. But every instance of self-denial is an interruption of some natural act. The man who virtuously contents himself with a look at a beautiful woman is conscious of such an interruption. The lover who stops at a kiss denies himself a natural progression. It is an easy, descending grade through all the approaches of sexual love, from the first touch of respectful friendship, to the final complete amalgamation. Must there be no interruption of this natural slide? Brutes, animal or human, tolerate none. Shall their ideas of self-denial prevail? Nay, it is the glory of man to control himself, and the Kingdom of Heaven summons him to self-control in ALL THINGS. If it is noble and beautiful for the betrothed lover to respect the law of marriage in the midst of the glories of courtship, it may be even more noble and beautiful for the wedded lover to respect the laws of health and propagation in the midst of the ecstacies of sexual union. The same moral culture that ennobles the antecedents and approaches of marriage will some time surely glorify the consummation.

Further Reading

Foster, Lawrence. *Women, Family, and Utopia: Communal Experiments of the Shakers, the Oneida Community, and the Mormons*. Syracuse, NY: Syracuse University Press, 1991.

Kern, Louis J. *An Ordered Love. Sex Roles and Sexuality in Victorian Utopias: the Shakers, the Mormons, and the Oneida Community*. Chapel Hill: University of North Carolina Press, 1981.

Klaw, Spenser. *Without Sin: the Life and Death of the Oneida Community*. New York: Allen Lane, 1993.

Quinn, D. Michael. *Same-sex Dynamics among Nineteenth-century Americans: a Mormon Example*. Urbana and Chicago: University of Illinois Press, 1996.

Stein, Stephen. *The Shaker Experience in America: a History of the United Society of Believers*. New Haven, CT: Yale University Press, 1992.

Thurman, Suzanne. "Shaker women and sexual power: heresy and orthodoxy in the Shaker village of Harvard, Massachusetts." *Journal of Women's History*, 10 (Spring 1998), 70–88.

5

Ministerial Misdeeds

Introduction

Patricia Cline Cohen's essay addresses a nineteenth-century incident of unwanted sexual behavior that we would now call sexual harassment. If that term was lacking in the 1840s, such conduct was all too present. Cohen examines the Onderdonk trial, in which the Episcopal Bishop of New York, Benjamin T. Onderdonk, was accused by several women of groping them beneath their shirts and fondling their breasts. The representation and interpretation of Onderdonk's behavior by the victims, their families, and the public speaks volumes about the expectations of male and female sexual behavior and the limitations endured by white women attempting to maintain polite decorum. Ironically, social convention discouraged women from discussing such delicate matters, yet the trial itself turned on the abused women's ability to report and document Onderdonk's offenses.

Onderdonk's trial and an ensuing flurry of pamphlet publication involved issues of race as well as gender. In one pamphlet, for example, the offending bishop was presented in blackface; that is, in a demeaning caricature of African Americans. If Onderdonk's improper sexual fondling seemed bizarre to white contemporaries – he did it in public, with no apparent expectation that it would lead to further sexual gratification – then imagining the incident in blackface seemed to make the circumstances more "natural." Given the racist climate, even in the antebellum North, it proved far easier for white audiences to envision a black man engaging in such childish and injudicious deportment than a respectable white minister, indeed an Episcopal bishop. White sexual and racial fantasies, then, merged with notions of appropriate female responses to male aggression and fundamentally shaped the public's response to both the victims and Onderdonk during the trial.

Ministerial Misdeeds: the Onderdonk Trial and Sexual Harassment in the 1840s

Patricia Cline Cohen

In late 1844, the Right Reverend Benjamin T. Onderdonk, Episcopal Bishop of New York, was brought to trial before an ecclesiastical court of his peers on nine counts of "immoralities and impurities" committed against Episcopal women. Followed with intense interest by the public and covered with rapt attention in the secular and religious press, the Onderdonk case generated a best-selling trial report and a heated pamphlet war, focusing sharply on questions of correct gender deportment between ministers and female parishioners. To his supporters, Onderdonk was a man wrongfully accused by enemies within his church who really opposed his theological politics. To his antagonists, the bishop was a powerful man who abused his position to prey on women within his circle. The Onderdonk controversy has all the hallmarks of what today would be called a case of sexual harassment. But lacking a concept of sexual harassment to frame the issues, commentators on both sides of the case remained perplexed and at odds about how to interpret Onderdonk's intimate touches.

The story unfolded in a place and time already alert to serious charges of misconduct by the clergy. News of an apparent epidemic of clerical vice oozed from the presses in antebellum America, from the urban penny newspapers to the respectable secular and religious papers. Several features of the sociology of antebellum religion promoted a climate of fear about increased sexual temptation. The rapid growth of denominations in the wake of the Second Great Awakening created space for irregularly trained ministers to make their way in the world; lax educational and licensing requirements inevitably allowed an occasional charlatan to move into a position of trust. An adversarial denominational

Excerpted from Patricia Cline Cohen, "Ministerial Misdeeds: the Onderdonk Trial and Sexual Harassment in the 1840s," *Journal of Women's History*, 7 (Fall 1995), pp. 34–57.

press stood ready to publicize questionable behavior as a way of discrediting the competition.

The emotional style of the evangelical movement further encouraged an atmosphere conducive to sexual disorder. Evangelism often brought passion and sensuality to the fore in a spirituality that manifested itself in ecstatic moments, altered states of being, uncontrolled weeping, or speaking in tongues. Camp meetings and all-night revivals provided a new kind of mixed-sex social space where older rules of gender deportment might be held to less rigidly. Emotional religion allowed for more unrestrained touching, embracing, and general physical intimacy among adherents than did the traditional orthodox churches. Even among those staid denominations, the renewal of religious fervor and the necessity to compete with charismatic clerics inevitably led to a greater cultivation of ministerial showmanship. Some men might ease into the presumption that their spiritual magnetism, displayed so dramatically in the pulpit, betokened sexual magnetism as well.

Whatever the causes, antebellum religious leaders were coming to realize that sexual temptation posed an important occupational hazard for clergymen. No other male occupation offered such easy proximity to women. Protected by an assumption of unimpeachable morality, ministers could approach strange women in public without benefit of introduction; for other men, this was rude or risky forwardness. ("Ah, your parsons know the way to the women! Would that I did!" wrote an envious young bachelor in his diary on an Erie canal boat trip in 1833, upon observing a minister approach some likely young women and propose a checkers game.[1]) Ministers were entitled to converse with women about intimate matters in private spaces – the parlor, the sickbed room, the minister's study. They were supposed to be above the ordinary temptations of life; but some succumbed to sin.

The Onderdonk case, however, was sharply different from the several dozens of tales of ministerial misconduct retailed in the press. No actual sex crime – seduction, rape, attempted rape – was ever alleged. The behavior that the women complained of was universally regarded as inappropriate; there was no possible innocent interpretation for a man's burrowing his hand into a woman's neckline and fondling her naked breast. But in context, the behavior made no sense to the 1840s commentators, because Onderdonk pursued his frontal assaults in public places, when male protectors of the women were nearby. His defenders were thus sure that some less intimate act of tenderness had somehow been misconstrued.

Rarely, before the twentieth century, have such minute, gendered interchanges of body language been the subject of so much discussion in print. Not surprisingly, the trial report created a sensation. The entire transcript was published in a 330-page soft cover book within three weeks of the verdict. At least a dozen pamphlets debated the case, as did local and national news publications. The fullness of the testimony and its wide distribution allowed a throng of people to participate in defining, interpreting, rationalizing, or condemning sexual harassment.

Two themes dominated the public discussion. One focused on the women's testimonies and the inappropriate familiarities. Why did the women not complain at the time? Why did their male relatives fail to defend them? What could the Bishop have possibly had in mind? Under what circumstances could a man presume a woman's willingness to engage in intimate touching? As so often happens in modern sexual harassment cases, questions were raised about the encouragement some of these women might have given the Bishop.

The other significant and weighty subject of discussion was the issue of warring factions within the Protestant Episcopal church. The present-ment for trial came in November of 1844, just one month after the most searing General Convention the Episcopal Church had ever witnessed in America, where the controversy over the English "Oxford Movement" erupted. The struggle pitted High Church adherents against Low Church defenders, the former group advocating a Romanizing move in the direction of Catholic doctrine and especially liturgy.[2] The debate turned on symbolic ritual acts: the lighting of candles, kneeling at the mention of Jesus's name, the color of the surplice worn, facing the congregation or not. Bishop Onderdonk was on record as a strong supporter of the High Church (or Puseyite) position, a minority view in American Anglicanism. The bishop's supporters claimed that the morality charges were a smokescreen for a sinister ulterior plot to oust the bishop and divest the church of Catholic leanings.

The modern experience of adjudicating sexual harassment grievances suggests that the two motives to unseat Onderdonk were not mutually exclusive, as commentators in the 1840s thought. Women who suffer sexual harassment often get heard more quickly and clearly when the harasser already has acquired powerful enemies on other grounds. The theological dispute, then, could well have been an important precondi-tion that enabled the charge of immorality to be taken seriously. And of course, to some, the two objections were not completely unrelated: ornate High Church ritual and aberrant sexuality could be seen as dual manifestations of an aristocratic posture now under attack by an increas-ingly bourgeois American Episcopalianism.

Onderdonk's defenders would naturally never agree that elaborate liturgy had anything to do with sexual irregularities. They insisted that a theological attack was being mounted under the guise of spurious and scandalous charges. And there was some foundation for this view. In the

complicated religious and political terrain of antebellum America, gendered ideas were often invoked as a strategy to distill debates and
simplify disagreements. Stereotypes of masculinity and femininity tend
to be widely shared in a culture and can thus be used as a kind of
shorthand to make accessible other, more complicated ideas. For example, depicting the concept of Liberty as a white woman in revolu-
tionary-era political cartoons conveyed in a glance the idea that liberty
was vulnerable to attack and in need of male protection. Fundamental
ideological tensions between the emerging political parties of Andrew
Jackson and John Quincy Adams in the 1828 election became readily
accessible to voters in the famous campaign fight over Jackson's alleged
adulterous marriage.[3] And impugning the masculine honor and sexual
purity of a clergyman was a quick way to bring him down.

The difficulty in the Onderdonk case was that using stereotypes of
masculine and feminine behavior did not simplify things. Gendered
behaviors lay at the heart of the case; they were not metaphors for larger
questions of character. But they eluded quick comprehension. Onderdonk did not fit the mold of a lecherous man out to seduce a woman; the
women also behaved unintelligibly according to 1840s notions of female
delicacy, by keeping quiet for years. Without a vocabulary of sexual
harassment, of the intricate interrelations of sex and power, commentators of the 1840s were at a loss. Ultimately, only one interpretative
strategy succeeded: a translation of the Onderdonk phenomenon into
blackface, where racist stereotypes distilled and simplified the complex
issues the Episcopalians struggled with. Where gender metaphors no
longer sufficed, racial metaphors worked.

In order to capture the perplexing nature of the incident with its
gendered and racialized configurations, we must first reconstruct the
players and the stage and hear the testimony of the women themselves.
Then we will turn to the contested explanations and interpretations,
nearly all offered by men, from lawyers and clergy to acknowledged
libertines and the jokester-creators of "Black Under-Donk-En Doughlips; or, De Feelin Deacon." The celebrity of the Onderdonk case
derived from its famed centerpiece personality, the Bishop of New
York; but this was far more than a seamy tabloid story of an individual
public figure's fall from grace. Its richness derives from its resonance
with complex public attitudes about sexuality, gender and race that
preoccupied antebellum America.

Benjamin T. Onderdonk, 53, was born in New York City of an old
Long Island Dutch family. Both he and his brother Henry attended
Columbia and became ordained ministers in the Protestant Episcopal
Church. He married at 22, fathered seven children, and spent his whole
career in New York City. Onderdonk was an ambitious leader, and in

1830, at the relatively young age of 39, he was consecrated Bishop of New York. His brother Henry rose to be Bishop of Pennsylvania in 1836.[4] Both men were articulate and powerful proponents of the High Church party; both made enemies.

In the fall of 1844, the controversy over the Oxford Movement erupted at the Episcopalian convention in Philadelphia. Tense delegates hammered out a set of new procedures governing dismissals of bishops. Henry Onderdonk had recently been persuaded to resign his bishopric on grounds of habitual intemperance. Within a month, the new procedures were invoked against Benjamin Onderdonk, and in December the trial to unseat him on nine charges of sexual immoralities opened in New York City.

The first woman to testify was the daughter of an Episcopal minister who had known the Bishop since her childhood. Onderdonk came to Syracuse in June 1837 to ordain her newlywed husband, Clement Moore Butler. The couple met him in Ithaca and drove all night with him in a two-seat wagon, the 20-year-old Mrs Butler in the back seat with the Bishop, and her husband and the driver in front. According to Mrs Butler, Onderdonk had had too much to drink, and as the sun set, he became unusually attentive, which alarmed her.

> He first put his arm around my waist and drew me towards him; this he repeated once, perhaps twice. He had often done this when I was unmarried, and I had permitted it, although always disagreeable to me; because I believed him incapable of wrong. At this time, however, I removed his hand each time, because I saw that he was not himself. I was exceedingly fearful lest our driver should discover it; . . . The bishop persisted in putting his arm about me, and raised his hand so as to press my bosom. I then rose and withdrew the arm from behind me, and laid the hand upon his knee, and said to him in a raised tone of voice . . . that a Bishop's hands were sacred in my eyes, and that his were particularly so, because they had been laid upon the heads of many I loved in confirmation, and were about to be laid upon my husband's head in ordination. He made but little answer, but for some little time let me alone.

Mrs Butler hoped it was just the alcohol and that the bishop meant no intentional insult. But

> while sitting in thought, I found he was again moving: I waited to see whether he might not be merely steadying himself in his seat, as the roads were rough, when he suddenly and violently again brought his hand upon my bosom, pressed and clasped it. In some horror I struck the hand with all my force, and he withdrew it; but immediately grasped my leg in the most indelicate manner.[5]

This was too much; Mrs Butler clambered into the front seat onto her husband's lap and whispered her fears to him. Mr Butler got the impression the bishop had actually lifted her skirt and touched her naked leg. At a rest stop he and his wife debated what to do. Mr Butler, very agitated, wanted to confront the man, but Mrs Butler, mindful of the ordination ceremony just hours away, counseled silence.

Under oath, Mr Butler confirmed his wife's story. He coldly avoided the bishop after his ordination. He divulged his painful story to other ministers only after hearing rumors of similar incidents. His wife broke her silence by confiding in her sister-in-law, a close female friend, and later her father, who did not believe her. The Butlers' complaint constituted two counts: undue familiarities and improper inebriation.

The third formal charge against Onderdonk involved an unknown woman, about 25, who shared a stagecoach with him in upstate New York in 1838. Also on board was another minister, a reluctant witness who now clearly wished to minimize the incident. Onderdonk, he testified, had put his hand over the woman's on her armrest. She blushed and withdrew the hand, but the bishop took it a second time. At the next stop the woman disembarked before reaching her stated destination. The witness observed the woman's discomfort but rejected the notion that Onderdonk had impure motives: "in a notoriously bad man such conduct would have been indicative of a bad design; but it did not occur to me, nor do I think, that the Bishop had any impure or lustful desires towards this woman." Nevertheless, the clergyman was sufficiently uneasy that he mentioned the event to another minister, whence the story spread.[6]

The next witness was Helen Rudderow, who had shared an eight-block ride from church to her home with the bishop in 1841, when she was 29.

> We had not proceeded very far from the church, when Bishop Onderdonk put his arm around my neck, and thrust his hand into my bosom: this he continued to do. I was very much surprised and agitated, and would have jumped from the carriage, had it not been for exposing him to the Rev. Mr. Richmond [then driving]. He kept repeating the offense until we reached home, where he was to dine with us.[7]

Careful questioning elicited the information that his hand was well below her neckline on her naked breast, under her shawl. Remarkably, the bishop continued to converse with Mr Richmond all the while. Once home, Helen sought out her sister. "I entreated her to go down and entertain him, as the family were not yet prepared to do so; she consented, upon condition that I should follow as soon as I could sufficiently compose myself." Jane Rudderow greeted the bishop in the drawing room, whereupon he led her to the sofa and there "thrust his hand in my bosom." Jane backed away, but the bishop attacked her again, withdrawing only when a sister-in-law entered the room moments later. Jane said she did not cry out, because her brothers were close by in the hall: "I was fearful for his personal safety, and did not expose him for the sake of the Church." Significantly, both Helen and Jane thought first of protecting him.

Jane's ordeal was not over. Despite great "fright and astonishment," she and Helen sat through a midday meal with Onderdonk and the family, remaining mostly silent while their mother chattered on with the distinguished guest. After dinner the bishop twice more maneuvered to be alone with her for just a few seconds and again plunged his hand inside her neckline, she testified.

The sisters commiserated with each other that day and told a sister-in-law a few weeks later. But they waited six months to tell their mother, and did not tell their brothers at all until they were called to produce affidavits in late 1844, for fear that the brothers would deliver "an ignominious if not bloody vengeance."[8]

The next charge against Onderdonk was dropped when the complainant, a young governess, suddenly refused to cooperate. Her pre-trial affidavit recalled a meeting five years earlier, when the bishop steered her aside in a Westchester garden and suddenly put his hand into her bosom.[9] Her refusal to testify underscores the difficulty these young women had withstanding close questioning by sharp trial lawyers about deeply embarrassing incidents before a roomful of Episcopal bishops, including of course Onderdonk.

The last witness was Charlotte Beare, wife of the Rev. Henry Beare of Bayside, Long Island. Like Mrs Butler, Mrs Beare was a recent bride in 1842 when the bishop accosted her. Mrs Beare sat next to Onderdonk in a carriage on their way to her husband's church, with her mother-in-law and nephew in front. When the bishop put his arm around her and pressed her bosom, she shrank away from him. She told her husband soon after, who tersely advised her to keep civil but distant.

Onderdonk accompanied them home for dinner. There, in the presence of her mother-in-law, the bishop lifted Mrs Beare's chin and kissed her, calling her "my daughter." The young wife reflected that "I had too much confidence in him to suppose that he would offer me an insult in my own house."[10] Yet she was unsettled and wary. Hours later, in another carriage ride with the husband and nephew in the front seat, Mrs Beare came under assault:

> The Bishop put his arm around my waist; then raised it, and put it across the back of my neck; he thrust his hand into the neck of my dress, down in

my bosom. I threw his hand from there; he immediately put it upon the lower part of my person. I pushed it aside from there, and he then with the other hand repeated the same upon the other side of my person; but removed it towards the centre of my person.[11]

The carriage was in the lane at the Beare's house at this point, and the wife alighted and sought her husband's help. He still counseled caution: "say no more now; let us join the family, and have our evening devotions." The bishop stayed the night, and Mrs Beare kept her distance. Except for her husband, she told no one of her concerns until eighteen months later, when she confided in three aunts.[12]

These, then, formed the substance of the first eight charges against Bishop Onderdonk. The ninth and last was a dark hint of a continuing pattern of immorality: "that at sundry times . . . [he] has impurely and unchastely laid his hands upon the bodies of other virtuous and respectable ladies, whose names have come to the knowledge of the said Bishops, so that he is of evil report within the limits of the said Diocese."[13] The sense of a larger field of victims was aptly conveyed in a pamphlet by Rev. James Richmond, who drove with Helen Rudderow and the bishop, and who, it develops, played a key role in marshaling all of the witnesses' affidavits and orchestrating their testimonies.

> Where is the presbyter who walked on the banks of the Hudson, and related to a fellow clergyman that gross insult to his family, (worse than any on the trial,) which will yet be dragged to the light, unless all parties make up their minds to abandon so forlorn a hope as this man's *restoration?* Where is the lady in Bond-street who related to me her daughter's refusal to be confirmed these four years? Where the bevy of young ladies on Long Island who declared, if the spiritual father was coming, they could escape by wearing dresses high in the neck? . . . Where is the other young lady on York Island, who long refused to be confirmed, and at last actually tittered, as she went up, at the sad and yet ludicrous idea, that he might make a mistake, through old habit?[14]

If it was true that a bevy of young women on Long Island shared lore about the bishop's unusual interest in necklines, we are here tapping into a collective female response to sexual harassment in the 1840s: the girls practiced avoidance, deterrent dress, and sororal humor, assuaging individual embarrassment by a shared knowledge of the bishop's habitual behavior. Evidently such girls were unwilling to be witnesses, however; they did not appear at the trial.

The four women witnesses together constituted the first interpretative gloss on Onderdonk's strange behavior. Singly, each woman reported confusion and disbelief; each kept quiet for fear of bringing dishonor on their bishop and their church. The married women put their husbands' careers first. The Rudderow sisters feared their brothers would seek vengeance. Mrs Beare's husband was at first unreceptive to her concern, and Mrs Butler's father, himself a minister, flat-out refused to believe her. So the women confided in trusted females and abandoned the idea of correcting the bishop. Together, at the trial, their individual experiences still perplexed them, but their conviction of Onderdonk's immorality was validated by knowing that three other woman had been through same experience.

Lawyers were the next in line to attempt a coherent account of the puzzling actions. Onderdonk opted to hire top professional lawyers, not customary in church trials, and the presenting bishops were forced to follow suit. Lawyers brought their sense of constitutional rights and legal wrongs to the case; evidence was held to a strict standard, and undermining the women's credibility became the prime defense strategy. The charge involving the unknown woman on a stage was immediately tossed out, since no one could name the woman. The ninth charge, of a broad pattern of immoralities and general "evil report," was similarly dismissed for lack of sworn evidence. What were left were four women, testifying to events many years in the past.

The lawyers' main defense strategy invoked gender stereotypes: none of the women had responded as an insulted woman of true virtue. None summoned help, even though help was nearby. Mrs Butler's concern to keep quiet for the sake of the driver was dismissed as ludicrous beyond belief. Much was made of the Butlers' confusion as to whether the bishop's hand was on top of or under her skirt, suggesting they had not gotten their concocted story straight. Maybe, the lawyers postulated, the jolting of the carriage on the bad roads out of Ithaca fully accounted for Mrs Bulter's complaint. Mrs Beare had only to lean forward and tug on her husband's sleeve when she apprehended the bishop's hand moving up her leg; Jane Rudderow could have leaped from the couch and run to her brothers in the hall.

What is more suprising, the lawyers said, was that the women continued to be civil to him. Why would Helen Rudderow send Jane down to be alone with him? How could they possibly dine with him, as did Mrs Beare? Helen Rudderow even visited him months later in a delegation of young women pleading support for a charitable activity, a point established at great length in the trial. Why had all of these victims failed to complain in a timely fashion?

The defense lawyers' narrative of uncredible women in the end did not persuade. The presiding bishops found Onderdonk guilty on a vote of 11 to 6. Apparently it was hard to imagine a conspiracy of perjury large enough to encompass all the ministers, wives, and parishioners who had testified. On the question of punishment, the vote was also 11 to 6, this time 11 voting for indefinite suspension of the bishop from his duties, while six voted for the harsher sentence of complete deposing from office. (The six who had voted for acquittal and lost now shifted their votes to the lesser penalty of suspension.) The Diocese of New York was put into ecclesiastical limbo, its leader suspended from all priestly functions but still technically occupying the office.

The verdict in, the pamphlet war began, each of the dozen writers – mostly clerical leaders – vying with the last to impose a credible account on the evidence. While the trial had limited itself to the women's allegations of immoralities, the pamphlets opened up the ulterior theological motives.

Bishop Onderdonk, silent at the trial, produced his own carefully crafted "Statement of Facts." He avoided comment on the women's particular charges, except to say that it was his impression that Mrs Butler was unwell and had gratefully leaned on him in the carriage out of Ithaca. The charges were all very old, brought up now as a conspiracy against him instigated by Rev. James Richmond, in revenge for a bad letter of recommendation Onderdonk had once written for him.[15]

James Richmond in his two pamphlets denied any personal grudge, just as he denied that animosity over High Church/Low Church differences formed his motive. Sexual sin was his chief concern. Richmond had driven the carriage with Helen Rudderow in 1841, uneasy about what was going on behind him – but too timid to turn and look. After hearing rumors of the bishop's unchaste attentions to other women, he returned to the Rudderow home in 1843 and boldly asked the women pointed questions. Richmond quoted a letter he wrote to his brother that year, warning that Onderdonk's indecencies were "now a matter of notoriety in the female portion of the Diocese, here, there, and everywhere. I know no man whom I would watch *so closely, every minute* in my house. No lady is safe from the grossest, most palpable, and almost open insult."[16]

Soon thereafter, at a dinner party of ministers and deacons, Richmond turned the conversation to "Pope Benjamin I," hinting at his intemperate, licentious ways. The other diners became instantly tense; some cautiously asked him what he meant, while others called "order! order!" to shut him up. "I looked through my fingers, and said to one and another, 'you know; *you know*,' and some of them did know." A nearby cleric said darkly to another: " 'Don't ask him . . . for he will tell you.' "[17]

To challenge that obstinate denial at the highest levels of church hierarchy, Richmond commenced gathering women's stories and securing agreements to testify. Most turned him down, he reported; this countered the complaint of Onderdonk supporters that the women witnesses were insufficiently modest. With good reason, women were reluctant to go public, for their own reputations were called into question. One writer tried to be kind, claiming that Mrs Butler and Mrs Beare, "ardent and impulsive" brides presumably in the fresh bloom of sexual awakening, might well misinterpret affectionate gestures that they would have innocently accepted when unmarried. Recall, this was intended to be a defense of the bishop – that his accusers confused his pure caresses with the preliminaries of lovemaking, simply because they were delicately ripe for sex.[18]

Much harsher treatment of the women came from a New York literary writer editorializing in the *New York Evening Mirror*. Nathaniel P. Willis set out "A Man of the World's View of the Onderdonk Case."

> In our opinion, no modest woman has ever been outraged by such liberties as are charged upon the Bishop.... Every man knows – and the most vicious man knows it best – that no woman is ever invaded till the enemy has given a signal from within!...We declare our belief that no woman whose virtue is above suspicion, was ever insultingly spoken to – far less, insulting touched – by a man in his senses.... The look of surprise only, with which the first shade of a questionable sentiment is met by a completely pure woman, is enough to arrest, and awe from his purpose, the boldest seducer.[19]

Profligate men all over New York City, Willis knowingly reported, were laughing to think that a woman could be surprised when a man put a hand on her breast. Worse still, Willis declared that clergymen everywhere would of course sympathize with Onderdonk, because of "the caressing character of the intercourse between the clergy and the women in their parishes whose affections are otherwise unemployed." Worldly men all knew that ministers frequently took advantage of affection-starved women.

Indignation greeted Willis's article. The secular press castigated him as a vulgar libertine who had libeled all of American womanhood. Willis's essay provoked a sharp reply from female pens as well, from the women editors of the bi-monthly *Advocate of Moral Reform* who had thus far steered clear of the Onderdonk case. To think that a look of surprise alone was sufficient to deter harassment was ridiculous, the editors wrote. Willis was in effect saying that women, not men, were to blame for sexual sin.[20]

The inexplicable failure of the victims to raise an outcry seems to have been the sticking point for many commentators. An anonymous pamphlet, by "Spectator," produced the most closely reasoned analysis of the complex power dynamics at work. As individuals, he pointed out, the women must have feared their accusations would not be believed; even four together testifying under oath were still met with skepticism. With no possibility of official redress, they took the only other path: avoidance and aloofness.

"Spectator" had a grasp of what prevents harassed women from complaining. But he could not explain the bishop's conduct; no one could, because of a persistent resort to the models of courtship or sex crimes as the context for interpreting his actions. One Onderdonk supporter, the Bishop of New Jersey, dismissed the alleged acts of immorality by simply asking, "What was to come of it?" With people all around, the bishop could not have intended to carry his misdeeds any further, so even if he touched a breast, there was no true evil intent. *The Churchman*, the official national publication of the Episcopal Church, urged the faithful to absolve the bishop because his sins were "comparatively light."[21] Even "Spectator" assumed that sexual intercourse was the ultimate goal of a man with roving hands. "Every body ... knows that seduction is insidious in its beginning, gradual in its progress, and because insidious ... and gradual, the more sure in its end. It always begins in 'passages that lead to nothing' in the eyes of its victims."[22]

Feelings ran high on the Onderdonk case precisely because it was hard, in the 1840s, to create a narrative that accounted for the bishop's conduct and the women's silence. To the bishop's High Church supporters, the only explanation that made sense was a conspiracy by theological opponents. His normally affectionate manner toward women had been misinterpreted; whatever he had done, he had no ultimate evil intent to seduce or rape. From the victims' point of view, the story was equally puzzling. How could such a touch be anything but immoral? Why would he touch them without trying to do more? Why would he take such a risk with people nearby? The ambivalent outcome – removing Onderdonk from duty without removing him from his bishop's office – perfectly reflected the bafflement religious leaders felt.

Framing the events through the lens of modern sexual harassment concepts helps bring several features of the case into focus. The four women, widely separated in location, each reported a very similar experience, suggesting a pattern of behavior indulged in by the bishop. He had enormous institutional power over his victims, and, as importantly, over their male relatives. He picked virtuous churchwomen – wives of ministers, single women active in church circles – to make sure of their allegiance to the larger entity of the church. He picked wives of young clergymen at precisely the point of their husband's greatest vulnerability to pressure, the moment of ordination or of grand visitation. Onderdonk's preference for apparently risky situations, with male protectors close by, actually ensured silent acquiescence from his victims. If no one had been within earshot, the women would have been freer to complain to him, to push him away, to make a scene. But these women well understood the cultural pressure for male protectors to respond with violent anger, and they thus feared for their bishop's safety and by extension the reputation of the church.

Onderdonk probably had no intention to seduce or rape; the quick, unauthorized plunge into forbidden territory carried a sexual charge and enhanced his sense of power over women. His thrill was to touch naked bosoms in crowds and get away with it. Over many years, he had gotten away with it, by picking his moments and victims carefully. During the years of rumors, his fellow clerics deliberately looked the other way; they really hoped James Richmond would not tell them anything unpleasant at that rancorous dinner party. Women told their war stories chiefly to other women, rarely to men, and never to authorities, knowing that the outcome of telling would be bad for them and bad for the church they respected.

But not everyone was baffled. Cynics and libertines in New York's night spots had a laugh over Onderdonk's scandalous plight. The *Herald* reported that at intermission at Niblo's, a popular New York City music hall on Broadway, four or five copies of the Onderdonk trial report were seen circulating through the audience and made the basis of choice humor. One mild joke that did make it into print told of a fancy evening party where the gas lights went out all of a sudden. "Ladies, don't be afraid, the Bishop is not here!" called out a man's voice in the darkness, "followed by an ungenerous burst of laughter."[23]

Nathaniel Willis, the self-appointed spokesman for libertine men, found the bishop's actions completely comprehensible: affection-starved women subtly but surely invited his caresses. A somewhat different humorous take on the libertine world-view was offered by George Thompson, a racy fiction writer and some-time radical social critic, who devoted a chapter to licentious clergymen in his 1848 book *New-York Life*. Thompson characterized Onderdonk as "a man so full of wine and lust – a high liver, a full eater of flesh, and a man of fleshly lusts, which war against the soul." Women were innocent victims of such men, Thompson claimed. Evil ministers easily seduced young women into believing that pleasing God and pleasing the minister were closely related undertakings. They knew how to excite tender feelings, both religious and sexual, in young women: "So far from a sin, it seems to be an act of duty and of piety to submit to his desires, and when the object is once accomplished, the reward is a devout blessing and thanks-giving, that removes every scruple of conscience and the pleasing duty of comforting a beloved pastor is performed as an act of religious merit." In Thompson's view, unscrupulous men under the camouflage of clerical robes took advantage of incredibly naive girls, who remained naive even after sexual favors were cleverly coaxed out of them. As absurd as that seems, Thompson's fantasy spoke to a deep and abiding male desire, even among libertine men, to maintain an illusion of female sexual innocence.[24]

The most interesting and on-the-mark social commentary interpreting the Onderdonk case took the form of a blackface parody of the bishop's carriage rides. It appeared in an 1845 scurrilous Philadelphia Almanac, titled "De Darkie's Comic Al-Me-Nig." The illustrated story, "Black Under-Donk-En Doughlips; or, De Feelin Deacon," recounted in exag-gerated Negro dialect the tale of a buggy driver who drove Deacon Doughlips to a purity meeting along with another clergyman and his wife. First the driver hears sounds "berry much like niggar lips comin in contract." He turns and sees the Deacon kissing the clergyman's wife. Next he hears the sound of a dress coming undone, and beholds "a sample ob dark underdonkation to parfection: dar was Mrs. Frogpaw's bare black beautiful bosom fast in de Deacon's boff hands, an his black fist war worken its way along like a black snake under de loose bark ob a gum tree." The text and accompanying illustration make clear that the black clergyman in the front seat looks on the whole scene of his wife and the bishop with full approval. The woman, in contrast, looks utterly astonished.[25]

The almanac of course was the production of whites, for a white audience, just as blackface minstrelsy in theaters of the 1840s involved whites speaking to other whites using the semantics of race. The media-tion of race transposed the bishop's behavior from the realm of privi-leged, religious whites – where it seemed to make no sense – to the realm of black burlesque and broad comedy, where infantile jokes and wishes could be given full expression. Rendering the Onderdonk story in black-face allowed white men to indulge in the forbidden fantasy of touching a woman's breasts at will and without punishment. The female victim as black woman is understood to be open game for sexual attack; no system of patriarchy protects her, as it would white women. This black woman victim has a husband, to be sure, but he looks on with approval and enjoyment, since the conventions of blackface exaggerate his prurient sexuality, along with his dialect and facial features.

In the world of privileged whites, men could not touch women dis-respectfully as a social rule, and if they did, male relatives were supposed to spring to the women's defense. Even harboring the thought of such an invasive action was so foreign – forbidden – to white commentators in the Onderdonk case that they could not imagine why the bishop might do it in actuality. In the negative figuration of blackface, immature and inappropriate fondling could be seen now to be an end in itself, an infantile compulsion and not a preliminary to serious seduction or courtship as might be expected from a grown man. The child-like and stupid black caricatures served to mark Onderdonk's behavior as child-like, a giving way to an impulsive urge that most men in real life would quickly censor were they even to allow the thought to creep into their heads. "Deacon Under-Donk-En" revealed the sexual fantasy for the forbidden thrill that it was. The racial inversion played off of an ambivalent identification some whites felt for blacks and black culture in the 1840s, a potent mixture of fear, ridicule, and desire. The caricature also expressed a sense of cross-race male solidarity at the expense of women: the almanac story invited masked men, white or black, to take delight in a sexual insult to women. This is why the black woman in the illustration must look surprised and scared – a reversal of the prevailing stereotype of black women's freer and easier sexuality, usually invoked to justify sexual advances. The thrill of the Onderdonk grab relied precisely on the fact that the victim felt great consternation and distress.

Bishop Onderdonk was suspended from office but his friends in the New York diocese refused to turn him out completely. He continued to occupy the bishop's house near Trinity Church and to draw his full bishop's salary. He attended church daily and led the procession to communion. He ceased all social life, rarely left his house, and retired from church politics. The confusion occasioned by having a suspended bishop finally led to the appointment of an interim bishop, and the death of this substitute in the late 1850s prompted Onderdonk's supporters to try, yet again, to have the suspension lifted. But the Convention of Bishops refused, and in 1859, the cleric died, unrepentant and officially unforgiven. His supporters installed an elaborate marble memorial, with an unintentionally multivalent symbol chiseled on it, depicting a "serpent darting his venomous fangs at the bishop," in the All Saints' Chapel in Trinity church.[26] On-lookers and mourners could wonder whether the serpent represented the external enemies (the snakes) who drove the man from power or the internal temptations of serpentine sexuality that bedeviled him.

The power of the Onderdonk case to amaze, in 1845 as surely now, is that it emerged in the midst of one of the most traditional, hierarchical, and ritual-bound religious institutions in America. Theological controversy for the Episcopalians involved struggles over minute details of ritual; the new and "radical" opinion lay with the High Church proponents, who wanted more symbolic punch in their liturgical arrangements. This was not a religion turned topsy-turvey by democratizing forces.

Americans in the 1840s were more prepared to find altered gender relations and aberrant sexuality among the liminal, anti-ritual, democratic religious groups pioneering on the margins of the major denominations. The religious upheavals of the antebellum period opened the doors to divergent styles of gendered interactions between a largely male clergy and an increasingly feminized congregation. Some of these new movements forged deliberately new styles of sexuality – the Oneida Community, the Shakers, and the Mormons, to name three very distinct examples. Fragmentation lessened the possibility for institutional oversight and control. Irregular ministers had the irregular lives, insisted the religious press; it was most comfortable to isolate unbridled sexuality on the margins of society.

But when the figure of the clerical seducer emerged in the highest pillar of respectable society, different explanations had to be invoked. For his Low Church opponents, Bishop Onderdonk's sponsorship of neo-Catholic symbolism was congruent with his sexual lust in that both were expressions of an indulgent sensuality – the man who ate rich foods during Lent and argued for opulent surplices also had fleshly desires he could not control. They framed their explanation in terms of undisciplined desire; but they could not fully comprehend the peculiar form his desire took, the quick and compulsive grab, that seemingly accomplished so little and yet incurred such risk.

But in the frame of modern understandings of sexual harassment, a pattern takes shape. The bishop preferred a church that maximized hierarchy and consolidated lines of authority to the top, one that contained women and men congregants within ritual forms. Elaborate liturgy distanced the minister from the congregation and operated as a symbolic language to express social arrangements honoring status and privilege. Individual congregants did not have individual voices within his institution, and so they found it hard to speak back to authority figures. Onderdonk's compulsion to grab breasts was at heart idiosyncratic and unrelated to any aspect of religion, but his insistence on a vast privilege and power inherent in a clerical elite gave him scope and cover to indulge with a remarkable degree of security his intimate frontal attacks. His authority and eminence became his safety net, giving him a sense of entitlement to do as he did and assuring him that no one would ever believe him capable of it. And it very nearly worked.

Notes

1   Julia Hull Winner, ed., "A Journey Across New York State in 1833," *New York History*, 46 (Jan. 1965), 60–78.

2   William Stevens Perry, *The History of the American Episcopal Church, 1587–1883*, 2 vols (Boston: James R. Osgood and Co., 1885), 269–282.

3   Norma Basch, "Marriage, Morals, and Politics in the Election of 1828," *Journal of American History*, 80:3 (1993), 890–918.

4   See entries on both brothers in the *Dictionary of American Biography*; and Elmer Onderdonk, *Genealogy of the Onderdonk Family in America* (New York, 1910), 104–5.

5   *The Proceedings of the Court Convened Under the Third Canon of 1844, on Tuesday, December 10, 1844, for the Trial of the Right Rev. Benjamin T. Onderdonk, D. D. Bishop of New York, on a presentment made by the Bishops of Virginia, Tennessee, and Georgia* (New York, D. Appleton & Co., 1845), 15.

6   Ibid., 30–39.

7   Ibid., 40.

8   Ibid., 39–62. James Richmond, *The Conspiracy Against the Late Bishop of New-York, Unravelled by one of the Conspirators* (New York, 1845), 10.

9   *Proceedings*, 7, 139–40.

10 Ibid., 63, 64, 73.

11 Ibid., 64.

12 Ibid., 65, 66.

13 Ibid., 8.

14 James Richmond, *Mr. Richmond's Reply to the "Statement" of the Late Bishop of New York* (New York: Burgess, Stringer and Co., 1845), 9–10.

15 Benjamin Onderdonk, *A Statement of Facts and Circumstances Connected with the Recent Trial of the Bishop of New York* (New York, Henry M. Onderdonk, 1845), 7.

16 Richmond, *The Conspiracy Unravelled*, 5, 6, 8–9. "James Cook Richmond," *Appleton's Cyclopedia of American Biography* (New York: D. Appleton & Co., 1888).

17 Richmond, *The Conspiracy Unravelled*, 7.

18 Anon., *An Appeal from the Sentence of the Bishop of New York, in Behalf of his Diocese; Founded on the Facts and Improbabilities Appearing on Both Sides in the Late Trial* (New York: James A. Sparks, 1845), 7, 14.

19 Quoted in both the *New York Herald*, Jan. 11, 1845, and *The Advocate of Moral Reform*, 11 (Feb. 1, 1845), 20.

20 *Advocate of Moral Reform*, 11 (Feb. 1, 1845), 20–21.

21 *The Churchman*, Dec. 21, 28, 1844; Jan. 11, 1845.

22 Spectator, *The Verdict Sustained at the Bar of Public Opinion* (New York: James Trow & Co., 1845), 10; *Proceedings*, 291.

23 The *New York Herald*, Jan. 31, 1845; *The Verdict Sustained*, 9.

24 Paul de Kock [George Thompson] *New-York Life, or the Mysteries of Upper-Tendom Revealed* (New York: Charles S. Attwood, n.d.), 54.

25 *De Darkies Comic Al-Me-Nig for 1846* (Philadelphia: Colon & Adriance, 1845).
26 William Hale Smith, *Sunshine and Shadow in New York* (Hartford, CT: J. B. Burr and Co., 1869), 584–85.

Documents

The first documentary selection contains direct questioning and cross-examinations of Jane Rudderow, one of two sisters who filed a complaint against the bishop Benjamin Onderdonk in 1844. It illustrates both friendly and hostile approaches to the witness, as first Jane Rudderow's lawyer questions her politely, followed by a severe grilling by Onderdonk's legal team. They ask her to recount a minutae of details, a lawyerly tactic most likely designed to elicit mistakes, which could discredit her testimony. How does Rudderow's interpretation of events implicate Onderdonk? How might a cross-examination of the sort endured by Ruddorow discourage other women from making complaints of this nature and testifying at such trials?

The Trial of the Right Rev. Benjamin T. Onderdonk, D.D., Bishop of New York

The Counsel being admitted,

MISS JANE O. RUDDEROW was again called up as a witness by the Counsel for the Presentment.

Direct Examination

1. Where do you live?
At the foot of Fiftieth street, on the East River.
2. Are you a member of the P. E. Church, in full communion with that church?
I am. I have been a communicant nine years.

Excerpted from *The Proceedings of the Court Convened Under the Third Canon of 1844, on Tuesday December 10, 1844, for the Trial of the Right Rev. Benjamin T. Onderdonk, D.D., Bishop of New York, on a Presentment Made by the Bishops of Virginia, Tennessee, and Georgia* (New York: D. Appleton & Co., 1845), pp. 51–60.

3. Did the Rt. Rev. Bishop Onderdonk of this diocese ever, and when, take improper liberties with your person? If he did, please state what they were particularly, and the time when.

On the 13th of June, 1841, Bishop Onderdonk visited St. James's Church, in this city. I left church before the close of the morning service, in consequence of a nervous headache. He returned with my sister Helen to dine, at the house of my brother, at the foot of 61st street, on the East River. I went down into the drawing room, at sister Helen's request, to see him. He was standing by the centre-table when I entered. He advanced to meet me with extended hand, and said, "My daughter, I must cure you of these nervous headaches," and led me to the sofa. I sat down in the centre of the sofa. Bishop Onderdonk immediately insulted me.

4. Please say what he did?

He thrust his hand in my bosom. I moved to the other end of the sofa. He followed me, and repeated the insult. I was afraid to scream, or even reprove him; for my two brothers were in the hall. I was fearful for his personal safety, and did not expose him for the sake of the Church. I was relieved by the entrance of my sister-in-law, Mrs. John Rudderow. We were summoned to dinner. I was reserved at the table, for I could scarcely keep from tears. After dinner we went on to the piazza. Bishop Onderdonk requested me to show him Mr. Schermerhorn's house; which I did by walking to the north end of the piazza. He threw his arm around my neck; I retreated into the drawing-room; where my mother, and sister, and sister-in-law immediately followed me. It was a stormy day; and I went to the window-shade to go underneath it, but not to raise it, to see if it had ceased raining. We were determined to go to Sunday-school, though we expected but few children to be present. Much to my surprise, Bishop Onderdonk was immediately by my side, and repeated the insult in the same manner as I stated before. I threw his hand away from me, and retreated from underneath the shade. I observed my mother regarding me intently. We repaired to the Sunday-school, and left my mother and sister-in-law to entertain him.

5. Please state how far the Bishop put his hand in your bosom?

The first time not very low down. The second, very low.

6. Did he, or not, put his hand on your naked bosom?

He did.

7. Was the back, or the palm of his hand, *next* to your naked bosom?

The palm of his hand.

8. Did he, or not, grasp your naked bosom?

The second time he did.

(Objected to after answer.)

9. What use did he make of his hand when in your bosom? Please state particularly.

He pressed it.

10. Any thing more?

No.

11. In what way did he press it?

It is scarcely in my power to describe.

12. How long had you known Bishop Onderdonk before this occurrence?

About ten years.

13. Did he confirm you?

He did.

14. Did he confirm your sister Helen?

He did, at the same time that I was confirmed.

15. When and where?

In the year 1835, in St. Paul's Chapel.

The *cross-examination* of Miss Jane O. Rudderow then proceeded.

51. When your sister returned from Church on the 13th of June, 1841, did you see her before you had met the Bishop in the house?

I did.

52. Where?

In our bedroom, where I was sitting.

53. Did she tell you, or give you any account of an insult alleged to have been offered to her by the Bishop?

She did.

54. Upon her requesting you to go down and see the Bishop, did you refuse to do so?

Yes; I told her I was afraid.

55. Were any of your brothers in the house at that time?

Both were.

56. In what part of the house?

In the hall.

57. When you met the Bishop, was he in a drawing-room opening from the hall?

He was.

58. Was he alone in the room?

He was.

59. What were your brothers doing in the hall?

I cannot answer.

60. Did they remain in the hall while you and the Bishop were together in the room?

They did.

61. Was the door leading from the hall into the room open or shut?

It was wide open.

62. In what part of the room was the sofa?

Between the door which led into the hall and the front window.

63. Did it extend nearly to the casing of the door?

It did quite.

64. Was the table, at which the Bishop was standing when you entered the room, in the centre of the room, fronting the door?

It was.

65. What was the Bishop doing when you entered the room?

He was standing by the centre-table, with a book in his hand, I think.

66. Had he his face or his back towards you, as you entered the room?

He had his face towards me.

67. Can you inform me what was the distance between the table and the door at which you entered?

About eight or ten feet.

68. Who spoke first, you or the Bishop?

The Bishop.

69. When he led you to the sofa, did you pass near the door?

I did.

70. How did he lead you to the sofa?

By one of my hands.

71. Did you feel no alarm at that act, after what your sister had just told you?

I did not, for I was in my own house.

72. What kind of a dress had you on?

I had a *high-neck* dress on.

73. Did it cover your shoulders, as the dress you now have on does?

It could not be considered a high-neck dress unless it did.

74. Did it come pretty close around your throat?

Not close around my throat, but as high as ladies' dresses usually are.

75. How was it fastened around your waist and chest?

The dress was hooked behind, as ladies' dresses usually are.

76. Was the dress open upon your chest?

Yes, a little way down, about the top of the chest-bone.

77. Was it a close or loose dress around your waist and chest?

It was a close dress, hooked behind.

78. When you took your seat on the centre of the sofa, as you have described and the Bishop thrust his hand into your bosom, was he standing or sitting?

He was sitting.

79. On which side of you was he sitting?

On my right, between me and the door.

80. Did the door continue wide open during the aggressions of the Bishop, which you have described?

It did.

81. When the Bishop first put his hand in your bosom on the sofa, did you remonstrate with him in any way?

I did not; I was afraid my brothers would hear me.

82. Did the Bishop accompany the first act with any remark?

He did not speak during the act.

83. Did he say any thing before the act, except what you have stated in your direct examination?

Not that I recollect.

84. Did the Bishop, during any portion of these transactions, unhook your dress?

He did not.

85. When you moved to the end of the sofa, after the first act, was it immediately repeated by the Bishop, without any remark on his part?

It was.

86. How did you disengage yourself at that time from him?

My sister-in-law came into the room almost directly after, and the Bishop started and moved to the other end of the sofa.

87. Did you see your sister-in-law until after she had entered the room?

I did not see her, but heard her coming.

88. Had the Bishop moved away from you when you first saw your sister-in-law in the room?

He moved away as soon as he heard her coming.

89. You say that the reason why you did not scream, nor reprove the Bishop, was that your two brothers were in the hall; how did you know that they were in the hall?

I saw them there when I came down stairs; and when I first came into the room I heard them.

90. Do you feel confident that they were in the hall during the whole time?

I do not: it is not possible for me to answer.

91. How many inmates were there in the house at the time?

My mother, brother and wife, my other brother and sister, my aunt, a female cousin who was staying with us, my brother's four children, and three servants.

92. Where, relatively to the drawing-room, was the dining- room?

It was opposite; but the doors were not opposite; the dining-room door was about a yard nearer the front of the house.

93. Were the preparations going on for dinner while you and the Bishop were in the room?

They were.

94. Describe the preparations going on.

I could scarcely do that; the entrance from the kitchen to the dining-room was on the other side, and not by the hall.

95. Was the dining-room door open as you passed into the drawing-room?

I did not notice.

96. Were you summoned to dinner immediately after the entrance of your sister-in-law into the drawing-room?

In about a quarter of an hour.

97. Did you remain in the room during the whole of that time?

I do not recollect – I presume I did.

98. Did your sister-in-law remain?

She did; my mother likewise, and my sister Helen.

99. When did your mother and sister enter the room?

Almost immediately after my sister-in-law did; my mother entered first.

100. Was there a general conversation in the room, before dinner?

I do not recollect.

101. Did your nervous headache continue until dinner-time?

I think it did. My nervous headache, if I had any at that time, was so absorbed in the fright and astonishment, that I cannot recollect.

102. Who composed the party at dinner that day?

My mother, my sister-in-law, my sister Helen, and I do not recollect whether my cousin was present or not; my brothers were not there; the Bishop and myself were also present.

103. Do you remember how long the dinner lasted?

I do not – it was about half an hour or three quarters.

104. Was there a general conversation kept up at the dinner-table, in which you and your sister participated?

My sister and myself did not take much part in the conversation; it was mostly carried on by my mother and the Bishop.

105. You said in your direct examination, "After dinner we went on the piazza." Who went?

My sister Helen, and, I think, my mother, and my sister-in-law, the Bishop and myself.

106. Who took the Bishop's arm?

I do not know that any one did.

107. Did you all go out to the piazza immediately from the dinner-table?

We did.

108. Had you any conversation with the Bishop on the piazza, excepting what you have stated?

I do not recollect.

109. When you walked to the north end of the piazza with the Bishop, were any of the other persons you have mentioned on the piazza?

They were all there.

110. Did they all continue upon the piazza until you retreated into the drawing-room?

I think they did.

111. Was this piazza entirely open from one end to the other?

It was.

112. Was there any lattice-work on either side?

On the south side there was, but the north side was open.

113. When the Bishop threw his arm around your neck at that time, as you have stated, was there any thing said by you or by him?

I do not recollect.

114. Which way were you looking when the Bishop threw his arm around your neck?

I was looking towards the north.

115. Which way did the Bishop look then?

I do not know.

116. Do you mean that he had his arm around your neck before you knew which way he was looking?

I did not look at the Bishop at all; I only knew he was along-side of me.

117. Was his back or his face towards you?

I presume his face was towards me; I did not look at him. As I said before, I cannot tell which way he was looking.

118. Did you and he walk together to the end of the piazza?

We did certainly, as he asked me to show him Mr. Schermerhorn's house.

119. Did he put his arm around your neck immediately upon reaching the end of the piazza?

I think he did.

120. When you say you retreated into the drawing-room, do you mean that you abruptly disengaged yourself from the Bishop, and left the piazza?

I do.

121. Was this observed by any of the other persons upon the piazza?

I do not know; for they were plucking roses at the other end.

122. Did the Bishop follow you into the drawing-room, before you went to the window-shade?

He did.

123. Did he *approach* you before you went to the window-shade?

We were all seated in the drawing-room, before I rose to go to the window-shade ...

148. Did you tell this story to your sister on the way to the Sunday-school?

I did.

149. Did you tell it to any other person that day?

I did not.

150. When and to whom did you first tell it after that day?

To my sister, Mrs. Brown, a few weeks after. I cannot be more precise than that.

151. Did you ever tell it to your mother, and when?

I did, the following fall.

152. Did you tell it to your brothers at any time, and when?

At the time we sent our affidavits to Philadelphia, in October last.

153. Did you tell it to them before you made the affidavits, or after?

Before.

154. Who prepared your affidavit?

The Rev. James C. Richmond.

155. Did he request you to make an affidavit of the facts?

He did.

156. When did you first communicate to Mr. Richmond the facts you have stated?

It was in May or June, 1843, when he asked us the question. He asked sister Helen first, and then I communicated *my* statement to him.

157. Have you accompanied Mr. Richmond to any other person, to obtain an affidavit against the Bishop?

I did.

158. When Mr. Richmond asked you to make the affidavit, for what purpose, and for whom, did he represent it as being intended?

The purpose was, for the sake of truth, and for the sake of the Church.

159. To whom did he say the affidavit was to be sent, and what use did he say was to be made of it?

We understood it was to be sent to the House of Bishops.

160. Did Mr. Richmond tell you so?

He did not directly, sir; he simply stated that this thing was going on – that affidavits were being sent in to the House of Bishops; and of course we understood, by that, that ours would be sent likewise.

161. Did you know at that time that Mr. Richmond had expressed a hostile feeling towards the Bishop? (Objected to, and waived for the present.)

162. When you accompanied Mr. Richmond to the other person referred to, for the purpose of getting an affidavit against the Bishop, did he go at your request, or you at his?

I proposed going with him.

163. Did you know at that time that Mr. Richmond was desirous of getting affidavits against the Bishop?

It was painful for Mr. Richmond to collect any affidavits, but he had been told where they could be obtained.

164. How do you know that it was painful to Mr. Richmond?

He expressed himself so.

165. What was the state of the weather when you were out on the piazza?

I have stated before that it was a stormy day; but it had ceased raining then.

166. At what time in the fall of the year in which the occurrences you have testified to took place, did you tell the story to your mother?

It was one of the three months of autumn – I cannot recollect which.

167. Was that before or after Mr. Richmond went to Europe?

I think it was after he sailed. I do not recollect.

168. Do you remember when Mr. Richmond went abroad?

I do not. I believe, however, it was the autumn of 1841. I think it was – I will not be certain.

169. Do you know when he returned?

He arrived in Boston on Easter-day, 1842. I did not see him until just before my mother's death, which occurred on the 2d of July, 1843.

170. Do you know that Mr. Richmond returned sooner than he expected? (Objected to, and waived for the present.)

171. Were you present when your affidavit was drawn up by Mr. Richmond?

I was.

172. After your return from your visit to the Bishop at his study, in 1842, did you express yourself to the Rev. Mr. Dowdney gratified, or otherwise, with your visit?

I do not think I said any thing to him about it.

173. Did you ever say any thing to Mr. Dowdney in relation to that visit?

I do not remember.

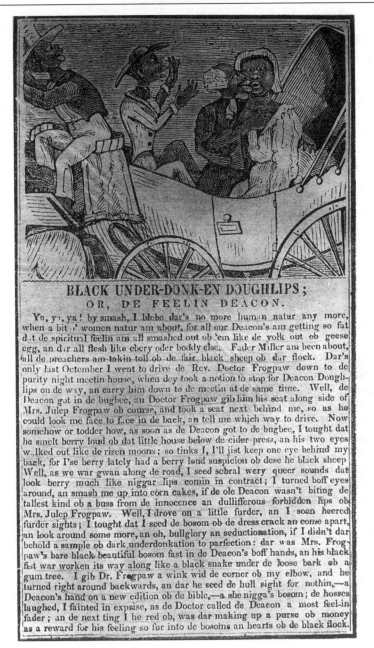

Excerpted from *De Darkie's Comic All-Me-Nig* (Philadelphia: Colon & Adriance, 1845). Courtesy American Antiquarian Society.

De Darkie's Comic All-Me-Nig

The picture on the previous page, taken from an 1845 almanac, casts the Onderdonk incident as an episode in blackface, a derisively comic representation of blacks. Patricia Cline Cohen argues that this racist version of the story, titled "Black Under-Donk-En Doughlips; or De Feelin Deacon," offered white audiences the freedom to laugh mockingly at the controversy, tarring all participants with the same racist brush. Onderdonk's blackness here both ridicules the bishop and explains his lewdness, while the woman victim's surprise may play against racist stereotypes. If the cartoon parodies Onderdonk and those he harassed, what does it say about white stereotypes of African Americans? How is white racism expressed in sexual terms here?

Further Reading

Arnold, MaryBeth Hamilton. " 'The life of a citizen in the hands of a woman': sexual assault in New York City, 1790–1820." In Kathy Peiss and Christina Simmons (eds), *Passion and Power: Sexuality in History*. Philadelphia: Temple University Press, 1989, pp. 35–56.

Block, Sharon. "Lines of color, sex, and service: comparative sexual coercion in early America." In Martha Hodes (ed.), *Love, Race, Sex: Crossing Boundaries in North American History*. New York: New York University Press, 1998, pp. 141–63.

Cohen, Patricia Cline. *The Murder of Helen Jewett: the Life and Death of a Prostitute in Nineteenth-century New York*. New York: Alfred A. Knopf, 1998.

Lindemann, Barbara. " 'To ravish and carnally know': rape in eighteenth-century Massachusetts." *Signs: Journal of Women in Culture and Society*, 10 (1984), 63–82.

Somerville, Diane Miller. "Rape, race, and castration in slave law in the colonial and early South." In Catherine Clinton and Michele Gillespie (eds), *The Devil's Lane: Sex and Race in the Early South*. New York: Oxford University Press, 1997, pp. 74–89.

Srebnick, Amy Gilman. *The Mysterious Death of Mary Rogers: Sex and Culture in Nineteenth-century New York*. New York: Oxford University Press, 1995.

6

White Women, Black Men, and Adultery in the Antebellum South

Introduction

Martha Hode's essay addresses the issue of interracial sex between white women and black men in the antebellum South. One of the legacies of slavery was the postbellum fiction that such liaisons were largely circumstances of rape. Hodes argues that interracial relationships of this nature, both before and after the abolition of slavery, were not forced; white women chose black men as partners, and though sex between such couples was legally prohibited, the community was more tolerant of such affairs than we might expect. White husbands could divorce their wives in such situations, but only if they could prove that the illicit relationship had caused more harm than would result from the ultimate dissolution of a white family. In the case Hodes describes here, a white husband, Lewis Bourne, sought divorce in 1825 in Virginia because his wife Dorothea and her black lover Edmond had at least one child together (maybe more), and Bourne sought to escape financial responsibility for them. Apparently his arguments proved insufficient, and his petition for divorce was denied.

Proper deportment between husband and wife was as important to this case as societal attitudes toward interracial sex and adultery. Lewis Bourne lost, in part, because he had been abusive toward his wife. If he had been successful in terrorizing his wife through his beatings and if he had then been able to frighten his wife into ceasing her adulterous affair, the case may never have appeared in the court, and historians would never have heard of these people. The case entered the records because, despite physical abuse, Lewis was unable to control his wife. Interestingly, the litigation presumed that Dorothea, and not the slave Edmond, was the party on trial. Edmond's voice never entered the historical record, and so we can only surmise his thoughts, feelings, and motivations. He does not seem to have been the victim of violence or recriminations; ultimately, this affair was Dorothea's transgression. As a dependent woman, she defied her husband's authority, and by bearing a mixed race child she challenged the Southern patriarchy as well.

Adultery: Dorothea Bourne and Edmond
Martha Hodes

If a married white woman in the antebellum South gave birth to a child whose father was presumably black, she was likely to be the subject of considerable scrutiny and judgment. Even without pregnancy and child-birth, suspicion of a white woman's adulterous liaison with a black man could become a fervid topic of local conversation. The seriousness of the matter and the actions taken, however, would depend more upon the woman's white husband. If he chose to remain silent, there might be talk but no concerted effort either to prove the transgression or to put a stop to it. If, instead, the white husband presented himself as a wronged man, friends and neighbors would be apt to cooperate in the legal investigation to support his claims. A white husband who proved his wife guilty of adultery with a black man was usually granted the divorce he requested, precisely because authorities had been swayed that the white wife was at fault. Yet white husbands were not guaranteed divorces under such circumstances. The gravity of breaking up a white family through divorce could outweigh the gravity of illicit sex between a white woman and a black man. Regardless of the verdict, antebellum divorce cases and other recorded instances of adultery based on the transgressions of white wives with black men confirm a marked absence of white outrage and violent retribution toward the participating black man, whether slave or free.

In 1824, an elderly white man named Lewis Bourne asserted publicly that his much younger wife, Dorothea, also called Dolly, made a habit of

Excerpted from Martha Hodes, "Adultery: Dorothea Bourne and Edmond," in *White Women, Black Men: Illicit Sex in the 19th-century South* (New Haven, CT: Yale University Press, 1997), pp. 68–95.

associating with black men in their Virginia piedmont neighborhood and specifically that she had been sexually involved with Edmond, one of John Richardson's twenty-five slaves, for the past six or seven years. Thus sex between a white woman and a black man entered the historical record as an offense of adultery. There were no accusations of rape, either by Dorothea, her husband, or any other white person, and [in fact] white neighbors blamed the white woman from the beginning. Dorothea was both bullied and shunned, yet in the end the circumstances were not grave enough to permit Lewis a divorce. The story of Dorothea and Edmond presents...a case of white people's uneasy endurance of a sexual liaison between a white woman and a black man in the slave South. Their story...involves dominant ideas about the sexuality of marginal white women, the precedence of a slaveowner's property rights over any other white person's reaction to the sexual transgressions of a valuable slave man, and the problem of free children of partial African ancestry.[1]

Denial of Divorce

...The evidence from Dorothea and Edmond's neighborhood reveals local knowledge of the illicit liaison. Many whites testified to familiarity with Dorothea Bourne's transgressions with more than one black man, but especially with John Richardson's slave Edmond. According to Dorothea's husband, there was "no room to doubt that an illicit intercourse" was "regularly kept up between them," precisely because so many "respectable persons" knew about it. Indeed, people said that Dorothea had "taken up with" a black man, "was intimate with" other men, and had been seen "in company with" Edmond. Others noted that she had children "by a slave" or that some of her children were "mulatto."[2] The Bourne and Richardson families resided in the southeastern corner of Louisa County and the bordering western section of Hanover County, a region that contained both farms and plantations....Lewis Bourne...counted himself among the small propertyholding yeomanry...who depended little on the market economy of the slave South.... For the last fifteen years of his life, Lewis owned seventy-five acres of land, placing him squarely among the county's middling folk. Just before he married Dorothea in 1812, he had been able to purchase one slave, though economic straits later forced him to sell his chattel and move in with a brother. By contrast, the Richardsons, who lived within half a mile of the Bournes, owned more than four hundred acres of land in addition to their many slaves.[3]

The white people whom Lewis Bourne selected to tell the story of Dorothea and Edmond agreed on its broad outlines. The blacksmith

Peter Wade, for example, noted of Dorothea that "she generally keeps the company of Negro slaves." Nathan Ross similarly testified that Dorothea kept "the company of negro slaves as often or perhaps oftener than any other company." The narrators also agreed that Dorothea consorted in particular with Edmond. Richard Woodson had "witnessed considerable intimacy" between Dorothea and Edmond, and Edmond's master himself believed that Dorothea had "quit" her husband and taken up with Edmond because the slave man was younger and more handsome than her spouse. Dorothea and Edmond had even been caught in the act. One winter's night in 1823, Lewis's brother and his servant-woman had found Dorothea and Edmond in bed together on the Bourne property. Dorothea and Edmond also carried on their illicit liaison in Edmond's quarters and had been caught there, too. John Richardson's wife, Judith, said she had "often seen Dolly Bourne lurking about her negroes' houses."[4]

Neighbors had also witnessed affection, at least on the part of Dorothea. When Daniel Molloy hired Edmond to travel to another town, he observed Dorothea's sorrow at the separation. Thomas Pulliam, who had known Lewis for twenty years, averred that Edmond and Dorothea "live together almost as man and wife." Another witness used the same phrase, adding that Dorothea washed and mended for Edmond in her own home. Dorothea had in fact ceased to cohabit with Lewis, and resided instead in a dwelling "on a corner of his land." Some white people believed that Lewis consented to this arrangement so that Dorothea "might have it in her power to have a more uninterrupted intercourse" with Edmond. Finally, the storytellers largely agreed that Edmond was the father of some of Dorothea's children; one of these had died in 1823 at about age three, and rumors of others had made their way around the neighborhood. Peter Wade had "seen the children of Dolly Bourne" and had "no doubt of some of them being colored." Joseph Perkins swore that Dorothea had "children by a slave," adding that "no person in the neighborhood doubts it." John Richardson believed that Dorothea's last child was "by my man, Edmond." Such statements were echoed by others, including relatives of Lewis and a man who testified that he had made a coffin for the deceased child.[5]

... The liaison between Dorothea and Edmond was tolerated by white neighbors to a point. There is no way to know whether, if Dorothea's husband had never spoken up, the liaison might have continued without entering the annals of the antebellum South. But because Dorothea and Edmond had a living child or children, Lewis Bourne ultimately decided to seek a divorce from his wife.... Any offspring of Dorothea, including any by a man other than her husband, would have been a burden to Lewis, for the children of adulterine bastardy were the responsibility of the spurned husband. Advising Lewis on the divorce proceedings, the county sheriff had pointedly told him: "You had better do it, Lewis, otherwise you will have them mulatto children to support all your life."[6] The presence of one or more children believed to belong to Dorothea and Edmond thus sparked Lewis's plea for divorce, thereby precipitating a local crisis. Only after Lewis decided on that course of action did a group of white neighbors confront the fact of the illicit liaison in a unified and zealous manner. From the start, it was the guilt of the white woman that the neighbors set out to prove.

When Lewis presented his divorce plea before the Virginia legislature in 1824, he had already been gathering depositions about his wife's transgressions for almost two years. The story of Dorothea Bourne and Edmond came to be recorded in that collection of narratives, for which caution and speculation are required in the re-creation of events and sentiments. It is not possible to know all that occurred before Lewis Bourne began to gather his sworn statements intended to justify the legal dissolution of the marriage. In a divorce petition such as Lewis filed, the voice of the wronged husband is easily discernible, and the voices of those who sided with him ring equally clear. Almost none of the witnesses who spoke on behalf of Lewis owned as many slaves as John Richardson, but for the most part, neighbors of good economic standing and status came forward to support a man of precariously middling circumstances. The voices of the transgressors themselves come through haltingly, if at all. The lone person who defended Dorothea was a midwife named Keziah Mosely, a woman who headed her own household. Although Keziah claimed to have delivered all of Dorothea's children and asserted that none had a black father, her testimony was refuted by three men who either countered that Keziah had previously pronounced one of Dorothea's children to be "black" or insisted that Keziah had not been present at every birth. The other six women who filed depositions sided with Lewis, as did the twenty-nine men who gave sworn testimony (there was also one anonymous witness).[7] Of course, because Lewis was the gatherer of the depositions, it is impossible to determine how many white neighbors may have defended Dorothea in their own minds. Dorothea commanded no power to call her own defense both because she was female and dependent and because she had transgressed too many boundaries. In any event, local authorities would likely have considered any supporters unrespectable outcasts. Opinions of the other slaves in John Richardson's household or in the neighborhood are equally difficult to discern. Those who knew the facts may have admired Edmond's defiance or held him in contempt for stooping to consort with a white woman.

In the process of proving himself wronged, Lewis Bourne ran into some trouble, for his wife did not wish for the divorce. And although Lewis was able to gather a considerable party of supporters, not all of their recollections worked in his favor. Lewis's probable violent treatment of Dorothea was crucial to the outcome, even though most petitioners painted a favorable portrait, proclaiming Lewis peaceable, honest, industrious, and "never... disposed to use his wife badly." One such speaker was the public notary, Anderson Bowles, who had been Lewis's neighbor for twenty-nine years. Another was Joseph Anderson, who had known Lewis from "infancy." Lewis was said to provide adequately for his family – he and Dorothea had one or two children of their own – except that Dorothea supposedly gave away food and clothing to the black men with whom she fraternized, leading the Bournes into poverty.[8]

But Thomas Anderson, who lived within a few miles of the Bournes, also stated of Lewis, "I believe had he married a virtuous woman, he would have made as kind a husband as any man," thereby implying that Lewis did not always treat Dorothea with complete forbearance. Other notes of suspicion also crept into the testimony, echoing this observation. Hannah Bourne, Lewis's niece who lived next door, said that her uncle "never was disposed to be unfriendly to his wife until she had taken to such an infamous course." Joseph Perkins, who had known Lewis for forty years, agreed that Lewis "would have made his wife a good husband... if she had conducted herself tolerably well." When Joseph Anderson testified to Lewis's good behavior as a husband, he pointed out that Lewis hadn't known Dorothea was "a strumpet" until after their marriage. Finally, eleven men, all neighbors of the Bournes, came forward on behalf of Lewis to opine: "We... think the many indignities offered Lewis Bourne by his wife has been sufficient to produce one of the few causes in which a husband might feel justified in whipping his wife." It is clear that at least some of the white neighbors considered domestic violence an appropriate course of action for a white husband whose white wife dishonored him by carrying on an affair with a slave, though there is no reason to believe that such violence would not also have been sanctioned if Dorothea had consorted with a white man.[9]

Although divorce in the nineteenth-century South was neither a common nor a swift process, adultery was one of the grounds for which most state legislatures and courts considered the proceeding justifiable. Yet despite evidence about Dorothea's sexual transgressions with a black man, despite the serious charge of adultery, and despite Virginia laws prohibiting sex between white women and black men, Lewis Bourne was denied his divorce. Lewis's inability to control his wife in spite of his probable violent behavior seems to have settled the matter in his wife's favor. If the beatings had stopped Dorothea's transgressions, there might have been no divorce plea; because they did not, Lewis became the party at fault.[10] . . .

Yet in the eyes of Lewis Bourne's friends the disgraceful conduct of his wife justified whatever abusive behavior he may have displayed, and made Lewis entitled to divorce. To the Virginia legislature, on the other hand, Lewis's abuse was at least as reprehensible as Dorothea's transgressions. Perhaps legal minds reasoned that breaking up a white family could only magnify weaknesses in Southern hierarchies of gender and race, hierarchies that were not so gravely threatened by a liaison between a white wife and a black man, at least as long as patriarchal authority still operated to some degree within the household, and especially as long as the institution of slavery remained intact. The institution of marriage thus might on occasion require legal preservation to shore up the structure of patriarchy that undergirded racial slavery.

Divorce laws were liberalized in the first half of the nineteenth century in the South, principally through a more flexible interpretation of what made a marriage unendurable and a broader definition of what constituted cruelty. This was fostered largely by the development of an ideology that cast women as more virtuous than, but physically inferior and legally subordinate to, men and therefore potential victims of their husbands. Divorce laws were formulated largely with the protection of women in mind, and most divorces in the antebellum era were requested by wives. Dorothea Bourne . . . and . . . other white women whose husbands lost their cases were understood by the law to be victims of their husbands' abusive treatment, a circumstance that was apparently more dangerous than their own adulterous behavior, even with black men. The view that it was a husband's duty to control his wife – which contradictorily could also sanction the physical abuse of wives – was also central to these verdicts. . . . At the same time, the fact that many white husbands whose white wives had transgressed with black men were indeed granted divorces indicates that convictions about white female virtue and victimization were never uniformly entrenched in antebellum culture, for those convictions did not always or necessarily apply to white women outside the planter classes or to white women who consorted with black men. Thus if the white wife were judged to be depraved, the husband might win; but if the wife were depraved and at the same time experienced severe abuse in her marriage, the husband could lose. Or to put it another way, if a severely abusive husband was unable to halt such depravity, he could be denied a divorce.

Although Lewis and his friends made Dorothea suffer for her transgressions, Lewis had also relinquished more than a measure of his patriarchal authority over his wife. . . . Whatever children belonged to Dorothea and the enslaved Edmond certainly threatened both the community's racial categories and its racial hierarchy, especially given that white people already considered Edmond to be a very light-complexioned slave. Dorothea's liaison with Edmond might not by itself have mattered to Lewis Bourne in any degree that made it worth his while to seek a divorce from her, especially in light of his ostensible exercising of disapproval through domestic violence. But the "black" children born to Dorothea, who required Lewis's economic support, forced him to take legal action and therefore put the case on record.... Precisely because no one had stopped Dorothea and Edmond early along, they had produced offspring that made apparent some of the fallibilities of the larger slave society within which they all lived.... The children of Dorothea and Edmond illuminated an erosion of patriarchy as well as an erosion of the racial categories of "black" and "white": free children of partial African ancestry eroded categories of slavery and freedom based upon race.

... The problem of the children had brought an illicit liaison between a white woman and a black man out of the realm of gossip and scandal and into the realm of law. Yet ultimately Virginia legal authorities understood Lewis to be at fault. Lewis's inability to govern as a patriarch, they may have reasoned, had produced free children of partial African ancestry. Although the presence of such children created problems for a society based on racial slavery, perhaps the judges felt that to leave Dorothea Bourne with no husband would allow her only to cause more trouble both within her community and in Southern society as a whole.

The Crimes and Defiance of Married White Women

Although white women's requests for divorce in the antebellum South were usually based on charges of cruelty or desertion, white men's were usually based on charges of adultery or premarital sex. Lawmakers were more likely to consider a middling or well-to-do woman requesting divorce to be the victim of her husband's ill treatment, and more likely to deny a poorer woman such a ruling. As one legal scholar sums it up, "A divorce decree was, in theory, a reward for an innocent and virtuous spouse, victimized by an evil partner." For divorces initiated by white husbands in adultery cases, that was certainly so.[11]

The liaison between Dorothea Bourne and Edmond was not an anomaly in the antebellum South.... For those white husbands who did act against transgressing wives, the petition for divorce followed a particular script: first the man enumerated the good qualities of the woman he had once chosen to be his bride (he might note her industrious nature and would be certain to describe her as virtuous). There

followed a description of the harmonious marriage that had ensued, including the husband's unfailing fulfillment of his duties. Astonishment came next, when the husband learned of his wife's egregious conduct, in these cases either the birth of a child whose father was black, or the rumor or discovery of illicit congress with a black man or men. In language filled with pain ("he has experienced the heart-rending mortification of the most certain evidence of infidelity," for example) the husband would name the newly discovered flaws of his wife: she was lewd, licentious, depraved, corrupt, profligate, even notorious in the neighborhood. Sometimes this description was followed by a sketch of the husband's futile suggestion for his wife's reform or of his own attempts at reconciliation. At the end, the plea for divorce was put forth. In all, the men's language gave explicit agency to their wives....
Although Lewis Bourne was unable to convince the legislature that he was the victim of his straying white wife by invoking this formula, other white men in the antebellum South had greater success. In many cases of adultery with black men, courts or legislatures were persuaded of the wife's depravity, and on those grounds granted divorces to the pleading husbands....

Ending a marriage – even an abusive one – had serious consequences for white women in a society in which there existed few alternatives, either social or economic, to the family and household. Most married white women who entered into liaisons with black men must have attempted secrecy at first, and those who succeeded also kept their actions out of the historical record. But secrecy was not always possible, especially in small, tightly knit communities, and evidence from other cases reveals that sex between a married white woman and a black man sometimes (as with Dorothea and Edmond) achieved the status of general knowledge....

Although the choices for a married white woman who engaged in an illicit liaison with a black man were few, there were nonetheless various points at which she could decide among different courses of action. In spite of the hard fact that Dorothea Bourne had been caught (both with Edmond and by virtue of offspring to prove the liaison), her first recorded response was simple denial. In January 1824, a white man named David Johnson, upon entering Lewis's home during the night with the motive of catching the white woman and the slave, found Edmond "undressed ... either going to bed or retreating from there." Late one night in November of the same year, Dorothea was discovered by neighbors and forcibly removed from a bed in the Richardson slave quarters. When one of the men in the party told her to run, she followed his advice, only to be overtaken and detained in the house of another neighbor. There the barefoot Dorothea, who also lacked hat or cape, claimed that she had not in fact been in bed with Edmond but, when threatened with appearance before a magistrate, relented and "promised to quit her bad practices." She then signed a statement admitting that "I was caught in a Negro quarter of John Richardson, in bed with one of his Negroes." The purposes of Lewis's allies had been accomplished, and more supporting depositions for the divorce petition could thenceforward be gathered. All this suggests that Dorothea and Edmond had been observed together before, since neighbors knew where to find them; indeed, John Richardson's wife had admitted as much when she confessed that she had "often seen Dolly Bourne lurking about her negroes' houses."[12]

It is impossible to know what other courses of action Dorothea may have taken before her rather pathetic attempt at denial. Like an unmarried white woman who transgressed across the color line, a married one might also try to terminate a pregnancy, especially if she were certain that the child was not her husband's. Foregoing that route, or failing at it, she might resort to infanticide.... If a transgressing white woman had financial resources or relatives willing to come to her aid, she might flee the community. A deserting wife may have been acting out of humiliation and ostracism or in order to escape an unhappy or abusive marriage; alternatively, she may have been acting on orders from her husband, who would later cast himself as a victim....

If a white woman caught in an adulterous liaison with a black man had nowhere to go or no means to get there, she might own up to her actions and amend her ways. If her husband subsequently took no legal action, the woman's misdeeds would never go on record....

Alternatively, an adulterous white woman could own up to her actions and, rather than seek forgiveness, present herself with a measure of defiance. After her lame denial when caught in Edmond's quarters, Dorothea Bourne chose this course by offering an alternative set of facts about her husband's motives and the motives of other witnesses who supported his allegations. Though Dorothea was unhappy with Lewis and very possibly abused by him, she hoped to remain married at least for the sake of her economic well-being. Dorothea accused Lewis's brother, William, of instigating the divorce proceedings and charged Lewis with selling off her dower (including land and livestock) to William in order to maintain himself and their legitimate children on the money. "The deep interest then which William Bourne feels in this question of divorce between my husband and myself is so palpable," noted Dorothea in a petition of her own (written out by someone else and signed with an "x"), that she felt William's testimony should not be admitted in the case, and neither should that of his "poor laboring dependent" servant-woman, Pleasants Proffit. Dorothea made a final and significant plea: in addition to two children she claimed were by Lewis, she had a third child, a babe in arms (she did not name the father), and she trusted that the legislators would not permit her to go unprovided for. Thus while Lewis did not want to support another man's children, Dorothea successfully invoked the lives of her children without specifying paternity in order to move the legal proceedings in her favor. If Lewis did not support Dorothea and the children, the burden would presumably fall on the community.[13]

Other white women who carried on adulterous liaisons with black men demonstrated decidedly more defiance than Dorothea Bourne. There were those who talked back, professed love for black men, and leveled more severe counteraccusations, though they did not always succeed in their endeavors. . . .

The whole demeanor of Elizabeth Fouch from the Virginia piedmont, for example, expressed an extraordinary level of defiance. Three years after their marriage in 1802, the millwright Isaac Fouch described his wife as "of a lewd, incontinent, profligate disposition and practice." Isaac's kindness and admonitions only "produced a contrary effect" in Elizabeth, he said, and twice he found her in bed with James Watt, a free man of color. Moreover, the Fouch servant, Jane Campbell, had witnessed "a very particular fondness and intimacy" between Elizabeth and James, and more than once Jane had peered through an opening and "seen them . . . in the very act"; at other times, Elizabeth and James "went up the loft together." When Elizabeth suspected the servant-woman of spying, she merely fastened the door and plugged up the hole. When Isaac finally walked out, Elizabeth remarked that he would probably never return. "She asked me if I did not pity her," the servant-woman recalled, adding: "However, she appeared very cheerful and easy on the occasion." Jane, who had been hired by Isaac rather than by Elizabeth, may have testified as she did either out of loyalty or under pressure; in any case, Isaac was granted his divorce, possibly in this instance to the satisfaction of his wife.[14]

A married white woman also had the choice to accuse a black man of rape, and some who had given birth to children that proved their illicit actions did so, though the strategy was not guaranteed to be successful. When a slave named Jefferson was accused of raping the married Elizabeth Rodgers in the North Carolina piedmont in 1845, he told the court . . . that "this intercourse by consent took place before the alleged rape and was regularly continued for several months" and that "he verily believes that she is now pregnant by him." Other slaves had observed physical intimacy between Elizabeth and Jefferson, but the court excluded this testimony. When a white man testified that Jefferson had confessed the rape, Jefferson was found guilty. On appeal, however, the state supreme court ruled that a man accused of rape, presumably including a black man, was permitted to give evidence "that the woman had been his concubine, or that he had been suffered to take indecent liberties with her" (making apparent the inability of nineteenth-century law to imagine rape within a consensual relationship).[15] A married white woman who consorted with a black man and found herself pregnant surely fretted over whether the child belonged to the white husband or the black partner; some must have prayed fervently that it would be impossible to tell if the child had a black father. Perhaps a rape accusation was less pressing for a married white woman, for a pregnant wife was not yet inherently guilty of anything. There may have been a chance that the child belonged to her husband, and there was always a chance that it would be presumed white by the community.

Although these white women suffered economic and social consequences for their liaisons with black men, not all set out to reform their behavior. Perhaps they felt they had less to lose than unmarried white women in the same circumstances: single women always had the possibility of a brighter future if they could allay rumors about past misconduct. Although some of the behavior of the married women after the discovery of their offenses was defiant, those women were presumably forced into such a stance by the discovery itself; the defiance was a last resort.... The documents remain largely silent as to motivations, yet in their behavior these white women jeopardized their marriages and livelihoods, and suffered the consequences of ostracism and poverty. Perhaps for white women in unendurable marriages, such actions were merely one bleak choice among a limited number of equally bleak choices. The conviction that a white patriarch was responsible for his wife's illicit actions did not make the gossip any less vicious. White women were still subject to patriarchal control, and local authorities branded transgressors harshly. Yet it is crucial to realize that even when legal authorities and white communities alike understood dishonorable white wives like Dorothea Bourne to be the victims of abusive white husbands, neither the law nor the white neighbors cast those adulterous white women as the victims of the black men with whom they had sex.

The Silence and Defiance of Black Men

The liaison between Dorothea and Edmond was common knowledge, but only when Dorothea's husband entered a divorce plea did his friends and neighbors act. Their purpose was to prove Dorothea's guilt, and although this was readily accomplished, the Virginia legislature denied Lewis Bourne his divorce. While there was no doubt that Dorothea had carried on a liaison with a black man, there was sufficient suspicion that

Lewis had abused a wife he was unable to control, and that factor outweighed other evidence. This reiteration of facts is to say that the contest was between the transgressions of Dorothea, the white wife, and the transgressions of Lewis, her white husband. The behavior of Edmond, the black man, was not a factor in the minds of either local or legal authorities.

The fates of some of the black men in adulterous liaisons can be gleaned, but their motivations and sentiments are more difficult to discern. Dorothea had a petition of her own among the collection of documents on the Bourne divorce case. Edmond's voice is a great deal more elusive. Because black men in such circumstances were not called upon to explain their transgression in any public forum, they wisely offered nothing to white people. Within his own family or community, Edmond surely dealt with the consequences of a liaison with a white woman, but just about the only thoughts attributed to Edmond (or any black person) in the documents come from his master, John Richardson, who recounted: "I have good reason for believing this man of mine has been disposed to forsake this woman, which has produced considerable discontent in her, and has been the cause of her often visiting my negro houses and staying all night in the quarters." If this story is true, Edmond was less than a completely willing partner in the liaison with Dorothea, and Dorothea imposed herself on Edmond at least some of the time.[16] Not only is it impossible to trace events on this point, but Dorothea and Edmond themselves probably understood the circumstances of their liaison in different ways. From Edmond's point of view, consenting to sex with a white woman may have contained an element of defiance. No matter what various people thought had transpired over the two years or longer in which Dorothea and Edmond had sex, Edmond was likely neither a complete victim nor as an enslaved black man in the antebellum South could he have been a free agent. For Edmond, too, the liaison with Dorothea may have been one choice among bleak and limited choices. Perhaps he deemed an enduring relationship with a black woman too risky, for example, entailing the possibility of separation through sale, or of his own powerlessness in the face of white sexual abuse or violence toward her.

A clue may lie in two depositions filed on behalf of Lewis Bourne, if taken in conjunction with John Richardson's story that Edmond at some time wished to "forsake" Dorothea's affections. First, the eleven neighbors who felt Lewis was justified in beating his wife came forward to refute rumors that Lewis had once ordered Dorothea whipped by a black man. Second, Joseph Perkins, who had known Lewis for two decades, recalled hearing of a fight that took place a few years past between Dorothea and a slave belonging to Lewis's brother, in which Dorothea came away with "some bruises."[17] These witnesses wished to assert that

Lewis had never set a slave violently upon his wife, opening up the possibility that the elderly Lewis had done exactly that in his efforts to get his aberrant wife to obey him. But it is also conceivable that this testimony points to a scenario of conflict between Dorothea Bourne and another slave man in the neighborhood, thereby possibly backing up John Richardson's version of the liaison between Dorothea and Edmond. Edmond's master had good reason to paint Dorothea as the perpetrator, leaving his slave property safe from a bad reputation, but it is not completely out of the question that the slave who beat Dorothea had been coming to the defense of Edmond or trying to put a stop to unwanted advances toward himself. All that is certain is that Dorothea suffered in some measure, perhaps severely, as a result of the liaison, and that Edmond himself may have suffered a great deal as well.

Edmond's voice may remain largely inaudible on the dynamics of this liaison, but in a few other antebellum cases the voices of black men, both slave and free, have been preserved. In these instances the level of defiance matches that of some of their partners. In 1847 in the North Carolina piedmont, a slave named George was charged with the murder of a white man named James Meadows. George had not only stabbed and beaten James but also, "with both his hands . . . fixed and fastened about the penis and testicles" of James, he "did violently squeeze." James's wife was named an accessory in the crime, and witnesses noted that Mary Meadows had shown "hostility to her husband" and that there was evidence of "a guilty connexion" between Mary and the slave man. George was sentenced to death in county court, but on appeal the judgment was reversed on technicalities regarding the evidence of a conspiracy between Mary and George.[18] The case of Redding Evans in southern Georgia in the volatile late 1850s reveals a stark example of defiance on the part of a black man who entered into an adulterous liaison with a white woman. Redding was a free man of color who kept the company of a woman named Mrs. Smith, who lived apart from her husband, James. Redding Evans and James Smith had an antagonistic relationship "on account of Evans' criminal intimacy with Smith's wife." When James Smith complained that Redding Evans's chickens were eating his corn, for example, Redding told the white man to leave those chickens alone or he might kill him. On another occasion, Redding promised to cut the white man's throat "if he bothered him." One day when Redding Evans and Mrs. Smith were in bed together, James Smith ordered the black man out of the house. Failing in this demand, James Smith departed, but Redding Evans "followed him and knocked him down, and made him come back in the house and sit down, and Evans went back to bed with Smith's wife, in the presence of Smith and his children." Another morning James Smith tried to retrieve his children, because he had heard that Redding Evans "was going to run away with his wife." At the same time, the black man was approaching the house. The white man pulled his shotgun and fired at the black man; Redding Evans, wounded, then fired at James Smith five times, killing him.[19]

In these two cases the black men were on trial, not for sex with a white woman, but for violence toward a white man. Although that may not have differed had the black men been white men, the conscious resistance to white authority behind the actions of these transgressing black men caught in an already dangerous endeavor is significant if not remarkable. The slave, George, was allowed to live, almost certainly because of his value as property. The free man, Redding Evans, was convicted of murder in 1861, as white Southerners clamped down on free people of color with the coming of war. The execution was presumably carried out. As for local white people's reactions to black men who consorted with married white women, neither indignity nor outrage are detectable in the documents. To be sure, white husbands in some of the divorce cases explicitly indicated that adultery with a black man was more deplorable than the same crime with a white man. . . . Isaac Fouch, for example, first wrote about his wife's illicit partner by name and later inserted the words "a man of color," indicating the salience of race to his quest for divorce.[20]

Nonetheless, taking offensiveness for granted did not warrant violent reprisal toward black men who were sexually involved with white women. Recall the winter's night scene in 1823 in which white neighbors ensnared Dorothea and Edmond in Edmond's slave quarters. Not only was Dorothea the target of the trap, but capturing Edmond did not concern those who participated in the vigilante episodes that followed: no mob went after the slave man. When Dorothea was forced from Edmond's bed in the Richardson slave quarters, it was she who was chased and captured, precisely because her husband hoped to use the evidence for his divorce plea. That the neighbors chased Dorothea into the night indicates that they were not seeking out Edmond for punishment, at least not at that moment, nor at any other moment recorded over two years in all the descriptions of that illicit liaison. Of course, because Edmond was the property of another white person, neither Lewis nor anyone else could take revenge without intruding on John Richardson's rights, and it is certainly possible that Edmond suffered violence at the hands of his master, even though John Richardson would later defend his slave by blaming Dorothea for the liaison. Still, the detailed narratives in the many depositions contain no hint of any public or private violent retribution toward Edmond, nor of white neighbors' wishes for violent retribution to be carried out by Edmond's master. Nor do the documents contain the least expression of white outrage, nor even a glimmer of the most casual disapproval toward the slave man for his liaison with a white woman.

Indeed, other black men were named in their antebellum Southern communities as transgressors with white women, and as with Edmond there is no record of white people seeking these men out for violent revenge. The partner of the defiant Elizabeth Fouch, for example, was identified as James Watt, a free man of color whom one witness had known "from his infancy." When Isaac Fouch finally left his wife, Elizabeth set off with the remaining household possessions loaded onto a wagon, and James Watt "followed her in a little time after." The two were followed in turn by a constable, but all he wanted was a portion of the Fouch property that Isaac owed someone.[21] In the case of Rebecca Baylis, also of the Virginia piedmont, her husband proclaimed her to be guilty of living "in open adultery with a free man of color named Wilford Mortimer," with whom she continued to live after her husband sought a divorce. William Howard of the Virginia piedmont had found his wife "undressed and in bed with a certain Aldredge Evans, a man of color." ... The 1824 petition of shoemaker Lewis Tombereau in eastern North Carolina told of finding his wife, Peggy, cohabiting "with a certain mulatto barber named Roland Colanche then living in Williamston," with whom she had one child. Rather than describing a violent conflict, however, the cobbler explained how his own poverty prevented him from exacting any redress without making a fool of himself.[22] ... The foregoing documents indicate unequivocally that the black men in these adulterous liaisons were named and known. ... On the other side, it seems that if no one beyond the white woman herself knew which black man had been her illicit partner, white neighbors made no attempt to identify or find the male transgressor. ...

It is not possible to know all that came to pass prior to the recording of any liaison, yet not a shadow of an enraged white person, not an inkling or an intimation of vigilante violence, not a faint or distant echo of a call to physical revenge appears in any of the recorded cases. If the man were enslaved, white people probably considered his offenses to be within the purview of his master, and some of these men may well have suffered within their own quarters. Again, it is impossible to know if John Richardson beat Edmond on discovering his liaison with Dorothea Bourne or threatened to sell away loved ones or tormented him in some other way. At the same time, because the white women in these cases were married, the matter of the transgressing man was likely considered to be within the purview of the white husband, and black men (like white men who had sex with married white women) may have suffered at the hands of angry white patriarchs, although once again no evidence whatsoever exists to support that conjecture. Although white Southern men did not take the matter of adultery between a white woman and a black man lightly or in stride – just as they did not take any sexual transgression of white women in stride – neither did rage and retribution, based on the race of the man, inevitably follow from local knowledge. . . . The lack of inevitable white violence in cases of adultery between white women and free black men may have stemmed in part from the value of the men as low-wage workers. The execution of the free Redding Evans (who owned at least his own chickens) indicates that white people considered free black men who enjoyed some economic independence more dangerous; in fact, Redding's death sentence foreshadows the fate of black men after the Civil War, when whites conflated black male autonomy with sexual transgressions across the color line.

Finally, because these white women were married, local authorities were less concerned with the support of bastard children. Instead, the white husbands would have to take responsibility, as did Lewis Bourne, whom the sheriff warned about having to care for "them mulatto children" for the rest of his life. . . . Yet although Edmond was not free, one of the white witnesses had heard Dorothea tell Edmond that "he must take the child she had and provide for it, as it was his child." Edmond's voice emerges here, for he agreed to do so if Dorothea "would tell him it was his child," meaning if Dorothea were absolutely sure that the child was not her husband's. Of course, as a slave, it is hard to know how Edmond could have provided for a child; perhaps Dorothea imagined the child being raised in the slave quarters and cared for by the Richardsons.[23]

There were, then, black men in the antebellum South who participated in liaisons with married white women, who lived with married white women or with their illegitimate children by those women, or who ran away with married white women. Only if a black man took revenge on a white husband in the form of violence (as the enslaved George and the free Redding Evans had done) were they sure to be called into court. Even then, the cause of that court appearance would be violence toward a white man. Although they consorted with white women, these black men were not automatically assumed by their white neighbors to be rapists or even seducers of white women. They were not systemically sought out in a white frenzy if no one knew their identity, and they did not suffer public retribution if anyone (or everyone) did. . . .

When Lewis Bourne filed for divorce, his major concern was the support of children not his own. Lewis's ineffective control over Dorothea illuminated an imperfectly functioning patriarchy, which in turn produced free children of partial African ancestry, children who then served to expose some of the imperfections of racial slavery. White neighbors and acquaintances all along cast Dorothea Bourne as the guilty party, but the Virginia legislature did not agree with that judgment. Although white community members had judged Dorothea to be the victim only of her own depraved sexual nature, legal authorities viewed her also as the victim of her white husband. Neither local nor legal authorities cast Dorothea as the victim of Edmond, the black man. And although Lewis did not get his divorce, white husbands under the same circumstances were often granted their wishes precisely because their white wives were understood to be so degraded. That a white woman's illicit partner was a black man in no way indicated to white authorities that she had been forced into the crime.

Because Lewis Bourne was not granted a divorce, Dorothea's life with her husband probably continued much as it had before. The liaison with Edmond may have continued, or perhaps once the community became enmeshed in the scandal, it came to an end. Or if John Richardson was correct, perhaps Edmond was an agent in ending the liaison. Whatever sentiments Edmond may have had toward his children went unrecorded. After Lewis's death in the mid-1830s, Dorothea and her children surely suffered economically. In his will, Lewis left all his land to his son, Thomas, the only child he called his own. Lewis referred to each of the two other children, Fanny and Mary Bourne, as "my wife's daughter which I do not believe to be my child," and left each girl a dollar. Dorothea inherited nothing.[24] ...

No white person ever considered taking the life of John Richardson's valuable slave because he had had sex with a disreputable white woman in the neighborhood. In the case of Dorothea and Edmond, all that was at stake was the financial situation of a white husband who had long ago relinquished his honor, as well as his authority, over his transgressing white wife. Still, ... the consequences of the liaison, rather than the liaison by itself, spurred local whites to action. Those consequences were the offspring of a white woman and a black man. That is not to say that white husbands tolerated their wives' affairs with black men (nor with white men) if no children were produced. But when children were born to a white woman and a black man, there was so much more at stake. No one had stopped Dorothea and Edmond until Dorothea's husband decided he didn't want to support another man's children. Dorothea and Edmond's liaison did not stir up white rage, but it did unsettle the local social order. The children of Dorothea and Edmond gave the lie to the infallibility of the Southern social structure.

In Edmond's children with a white woman, the effort to keep people of African ancestry in slavery was unsuccessful. Their existence eroded not only categories of race based upon color but also categories of slavery and freedom based upon racial designations. Everyone in town knew that those children were of partial African ancestry... and yet they were free. As such, they were troublesome to whites in a way that the enslaved children of a white man and a black woman could never be. And yet ultimately it did not matter so much, except for those who wished to help out Lewis Bourne, because the institution of slavery for the most part kept people of African ancestry in slavery – even where that ancestry might be invisible. Thus, the contradiction: the liaison between a white woman and a black man did not sufficiently threaten the institution of racial slavery, but the production of children made apparent defects in the Southern social structure.

Notes

1 Lewis Bourne Divorce Petition, Louisa County, Dec. 16, 1824, #8218, LPP, LVA; and statements of Lewis Bourne, Dec. 25, 1823, Jan. 17. 1825, and receipt for advertisements, Sept. 10, 1824, in Lewis Bourne Divorce Petition, Louisa County, Jan. 20. 1825, #8305, Legislative Papers, Petitions, Library of Virginia, Richmond.

2 Bourne Divorce Petition #8218; Depositions of Joseph Anderson, Jan. 22, 1824; Thomas Pulliam, Jan. 29, 1824; [no name], Jan. 20, 1825; Anderson Bowles, Jan. 6, 1824; and Joseph Perkins, Jan. 17, 1824.

3 Louisa County Land Tax Books, 1820A–1835A. Will of Lewis Bourne, Louisa County Will Book #9, Nov. 10, 1834, pp. 174–75, LVA. John Richardson, Hanover County Land Tax Book, 1824A, 1825A, LVA.

4 Depositions of Peter Wade, Mar. 26, 1823, and Nathan Ross, Dec. 26, 1823 (company of slaves); Richard Woodson, Jan. 28, 1824, and John Richardson, Jan. 18, 1825 (Dorothea and Edmond); William Bourne and Pleasants Proffit, Nov. 25, 1823 (being caught); Judith Richardson, Dec. 26, 1823 (Edmond's quarters).

5 Depositions of Daniel Molloy, Jan. 28, 1824 (affection); Thomas Pulliam, Jan. 29, 1824, and [no name], Jan. 20, 1825 ("man and wife"); Thomas Anderson, Jan. 23, 1824 (Dorothea's house); Hannah Bourne, Dec. 25, 1823; Thomas Anderson, Jan. 23, 1824; John Conway and Daniel Molloy, both Jan. 28, 1824; Thomas Pulliam, Peter Wade, and Stephen Pulliam, all Jan. 29, 1824; John Richardson, Jan. 18, 1825 (all re: dead child); Peter Wade, Mar. 26, 1823 (quotation); Joseph Perkins, Jan. 17, 1824, and John Richardson, Jan. 18, 1825 (children by a black man).

6 Deposition of William Bourne, Jan. 16, 1824.

7 Depositions of Keziah Mosely, Jan. 27, 1824; Peter Wade and Stephen Pulliam, both Jan. 29, 1824; Thomas Sayne, Peter Wade, Stephen Pulliam, all Jan. 29, 1824.

8 Depositions of Judith Richardson, Dec. 26, 1823 ("never disposed"); Anderson Bowles, Jan. 20, 1823, Jan. 16, 1824; Joseph Anderson, Jan. 22, 1824;

Thomas Anderson, Jan. 23, 1824, and Thomas Pulliam, Jan. 29, 1824 (providing adequately).

9   Depositions of Thomas Anderson, Jan. 23, 1824; Hannah Bourne, Dec. 25, 1823; Joseph Perkins, Jan. 17, 1824; Joseph Anderson, Jan. 22, 1824; and 11 men, Jan. 20, 1824.

10   *Journal of the House of Delegates*, Jan. 26, 1825, p. 184.

11   Lawrence M. Friedman, *A History of American Law* (New York: Simon and Schuster, 1985), 207.

12   Depositions of D. B. Johnson, Jan. 28, 1824; and Anderson Bowles, Delphy Hooker, and Shandy Perkins, all Jan. 18, 1825; statement of Dorothea Bourne, Nov. 7, 1824; deposition of Judith Richardson, Dec. 26, 1823.

13   Petition of Dorothea Bourne, n.d.; deposition of William Bourne and Pleasants Proffit, Nov. 25, 1823.

14   Isaac Fouch Divorce Petition, Loudoun Country, Dec. 22, 1808, #5321A, LPP, LVA; *Journal of the House of Delegates*, Jan. 28, 1809.

15   *State v. Jefferson*, Mecklenberg County Superior Court, SSCMR #3699, NCDAH, and 28 N.C. 305 (1846).

16   Deposition of John Richardson, Jan. 18, 1825.

17   Deposition of 11 men, Jan. 20, 1824; deposition of Joseph Perkins, Jan. 17, 1824.

18   *State v. George*, Granville County, SSCMR #4188, NCDAH, and 29 N. C. 321 (1847).

19   *Redding Evans v. Georgia*, 33 Ga. 4 (1861).

20   Fouch Divorce Petition.

21   Depositions of Colmore Brashears, James and Ann McNeilege, and Jane Campbell, in Fouch Divorce Petition.

22   William Baylis Divorce Petition, Fairfax County, Dec. 8, 1831, #9781, LPP, LVA. William Howard Divorce Petition, Amherst County, Dec. 6, 1809, #5370, LPP, LVA. Lewis Tombereau Divorce Petition, Martin County, Nov. 19, 1824, General Assembly Session Records, 1824–25, NCDAH.

23   Deposition of William Kimbrough, Nov. 25, 1823.

24   Will of Lewis Bourne. 1850 census, Louisa County, Va., household #377, p. 385.

Documents

In this set of documents excerpted from the records of an 1825 court case, we can see the ways in which different members of the community stood up for either Lewis Bourne or his wife, Dorothea. Those who testified on behalf of Lewis cast him as honest, a solid provider, and potentially a good husband if only he had married someone more virtuous than Dorothea. Dorothea's only supporter, a midwife who had delivered her children, focused not on her personal characteristics but on whether or not the child she delivered was white or black. Dorothea's own words speak not to the morality of her indiscretions but rather to the financial claims of her case. According to these documents, what were Dorothea's trangressions as a wife? How has Lewis Bourne represented her? How was Edmond, the slave father of Dorothea's child, portrayed? Whose fault was the entire affair, according to these documents, and what part of Southern society is being protected by the court?

Lewis Bourne Divorce Petition

Deposition of Judith Richardson, Dec. 26, 1823

" . . . she has often seen the children of Dolly Bourne the wife of Lewis Bourne and has no doubt of two of them being coloured, that she believes she had those children by one of her slaves, that is the slave of her husband, John Richardson, that she has often seen Dolly Bourne lurking about her negroes houses, has never seen her in the negroes houses tho firmly believes she is often in them, that she believes Lewis Bourne never was disposed to use his wife badly." No signature.

Deposition of Eleven Men, Jan. 20, 1824

"We neighbours of Lewis Bourne do hereby certify that we have known Lewis Bourne for many years, believe him to be an honest industrious peaceable citizen. . . . We are informed there is a report of his having ordered his negro man some few years past to whip his wife which order his negro man executed. We . . . believe this report is entirely without foundation. During our lengthy acquaintance with Lewis Bourne we never did hear it hinted or insinuated that he was in the smallest degree unkind to his wife until a few days ago. We . . . think the many indignities offered Lewis Bourne by his wife has been sufficient to produce one of the few causes in which a husband might feel justified in whipping his wife. Yet we verily believe he has never given her a stripe nor been instrumental in its being done. We feel the fullest assurance that if the

Excerpted from Lewis Bourne Divorce Petition, Louisa County, January 20, 1825, #8305, Legislative Papers, Petitions, Virginia State Library and Archives, Richmond. (Spellings of names vary in the original documents, and have been standardized here. All other errors appear as in the original documents.)

Senate of Virginia was in possession of all the facts connected with this case their [*sic*] would . . . be but one opinion on this subject. That she has child by a coloured man [the word "slave" is crossed out] we have no doubt and believe its doubted by no person who knows anything of the parties." Signed by eleven men, one with an "x."

Deposition of Thomas Anderson, Jan. 23, 1824

"I hereby certify that Lewis Bourne and myself was [illeg.] [ajoining?] that I think we have never lived more than three miles apart, have no hesitation in saying he is an honest peaceable citizen. I believe had he married a virtuous woman he would have made as kind a husband as any man. I believe he thought at the time of his marriage & for some time after he had married a good woman indeed. I think he continued this belief until he had the best of proof to the contrary. His wife's first child Lewis Bourne as well as the second altho a white one, he disowns. I believe no person in this neighborhood believes that child to his. Lewis Bourne was in the habit of providing a plenty of holsome food for his family and to my knowledge was making money as he purchased a negro man of me a little time previous to his marriage. I believe Lewis Bourne's wife had entire access to his provisions until he discovered she was in a constant habit of disposing of it among negroes with whom she almost entirely associated. I am informed and believe she traded of his clothes until she had reduced him almost to a state of nakedness, Lewis Bourne having lost the only slave he had and is now old and infirm. I confidently believe he was from a plentiful living brought to suffer until Wm. Bourne rec'd him into his house since which time there is a great change in his appearance for the better. At the time Lewis Bourne's wife lived on a corner of his land I believe and believe its the opinion of all the neighbors it was his wish so that she might have it in her power to have a more uninterrupted intercourse with a mulatto man of John Richardson by whom its believed she had her last child. This slave is so bright in his colour, a stranger would take him for a white man. Her child which died last summer from its colour must have been by a black negro. I verily believe the report of Lewis Bourne having whipt his wife or its being done by his direction or consent is without foundation." Signed.

Deposition of Kezia Mosely, Jan. 27, 1824

". . . appeared before me a Justice for County made Oath that she has acted as Midwife for Dolly the wife of Lewis Bourne with every child she has had since her Marriage & that she never delivered her of a coloured child & that the child she now carrys in her arms before me is the child she last delivered her of."

Deposition of John Richardson, Jan. 18, 1825

"I live in the County of Hanover and I think within a half mile of Lewis Bourne both of our plans of residence we have lived at ever since my earliest recollection. I am now about 61 years old. I know Lewis Bourne well & have no hesitation in saying he is an honest peaceable man and would have made his wife as good a husband as men in his power if she had of conducted herself only tolerably well. I do firmly believe her last child is by my man Edmund who is as white as any white men generally are. For some time past I have good reason for believing this man of mine has been disposed to forsake this woman which has produced considerable discontent in her and has been the cause of her often visiting my negro houses and staying all night in the quarters. She had a child which died perhaps about two years ago which I confidently believe was a black one. I believe the only cause of Lewis Bourne wife quitting him and taking up with this slave man, that the slave was much younger and a likely man than Bourne there being a great difference in the age of Lewis Bourne and his wife." Signed.

Deposition of Dorothea Bourne, No Date

"Dorothea the wife of Lewis Bourne now preying for a divorce after referring to his petition allready presented to the Honorable speaker & members of the Senate for the commonwealth of Virginia which petition remains yet uncontradicted begs leave to inform your hon.ble body that the Testimony last taken in this cause on Friday the 16th inst. was taken without giving her any notice. Lewis Bourne, but more especially William Bourne who your Petitioner charges with being the prime mover & instigator of this prosecution, had his reason for acting thus for had your petitioner been present she could have proven that neither William Bourne nor Lewis could have dared to deny, that Lewis Bourne had sold to William Bourne all the land she ownes and that our son Thomas (a boy 8 years old) shall be of age & if Lewis shall then receive for and during the term of said Lewis's life & that the sd. Lewis has sold sd. William Bourne all his personal property of every description consisting of houses cattle & steers with all the household & kitchen furniture plantation [illeg.] &c. & that the sd. William Bourne was at this time in the actual possession of the house & all the above mentioned property & all which William Bourne is to pay for this property is to maintain Lewis Bourne during his life and one son Thomas till he is of age. Your

Petitioner can also prove that Lewis Bourne has contracted with William Bourne to sell him a . . . title to one half of all the land she owns (150 acres) & all that William Bourne is to pay for it is to support our Daughter Fanny a girl 7 years old till 21. The deep interest then which William Bourne feels in this question of Divorce between my husband & myself is so palpable that your Petitioner prays the whole of William Bourne's testimony to be thrown out of this cause, as to the testimony of Profitt your Petitioner can only say that she is a poor labouring dependant of William Bourne & utterly under his contract & with the strong motives that govern William Bourne in this cause what might she not necessarily be suspected of doing with a man, situated as Profitt is. & a Negro fellow to aid him, whereas she had dared to [allude such untrusted?] testimony as his own upon your Honorable body. Your petitioner will only add that she had three children the two first Thomas & Fanny above mentioned & that she [houseless?] & unprotected carrys the youngest in her arms relying with confidence on the Justice & humanity of the tribunal she adduces & trusting your decree will be that her husband living she shall not be unprovided nor dying unprovided." Signed with an "x."

Further Reading

Bederman, Gail. *Manliness and Civilization: a Cultural History of Gender and Race in the United States, 1880–1917*. Chicago: University of Chicago Press, 1995.

Clinton, Catherine, and Nina Silber. *Divided Houses: Gender and the Civil War*. New York: Oxford University Press, 1992.

Gaspar, David Barry, and Darlene Clark Hine. *More than Chattel: Black Women and Slavery in the Americas*. Bloomington: Indiana University Press, 1996.

Hall, Jacquelyn Dowd. " 'The mind that burns in each body': women, rape and racial violence." In Ann Snitow, Christine Stansell, and Sharon Thompson (eds), *Powers of Desire: the Politics of Sexuality*. New York: Monthly Review Press, 1983, pp. 328–39.

Hodes, Martha. *White Women, Black Men: Illicit Sex in the Nineteenth-century South*. New Haven, CT: Yale University Press, 1997.

Roberts, Dorothy. *Killing the Black Body: Race, Reproduction, and the Meaning of Liberty*. New York: Pantheon Books, 1997.

White, Deborah Gray. *Ar'n't I a Woman? Female Slaves in the Plantation South*. New York: Norton, 1985.

Part III
Early Twentieth Century

7

Hysteria

Introduction

"Hysteria" and womanhood have been inextricably linked since early twentieth-century psychiatrists diagnosed the sexualized symptoms of the disease.
In this essay Elizabeth Lunbeck examines the relationship between hysteria
and what it meant to be a "good" woman. The "hypersexual" women denoted
a deceitful, cunning creature out of control, yet her symptoms bordered on
the "normal," because so many men expected this female behavior. The
hysteric, on the other hand, clearly had more serious problems. She retreated
from sex for any number of reasons and thus threatened the heterosexual
order and demanded a cure. Hysterics had to describe their symptoms in
ways intelligible to male psychiatrists; in the process they perfectly realized
cultural constructions of sexual norms, which featured aggressive males and
passive females.

The women who voluntarily visited Boston's Psychopathic Hospital for
hysteria described a variety of physical symptoms as well as a range of sexual
experiences, from enduring sexual abuse at the hands of male relatives to
complete sexual innocence and withdrawal from men. As Lunbeck illustrates,
the stories they told psychiatrists were framed by notions of female seduction
and male aggression. Indeed, male aggression was so common that some
women had trouble distinguishing between rape and "normal" male desire.
Women often saw their own behavior as problematic, and their psychiatrists
concurred, convinced that women's seductive nature and repressed desires,
and not men's assaults, were to blame for any scenario that turned sour.
Psychiatrists may have thought they were pulling female desire out of the

dark, repressive Victorian age, but how do you think they might have merely substituted one oppressive sexual ethos for another?

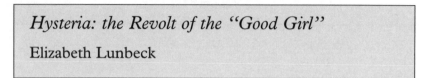

Hysteria: the Revolt of the "Good Girl"

Elizabeth Lunbeck

In hysteria, as psychiatrists conceived of it and as the young women whom psychiatrists diagnosed as hysterics experienced it, the broad-based early-twentieth-century sexualization of womanhood that was manifest in the category of female psychopathy reached its apogee: In hysteria, every thought, every symptom was linked to sex. The flamboyant eroticism of the hysteric had a long and distinguished history; psychiatrists fascinated with Freud and emboldened by his frankly sexual discourse could even propose that the hysteric's convulsions were "equivalent to a sexual climax" and were "of the nature of an orgasm."[1] Although this rather indelicate formulation enjoyed only fleeting currency, Freud's positing of an entirely sexual etiology for hysteria – his conceiving of hysterical symptoms as expressions of repressed sexual conflicts – gave early-twentieth-century psychiatrists license further to eroticize this female malady. It served, too, to reinforce its deep-rooted and multifaceted association with women and the worst of womanliness, an association manifest most literally in the term's etymology (from the Greek *hysterikos*, or womb) and more metaphorically and powerfully in the many damning resonances the term's use as an epithet evoked. To act hysterically had long meant to act as a woman. What it meant to act as a woman was now, however, up for grabs, and the confrontation between psychiatrists and the women they diagnosed as hysterics was correspondingly confused.

The hysteric's tale, as she told it and as psychiatric theory constructed it, was a narrative of seduction. This seduction was from the start double-edged, the question of who was seducing whom implicitly posed but never addressed. The coquettish, swooning young woman was central to the iconography of hysteria as the Parisian physician Jean-Martin Charcot, working in the 1870s, constructed it. Charcot

Excerpted from Elizabeth Lunbeck, "Hysteria: the Revolt of the 'Good Girl'," in *The Psychiatric Persuasion: Knowledge, Gender, and Power in Modern America* (Princeton, NJ: Princeton University Press, 1997), pp. 209–28.

embellished the overtly erotic photographs he took of the fifteen-year-old hysteric Augustine, who had been raped by her father's employer, with such suggestive titles as "Extase" and "Erotisme."[2] In Freud's writings, too, seduction was ambiguous. Although, as he told it, his "discovery" of psychoanalysis – of the unconscious, the repressive mechanisms, and the transference – was predicated on his interpretation of the hysteric's account as one of infantile sexual trauma, of unwanted seduction,[3] and although he would later envision this seduction more equivocally, substituting a universally desired, fantastic coupling with the parent of the opposite sex for the actual seduction he had earlier hypothesized lay at the root of hysteria, the ambivalence of seduction was there from the beginning. From the mutually imagined seduction of Anna O. and Freud's early collaborator Josef Breuer, which culminated in her hysterical pregnancy and his fleeing the scene of the imagined crime, through Freud's seduction at the hands of Dora, who was at once antagonist and object of desire, the sexuality of the seduced – the hysteric – was never so passive as the manifest tale would have it. Yet so subversive was the sexual subjectivity of the hysteric that Freud could never directly confront it.

This sexual subjectivity – this desire to act rather than be acted upon – was evident in the tales the young women themselves told, though here, as in Freudian theory, it was subsumed within a sexual drama more compelling (because more orthodox) in both professional and popular estimation. This was the Victorian sexual drama, of which the hysterical girls and women who came to the attention of the Psychopathic Hospital psychiatrists were, for the most part, captives, engaged in debilitating struggles to establish their status as "good girls." This drama's stark casting of womanhood in terms of female virtue and female ruination appeared especially compelling to them, and they struggled mightily, against men and against their own desires, to maintain their virtue. Many of them wanted to participate in the sexual sphere, but found themselves – by reason of sexual abuse, traumatic heterosexual experience, or delicate temperament – psychically, and sometimes even physically, paralyzed and unable to act. These hysterics were self-described good girls in an increasingly sexualized world, girls suffering, in the words of one, from their modesty.[4]

Just as hypersexuality was the bad girl's ailment, hysteria was the good girl's. And just as psychiatrists worried that the former were too active sexually, they were concerned that hysterical women would withdraw from heterosexuality altogether. To psychiatrists, the hypersexual and the hysteric were two sides of the same coin of female desire. They confronted both on the uncertain terrain of female subjectivity. Around both they spun cautionary tales of feminine deceitfulness and tried out various visions of modern womanhood. And in both, the normal and the pathological were mixed. In the end, however, psychiatrists found the hypersexual – that cunning ruiner of innocent men – far more palatable than the hysteric, even though the hypersexual not only rejected the diagnosis but also impertinently questioned their authority. The hysteric, by contrast, not only acquiesced in the diagnosis of hysteria, she invited it. In the psychiatric encounter, the hypersexual's malady – attested to by advance reports detailing her every transgression – was in danger of simply disappearing, eclipsed by the normality psychiatrists were disposed to see in her. The hysteric resisted normalization. She came to psychiatrists having already constituted herself, through her symptoms, as a hysteric, and in the encounter, as she detailed the sordid transgressions of others and enacted her symptomological responses thereto, her malady appeared more, not less, substantive. Indeed, the validation that psychoanalysis offered is precisely what she sought....

Psychopathic Hospital psychiatrists professed only disdain for sexual Victorianism and urged on hysterical women a modern, rationalist sexual ethos structured not around the polarities of good and bad (which were, to their minds, ideological remnants from the past), but on the supposed sexual equality of women and men. But these women, even as they elicited from psychiatrists a vision of the battle of the sexes as fair, balanced, and straightforward, posed a serious challenge to that vision. Although she sometimes envisioned it otherwise, the hysteric told a tale that was a narrative of seduction at the hands of men, and the psychiatrists, although fierce proponents of modern sexual ethics, unwittingly adopted that narrative's conventions. The pleasing complementarity of male aggression and female passivity structured this narrative, in which the man, possessed of an uncontrollable sexual appetite, used the passionless woman for his pleasure while she, feigning indifference, coyly teased him. This scenario was so deeply culturally embedded that both the psychiatrists and the women who endeavored to envision an alternative sexual politics found themselves constrained by its terms. Psychiatrists could condemn the stratagems of "old-fashioned" courtship, which depended on a sort of male libertinism and female artifice that was anathema to them. But the best they could propose as an alternative was that women become as sexually knowledgeable, assertive, and even as aggressive as men. As psychiatrists conceived it, the rules of the marketplace (or, in a more pointed formulation, of the battlefield)[5] governed heterosexual relations; equally endowed men and women should be left the freedom to resolve their differences, to fashion mutually pleasing accommodations. Psychiatrists thus committed themselves to the aim of achieving a parity of sexual power between men and women. They would educate women in the ways of sex and attempt to curb the worst of male sex abuses – incest, rape, assault. Paradoxically, however, as psychiatrists began to define these relatively common acts of aggression against women as beyond the range of the "normal," they incorporated within that range a level of male sexual aggression that many women found vexatious, a level that gave the lie to their conception of the battle of the sexes as a contest of equals. Male sexual aggression was so deeply ingrained in the culture of heterosexuality that only at its worst was it available for inspection as pathology. To psychiatrists, then, hysteria was a malady suffered by undersexed prudes in a sexualized world. To "hysterics" themselves it represented a dramatic protest against the general cultural precept that the woman's body was fair game.

Sex, Lies, and Claims of Rape

Although Psychopathic Hospital psychiatrists made the diagnosis of hysteria infrequently, conferring it on fewer than 1 percent of their female patients, hysterical girls and women constituted perhaps one-quarter of the patients of the hospital's Freudian, L. E. Emerson, and occupied a disproportionate amount of his time and interest. Most of the women who were diagnosed as hysterics considered here were institutionalized at least once, for from one week to several months. Emerson later treated a number of them, as well as some who were never hospitalized, as outpatients, seeing them several times a week. Nearly all were registered as voluntary patients, and although some were brought to psychiatrists' attention by their mothers or fathers, there is little evidence that any objected to the diagnosis or the treatment. By contrast, several told Emerson that they found the treatment helpful; "This is just want I wanted – I've never talked things over with anyone," said one.[6]

The typical woman manifesting hysterical symptoms was young, single, native-born, and white. Most were between the ages of eighteen and twenty-three, although some were in their mid- thirties and even early forties; their median age was twenty-one. Although psychiatrists diagnosed a few married women as hysterical, the group was overwhelmingly single, in part because it was so youthful but also in part because many of the older women diagnosed as hysterics had purposely avoided men and marriage. Approximately half of those for whom occupational information is available labored at working-class occupations, in factories, as domestic servants, or as cooks or hospital attendants; 40 percent held low-level white-collar women's jobs as clerks in stores or as office workers; several were teachers. These women suffered from a range of psychic and bodily ailments. Spells of depression and crying temporarily incapacitated some; severe, inexplicable pains plagued others; vertigo, fainting spells, temporary paraplegias, twitching, tremors, and convulsions beset the most severely afflicted.

Most of these women told psychiatrists tales of sexual contest and conquest. Their tales fall into three groups of equal size that can be arrayed along a spectrum of sexual activity, ranging from outright sexual abuse at the one extreme, through active but vexed engagement in the middle, to almost entire withdrawal from heterosexuality at the other extreme. Into the first group fell young women who told of being sexually assaulted, subjected to incest at the hands of brothers or fathers, or raped by strangers. The middle group encompassed women who told of experiencing what men, and their culture, considered "normal" heterosexuality – whether it was the boss's hand surreptitiously slipped up the leg or the boyfriend's acting on his assumed right to her body – as unwanted aggression. The third group was composed of women, by the time they came to psychiatric attention, who had experienced the terrors of womanhood – from the facts of life to the ethics of courtship – so acutely that they had withdrawn almost entirely from the field of heterosexual play in which most of them wanted desperately to be engaged.

These women, however diverse their experience, shared a language with each other and with psychiatrists. So compelling, and so common, was the drama of seduction, so familiar were its players, that these women unwittingly adopted its terms even as they protested against it. The woman "gave way" to the man in the traditional sexual scenario, the language casting her as passive; at the same time all felt she was likely responsible for inciting his passions to a level that would demand her submission. One of Emerson's patients, for example, who complained of being constantly apprehensive, plagued by pains in her heart and weakness in her knees, and so afraid she would commit suicide that she had her mother put the kitchen knives out of reach, told him that prior to her first "breakdown" she "gave way" to a man and engaged in regular coitus interruptus with him for a year. Even though he sometimes prevailed upon her to have sex when she was less than willing, she worried that she had "led him on, more or less, teased him, etc.," and though of him as "a good fellow" because he was prepared to marry her should she become pregnant.[7] This woman experienced heterosexuality as aggression. Others told of interpreting aggression as normal, routine heterosexuality. For example, a woman who came to Emerson suffering from throbbing head pain told him, through her tears, that she thought she had been indiscreet in accepting a man's offer to escort her home late at night and that she had led him to do "something wrong with her" – he had raped her, her first brush with sex.[8] Another, a forty-four-year-old businesswoman who had turned down many proposals of marriage, was haunted by memories of a "compromising drive" she had taken at age nineteen.[9] And twenty-year-old Laura Jean Harper described being raped by an acquaintance in terms of "submission to sexual intercourse." As she recounted it, the "man drew her into a room and she lay down and prepared herself." That she could comment that at the time she felt, as sexual Victorianism prescribed, "little pleasure, some pain," is tellingly indicative of just how conflated were heterosexuality and male sexual aggression, for some women could neither envision nor experience them as discrete phenomena.[10]

Psychiatrists were only beginning to conceive of the male sexual aggression expressed in such acts as rape, incest, and forceful attack as apart from the ordinary, intermittently classing as instances of sexual assault what their culture comprehended in terms of seduction.[11] Rape and assault were, to be sure, recognized by the law as crimes, but physicians and other authorities met women's claims of violation with immense skepticism. That men actually assaulted women was given short shrift in the scant medico-legal literature on the subject, which focused instead on women's ruinous lies – their misstatements, untruths, staged accusations, and simulated hysterical attacks – and upon, in the rare instances where rape was determined to have occurred, their acquiescence. Do not believe a woman who cries rape, the authorities roundly warned, for more likely than not she was oversensitive and hysterical, making of "innocent playfulness" a serious offense, like the girl "roughly handled by some young man of the neighborhood, although with no evil intent," who falsely accuses him of assault.[12] "Truth is told about once in thirteen cases," maintained one self-proclaimed expert; the prisons are filled with innocent men falsely accused of rape, declared another.[13] That "the mere crossing of the knees absolutely prevents penetration" was apparently common belief among physicians, for, as one wrote, "every competent physician knows" that "sexual assault is physically impossible without consent."[14] In this literature, the paradigmatic case of "rape" – wrongly labeled as such, of course – involved two intimates engaged in heated "amorous sport." The *via voluptatis* pleasurably and mutually traversed; the man ready to claim what was naturally his; the girl – ignorant, like most, of male physiology and suddenly aware of "adverse considerations" – suddenly, inexplicably indignant, said no. "In a state of sexual hyper-excitability," the man pressed on, unfairly bringing on himself the charge of rape. . . .

To Emerson, the hysteric's symptoms were of interest not in themselves, but for the stories they encoded. He spent little time quizzing hysterics about the particulars of their symptoms, and he rarely, if ever, asked them to explain or account for their convulsions, tics, and twitching. Instead, he encouraged patients to dredge their pasts for incidents that might bear on their present distress. "Do for yourself just what you have learned to do with me," he wrote to one young woman. "Just sit in your chair and close your eyes and think, and look to see what you see."[15] Much of what Emerson elicited from patients had to do with sex. This is what he, as a Freudian, expected, and although it is impossible to reconstruct the mix of subtle suggestion and emotional incentives that in nearly every case yielded the information he sought, it is clear that, in theory at least, he maintained that it was "bad to work up a whole lot of theories in your own mind and then try to inject them into the patient." Still, on occasion he admitted to impatience.[16] Barely three weeks into the treatment of a woman suffering from blurred vision who thought analysis was "silly," he noted that he could "get no sign of any consciousness of any sexual experience or thought sufficiently adequate to explain trouble." "Chews the rag," he noted during one session in which, like many others, she produced little with which he could work.[17]

Bluntly asserting that "all hysterics tell untruths; some hysterics lie," Emerson argued that it was up to the psychoanalyst to discriminate truth from fiction. He was confident he could do so. Yet philosophically a pragmatist, he held that truth was neither final nor absolute, always representing a compromise. Truth, he maintained, "means the agreement of our ideas with reality," which was not to be opposed to unreality but considered as "a matter of immediate experience."[18] What he called the "subjective truth" of the hysteric's account, which the analyst could glean from her "manner and attitude," was to his mind of greater psychological consequence than any impossible-to-corroborate "objective truth."[19] Philosophy aside, it is clear that, in practice, Emerson believed much of what his hysterical patients told him (and he sometimes excoriated others who did not believe the stories). That the hysteric's symptoms waxed and waned in concert with the narratives of assault and trauma that she painfully patched together in analysis was evidence enough for him of her essential truthfulness. Still, he was well aware that Freud no longer maintained that actual assaults were implicated in the etiology of hysteria. Although social workers did corroborate several accounts of assault (and police several others), and although several men told of visiting upon their sisters the sorts of sexual abuses of which some of these young women complained, the historian of hysteria has no choice but to adopt Emerson's stance vis-à-vis the truth of the hysteric's account. "The patient herself fully believed what she said"; lacking evidence to the contrary, so might we.[20]

Good Girls, All

The consequences of sexual assault for many of the one-third of hysterical women who claimed to be its victims was hysteria in its most severe, debilitating, and classic form. Theresa Cellini, for example, a twenty-one-year-old office worker of Italian descent who was brought to the Psychopathic Hospital by her parents in 1912, complained of twice-weekly attacks of dizziness, shooting abdominal pain, headaches, nausea, blurred vision, and transient paraplegia. Although she appeared to be a normal girl who could hold a job and who took flight, like others, into the pulp fiction "world of fancy and romance," she was in fact deeply troubled by the sexual abuse to which she tearfully told Emerson she had been subjected since an early age. Her great-grandfather had "monkied" with her – put his penis in her, fingered her, urinated on her – from childhood until she was seventeen; a man had attempted, unsuccessfully, to penetrate her at age thirteen (she had been left to cry while he then "sat on a lounge and worked himself off by masturbation"); and she had had a series of sexual encounters with men she had pleased, but she had been left unsatisfied. It is hardly surprising that Cellini thought of intercourse a lot, or that she was overcome with "a queer sensation" as she dreamed of a man giving her plenty of money, taking it back, and then "fooling" with her as they argued. Like many girls subject to sexual abuse she had turned to promiscuous, passionless sexual activity, making her body available to men and getting her own satisfaction only solitarily – she could "get the thrills" if she dwelt on the subject of sex.[21]

Cellini was in this respect more fortunate than the other women who told of being so traumatized by sexual violation that they spurned sexuality altogether. Thirty-six-year-old Margaret Knight, for example, a self-described Catholic "good girl" who had been "running away from marriage" all her life and who suffered from what she called nervous prostration, told Emerson of a man hugging her several times when she was ten years old, of another exposing himself to her and a friend when she was fourteen, and of being traumatized, at age thirty-two, after she had allowed a man to fondle her breasts, having stopped him when he wanted more. "There is no such thing as love," she observed to Emerson, turning over the possibility of entering the convent.[22] And forty-year-old Emily Patton, who opened her first session with Emerson by disclosing that at age fourteen she had been drugged and raped by an elderly neighborhood man, an experience she felt "had ruined her life," told of keeping company in her youth with a man she loved, who wanted her to submit to him, but of being unable to act: "I was burning all over, I wanted to give in to him, but I couldn't." Her life "gone for nothing," she mused that she could have "got married, and brought great children in the world."[23] These and several other sexually traumatized women who repudiated sexuality altogether found themselves, in middle age, still plagued by ambivalence and unresolved desires. A number of them considered entering the convent, which held the promise of psychic and social salvation, representing the obliteration of sex conflict and offering community to women on their own. "To live in a convent is grand – they have good food," Knight exclaimed to Emerson, but she and all the others decided against it. One woman's explanation that as a girl she had thought "there were only three vocations: marriage, single, and convent life," and her admission that she had not known exactly where she fit in, only underscored how paltry yet how full of significance were the good girl's choices.[24] ...

In a culture that nurtured male sexual aggressiveness and in which even heterosexual couplings that had been openly entered into were suffused with this aggression, it was sometimes difficult for women to draw a firm line between abuse on the one hand and consensual sexual activity on the other. Sexual mores were in flux, and this only blurred the already tenuous distinction. One-third of the women who manifested the symptoms of hysteria told of being subjected to unwanted male sexual aggression that fell just short of outright rape or assault. Yet so powerful was the paradigm of seduction that even as these women conveyed to Emerson and to psychiatrists that what they were experiencing was aggression, they could not articulate it as such. The language of seduction – of feminine wiles masquerading as feminine submission – sustained the widely accepted fiction that women had the upper hand in the negotiations of heterosexuality, and it imputed an aura of contingency to those negotiations that veiled only imperfectly their inevitability: if in social fiction women directed them, in social fact women were relatively powerless.

The saga of twenty-eight-year-old Sally Hollis, who came to psychiatric attention complaining of a fear of crowds, shows how debilitating the consequences of "normal" heterosexuality could be. Hollis had been working since the age of seventeen, living on her own at the Frances Willard Settlement. She told Emerson, who quickly took charge of her case, of being irritated all the time and of suffering from "an awful feeling at the pit of [her] stomach" – "my breath is tied up and my stomach is sick." Years before she had been going with a young man, Walter, who worked in the same shop as she; from the beginning of their relations, she said, "I was working against my own feelings." Very quickly he began to get "fresh"; he kissed her within a month, within two he was feeling up her legs, within three, taking off her garter, and on one occasion he ripped her drawers in "trying to get at her." "Before I

marry a girl I'm going to find out what she's made of, how she's built,"
he boasted to her as he forced her to have intercourse. Hollis thought of
herself as "queer" and felt unable to resist this man's advances; the only
protest she could mount was symptomological – she began to vomit.
Hollis paid a high price for her desire to participate in the world of
heterosexuality. After Walter left the scene, having impregnated another
young woman and been forced into marriage, she took up with another
young man. Although he was less of a sexual bully, she still felt deeply
torn. For several years, during which he masturbated her twice weekly,
their relations were pleasant and uneventful. She was terribly shaken,
however, one morning after he had almost "seduced" her, and could
only try to put the memory out of her mind. This man, like the first,
eventually left her, informing her by letter that he was going with another
girl he liked better.[25]

Hollis knew she had been wronged, subjected to unwanted male
sexual aggression, but she could only cast the issue in terms of her own
reticence, not men's bullying. The materials from which she might have
constructed an alternative sexual politics were not at hand; the sexual
aggression of courtship was not a pressing social issue in the way that
female aggression was. Her illness – her hysteria – testified to the psychic
toll this ideological inversion of the actual power relations of heterosexuality between the sexes could exact. Psychoanalytic treatment only reinforced the power of this inversion. On one occasion, for example, she
dreamed she had been in a hammock when, she related to Emerson,
"some fellow came alongside of me and put his arm around me and
kissed me." "Then I thought of you," she told Emerson. "Then I
thought you said 'you shouldn't allow a person to kiss you. It was
encouraging them.' But I couldn't help it," she protested, "it was he
that kissed me!"

As they delimited a range of unacceptable male aggression, psychiatrists tacitly sanctioned a broad range of male aggression the psychic
sequelae of which could be especially vexing – because so "normal" – to
women. Even girls and women who openly struggled against male aggression, like one fifteen-year-old who was referred to Emerson by another
physician because of the cutting abdominal pain from which she suffered,
could pay a high price for that struggle. This girl told of fighting until she
was "exhausted" with the boy she had been seeing for three years the first
two or three times they had had intercourse. After that, she claimed, she
"didn't care," even "rather enjoyed it." Still, when he forced himself on
her when she was unwilling, she fought back by calling him "son of a
bitch" and "bastard." She knew she had been wronged. Men "shouldn't
have to fight to do it," she claimed authoritatively. But Emerson could
only engage with her failings, not his; she, after all, was the patient. He

assessed her as "*very repressed*" – this, concerning a girl who told him she was "dreaming of intercourse all the time" – and homed in on the conflict between her conscious and unconscious desires.[26]

That the ethic of seduction was as pervasive in the workplace as in courtship was especially confusing, even galling, to women. A colleague of one twenty-eight-year-old teacher, for example, told her over lunch that she "needed to be waked up" and invited her to meet him in a hotel.[27] Another woman, who began to work at age thirteen, told Emerson of a man hugging and squeezing her at work, and "going through coitus-like movements," a traumatic experience she kept to herself.[28] And forty-four-year-old Ada Buxton, who had worked as a proofreader when younger, related to Emerson that an older man in her office "had put his arms around her waist several times." She was mortified and was still ashamed of the incident; the man was let go for unrelated reasons but the one who replaced him, she felt, always "looked at her as if he thought there might have been something wrong going on." "I was so afraid someone would think I was immoral," she admitted.[29] Whether occasioned by her own heightened sensitivity or by the man's leering glances, Buxton's fears are indicative both of how hysterical women tended to fault themselves – not the men whose advances they rebuffed – in sexual negotiations, and of how little the sexual ethics of the business world differed from those of courtship: the paradigm of seduction was as compelling in the former as in the latter context. Seduction, which encoded the male belief that women wanted sex whether they admitted to it or not, and which cast a woman's hauteur as but one pose in her repertory of come-ons, gave men license to grope and fondle. An aloof manner and professional bearing offered women little protection against predatory workmates and employers. Harriet Andrews, a stenographer, described herself as "very ambitious": "I have plenty of ability, I am very able." But Andrews did not "take well with men in business. They like my work but they don't like me." Andrews displayed an unusual, even unseemly, degree of self-confidence for a working woman. She had nevertheless several times been subjected to unwanted sexual advances – hugs, kisses, leering looks, and groping hands – from the men who spurned her as too professional. Her employer proclaimed that "girls were likely to go astray if they didn't have work," but men acted as though the reverse was just as true, interpreting a woman's working as a sure sign of her desire to be led astray.[30]

The one-third of women diagnosed as hysterics who had little or no experience with boys and men provide evidence that the struggle to be a good girl could be waged on an entirely psychic front. Twenty-four-year-old Ethel Bowen, for example, dated her "awful dread of men" to age six or seven when she used to make the rounds with her father, who had a milk cart. Even now she was extremely sensitive to the presence of boys. Sometimes she could "meet them all right," but at other times she was too self-conscious. It worried her that she was unable, like other girls, to go out and feel free to talk to boys.[31] Likewise, eighteen-year-old Helen Haley, who characterized herself as sensitive and shy, wanted to go with boys but could not talk to anyone outside her family without becoming "terribly nervous and sick in every fibre of her being."[32] And twenty-five-year-old Clara Hill, a mill worker raised by her maternal grandmother who had told her "never to marry and [that] girls are happier single," dreamed of dancing and of boys talking to her, but admitted to never having had a lover and never having kissed, except at a game of post office.[33] These young women had suffered the terrors of womanhood so acutely that they had withdrawn entirely from the field of heterosexual play.

Those terrors were legion. From the biological facts of womanhood – menstruation, pregnancy, childbirth – to the social strategies of hetero-sexuality, many young women's minds were filled with frightening mis-information that cohered into a great cautionary tale concerning the dangers of sex. Because many knew nothing of menstruation, the first sight of blood was terrifying; one fifteen-year-old, for example, thought she was bleeding to death, and another was "shocked and horrified beyond measure," thinking, until convinced otherwise by a schoolmate, that it could only have been "a horrible peculiarity of her family."[34] Pregnancy, which only some knew resulted from what one called "bad-ness between man and wife," was an even greater source of terror and mystery.[35] One girl thought a man "touched" a woman to impregnate her; what Emerson called the family fiction of another was that Indians brought babies; and yet another, whose father was "violently opposed to sex knowledge," thought a girl could become pregnant by being kissed or hugged or by sitting on a man's lap. Schoolgirls regaled each other with shocking tales – of "little girls who died from relating to boys," of neighborhood women who succumbed in childbirth, of babies being pulled out of mothers split open "from the navel down."[36] The truth offerred little solace. "I don't see how they can get out unless they cut through at the sides," a puzzled seventeen-year-old put it to Emerson. "Told her," the psychologist tersely noted. "I should think it would hurt," she responded.[37]

To the psychoanalytically inclined, it was an article of faith that sexual ignorance was harmful, knowledge beneficial. "It is the function of the analysis to show," wrote Emerson, "that virtue consists in virtuous acts, and not in barren purity of thought," such as that revealed in an exchange with a twenty-four-year-old who, when asked "what do you know about sex," could only reply she did not "know what the word means."[38] This woman's seemingly willful ignorance troubled Emerson, who, when confronted with the extent of girls' sexual ignorance and with the psychic distortions such ignorance wrought, felt compelled to enlighten them. "Sex knowledge almost nil," he wrote of one; "has no knowledge of meaning of menstruation or sex matters at all," he noted of another, a seventeen-year-old who "denied all curiosity," saying she "believed her mother would tell her all she needed to know."[39] A good Freudian, Emerson maintained that there was "sex running through everything," and to woman after woman he explained the facts of sex.[40] "Told her facts"; "talked with her and told her about sex, etc."; "told her of possible sex connection"; "explained the sex act somewhat" – scattered through Emerson's notes is evidence of his pedagogical project.[41] At least some women knew what they were facing. A woman friend of Ada Buxton's, for example, cautioned her that if she was to continue seeing Emerson, "the sex question would have to be met."[42]

Emerson's zealotry on the sex question stemmed in part from the psychoanalyst's conviction that the roots of hysteria lay in sexual conflict. He urged women to sift through their memories of the past for the unpleasant sexual experiences that might help explain their ailments, and he expected women would find, then divulge, these memories quickly. If they failed to do so, he was likely to judge them repressed, as he did one twenty-one-year-old Scotswoman who, to his mind, exhibited characteristic Scottish reserve because she had not told all within an hour of meeting him. "Told her the necessity of thinking all things," Emerson noted to himself; "trying to persuade her to look consciously at sex ideas." This woman – the perfect pupil – complied, and within a week she was reporting that she felt, somewhat improbably, "no repulsion to sexual understanding" and "wondered how she could have been so unobservant before."[43] But other women were less complaisant. Prompted by Emerson, one twenty-four-year-old asked her mother, from whom she had earlier tried to pry information, "about the difference between men and women," but her mother only upbraided her, telling her it was not nice to ask such questions and that she would know the answers soon enough.[44] . . .

Psychiatrists could complain that hysterics dragged them into the sordid morass of sexuality, but they were already there. Hysterical girls, like hypersexual girls, piqued their prurient curiosities. "I just want to know if she has been immoral," demanded Elmer Southard in the case of a sixteen-year-old factory worker who suffered from intermittent attacks of acute pain. Hysteric or hypersexual? The case "could be converted into a Freudian case," suggested Herman Adler, opting for the first diagnosis. Southard demurred, hoping "the whole thing could be managed without resort to buried complexes" – a vote for the second. He suggested psychiatrists could trick the girl – who claimed she had neither boyfriends nor girlfriends – into admitting she had been immoral by telling her they had discovered a physical disease in her that indicated she had been immoral but that could be cured, putting an end to her painful attacks, if she would only confess. Southard's colleagues rejected this tack and diagnosed the girl, who was by all accounts rather sad and lonely, as a hysteric.[45]

Some women objected to the psychiatric casting of them as wholly erotic. One felt Emerson was mistaken in characterizing her as passionate, preferring the less equivocal "strong-minded."[46] Another told Emerson she was sick of talking about sex all the time.[47] "The male, specialist or other, does not understand the true nature of the sexual life of the hysteric," wrote a female physician.[48] Few, however, could mount as explicit an attack on the assumptions that underlay psychoanalytic modernism as did Julia M. Dutton, who had attended Charcot's lectures at the Salpêtrière and who ran a sanitarium for neurasthenics. "I do not accept Freud's opinions as far as women are concerned," she wrote. "About men I do not know. Their minds are an unknown land to me." Dutton objected to the assumption that the source of one girl's maladies lay in sexual immorality. "Men do not realize women are receptive," she explained. "They have no sexual emotions till they are roused – I mean the vast majority of women."[49] Dutton's protest, although impassioned, was couched in the language of seduction (she defended the girl in question as clean-minded), showing how paltry were the resources women could call upon to counter the sexualization that psychiatry and psychoanalysis were proposing, and how hard it was to get beyond the terms of sexual Victorianism to fashion some sort of subjectivity for women.

A Female Malady

Nearly all of the women diagnosed as hysterics by Emerson and at the Psychopathic Hospital conformed to the classic picture of the disease, suffering from some sort of bodily malady – convulsions, tics, spells, and so on. But so deep and feminine were the cultural resonances of hysteria, and so underscored were these in practice by identification with a demographically quite homogeneous group of single women, that psychiatrists at times used the diagnosis less as a proxy for symptoms than as an epithet expressive of their disdain for troubling aspects of womanhood. The hysteric was for the most part compliant, willing to be tutored by psychiatrists in the ways of womanhood. Several, however, expressed nothing but contempt for psychiatric authority. Psychopathic Hospital nurses judged one, a sixteen-year-old, rude and impetuous. The only symptoms of hysteria she displayed – and these, the nurses were careful to note, only when a psychiatrist was present – were crying, shaking, and constant movement of her arms and legs. Always attracting attention to herself, she warned the other girls not to consent to gynecological examinations and made loud, disparaging comments about the nurses and psychiatrists – "Half the doctors here don't know what they are doing. They ought to be in an insane asylum themselves." Yet in the presence of the male authorities she was so quick to malign, she transformed herself, much to the disgust of the nurses, into a seductress – giggling, flirting, sulking, and, they noted, speaking pettishly. By the end of her short hospital stay she was buoyantly happy, walking arm-in-arm with other girls on the ward, talking, and singing ragtime music.[50]

It was this young woman's seemingly calculated obtuseness that evoked such a passionate response and fed the fears of those physicians to whom hysteria was no more than a weapon women deployed, willfully and unfairly, in the battle of the sexes. Hysteria appeared, in this formulation, as the ultimate expression of feminine wiles; the hysteric's symptoms – her "spells," paralysis, loss of speech – the modern substitute for the tears women had proverbially wielded in marital combat.[51] Psychiatrists were fascinated with hysterics on the one hand, contemptuous of them on the other. They found their youthful enthusiasm endearing. "The hysteric reacts in a lively manner to the events of life," Southard noted, the stolidity of the praecox patient, the torpor of the depressed, the wild mania of the manic-depressive serving as a flattering foil for her antics.[52] But the hysteric could also elicit psychiatrists' hostility. . . .

The hysteric evoked hostility in part because the psychiatric debate on hysteria was a debate on the worthiness of psychoanalysis itself. That most hysterics were single women both stirred up psychiatrists' anxiety and allowed them to trivialize the issues arrayed about the disorder. The women whom psychiatrists diagnosed as hysterics were neither so willful nor so resourceful as they imagined them. Nor were they so heroic as a strain of feminist thinking has considered them. They were, rather, a sad lot, and their collective experience was one of thwarted ambition, lonely passion, and psychic misery. A number of them told of feeling acutely that they were queer and different. One described herself as "the most miserable girl in the world";[53] another confessed that she felt she was "not like other girls – I don't feel myself, just what I'd like to be";[54] still another said she felt "like two persons, and the one cannot control the other."[55] None of these women made a name for herself in the public world, like Bertha Pappenheim (Anna O.) so successfully did in the world of reform and feminist activism. They were, by contrast, ordinary women, women who wished more than anything else to be normal, an aim as ambiguous as the term itself.

In psychiatrists' evolving discourse, the hypersexual and the hysteric served as emblematic representations of modern womanhood and its possibilities gone awry. Attempting to consign the frigid, prudish Victorian woman to the past, psychiatrists found it difficult to portray her successor along consistent lines, at least in part because the program she was meant to project was itself contradictory and not yet fully worked out. Psychiatrists' writings attest to their desire to normalize female sexuality, but in practice they located it in the hypersexual one moment, in the hysteric the next. Each could serve reflexively as foil to the other, obscuring any middle ground, as they did in Emerson's short treatment of the hypersexual Prudence Walker. Emerson was uncharacteristically censorious of Walker. He quickly summed her up as sentimental, a "mental light-weight," warned "her not to 'flirt,' " and laid out for her what he called the "possibilities of lack of self-control." "Syphilis, illegitimate baby or abortion, nervousness, or insanity" – Emerson's catalogue of horrors was *echt* Victorian, straight out of the textbooks he and his colleagues had long ago discarded, a stark contrast to the program of sexual modernity he pressed on the patients he deemed hysterics.[56] Hypersexual and hysteric: psychiatrists might have located normal womanhood somewhere between the two categories. They did not, falling back on the language of pathology as they went about charting the new territory of female desire that sustained both.

Notes

1 Case 5426, 1915, staff meeting; L. E. Emerson, "The Psychoanalytic Treatment of Hystero-Epilepsy," *Journal of Abnormal Psychology* 10 (1915–1916): 327 (comment in reference to epileptiform seizures in a male hysteric).

2 Elaine Showalter, *The Female Malady: Women, Madness, and English Culture, 1830–1980* (New York, 1985), pp. 147–55.

3 James Strachey, introduction to Josef Breuer and Sigmund Freud, *Studies on Hysteria*, ed. and trans. Strachey (New York, n.d.), p. 20.

4 LEE case 85, 1912. Citations to all of Emerson's numbered cases refer to handwritten – in a few cases typewritten – notes made on half sheets of paper during sessions with patients. Much of what he records appears to be verbatim transcriptions of patients' words – direct discourse; in several instances he incorporated grammatical errors, as in "Before that I never had no pain" (case 26).

5 Abraham Myerson, "Hysteria as a Weapon in Marital Conflicts," *Journal of Abnormal Psychology*, 10 (1915–16), p. 1.

6 LEE case 240, 1914.

7   LEE case 224, 1914.
8   LEE case 81, 1912.
9   LEE case 264, 1915.
10 LEE case 53, 1911–1915.
11 I found several uses of the term "sexual assault" in the records of women
    diagnosed as hysterics: case 5426, 1915, and LEE cases 70, 41, and 91
    ("sexually assaulted by a boy when abt. 4 years").
12 F. R. Bronson, "False Accusations of Rape," *American Journal of Urology
    and Sexology* 14 (1918): 541.
13 Gurney Williams, "Rape in Children and in Young Girls," *International
    Clinics* 23d ser., 2 (1913): 250; Charles C. Mapes, "Sexual Assault,"
    Urologic and Cutaneous Review 21 (1917): 431.
14 Williams, "Rape in Children," p. 259; Mapes, "Sexual Assault," p. 430.
15 LEE case 50, 1912, letter to patient.
16 Case 1002, 1913, staff meeting.
17 LEE case 244, 1915.
18 L. E. Emerson, "A Psychoanalytic Study of a Severe Case of Hysteria,"
    Journal of Abnormal Psychology 7 (1912–1913): 385–406; 8 (1913–1914):
    44–56; 8 (1913–1914): 180–207 (quotation from p. 199); L. E. Emerson, "A
    Philosophy for Psychoanalysts," *Psychoanalytic Review* 2 (1915): 426–27.
19 L. E. Emerson, "The Case of Miss A: A Preliminary Report of a Psycho-
    analytic Study and Treatment of a Case of Self-Mutilation," *Psychoanalytic
    Review* 1 (1913–1914): 42.
20 Emerson, "Case of Miss A," p. 42.
21 Case 677, 1912, case record, ward notes, patient's account of dream, and
    Emerson's notes of sessions with her.
22 LEE case 83, 1912–1916.
23 LEE case 26, 1911–1912.
24 LEE case 83, 1914; and 53, 1911.
25 LEE case 85, 1912, Emerson's notes and patient's letters.
26 LEE case 259, 1915.
27 Case 853, 1913, case history.
28 LEE case 256, 1915.
29 LEE case 264, 1915.
30 LEE case 45, 1911.
31 LEE case 78, 1912.
32 LEE case 242, 1914.
33 LEE case 27, 1911.
34 LEE case 254, 1915, and 264, 1915.
35 Quotation from Emerson, "Severe Case of Hysteria," p. 388.
36 "Misinformation" from LEE case 26, 85, 219, 236, and 244, among others.
37 LEE case 251, 1915.
38 Emerson, "Severe Case of Hysteria," p. 201; LEE case 263, 1915.
39 LEE case 242, 1914, and 238, 1914.
40 Quotation from LEE case 48, 1912.
41 LEE case 254, 81, 87, and 244.

42 LEE case 264, 1915.
43 LEE case 255, 1915.
44 LEE case 263, 1915.
45 Case 3800, 1914, staff meeting.
46 LEE case 45, 1911.
47 LEE case 262, 1915.
48 Margarethe Kossak, "The Sexual Life of the Hysteric," *American Journal of Urology and Sexology* 11 (1915): 505.
49 LEE case 244, 1915.
50 Case 7858, 1916, case history, ward notes.
51 Myerson, "Hysteria as a Weapon."
52 Quotation from case 1158, 1913, staff meeting.
53 LEE case 85, 1912.
54 LEE case 53, 1911.
55 LEE case 48, 1912.
56 LEE case 247, 1915; see also case 5370.

Documents

In the following case study, psychiatrist L. E. Emerson discusses "Miss A," a young woman afflicted with self-mutilation. Three parts are included here: Emerson's summary of her sexual history and her stories of past self-inflicted wounds; Miss A's own account of her cutting and the dreams she associated with it; and finally Emerson's analysis of the case. Emerson concluded that the mutilation symbolically substituted for masturbation, the pain she endured being a reminder of her early sexual trauma induced by forced masturbation. How does Miss A's telling of her own story and Emerson's rendering of her case help to construct the paradigm of the hysterical woman? What specific qualities characterized her as an hysteric? How does Emerson's reading of the causes of Miss A's mutilation help to define "normal" women's desires for a full life?

The Case of Miss A

L. E. Emerson

This is a case of self-inflicted serious injury. But Krafft-Ebing records only two cases of female masochism and one of these was in the "initial stages of paranoia persecutoria." *This patient was not insane.* For the purposes of this paper, therefore, perhaps it would be better to leave the question of definition and comparison undecided for the present. . . .

The patient was a young woman twenty-three years old. She came to the Hospital with a self-inflicted cut on her left arm. Her arm had many other scars, and there was one on her breast: she said she had cut herself twenty-eight or thirty times; and on the calf of her right leg was a scar forming the letter W.

Two problems presented themselves: Why did she cut herself? How could she be helped?

The physical and mental examination gave but negative results. The patient was quiet and completely amenable, showing excellent judgment, in her attitude in the ward.

The following facts were all gleaned from the patient, and so far as objective truth is concerned, are uncorroborated. *Objective* truth, however, is unimportant, in a psychological sense, and of the *subjective* truth of the account I was finally convinced by the manner and attitude of the patient, during daily conferences lasting over a month. The patient herself fully believed what she said.

Anamnesis

As a baby the patient was her father's pet, and was also much made of by the male boarders in the family. With the advent of other daughters, however, the father paid less and less attention to her. He was a cruel man. He used to thrash his sons unmercifully, often stripping and tying them to a bed post. Although he never thrashed the patient she lived in mortal terror lest he would do so. The thing she feared more even than the whipping, she said, was being stripped.

Excerpted from L. E. Emerson, "The Case of Miss A: a Preliminary Report of a Psycho-analytic Study and Treatment of a Case of Self-mutilation," *Psychoanalytic Review*, 1 (1913–14), pp. 41–6, 49–54.

One day, when about eight years old, she trampled on her father's garden, of which he was inordinately proud, and was seen by her uncle, one of the men boarders. He threatened to tell her father, which frightened her dreadfully; but promised not to tell if she would let him do as he liked. She did, and for many years (five or six) he was accustomed almost daily to masturbate her. She accepted it in a perfectly frigid manner although at first it was very painful, and from this time forth she hated her father, because fear of him made her submit to this degradation. Finally, at the age of fourteen, however, she learned that her uncle was attempting to do the same thing to her younger sister. Though she had never told any one, she became bold to do for her sister what she did not dare to do for herself, and threatened him with telling her father. She then discovered that he really was afraid lest she tell, and thus she escaped. But not until he had attempted coitus. This he did when she was only twelve years old.

As the patient matured she became abnormally stout. Her catamenia began when she was about thirteen, but were always very irregular. In the shop, for she was then working, the girls said irregular menses were the cause of either consumption or insanity. This she believed, more or less, because she was having severe headaches, and she attributed them to her irregular menses.

One day, about three years ago, as she was cutting bread, her cousin, boarding with her family at the time, attempted a sexual assault. In the scuffle she cut herself with the bread knife. This was enough for her assailant, who left her alone. It happened that at the time of this attempted assault the patient was suffering from an intense headache. After cutting herself, however, she noticed that the headache had left. She said she continued the cutting as a means of gaining relief from headaches, and from a *"queer feeling"* which she could not describe.

After a while the patient became aware that what she wanted more than anything else was a baby; but because of what she had passed through as a child, she regarded marriage as impossible. At a moment of intense mental agony over this more conscious conflict she took her brother's razor and cut her breast, thinking that if she could have no babies her breasts were useless. Here the sexual nature of her acts became apparent. After much thinking on the subject, and as the result of concrete advice, she determined to have a baby, without marriage. For this purpose, though she had never before done such a thing, she accepted the attentions of a man who had been soliciting her for some time. She stayed with him a short while but then left him because he "insulted" her. She did not become pregnant. Some time later another man wanted to marry her. She cared for him, and would have married him, but first, she felt it necessary to tell him all. As was natural, he then refused to marry her and called her a whore. She left him and went to her brother's room, and for the first and only time in her life took some whiskey, found his razor and cut on her leg the letter W. (In this relation Hawthorne's "Scarlet Letter" is interesting.)

After I had been working with the patient a short time I asked her to write for me a history of her self-mutilation. In her account one can get an idea as to the patient's natural intellectual ability. She was taken out of school and sent to work in a factory at about thirteen years of age and has worked there ever since. Some further idea of her family's sexual morality is suggested by the fact that she said all her brothers but one asked her for "connections" (*i.e.*, coitus). She denied gratifying their request. The following is in her own words:

"The first time I cut myself was about three years ago, and then I cut myself on the wrist of the left arm. It was not a very bad cut. A student at the Hospital took two stitches in it. Before I cut myself I had what I called a crazy headache, and after I had let blood my headache went away, and I thought that the cutting of my wrist, and letting the blood flow had cured it. I do not remember very clearly how I felt at the time.

"It was about three weeks afterwards that I decided I must cut myself again. All during the week I had been feeling queer, and I thought because I was feeling so queer it was because I did not have my menses regularly – it was six months since I had been unwell – so I'd deliberately made up my mind that I would do it. I went upstairs to my brother's room, and found his razor. I opened it, and held out my arm, and rested my arm on the dresser. I was shaking all over, it seemed to me that I would not have the nerve to do it even if my head did ache, and I did think that it would cure my headache, and help me to menstruate regularly like other girls did. I had about decided that I would not, when I happened to look up and saw myself in the mirror. That settled it, all my nerve came back. I remember distinctly that I sneered at my reflection in the glass and said something about nobody caring if I killed myself, much less if I only cut myself, so I drew the razor slowly across my wrist, and made a deep cut. It then took three stitches to sew it up. . . .

"It was quite a while before my head ached very badly again, and when it did ache I tried hard to control myself for I was getting a little bit afraid. It was about five o'clock in the morning. My head had been aching badly for two days. I had gone to bed very much discouraged. I slept badly, and had horrible dreams mostly of a sexual nature – at that time anything about sex was most repulsive to me – I woke about 4:30 o'clock, and lay there and thought about everything, everything disagreeable that had ever happened to me especially about what happened when I was a child, and about my cousin. At last I could not stand it any longer, and in a manner almost frantic I went into my brother's room and took his razor – he was working nights – and slashed at my arm. I did not do it slowly. I did it quickly, because I hated myself, and some other people, and in a way I felt that by hurting myself I was hurting them and also I was wishing that I could do it to them only I knew I could not even if they were where I could reach them, because I dislike to see people suffer. I felt so badly over cutting myself, and also so ashamed that I did not have it attended for about a day and a half. Dr. ———— took two stitches in it. He asked me why I did it. I told him I did it because I did not menstruate regularly. He told me lies, and treated me for about four weeks.". . .

Epicrisis

This case has interest for a number of reasons. In the first place it is doubtful if one could call it purely hysterical. There is no splitting of consciousness in the sense in which hystericals split their consciousness. The psycho-sexual traumas of childhood are repressed, but are also remembered. Even so, they are all-powerful. This proves that such traumas do not have to be forgotten to have an abnormal influence on the psyche.

In another way, however, the patient shows a closely similar reaction to that of an hysteric. She was unable to bear mental distress. The hysteric represses his unpleasant memories because they cause him mental distress and he is morally faint-hearted. There are two kinds of courage or endurance: the ability to bear spiritual distress or agony, and the ability to bear physical pain. The patient was not afraid of pain, but she was unable to bear mental anguish. To a certain extent she *chose* pain. Here she was imitating, in her own acts, *both* her father and mother. Her father used to beat and otherwise maltreat her mother; but her mother never struck back, or resented it. She could bear anything, in pain. On the other hand, her father could not bear the slightest pain without creating the greatest disturbance. To the patient, bearing pain increased her own self-respect, as contrasted with her father, and identified her with her mother; while in inflicting pain she satisfied her aggressive masculine impulses and identified herself with her father. In another respect the patient was very like an hysteric. She carried on an active process of day-dreaming, of fantastic creation, all having to do with babies, homes, and husbands. Night dreams, too, were of the same subject, though less idealized. . . .

Roughly, the cutting may be analyzed into five parts: (1) The pain; (2) the bleeding; (3) an aggressive act leading to (4) surgical and sympathetic treatment; (5) sexual relief through symbolical masturbation.

Pain alone is an insufficient motive. If it had been merely pain that the patient wanted she could have gotten it in many ways, more intense and not so destructive. But there was the pleasure in pain if it were not too intense. Freud says, "it has also been claimed that every pain contains in itself the possibility of a pleasurable sensation. Let us be satisfied with the impression that the explanation of this perversion is by no means satisfactory and that it is possible that many psychic efforts unite themselves into one effect." This multiplicity of motives has been found to be the case with the patient. Whether it is so generally could only be determined by the psychoanalysis of a great many corroborative cases. In the case under consideration, however, the pain element in itself may be regarded as almost negligible, but through association with her passive masturbation it gained tremendous power.

Thus cutting was a sort of symbolical substitute for masturbation. At first when she was masturbated it caused a good deal of pain. Hence pain and sexual stimulation were intimately related. Another motive for her painful self-mutilation was a desire to escape mental distress. Physical pain distracted her attention and was a means of escaping such distress. She also felt disgusted with herself and wished to punish herself, in a way, for her acquiescence as a child in what she instinctively felt were serious misdeeds.

The patient said she had masturbated herself only once, and never did so again because of the loathsome memory of what her uncle did.

Bleeding, as a means of medication, has a long history. Perhaps here we may get a glimpse of one of its roots. In the patient, bleeding had several psychic determinants. In the first place there was the desire for regular menstruation. The menses had always been irregular, and after the patient began cutting herself, she said she cut herself every four weeks. This correspondence to the catamenia period is obvious. The idea of vicarious actions bringing about a desired end is very primitive. From this point of view the pain element in the complex act would be a barrier to be overcome before the cutting could take place. The desire for regular menstruation together with other desires must overcome her aversion to pain. This desire for menstruation was also rooted in a desire to be like other girls and to function like other girls. Here the power of the herd instinct is suggested. Bleeding also occupied a peculiar double position in the mind of the patient. First it symbolized menstruation, and second it seemed a direct way of reducing her obesity. Her dislike of obesity also had a sexual ground. At about the age of seventeen she was so fat that some of the girls in the factory thought she was pregnant and used to taunt her with it. As it as a common thing for these girls to live loose lives there was nothing strange in their suspicions. Luckily, she said, she never lost a day at work during that year, otherwise the girls would have thought she had had an operation.

The third part of the analysis of the cutting concerns itself with the act as an aggression. From this point of view the act is masculine. This corresponds completely with a large part of the patient's character. She is decidedly masculine in many ways. Physiologically and psychologically the bisexual character of man and woman is established. Hence the right to say that the patient, as a man, committed an act of aggression, against herself, as a woman, thus following the double law of her being. Thus her sadistic impulses, probably strongly inherited from her father, got satisfaction while she satisfied at the same time her masochistic inclinations, inherited from her mother. Masochism, therefore, in this case at least, so far as it may be said to be masochistic, has a sadistic component. Similarly, sadism, in so far as others are really part of ourselves, has a masochistic component. This patient had strong sadistic impulses as was shown by her desire to kill her uncle and also to kill her father. These impulses, however, were repressed, or perhaps better said, were introverted, to use Jung's phrase, and thus became masochistic. Thus one fundamental root of masochism may lie in sadism. Certain oriental peoples kill themselves, thinking thereby most seriously to harm their enemy. So the patient sometimes cut herself, she said, to hurt her father.

It is worthy of note that any act of conscious aggression, whether directed inward or outward, implies the *overcoming* of certain psychic barriers such as pain or fear of reprisal. It must be a strong impulse which overcomes a strong resistance. Next to complete self-destruction comes partial self-destruction as the strongest deterrent possible to certain acts. On the other hand, the will to live a *full* life is perhaps almost as strong as the will to live at all. The patient's desire to live a full life is shown by her almost overwhelming desire for children, together with a strong desire to associate with, and receive consideration from, people superior to her inherited social environment. These various components of a complex total force were of course not clearly recognized or known. It was the work of psychoanalysis, just as the word implies, to analyze this complex into components and present them clearly to consciousness for consideration, judgment, and control. This necessary function of psychoanalysis implies an ethical and philosophical foundation. . . .

It was assumed that the patient had considerable psychic power, only introverted. She was encouraged to believe in her own capacity. Each step in the analysis was explained and discussed with her. She was told some of the theories and was asked if she corroborated them in her own feelings and thoughts. If not, they were revised to fit the facts. In this way she analyzed her own complexes and thereby gained much self-control. And, most important of all, opportunity for sublimation was obtained for the patient and she was given a chance. Nothing could be less helpful than two courses which might have been followed. A complete analysis, left there, would have been of little help to the patient, if she had been given no chance to sublimate or idealize her energies. Because she was poor, of lowly origin, and uneducated, it was necessary to provide such opportunities of idealization as would be unnecessary to more highly favored patients. Strictly speaking, this is not a function of the analyst, but like the doctor who prescribes a medicine too expensive for the patient and therefore must get it himself if it is absolutely necessary, so the analyst, if he wishes his work to last, must provide an adequate outlet for energies which, turned in, are self-destructive.

Another course which would have been not only futile but actively harmful was also avoided. I mean the assumption that what the patient was suffering from was lack of specific sexual satisfaction and advising sexual relations or masturbation. Such a course could only end in disaster. The reason is unassailable. The patient, herself, had already sublimated her sensual desires sufficiently to know that what she really wanted was children and not the sexual act merely. Hence only the highest ideals of love could satisfy, even approximately, her cravings and desires. Anything less than this could only throw her back into the childhood degradation, out of which she had already partially climbed.

So far the patient has responded to the treatment. While fourteen months, without a relapse, is too short a time upon which to base any prophecy of the future, yet it does give a certain ground for hope.

Further Reading

Cott, Nancy F. "Passionlessness: an interpretation of Victorian sexual ideology, 1790–1850." *Signs: Journal of Women in Culture and Society*, 4, 2 (1978), 219–36.

Degler, Carl. "What ought to be and what was: women's sexuality in the nineteenth century." *American Historical Review*, 79 (1974), 1479–90.

Groneman, Carol. "Nymphomania: the historical construction of female sexuality." *Signs: Journal of Women in Culture and Society*, 19 (Winter 1994), 337–67.

Lunbeck, Elizabeth. *The Psychiatric Persuasion: Knowledge, Gender, and Power in Modern America*. Princeton, NJ: Princeton University Press, 1997.

Maines, Rachel P. *The Technology of Orgasm: "Hysteria," the Vibrator, and Women's Sexual Satisfaction*. Baltimore: Johns Hopkins University Press, 1999.

Meyerowitz, Joanne. "Sexual geography and gender economy: the furnished rooms districts of Chicago, 1890–1930." *Gender and History*, 2, 3 (1990), 274–96.

Odem, Mary E. *Delinquent Daughters: Protecting and Policing Adolescent Female Sexuality in the United States, 1885–1920*. Chapel Hill: University of North Carolina Press.

Simmons, Christina. "Modern sexuality and the myth of Victorian repression." In Kathy Peiss and Christina Simmons (eds), *Passion and Power: Sexuality in History*. Philadelphia: Temple University Press, 1989, pp. 155–77.

Smith-Rosenberg, Carroll. *Disorderly Conduct: Visions of Gender in Victorian America*. New York: Knopf, 1985.

Stearns, Carol Z., and Peter N. Stearns. "Victorian sexuality: can historians do it better?" *Journal of Social History*, 18 (1984/5), 626–33.

8

Christian Brotherhood or Sexual Perversion?

Introduction

Definitions of gay and straight, as George Chauncey, Jr shows in this essay, have only recently been inscribed in our social and cultural imagination. In the early twentieth century, men had sex with other men, but this did not necessarily define them as homosexual. Chauncey has examined 3500 pages of testimony concerning a US Navy investigation for alleged homosexuality among sailors in Newport, Rhode Island. It is clear from the testimony that the sailors' perception of their own and others' sexuality was virtually unrelated to *who* they had sex with and deeply connected to *what* happened during the sex. Adopting feminine behavior on the street and in the bedroom ("taking the woman's part") defined a man as "queer," a "fairy," or "faggot." In contrast, assuming the role of the straight "husband" or acting as "trade" for a gay man's sexual satisfaction did not mark a man as queer. Indeed, during the Navy's investigation, ostensibly straight men posed as decoy trade, apparently without compromising their self- image as "normal" men.

The investigation was further complicated when naval officials charged a prominent Episcopal clergyman and a YMCA churchman with sodomy. Newport's clergymen came to the defense of these two and, in fact, broadly defended male intimacy among the clergy and their male followers while extolling the virtues of Christian brotherhood. Ministers were supposed to be emotional, like women, they argued; they created strong relationships with other men, cared deeply about them, and came to their aid when they were in trouble. As Chauncey demonstrates, the rules of appropriate masculine behavior – both sexual and emotional – were contested in the Newport trials. Straight sailors believed they were "normal" if they acted like men, even though they engaged in homosexual sex; ministers claimed they were "normal" if they refrained from sex but nonetheless forged intimate emotional bonds with other men.

Christian Brotherhood or Sexual Perversion? Homosexual Identities and the Construction of Sexual Boundaries in the World War I Era

George Chauncey, Jr

In the spring of 1919, officers at the Newport (Rhode Island) Naval Training Station dispatched a squad of young enlisted men into the community to investigate the "immoral conditions" obtaining there. The decoys sought out and associated with suspected "sexual perverts," had sex with them and learned all they could about homosexual activity in Newport. On the basis of the evidence they gathered, naval and municipal authorities arrested more than twenty sailors in April and sixteen civilians in July and the decoys testified against them at a naval court of inquiry and several civilian trials. The entire investigation received little attention before the navy accused a prominent Episcopal clergyman who worked at the YMCA of soliciting homosexual contacts there. But when civilian and then naval officials took the minister to trial on charges of being a "lewd and wanton person," a major controversy developed. Protests by the Newport Ministerial Union and the Episcopal Bishop of Rhode Island and a vigorous editorial campaign by the *Providence Journal* forced the navy to conduct a second inquiry in 1920 into the methods used in the first investigation. When that inquiry criticized the methods but essentially exonerated the senior naval officials who had instituted them, the ministers asked the Republican-

Excerpted from George Chauncey, Jr, "Christian Brotherhood or Sexual Perversion? Homosexual Identities and the Construction of Sexual Boundaries in the World War I Era," *Journal of Social History*, 19 (1985), pp. 189–212.

controlled Senate Naval Affairs Committee to conduct its own investigation. The Committee agreed and issued a report in 1921 that vindicated the ministers' original charges and condemned the conduct of the highest naval officials involved, including Franklin D. Roosevelt, President Wilson's Assistant Secretary of the Navy and the 1920 Democratic vice-presidential candidate.

The legacy of this controversy is a rich collection of evidence about the organization and phenomenology of homosexual relations among white working-class and middle-class men and about the changing nature of sexual discourse in the World War I era.[1] On the basis of the 3,500 pages of testimony produced by the investigations it is possible to reconstruct the organization of a homosexual subculture during this period, how its participants understood their behavior, and how they were viewed by the larger community, thus providing a benchmark for generalizations about the historical development of homosexual identities and communities. The evidence also enables us to reassess current hypotheses concerning the relative significance of medical discourse, religious doctrine, and folk tradition in the shaping of popular understandings of sexual behavior and character. Most importantly, analysis of the testimony of the government's witnesses and the accused churchmen and sailors offers new insights into the relationship between homosexual behavior and identity in the cultural construction of sexuality. Even when witnesses agreed that two men had engaged in homosexual relations with each other they disagreed about whether both men or only the one playing the "woman's part" should be labeled as "queer." More profoundly, they disagreed about how to distinguish between a "sexual" and a "nonsexual" relationship: the navy defined certain relationships as homosexual and perverted which the ministers claimed were merely brotherly and Christian. Because disagreement over the boundary between homosexuality and homosociality[2] lay at the heart of the Newport controversy, its records allow us to explore the cultural construction of sexual categories in unusual depth.

The Social Organization of Homosexual Relations

The investigation found evidence of a highly developed and varied gay subculture in this small seaport community and a strong sense of collective identity on the part of many of its participants. Cruising areas, where gay men and "straight" sailors[3] alike knew that sexual encounters were to be had, included the beach during the summer and the fashionable Bellevue Avenue close to it, the area along Cliff Walk, a cemetery and a bridge. Many men's homosexual experiences consisted entirely (and irregularly) of visits to such areas for anonymous sexual encounters, but some men organized a group life with others who shared their inclinations. The navy's witnesses mentioned groups of servants who worked in the exclusive "cottages" on Bellevue Avenue and of civilians who met at places such as Jim's Restaurant on Long Wharf.[4] But they focused on a tightly knit group of sailors who referred to themselves as "the gang,"[5] and it is this group whose social organization the first section of this paper will analyze.

The best-known rendezvous of gang members and of other gay sailors was neither dark nor secret: "The Army and Navy YMCA was the headquarters of all cocksuckers [in] the early part of the evening," commented one investigator, and, added another, "everybody who sat around there in the evening... knew it."[6] The YMCA was one of the central institutions of gay male life; some gay sailors lived there, others occasionally rented its rooms for the evening so that they would have a place to entertain men, and the black elevator operators were said to direct interested sailors to the gay men's rooms.[7] Moreover, the YMCA was a social center, where gay men often had dinner together before moving to the lobby to continue conversation and meet the sailors visiting the YMCA in the evening.[8] The ties which they maintained through such daily interactions were reinforced by a dizzying array of parties; within the space of three weeks, investigators were invited to four "faggot part[ies]" and heard of others.[9] ...

Within and sustained by this community, a complex system of personal identities and structured relationships took shape, in which homosexual behavior per se did not play a determining part. Relatively few of the men who engaged in homosexual activity, whether as casual participants in anonymous encounters or as partners in ongoing relationships, identified themselves or were labeled by others as sexually different from other men on that basis alone. The determining criterion in labeling a man as "straight" (their term) or "queer" was not the extent of his homosexual activity, but the gender role he assumed. The only men who sharply differentiated themselves from other men, labeling themselves as "queer," were those who assumed the sexual and other cultural roles ascribed to women; they might have been termed "inverts" in the early twentieth-century medical literature because they not only expressed homosexual desire but "inverted" (or reversed) their gender role. . . .

The inverts grouped themselves together as "queers" on the basis of their effeminate gender behavior,[10] and they all played roles culturally defined as feminine in sexual contacts. But they distinguished among themselves on the basis of the "feminine" sexual behavior they preferred, categorizing themselves as "fairies" (also called "cocksuckers"), "pogues" (men who liked to be "browned," or anally penetrated), and "two-way artists" (who enjoyed both). The ubiquity of these distinctions and their importance to personal self-identification cannot be overemphasized. Witnesses at the naval inquiries explicitly drew the distinctions as a matter of course and incorporated them into their descriptions of the gay subculture. One "pogue" who cooperated with the investigation, for instance, used such categories to label his friends in the gang with no prompting from the court: "Hughes said he was a pogue; Richard said he was a cocksucker; Fred Hoage said he was a two-way artist. . . . " While there were some men about whom he "had to draw my own conclusions: they never said directly what they was or wasn't," his remarks made it clear he was sure they fit into one category or another.[11]

A second group of sailors who engaged in homosexual relations and participated in the group life of the gang occupied a more ambiguous sexual category because they, unlike the queers, conformed to masculine gender norms. Some of them were heterosexually married. None of them behaved effeminately or took the "woman's part" in sexual relations, they took no feminine nicknames, and they did not label themselves – nor were they labeled by others – as queer. Instead, gang members, who reproduced the highly gendered sexual relations of their culture, described the second group of men as playing the "husbands" to the "ladies" of the "inverted set." Some husbands entered into steady, loving relationships with individual men known as queer; witnesses spoke of couples who took trips together and maintained monogamous relationships. The husbands' sexual – and sometimes explicitly romantic – interest in men distinguished them from other men: one gay man explained to the court that he believed the rumor about one man being the husband of another must have "some truth in it because [the first man] seems to be very fond of him, more so than the average man would be for a boy."[12] But the ambiguity of the sexual category such men occupied was reflected in the difficulty observers found in labeling them. The navy, which sometimes grouped such men with the queers as "perverts," found it could only satisfactorily identify them by describing what they *did*, rather than naming what they *were*. One investigator, for instance, provided the navy with a list of suspects in which he carefully labeled some men as "pogues" and others as "fairies," but he could only identify one man by noting that he "went out with all the above named men at various times and had himself sucked off or screwed them through the rectum."[13] Even the queers' terms for such men – "friends," and "husbands" – identified the men only *in relation to* the queers, rather than according them an autonomous sexual identity. Despite the uncertain definition of their sexual identity, however, most observers recognized these men as regular – if relatively marginal – members of the gang. . . .

Even before the naval inquiry began, Newport's servicemen and civilians alike were well aware of the queers in their midst. They tolerated them in many settings and brutalized them in others, but they thought they knew what they were dealing with: perverts were men who behaved like women. But as the inquiry progressed, it inadvertently brought the neat boundaries separating queers from the rest of men into question.

Disputing the Boundaries of the "Sexual"

The testimony generated by the navy investigation provided unusually detailed information about the social organization of men who identified themselves as "queer." But it also revealed that many more men than the queers were regularly engaging in some form of homosexual activity. Initially the navy expressed little concern about such men's behavior, for it did not believe that straight sailors' occasional liaisons with queers raised any questions about their sexual character. But the authorities' decision to prosecute men not normally labeled as queer ignited a controversy which ultimately forced the navy and its opponents to define more precisely what they believed constituted a homosexual act and to defend the basis upon which they categorized people participating in such acts. Because the controversy brought so many groups of people – working- and middle-class gay- and straight-identified enlisted men, middle-class naval officers, ministers, and town officials – into conflict, it revealed how differently those groups interpreted sexuality. A multiplicity of sexual discourses coexisted at a single moment in the civilian and naval seaport communities.

The gang itself loosely described the male population beyond its borders as "straight" but its members further divided the straight population into two different groups: those who would reject their sexual advances, and those who would accept them. A man was "trade," according to one fairy, if he "would stand to have 'queer' persons fool around [with] him in any way, shape or manner." The boundary separating trade from the rest of men was easy to cross. There were locations in Newport where straight men knew they could present themselves in order to be solicited. Even among "trade," gay men realized that some men would participate more actively than others in sexual encounters. Most gay men were said to prefer men who were strictly "straight and [would] not reciprocate in any way," but at least one fairy, as a decoy recorded, "wanted to kiss me and love me [and] . . . insisted and begged for it."[14] Whatever its origins, the term "trade" accurately described a common pattern of interaction between gay men and their straight sexual partners. In Newport, a gay man might take a sailor to a show or to dinner, offer him small gifts, or provide him with a place to stay when he was on overnight leave; in exchange, the sailor allowed his host to have sex with him that night, within whatever limits the sailor cared to set. The exchange was not always so elaborate: The navy's detectives reported several instances of gay men meeting and sexually servicing numerous sailors at the YMCA in a single evening. Men who were "trade" normally did not expect or demand direct payment for their services, although gay men did sometimes lend their partners small amounts of money without expecting it to be returned, and they used the term "trade" to refer to some civilians who, in contrast to the sailors, paid *them* for sexual services. "Trade" normally referred to straight-identified men who played the "masculine" role in sexual encounters solicited by "queers."[15]

Almost all straight sailors agreed that the effeminate members of the gang should be labeled "queer," but they disagreed about the sexual character of a straight man who accepted the sexual advances of a queer. Many straight men assumed that young recruits would accept the sexual solicitations of the perverts. "It was a shame to let these kids come in and run in to that kind of stuff," remarked one decoy; but his remarks indicate he did not think a boy was "queer" just because he let a queer have sex with him.[16] Most pogues defined themselves as "men who like to be browned," but straight men casually defined pogues as "[people] *that you can 'brown'*" and as men who "offered themselves in the same manner which women do."[17] Both remarks imply that "normal" men could take advantage of the pogues' availability without questioning their own identities as "straight"; the fact that the sailors made such potentially incriminating statements before the naval court indicates that this was an assumption they fully expected the court to share (as in fact it did). That lonesome men could unreservedly take advantage of a fairy's availability is perhaps also the implication, no matter how veiled in humor, of the remark made by a sailor stationed at the Melville coaling station: "It was common talk around that the Navy Department was getting good. They were sending a couple of 'fairies' up there for the 'sailors in Siberia.' As we used to call ourselves . . . meaning that we were all alone."[18] The strongest evidence of the social acceptability of trade was that the enlisted men who served as decoys volunteered to take on the role of trade for the purpose of infiltrating the gang, but were never even asked to consider assuming the role of queer. Becoming trade, unlike becoming a queer, posed no threat to the decoys' self-image or social status.

While many straight men took the sexual advances of gay men in stride, most engaged in certain ritual behavior designed to reinforce the distinction between themselves and the "queers." Most importantly, they played only the "masculine" sex role in their encounters with gay men – or at least claimed that they did – and observed the norms of masculinity in their own demeanor. They also ridiculed gay men and sometimes beat them up after sexual encounters. Other men, who feared it brought their manhood into question simply to be approached by a "pervert," were even more likely to attack gay men. Gang members recognized that they had to be careful about whom they approached. They all knew friends who had received severe beatings upon approaching the wrong man.[19] The more militant of the queers even played on straight men's fears. One of the queers at the Melville coaling station "made a remark that 'half the world is queer and the other half trade,'" recalled a straight sailor, who then described the harassment the queer suffered in retribution.[20] ...

As the investigation and trials proceeded, the men prosecuted by the navy made it increasingly difficult for the navy to maintain standards which categorized certain men as "straight" even though they had engaged in homosexual acts with the defendants. This was doubtless particularly troubling to the navy because, while its opponents focused their questions on the character of the decoys in particular, by doing so they implicitly questioned the character of *any* man who had sex with a "pervert". The decoys testified that they had submitted to the queers' sexual advances only in order to rid the navy of their presence, and the navy, initially at least, guaranteed their legal immunity. But the defendants readily charged that the decoys themselves were tainted by homosexual interest and had taken abnormal pleasure in their work. Reverend Kent's lawyers were particularly forceful in questioning the character of any man who would volunteer to work as a decoy. As one decoy after another helplessly answered each question with a quiescent "Yes, sir," the lawyers pressed them:

Q. You volunteered for this work?
A. Yes, sir.
Q. You knew what kind of work it was before you volunteered, didn't you?
A. Yes, sir.
Q. You knew it involved sucking and that sort of thing, didn't you?
A. I knew that we had to deal with that, yes, sir.
Q. You knew it included sodomy and that sort of thing, didn't you?
A. Yes, sir.
Q. And you were quite willing to get into that sort of work?
A. I was willing to do it, yes, sir.
Q. And so willing that you volunteered for it, is that right?
A. Yes, sir. I volunteered for it, yes, sir.
Q. You knew it included buggering fellows, didn't you?[21]

Such questions about the decoys' character were reinforced when members of the gang claimed that the decoys had sometimes taken the initiative in sexual encounters.

The defendants thus raised questions about the character of any man capable of responding to the advances of a pervert, forcing the navy to reexamine its standards for distinguishing "straight" from "perverted" sexuality. At the second naval court of inquiry, even the navy's judge advocate asked the men about how much sexual pleasure they had experienced during their contacts with the suspects. As the boundaries distinguishing acceptable from perverted sexual response began to crumble, the decoys recognized their vulnerability and tried to protect themselves. Some simply refused to answer any further questions about the sexual encounters they had described in graphic detail to the first court. One decoy protested that he had never responded to a pervert's advances: "I am a man.... The thing was so horrible in my sight that naturally I could not become passionate and there was no erection," but was immediately asked, "Weren't [the other decoys] men, too?" Another, less fortunate decoy had to plead:

> Of course, a great deal of that was involuntary inasmuch as a man placing his hand on my penis would cause an erection and subsequent emission. That was uncontrollable on my part.... Probably I would have had it [the emission] when I got back in bed anyway.... It is a physiological fact.[22]

But if a decoy could be suspected of perversion simply because he had a certain physiological response to a pervert's sexual advances, then the character of countless other sailors came under question. Many more men than the inner circle of queers and husbands would have to be investigated. In 1920, the navy was unprepared to take that step. The decision of the Dunn Inquiry to condemn the original investigation and the navy's decision to offer clemency to some of the men imprisoned as a result of it may be interpreted, in part, as a quiet retreat from that prospect.

Christian Brotherhood under Suspicion

The navy investigation raised fundamental questions concerning the definition of a "sexual relationship" itself when it reached beyond the largely working-class milieu of the military to label a prominent local Episcopal clergyman, Samuel Kent, and a YMCA volunteer and churchman, Arthur Leslie Green, as homosexual. When Kent fled the city, the navy tracked him down and brought him to trial on sodomy charges. Two courts acquitted him despite the fact that five decoys claimed to have had sex with him, because the denials of the respected minister and of the numerous clergymen and educators who defended him seemed more credible. Soon after Kent's second acquittal in early 1920, the Bishop of Rhode Island and the Newport Ministerial Union went on the offensive against the navy. The clergymen charged that the navy had used immoral methods in its investigation by instructing young enlisted men "in details of a nameless vice" and sending them into the community to entrap innocent citizens. They wrote letters of protest to the Secretary of the Navy and the President, condemned the investigation in the press, and forced the navy to convene a second court of inquiry into the methods used in the first inquiry. When it exculpated senior naval officials and failed to endorse all of the ministers' criticisms, the ministers persuaded the Republican-controlled Senate Naval Affairs Committee to undertake its own investigation, which eventually endorsed all of the ministers' charges.[23] . . .

When the navy charged that Kent's and Green's behavior and motives were perverted, many ministers feared that they could also be accused of perversion, and, more broadly, that the inquiry had questioned the ideology of nonsexual Christian brotherhood that had heretofore explained their devotion to other men. The confrontation between the two groups fundamentally represented a dispute over the norms for masculine gender behavior and over the boundaries between homosociality and homosexuality in the relations of men.

The investigation threatened Newport's ministers precisely because it repudiated those conventions that had justified and institutionalized a mode of behavior for men of the cloth or of the upper class that would have been perceived as effeminate in other men. The ministers' perception of this threat is reflected in their repeated criticism of the navy operatives' claim that they could detect perverts by their "looks and actions."[24] Almost all sailors and townspeople, as we have seen, endorsed this claim, but it put the ministers as a group in an extremely awkward position, for the major sign of a man's perversion according to most sailors was his being effeminate. As the ministers' consternation indicated, there was no single norm for masculine behavior at Newport; many forms of behavior considered effeminate on the part of working-class men were regarded as appropriate to the status of upper-class men or to the ministerial duties of the clergy. Perhaps if the navy had accused only working-class sailors, among whom "effeminacy" was more clearly deviant from group norms, of perversion, the ministers might have been content to let this claim stand. But when the naval inquiry also identified as perverted churchmen associated with such an upper-class institution as the Episcopal Church of Newport because of their perceived effeminacy, it challenged the norms which had heretofore shielded men of their background from such suspicions.

One witness tried to defend Kent's "peculiar" behavior on the basis of the conventional norms when he contended that "I don't know whether you would call it abnormal. He was a minister."[25] But the navy refused to accept this as a defense, and witnesses repeatedly described Kent and Green to the court as "peculiar," "sissyfied," and "effeminate." During his daily visits to patients at the hospital, according to a witness named Brunelle, Green held the patients' hands and "didn't talk like a man – he talk[ed] like a woman to me."[26] Since there is no evidence that Green had a high-pitched or otherwise "effeminate" *voice*, Brunelle probably meant Green addressed men with greater affection than he expected of a man. But all ministers visited with patients and spoke quiet, healing words to them; their position as ministers had permitted them to engage in such conventionally "feminine" behavior. When the navy and ordinary sailors labeled this behavior "effeminate" in the case of Green and Kent, and further claimed that such effeminacy was a sign of sexual perversion, they challenged the legitimacy of many Christian social workers' behavior. . . .

The ministers sought to defend Kent – and themselves – from the navy's insinuations by reaffirming the cultural interpretation of ministerial behavior as Christian and praiseworthy. While they denied the navy's charge that Kent had had genital contact with sailors, they did not deny his devotion to young men, for to have done so would have implicitly conceded the navy's interpretation of such behavior as salacious – and thus have left all ministers who had demonstrated similar devotion open to suspicion. . . . Rather than deny the government's claim that Kent had sought intimate relationships with sailors and devoted unusual attention to them, therefore, Kent and his supporters depicted such behavior as an honorable part of the man's ministry. Indeed, demonstrating just how much attention Kent had lavished on boys became as central to the strategy of the ministers as it was to that of the government, but the ministers offered a radically different interpretation of it. Their preoccupation with validating ministerial behavior turned Kent's trial and the second naval inquiry into an implicit public debate over the cultural definition of the boundaries between homosociality and homosexuality in the relations of men. The navy had defined Kent's behavior as sexual and perverted; the ministers sought to reaffirm that it was brotherly and Christian. . . .

The extent to which Kent's supporters were willing to interpret his intimacy with young men as brotherly rather than sexual is perhaps best illustrated by the effort of Kent's defense lawyer to show how Kent's inviting a decoy named Charles Zipf to sleep with him was only another aspect of his ministering to the boy's needs. Hadn't the decoy told Kent he was "lonesome" and had no place to sleep that night, the defense attorney pressed Zipf in cross-examination, before Kent invited him to spend the night in his parish house? And after Kent had set up a cot for Zipf in the living room, hadn't Zipf told Kent that he was "cold" before Kent pulled back the covers and invited him to join him in his bed?[27] The attorney counted on the presumption of Christian brotherhood to protect the minister's behavior from the suspicion of homosexual perversion, even though the same evidence would have seemed irrefutably incriminating in the case of another man.

Kent's defense strategy worked. Arguments based on assumptions about ministerial conduct persuaded the jury to acquit Kent of the government's charges. But Newport's ministers launched their campaign against the navy probe as soon as Kent was acquitted because they recognized that it had succeeded in putting their devotion to men under suspicion. It had raised questions about the cultural boundaries distinguishing homosexuality from homosociality that the ministers were determined to lay to rest.

But while it is evident that Newport's ministers feared the consequences of the investigation for their public reputations, two of their charges against the navy suggest that they may also have feared that its allegations contained some element of truth. The charges reflect the difference between the ministers' and the navy's understanding of sexuality and human sinfulness, but the very difference may have made the navy's accusations seem plausible in a way that the navy could not have foreseen. First, the ministers condemned the navy for having instructed young enlisted men – the decoys – "in the details of a nameless vice," and having ordered them to use that knowledge. The naval authorities had been willing to let their agents engage in sexual acts with the "queers" because they were primarily concerned about people manifesting a homosexual disposition rather than those engaging occasionally in homosexual acts. The navy asserted that the decoys' investigative purpose rendered them immune from criminal prosecution even though they had committed illegal sexual acts. But the ministers viewed the decoys' culpability as "a moral question ... not a technical question at all"; when the decoys had sex with other men, they had "scars placed on their souls" because, inescapably, "having immoral relations with men is an immoral act."[28] The sin was in the act, not the motive or the disposition. In addition, the ministers charged that the navy had directed the decoys to entrap designated individuals and that no one, no matter how innocent, could avoid entrapment by a skillful decoy. According to Bishop Perry, the decoys operated by putting men "into compromising positions, where they might be suspected of guilt, [even though they were] guiltless persons." Anyone could be entrapped because an "innocent advance might be made by the person operated upon and he might be ensnared against his will."[29] Implicitly, any clergyman could have done what Kent was accused of doing. Anyone's defenses could fall.

The ministers' preoccupation with the moral significance of genital sexual activity and their fear that anyone could be entrapped may reflect the continued saliency for them of the Christian precept that *all* people, including the clergy, were sinners subject to a variety of sexual temptations, including those of homosexual desire. According to this tradition, Christians had to resist homosexual temptations, as they resisted others, but simply to desire a homosexual liaison was neither a singular failing nor an indication of perverted character. The fact that the ministers never clearly elucidated this perspective and were forced increasingly to use the navy's own terms while contesting the navy's conclusions may reflect both the ministers' uncertainty and their recognition that such a perspective was no longer shared by the public.

In any case, making the commission of specified physical acts the distinguishing characteristic of a moral pervert made it definitionally impossible to interpret the ministers' relationships with sailors – no matter how intimate and emotionally moving – as having a "sexual" element, so long as they involved no such acts. Defining the sexual element in men's relationships in this narrow manner enabled the ministers to develop a bipartite defense of Kent which simultaneously denied he had had sexual relationships with other men and yet celebrated his profound emotional devotion to them. It legitimized (nonphysical) intimacy between men by precluding the possibility that such intimacy could be defined as sexual. Reaffirming the boundaries between Christian brotherhood and perverted sexuality was a central objective of the ministers' very public debate with the navy. But it may also have been of private significance to churchmen forced by the navy investigation to reflect on the nature of their brotherhood with other men.

Conclusion

The richly textured evidence provided by the Newport controversy makes it possible to re-examine certain tenets of recent work in the history of sexuality, especially the history of homosexuality. Much of that work, drawing on sociological models of symbolic interactionism and the labeling theory of deviance, has argued that the end of the nineteenth century witnessed a major reconceptualization of homosexuality. Before the last century, according to this thesis, North American and European cultures had no concept of the homosexual-as-person; they regarded homosexuality as simply another form of sinful behavior in which anyone might choose to engage. The turn of the century witnessed the "invention of the homosexual," that is, the new determination that homosexual desire was limited to certain identifiable individuals for whom it was an involuntary sexual orientation of some biological or psychological origin. The most prominent advocates of this thesis have argued that the medical discourse on homosexuality that emerged in the late nineteenth century played a determining role in this process, by creating and popularizing this new model of homosexual behavior (which they have termed the "medical model" of homosexuality). It was on the basis of the new medical models, they argue, that homo-sexually active individuals came to be labeled in popular culture – and to assume an identity – as sexual deviants different in nature from other people, rather than as sinners whose sinful nature was the common lot of humanity.[30]

The Newport evidence suggests how we might begin to refine and correct our analysis of the relationship between medical discourse, homosexual behavior, and identity. First, and most clearly, the Newport evidence indicates that medical discourse still played little or no role in the shaping of working-class homosexual identities and categories by World War I, more than thirty years after the discourse had begun. There would be no logical reason to expect that discussions carried on in elite journals whose distribution was limited to members of the medical and legal professions would have had any immediate effect on the larger culture, particularly the working class. In the Newport evidence, only one fairy even mentioned the favored medical term "invert," using it as a synonym for the already existing and widely recognized popular term "queer." Moreover, while "invert" was commonly used in the medical literature there is no reason to assume that it originated there, and the Newport witness specified that he had first heard it in theater circles and not through reading any "literature." The culture of the sexual under-ground, always in a complex relationship with the dominant culture, played a more important role in the shaping and sustaining of sexual identities.

More remarkably, medical discourse appears to have had as little influence on the military hierarchy as on the people of Newport. Throughout the two years of navy investigations related to Newport, which involved the highest naval officials, not a single medical expert was invited to present the medical perspective on the issues at stake. The only member of the original board of inquiry who even alluded to the published literature (and this on only one occasion during the Foster hearings, and once more at the second inquiry) was Dr E. M. Hudson, the welfare officer at the naval hospital and one of the decoys' super-visors. Hudson played a prominent role in the original investigation not because of his medical expertise, but because it was the flagrantly displayed (and normally tolerated) effeminacy and homosexuality of hospital staff and patients that first made naval officials consider undertaking an investigation. As the decoys' supervisor, Hudson drew on his training in fingerprinting and detective work considerably more than his medical background. Only after he became concerned that the decoys might be held legally culpable for their homosexual activity did he "read several medical books on the subject and read everything that I could find out as to what legal decisions there were on these cases."[31] But he never became very familiar with the medical discourse on sexual nonconformity; after his reading he still thought that the term "invert," which had first appeared in US medical journals almost forty years earlier, was "practically a new term," less than two years old.[32]

Moreover, Hudson only accepted those aspects of the medical analysis of homosexuality that confirmed popular perceptions. Thus he accepted as authoritative the distinction that medical writers drew between "congenital perverts" (called "queers" in common parlance) and "normal people submitting to acts of perversion, as a great many normal people do, [who] do not become perverts themselves," such as men isolated from women at a military base. He accepted this "scientific" distinction because it only confirmed what he and other naval officials already believed: that many sailors had sex with the queers without being "queer" themselves. But when the medical literature differed from the assumptions he shared with most navy men, he ignored it. Rather than adopting the medical viewpoint that homosexuals were biological anomalies who should be treated medically rather than willful criminals who should be deterred from homosexuality by severe legal penalties, for instance, he agreed with his colleagues that "these conditions existed and should be eradicated and the men guilty of offenses should be rounded up and punished."[33] In the course of 109 days of hearings, Dr Hudson referred to medical authorities only twice, and then only when they confirmed the assumptions of popular culture.

It thus appears more plausible to describe the medical discourse as a "reverse discourse," to use Michel Foucault's term, rather than as the central force in the creation of new sexual categories around which individuals shaped their personal identities. Rather than creating such categories as "the invert" and "the homosexual," the turn-of-the-century medical investigators whom Hudson read were trying to describe, classify and explain a pre-existing sexual underground whose outlines they only vaguely perceived. Their scientific categories largely reproduced those of popular culture, with "queers" becoming "inverts" in medical parlance but retaining the characteristic cross-gender behavior already attributed to them in popular culture. Doctors developed generalizations about homosexuals based on their idiosyncratic observations of particular individuals and admitted from the beginning that they were responding to the existence of communities of such people whose mysterious behavior and social organization they wished to explore. As one of the first American medical commentators observed in 1889, in explaining the need to study sexual perversion, "[t]here is in every community of any size a colony of male sexual perverts; they are usually known to each other, and are likely to congregate together."[34] By the time of the Newport investigation, medical researchers had developed an elaborate system of sexual classification and numerous explanations for individual cases of homosexuality, but they still had little comprehension of the complex social and cultural structure of gay life.

The Newport evidence helps put the significance of the medical discourse in perspective; it also offers new insights into the relationship between homosexual behavior and identity. Recent studies which have established the need to distinguish between homosexual behavior (presumably a transhistorically evident phenomenon) and the historically specific concept of homosexual identity have tended to focus on the evolution of people whose *primary* personal and political "ethnic" identification is as gay, and who have organized a multidimensional way of life on the basis of their homosexuality. The high visibility of such people in contemporary Western societies and their growing political significance make analysis of the historical development of their community of particular scholarly interest and importance. But the Newport evidence indicates that we need to begin paying more attention to *other* social forms of homosexuality – other ways in which homosexual relations have been organized and understood, differentiated, named, and left deliberately unnamed. We need to specify the *particularity* of various modes of homosexual behavior and the relationships between those modes and particular configurations of sexual identity.

For even when we find evidence that a culture has labeled people who were homosexually active as sexually deviant, we should not assume a priori that their homosexual activity was the determinative criterion in the labeling process. As in Newport, where many men engaged in certain kinds of homosexual behavior yet continued to be regarded as "normal," the assumption of particular sexual roles and deviance from gender norms may have been more important than the coincidence of male or female sexual partners in the classification of sexual character. "Fairies," "pogues," "husbands," and "trade" might all be labeled "homosexuals" in our own time, but they were labeled – and understood themselves – as fundamentally different kinds of people in World War I-era Newport. They all engaged in what we would define as homosexual behavior, but they and the people who observed them were more careful than we to draw distinctions between different modes of such behavior. To classify their behavior and character using the simple polarities of "homosexual" and "heterosexual" would be to misunderstand the complexity of their sexual system. Indeed, the very terms "homosexual behavior" and "identity," because of their tendency to conflate phenomena that other cultures may have regarded as quite distinct, appear to be insufficiently precise to denote the variety of social forms of sexuality we wish to analyze. . . .

The stigmatized image of the queer also helped to legitimate the behavior of men in Newport. Most observers did not label as queer either the ministers who were intimate with their Christian brothers or the sailors who had sex with effeminate men, because neither group conformed to the dominant image of what a queer should be like. Significantly, though, in their own minds the two groups of men legitimized their behavior in radically different ways: The ministers' conception of the boundary between acceptable and unacceptable male behavior was almost precisely the opposite of that obtaining among the sailors. The ministers made it impossible to define their relationships with sailors as "sexual" by making the commission of specified physical acts the distinguishing characteristic of a moral pervert. But even as the ministers argued that their relatively feminine character and deep emotional intimacy with other men were acceptable so long as they engaged in no physical contact with them, the sailors believed that their physical sexual contact with the queers remained acceptable so long as they avoided effeminate behavior and developed no emotional ties with their sexual partners.

At the heart of the controversy provoked and revealed by the Newport investigation was a confrontation between several such definitional systems, a series of disputes over the boundaries between homosociality and homosexuality in the relations of men and over the standards by which their masculinity would be judged. The investigation became controversial when it verged on suggesting that the homosocial world of the navy and the relationships between sailors and their Christian brothers in the Newport ministry were permeated by homosexual desire. Newport's ministers and leading citizens, the Senate Naval Affairs Committee, and to some extent even the navy itself repudiated the Newport inquiry because they found such a suggestion intolerable. Although numerous cultural interpretations of sexuality were allowed to confront each other at the inquiry, ultimately certain cultural boundaries had to be reaffirmed in order to protect certain relations as "nonsexual," even as the sexual nature of others was declared and condemned. The Newport evidence reveals much about the social organization and self-understanding of men who identified themselves as "queer." But it also provides a remarkable illustration of the extent to which the boundaries established between "sexual" and "nonsexual" relations are culturally determined, and it reminds us that struggles over the demarcation of those boundaries are a central aspect of the history of sexuality.

Notes

1   Murphy J. Foster presided over the first Court of Inquiry which began its work in Newport on 13 March 1919 and heard 406 pages of testimony in the course of 23 days (its records are hereafter cited as *Foster Testimony*). The second court of inquiry, convened in 1920 "to inquire into the methods employed ... in the investigation of moral and other conditions existing in the Naval Service; [and] to ascertain and inquire into the scope of and authority for said investigation," was presided over by Rear Admiral Herbert O. Dunn and heard 2500 pages of testimony in the course of 86 days (hereafter cited as *Dunn Testimony*). The second trial of Reverend Kent, *US v. Samuel Neal Kent*, heard in Rhode Island District Court in Providence beginning 20 January 1920, heard 532 pages of evidence (hereafter cited as *Kent Trial*). The records are held at the National Archives, Modern Military Field Branch, Suitland, Maryland, R. G. 125.

2   The term "homosociality" pertains to same-sex networks and associations; it is used here in contrast to same-sex associations that include overtly erotic and sexual behavior.

3   I have used "gay" in this essay to refer to men who identified themselves as sexually different from other men – and who labeled themselves and were labeled by others as "queer" – because of their assumption of "feminine" sexual and other social roles. As I explain below, not all men who were homosexually active labeled themselves in this manner, including men, known as "husbands," who were involved in long-term homosexual relationships but nonetheless maintained a "masculine" identity.

4   *Foster Testimony*, Ervin Arnold, 5; F. T. Brittain, 12; Thomas Brunelle, 21; *Dunn Testimony*, Albert Viehl, 307; Dudley Marriott, 1737.

5   Frederick Hoage, using a somewhat different construction than most, referred to them as "the inverted gang" (*Foster Testimony*, Hoage, 255).

6   *Foster Testimony*, Arnold, 5: *Dunn Testimony*, Clyde Rudy, 1783.

7   A man named Temple, for instance, had a room at the Y where he frequently took pickups (*Foster Testimony*, Brunelle, 207–8); on the role of the elevator operators, see William McCoy, 20; and Samuel Rogers, 61.

8   *Foster Testimony*, Arnold, 27; Hoage, 271; Harrison Rideout, 292.

9   Ibid., Hoage, 267; Rogers, 50; Brunelle, 185.

10   Ibid., George Richard, 143; Hoage, 298.

11   Ibid., Rideout, 69; see also, for example, Rogers, 63; Viehl, 175; Arnold, 3.

12   Ibid., Hoage, 313.

13   Ibid., Arnold, 5.

14   Ibid., Hoage, 269, 314; Rudy, 14.

15   Edward Stevenson described the "trade" involved in military prostitution in *The Intersexes: A History of Similisexualism* (privately printed, 1908), 214.

For an early sociological description of "trade," see Albert Reiss, Jr., "The Social Integration of Queers and Peers," *Social Problem* 9 (1961): 102–20.

16   *Dunn Testimony*, Paul, 1836; see also, e.g., Mayor Mahoney's comments, 703.
17   *Foster Testimony*, James Daniel Chase, 119 (my emphasis); Zipf, 375.
18   Ibid., Smith, 169.
19   See, e.g., the accounts of Hoage, *Foster Testimony*, 271–2, and Rideout, 87.
20   *Foster Testimony*, Smith, 169.
21   *Kent Trial*, defense attorney's interrogation of Charles McKinney, 66–7. See also, e.g., the examination of Zipf in *Kent Trial*, esp. 27–8.
22   Ibid., Zipf, 2113, 2131 (the court repeatedly turned to the subject). The "manly" decoy was Clyde Rudy, 1793.
23   The ministers' efforts are reviewed and their charges affirmed in the Senate report, 67th Congress, 1st session, Committee on Naval Affairs, *Alleged Immoral Conditions of Newport (R.I.) Naval Training Station* (Washington, DC: 1921), and in the testimony of Bishop Perry and Reverend Hughes before the Dunn Inquiry.
24   Hudson quoted in the Senate report, *Alleged Immoral Conditions*, 8: see also *Dunn Testimony*, Tobin, 723; cf. Arnold, 1712. For the ministers' criticism, see, e.g., Bishop Perry, 529, 607.
25   *Foster Testimony*, Hoage, 319.
26   Ibid., Brunelle, 216. He says the same of Kent on p. 217.
27   *Kent Trial*, interrogation of Zipf, 37–8.
28   *Dunn Testimony*, Reverend Deming, 42; Bishop Perry, 507.
29   Ibid., Bishop Perry, 678.
30   This argument was first introduced by Mary McIntosh, "The Homosexual Role," *Social Problems* 16 (1968): 182–92, and has been developed and modified by Jeffrey Weeks, *Coming Out: Homosexual Politics in Britain from the Nineteenth Century to the Present* (London: 1977).
31   *Dunn Testimony*, Hudson, 1630.
32   *Foster Testimony*, 300. The transcript does not identify the speaker, but the context strongly suggests it was Hudson.
33   *Dunn Testimony*, 1628, 1514.
34   George Frank Lydston, "Sexual Perversion, Satyriasis, and Nymphomania," *Medical and Surgical Reporter* 61 (1889): 254. See also George Chauncey, "From Sexual Inversion to Homosexuality: Medicine and the Changing Conceptualization of Female Deviance," *Salmagundi* 58/59 (Fall 1982/Winter 1983), 142–3.

Documents

The first document is an excerpt from the 1920 Senate subcommittee's investigation into allegations of homosexuality at the naval training station at Newport, Rhode Island. An earlier investigation had exposed an entrapment scheme whereby young navy recruits were ordered to lure prospective male partners in order to catch them performing homosexual acts. Whereas the first investigation into these activities exonerated the navy from any wrong-doing, this Senate report denounced the navy's methods for uncovering "alleged sexual perverts." What exactly did the Senate find objectionable with the navy's approach? Do the findings show concern for the men entrapped or for the decoys following naval orders?

Alleged Immoral Conditions and Practices at the Naval Training Station, Newport, Rhode Island

Various charges and allegations with reference to conditions at the training station at Newport were made by the leading clergymen of Newport. These were followed by seven separate and distinct allegations (in substance similar to those of the clergymen) made by the Providence Journal, as follows:

First Allegation

That young men, many of them boys in the naval service, have been compelled, under specific orders of officers attached to the Office of Naval Intelligence, to commit vile and nameless acts on the persons of others in the Navy service, or have suggested these acts to be practiced on themselves.

The evidence before this committee establishes the following facts:

(1) Forty-one members of the Navy personnel were from time to time after June 6, 1919, detailed by orders of Franklin D. Roosevelt, Assistant Secretary of the Navy, as members of a secret squad of investigators or detectives for the purpose of investigating sexual perversion in and about Newport.

(2) This section was known as section A, O. A. S. N. (Office of the Assistant Secretary of the Navy). The men assigned to this section were

---

Excerpted from the Report of the Committee on Naval Affairs, United States Senate, Sixty-seventh Congress, First Session, Relative to Alleged Immoral Conditions and Practices at the Naval Training Station, Newport, RI (Washington, DC: Government Printing Office, 1921), reprinted in Jonathan Katz, *Government versus Homosexuals* (New York: Arno Press, 1975), pp. 6–8, 26, 30.

placed under the direct command of Lieut. Erasmus M. Hudson, Medical Corps, United States Navy, and Chief Machinist's Mate Ervin Arnold, United States Navy, with headquarters arranged for in New York by Franklin D. Roosevelt, Assistant Secretary of the Navy. The ages of these men, with the single exception of Arnold, ranged from 16 to 32; 10 of the 41 men were between 16 and 19 years of age, and the remainder, except Arnold, ranges in age from 21 to 32. Arnold was 44 years of age.

(3) May 5, 1919, Assistant Secretary Franklin D. Roosevelt, in a confidential memorandum directed to Rear Admiral Albert P. Niblack, director of naval intelligence, asked that Lieut. Hudson and Arnold be attached to the Office of Naval Intelligence (the secret service of the Navy). The usual identification cards given to men attached to the Office of Naval Intelligence were immediately issued to Hudson and Arnold by order of Admiral Niblack and both men were ordered to New York. There is no evidence to show that these men were at some later date detached from Naval Intelligence, although they were subsequently detailed for special investigation duty to the Office of the Assistant Secretary of the Navy, in accordance with Naval Regulations.

(4) The evidence shows that members of this squad of young men and boys, known as section A, O. A. S. N., permitted the basest of vile acts to be performed upon them at the suggestion, instigation, instruction, or order, it matters not the designation, of Lieut. Hudson and Chief Machinist's Mate Arnold, immediately in command of them.

(5) The instructions given to these young men were: To frequent places where immoral practices were suspected of being carried on; to place themselves in a position where an alleged sexual pervert might make improper advances upon them; that they were at all times to remain passive and not take the initiative or solicit, and were to use their own judgment and discretion as to how far the improper advances of the alleged sexual pervert should be permitted.

(6) Such were the acknowledged official instructions issued to boys, some of whom were not over 19 years of age. It is unfortunately necessary to state that in some cases the men used their "judgment" and "discretion" and allowed to be committed upon themselves the most vile and unnameable acts.

Second Allegation

That the victims selected for traps of this character have been picked out in every case by Lieut. Erasmus Mead Hudson, of the Medical Corps, and Ervin Arnold, machinist's mate, both of whom have declared that they were able to recognize degenerates by the way they walk along the streets.

(7) The testimony of Arnold is clear that the names of suspected perverts or "a man that was under suspicion or some one told us he was acting peculiar," were given by him to the operators. These men were followed and the opportunity given them to commit lewd or immoral acts – in other words they were "trapped" within the police meaning of the word for the purpose of securing sufficient evidence to convict them.

(8) Arnold testified before this committee:

> I can take you up on Riverside Drive at night and show them [perverts] to you and if you follow them up nine times out of ten you will find it is true.

Hudson testified before the Dunn court of inquiry that he could recognize degenerates by their "looks and actions." He made practically this same statement to James De Wolfe Perry, jr., bishop of Rhode Island. Such statements as were made before this committee, before the Dunn court of inquiry, and before Bishop Perry would most naturally lead anyone to believe that Hudson and Arnold claimed the power, as charged by Bishop Perry and the Providence Journal, to recognize a degenerate at sight, and the committee are of the opinion that this construction placed upon the statements of Hudson and Arnold is not without ample justification....

The arrest and trial of a man of Kent's standing in Newport caused much indignation among the residents of that city. It was not so much a question of the guilt or innocence of the men accused as it was the methods that were being employed by the Navy Department to secure evidence. The facts became known at the Brown and Kent trials that young men, many of them boys, had received instructions to allow immoral acts to be performed upon them if in their judgement such an act was necessary to secure evidence.

It is but necessary to read the evidence before the committee to realize the dreadful state of affairs that was brought about as a result of the instructions issued to members of section A by their superior officers. Testimony at the second Kent trial in Providence, as well as testimony before the Dunn court of inquiry and before this committee, shows that these boys not only permitted one act to be performed upon them, but returned time after time to the same suspect and allowed a number of acts to be performed. Capt. Wainwright, when he investigated the activities of section A, reported to Capt. Leigh that one operator had acknowledged four completed acts, three other men three completed acts each, one two completed acts, and the remainder of the 11 men he questioned owned up to one act apiece. One lad stated that he had had one attempt made upon him but had not allowed a completed act.

On September 3, the Rev. Stanley C. Hughes and Hamilton Fish Webster, of Newport, called upon Franklin D. Roosevelt and in a general way explained to him the methods employed by men under the command of Hudson and attached to the office of the Assistant Secretary of the Navy while attempting to secure evidence. At this time they presented to Franklin D. Roosevelt a transcript of part of the testimony given at the Kent trial in Newport, and asked that a statement be made by the Navy Department exonerating Mr. Kent.

In this connection the committee wishes it understood that it has not inquired into the guilt or innocence of any of the men arrested, either among the enlisted personnel or civilians. The committee was not appointed for that purpose. It was named only to inquire into the alleged immoral practices of the enlisted personnel at Newport in their efforts to secure evidence against all alleged sexual perverts. . . .

(10) Lieut. Hudson and Ervin Arnold had knowledge at the time the acts were performed, that boys were lending their physical bodies for immoral purposes under the screen that they were acting for the good of the service. Official and semiofficial authority protected these lads from civil prosecution. They went forth into Newport and vicinity as a sacrifice to, and the prey of every degenerate and sexual pervert, male and female, in the city and at the training station.

(11) The details of this work, according to their own statements, were left to the arbitrary ideas of a totally unknown Navy doctor and an equally unknown petty officer. Neither of these men had had any practical experience fitting him for an investigation of this character, nor apparently any sense of moral obligation. Hudson was a full-fledged physician and knew something about finger-print methods of crime detection. Arnold's experience as a detective in Connecticut did not qualify him for the position he occupied as the officer immediately in charge of and directing the activities of these young and inexperienced men, and the committee is of the opinion that he is in no manner fitted to be in charge of men in any capacity.

(12) Many of these boys were immature in mind and experience. Their first instruction in the service was that orders were to be unhesitatingly and implicitly obeyed. Orders, to them, either expressed or implied, were orders in the strictest sense of the word. Before they were told what acts they were to perform, Arnold showed them the order of Capt. Campbell, detailing them to his (Arnold's) command. Then he explained the nature of the work. It matters not, in the minds of the committee, that not one boy declined the assignment. Under the circumstances, it is reasonable to believe that none refused the duty simply because he hesitated to decline in the face of the order signed by Capt. Campbell, detailing him to Arnold's command. One might

argue that each boy who accepted the assignment was himself a pervert. This, the committee does not believe. It does believe that these lads were practically forced into this duty because of their ignorance of naval procedure and civil law and their mental perspective regarding the obedience of any order given them by a superior.

(13) It is to be regretted that one connected with the Naval Establishment should have allowed such a situation to develop. Better far that perversion in Newport should have been stamped out by the arbitrary wholesale discharge of suspected perverts in the service, as at first suggested by Capt. Campbell, and the arbitrary running out of town by the Department of Justice of every suspected civilian pervert, male or female, as could have been done under the emergency war laws, than that one innocent boy in the naval service should have been placed in the position of allowing his body to be polluted – a crime perpetrated upon him which he will remember and regret to his dying day.

(14) The committee can not express in too strong language its condemnation of the methods of investigations at Newport from the time the Foster court of inquiry was organized in March, 1919, to the time when orders were given to Hudson to discontinue the work of section A, O. A. S. N., on September 20, 1919. Assistant Secretary Franklin D. Roosevelt, to whose office section A was attached, is, in the opinion of the committee, morally responsible for the orders issued by Hudson and Arnold.

The Intersexes: a History of Similisexualism

Edward Irenaeus Prime Stevenson

In this 1908 document, Edward Stevenson describes the two stereotypic profiles of homosexual men, or uranians, from the Greek goddess of love. Heavily indebted to Dr Richard von Krafft-Ebing, Stevenson collected and summarized much of the popular medical and lay research of the time. How might Stevenson have reacted to the naval investigation that Chauncey analyzes? How does his explanation of homosexuality in the military help to explain the incident?

Excerpted from Edward Irenaeus Prime Stevenson, *The Intersexes: a History of Similisexualism* (privately printed, 1908; reprinted New York: Arno Press, 1975), pp. 158–9, 212–14.

Two Leading Types of Uranian Youth

Two types of Uranian boyhood prevail. The child being in this the father of the man, as in other foreshadowings. One is the physically delicate youth, graceful, spiritual, and dreamy, highly impressionable. To this type also belong often detail of uncertain health, of shunning the ruder sports of lads, of indifference or dislike to the society of noisy male playmates; along with a proportionate relish for playing with girls, dressing in girls' clothing, and a natural ease of comporting oneself in it. A boy should never be permitted to "dress up" in female apparel, nor a girl allowed to travesty herself as a boy. To such a delicate boy-type, pertains the love of quiet, of solitude, tastes for reading and for arts, admiration of what is beautiful rather than what is rudely grand and heroic, and of intellect, not action. Above all, in such young Uranians occurs vivid appreciation of adult male beauty, the charm of mature male society, when the man concerned is gentle of temperament and gifted. These later traits are more or less recurrent in heterosexual youths. But they arrive at a proper proportion in normal lads as virile maturity advances and they do not have that sentimental tinge in normal boys that they possess in the young Uranian. This Uranian frequently matures to "passive" sexuality.

The second type of young Uranian has nothing feminine in his tastes. He is, on the contrary, averse to girlish interests in life. He, indeed, passionately attaches himself to friends. He perhaps is wholly careless of other relationships. Often he is noticed as concentrating his sentimental nature, so far as it is revealed, on one or another intimacy with a boy, no matter what be the masculinity of his general equipment. At least, this is frequently a trait in him. But in his case, as in that of the relatively feminine youth, there is the superseding sense of the beauty of the male physique and male character, indifference to girlish charms, and inner responsiveness to what is manly attractiveness. Perhaps it is all hid; reserved by the lad with great pains. Naturally, this type is far less easy to separate from the normal-natured lad growing up into a quite dionistic nature. But often it is strong "active" Uranianism, under a vigorously boyish veil. . . .

Military Prostitution

To the important topic of male prostitution in general an extended reference will occur in this book presently. But at this point must be noticed specifically military prostitution; particularly by young soldiers in large cities and garrisons. . . .

In some cases the young soldier is more or less constitutionally homosexual. He likes coition only with a male, and would seek that, even could he not expect to be paid for it, like any other harlot. In a proportion of examples he is bi-sexual. Perhaps he is too poor to give himself heterosexual relief through a brothel; or else is afraid of disease. In another proportion, the soldier is not at all homosexual. He sells his body to a stranger, or regular patron, simply as an easy though rather irksome avocation. A mercenary motive is probably the most common. . . .

We will suppose the lad tall, well-built, robust and from eighteen to twenty years old. He is probably not sexually "innocent." If he be so, and hears what is said among his fellows in the barracks, he soon loses in moral sensitiveness. As was said, he may not be – often he is not – a born homosexual. But he allows himself to drift into the practice of sitting in public resorts where strangers come: in the parks and restaurant-gardens, well-known for equivocal usefulness. He goes to certain baths, to cheap cafés and theaters, of like repute; letting friendly gentlemen scrape acquaintance with him. In a park or suburb, comes the classic aid of a cigarette. Complaisantly he "takes walks" into secluded corners of the place with affectionate strangers, or gets into the way of accompanying them to their lodgings, for an hour or so. The price of giving his physical beauty and sexual vigor, even if with no good-will for the act, to the embraces of some casual homosexual client brings him more money in half an hour than he is likely to receive as his whole week's pay, even at the low *quid pro quo* of two or three marks, a couple of florins, three or four lire, or a couple of half crowns, for his amiabilities. The "trade" aspect of it grows on him. – "Why not?" he asks himself. The commerce in a large town becomes easy, successful, and it is practically undetected. He soon discovers that whatever is suspected among his companions of him or of each other, little is said. So many of his fellows engage in the same by-trade of an evening! And as indicated, while soldier-prostitutes may vastly prefer sexual intercourse with women, and may make homosexual complaisances pay for normal gratifications, still, they are likely to lose repugnance to homosexual coitions. Many a young soldier grows into preferring it: he literally first "endures" then "embraces" it. Lasting intimacies are formed between soldier-prostitutes and civilians, when a particular regiment is stationed long in the same city.

Sexual Perversion, Satyriasis, and Nymphomania

G. Frank Lydston, MD

Delivered at the College of Physicians and Surgeons in Chicago, Illinois, this lecture unveils the popular medical position on homosexuality in 1889. The author argues for a biological interpretation rather than a strictly moral understanding of homosexuality, yet his moralistic language undermines his scientific intentions. How does the author create a distinction between "sexual perversion" and "the normal method" in this article? Does he suggest that this "vicious impulse" is hereditary, acquired, or both?

Gentlemen: The subject of sexual perversion, *Contrare Sexualempfindung,* although a disagreeable one for discussion, is one well worthy the attention of the scientific physician, and is of great importance in its social, medical, and legal relations.

The subject has been until a recent date studied solely from the standpoint of the moralist, and from the indisposition of the scientific physician to study the subject, the unfortunate class of individuals who are characterized by perverted sexuality have been viewed in the light of their moral responsibility rather than as the victims of a physical and incidentally of a mental defect. It is certainly much less humiliating to us as atoms of the social fabric to be able to attribute the degradation of these poor unfortunates to a physical cause, than to a wilful viciousness over which they have, or ought to have, volitional control. Even to the moralist there should be much satisfaction in the thought that a large class of sexual perverts are physically abnormal rather than morally leprous. It is often difficult to draw the line of demarcation between physical and moral perversion. Indeed, the one is so often dependent upon the other that it is doubtful whether it were wise to attempt the distinction in many instances. But this does not affect the cogency of the argument that the sexual pervert is generally a physical aberration – *a lusus naturæ....*

There is in every community of any size a colony of male sexual perverts; they are usually known to each other, and are likely to congregate together. At times they operate in accordance with some definite and concerted plan in quest of subjects wherewith to gratify

Excerpted from G. Frank Lydston, MD, "Sexual Perversion, Satyriasis, and Nymphomania," *Medical and Surgical Reporter,* 41 (September 7, 1889), pp. 253–6.

their abnormal sexual impulses. Often they are characterized by effeminacy of voice, dress, and manner. In a general way, their physique is apt to be inferior – a defective physical make-up being quite general among them, although exceptions to this rule are numerous.

Sexual perversion is more frequent in the male; women usually fall into perverted sexual habits for the purpose of pandering to the depraved tastes of their patrons rather than from instinctive impulses. Exceptions to this rule are occasionally seen. For example, I know of an instance of a woman of perfect physique, who is not a professional prostitute, but moves in good society, who has a fondness for women, being never attracted to men for the purpose of ordinary sexual indulgence, but for perverted methods. . . .

There is one element in the study of sexual perversion that deserves especial attention. It is probable that few bodily attributes are more readily transmitted to posterity than peculiarities of sexual physiology. The offspring of the abnormally carnal individual is likely to be possessed of the same inordinate sexual appetite that characterizes the parent. The child of vice has within it, in many instances, the germ of vicious impulse, and no purifying influence can save it from following its own inherent inclinations. Men and women who seek, from mere satiety, variations of the normal method of sexual gratification, stamp their nervous systems with a malign influence which in the next generation may present itself as true sexual perversion. Acquired sexual perversion in one generation may be a true constitutional and irradicable vice in the next, and this independently of gross physical aberrations. Carelessness on the part of parents is responsible for some cases of acquired sexual perversion. Boys who are allowed to associate intimately, are apt to turn their inventive genius to account by inventing novel means of sexual stimulation, with the result of ever after diminishing the natural sexual appetite. Any powerful impression made upon the sexual system at or near puberty, when the sexual apparatus is just maturing and very active, although as yet weak and impressionable, is apt to leave an imprint in the form of sexual peculiarities that will haunt the patient throughout his after life. Sexual congress at an early period, often leaves its impression in a similar manner. Many an individual has had reason to regret the indulgences of his youth because of its moral effect upon his after life. The impression made upon him in the height of his youthful sensibility is never eradicated, but remains in his memory as his ideal of sexual matters; for – if you will pardon the metaphor – there is a physical as well as an intellectual memory. As he grows older and less impressionable, he seeks vainly for an experience similar to that of his youth, and so joins the ranks of the sexual monomaniacs, who vainly chase the Will-o'-the-wisp: sexual gratification, all their lives. Variations of circumstance may determine sexual perversion rather than abnormally powerful desire. Let the physician who has the confidence of his patients inquire into this matter, and he will be surprised at the result. Only a short time since, one of my patients, a man of exceptional intellect, volunteered a similar explanation for his own excesses. Satiety also brings in its train a deterioration of normal sexual sensibility, with an increase, if anything, in the sexual appetite. As a result, the deluded and unfortunate being seeks for new and varied means of gratification, often degrading in the extreme. Add to this condition, intemperance or disease, and the individual may become the lowest type of sexual pervert. As Hammond concisely puts it, regarding one of the most disgusting forms of sexual perversion: "Pederasty is generally a vice resorted to by debauchees who exhaust the resources of the normal stimulus of the sexual act, and who for a while find in this new procedure the pleasure which they can no longer obtain from intercourse with women."

Further Reading

Berube, Allan. *Coming out under Fire: the History of Gay Men and Women in World War II.* New York: Free Press, 1990.

Chauncey, George. *Gay New York: Gender, Urban Culture, and the Making of the Gay Male World, 1890–1940.* New York: Basic Books, 1994.

Chauncey, George. "From sexual inversion to homosexuality: the changing medical conception of female 'deviance'." In Kathy Peiss and Christina Simmons (eds), *Passion and Power: Sexuality in History.* Philadelphia: Temple University Press, 1989, pp. 87–117.

Katz, Jonathan Ned. *The Invention of Heterosexuality.* New York: Penguin, 1995.

Somerville, Siobhan. "Scientific racism and the emergence of the homosexual body." *Journal of the History of Sexuality*, 5 (1994), 243–66.

Terry, Jennifer. *An American Obsession: Science, Medicine, and Homosexuality in Modern Society.* Chicago: University of Chicago Press, 1999.

Ullman, Sharon. *Sex Seen: the Emergence of Modern Sexuality in America.* Berkeley: University of California Press, 1997.

Wood, Mary. "How we got this way: the sciences of homosexuality and the Christian right." *Journal of Homosexuality*, 38 (2000), 19–40.

9

About to Meet Her Maker

Introduction

Leslie Reagan's essay examines a time in American history when having an abortion was illegal. Nevertheless, from the mid-nineteenth century to 1973, women still had unwanted pregnancies, and many chose to abort, often despite dire consequences. Though women were not usually prosecuted for aborting, they suffered greatly from botched medical procedures, and sometimes they died.

The state, eager to prosecute abortionists, sought women's dying declarations: statements of remorse made by dying women which named the illicit medical practitioner as well as the man who shared responsibility for the pregnancy. These declarations, recorded by doctors or hospital officials, were turned over to the state in the event of a woman's death. Doctors found themselves in a bind: some were eager to avoid prosecution themselves and thus encouraged women to name their abortionists; others concerned about confidentiality shielded their records from the state, refusing to act as police in this effort.

Attempts to attain dying declarations created and reinforced norms of "proper" sexual behavior. Women were asked personal questions about their sexual histories that went far beyond the information necessary to find abortionists. Though married women also had abortions, single women were pressured by state officials to reveal their lovers, and the male partners of single women only were arrested, jailed, and sometimes prosecuted as accessories to crime. Thus marriage was exalted, the only reasonable solution to the predicament of pregnancy.

"About to Meet Her Maker": Women, Doctors, Dying Declarations, and the State's Investigation of Abortion, Chicago, 1867–1940

Leslie J. Reagan

In March 1916, Carolina Petrovitis, a Lithuanian immigrant to Chicago, married with two small children, was in terrible pain following her abortion. Her friends called in Dr. Maurice Kahn. The doctor asked her, "Who did it for you[?]" He "coaxed" her to answer, then told her, "If you won[']t tell me what was done to you I can't handle your case." When Petrovitis finally revealed that a midwife had performed an abortion, Dr. Kahn called for an ambulance, sent her to a hospital, told the hospital physician of the situation, and suggested he "communicate with the Coroner's office." Three police officers soon arrived to question Petrovitis. With the permission of the hospital physician, Sgt. William E. O'Connor "instructed" an intern to "tell her she is going to die." The sergeant and another officer accompanied the intern to the woman's bedside. As the doctor told Petrovitis of her impending death, she "started to cry – her eyes watered." Sure that Petrovitis realized she was about to die, the police then collected from her a "dying declaration" in which she named the midwife who performed her abortion, told where and when it was done and the price paid, and described the instruments used. Later the police brought in the midwife and asked Petrovitis "if this was the woman," and she nodded "yes." A third police officer drew up another dying statement "covering the facts." He read that statement back to Petrovitis as she lay in bed "in pain, vomiting," and she made her "mark" on the statement. Then she died.[1]

Carolina Petrovitis's experience in 1916 provides an example of the standard medical and investigative procedures used in criminal abortion cases. This account, drawn from the Cook County coroner's inquest into Petrovitis's death, illustrates this essay's major themes: the state's interest in obtaining dying declarations in order to prosecute abortionists; the intimate questioning endured by women during official investigations into abortion; and the ways in which physicians and

Excerpted from Leslie J. Reagan, " 'About to Meet Her Maker': Women, Doctors, Dying Declarations, and the State's Investigation of Abortion, Chicago, 1867–1940," *Journal of American History*, 77 (March 1991), pp. 1240–64.

hospitals served the state in collecting evidence in criminal abortion cases.

Abortion had not always been a crime. During the eighteenth and early nineteenth centuries, early abortions were legal under common law. Abortions were illegal only after quickening, the point at which a pregnant woman could feel the movements of the fetus (at approximately sixteen weeks' gestation). In the 1840s and 1850s, abortion became commercialized and was increasingly used by married, white, native-born, Protestant women of the middle and upper classes. In 1857, the newly organized American Medical Association (AMA) initiated the ultimately successful crusade to make abortion illegal. Regular physicians, such as those who formed the AMA, were motivated to organize for the criminalization of abortion in part by their desire to win professional power, control medical practice, and restrict their irregular competitors, including homeopaths, midwives, and others. Hostility toward feminists, immigrants, and Catholics fueled the medical campaign against abortion and the passage of criminal abortion laws by state legislatures.[2] In response to the physicians' campaign, in 1867 Illinois criminalized abortion and in 1871 outlawed the sale of abortifacients (drugs used to induce abortions) without a prescription. The new statues permitted only therapeutic abortions performed when pregnancy threatened a woman's life. By the end of the century, every state had restricted abortion.[3]

The history of the nineteenth-century criminalization of abortion has been well studied, as has the movement to decriminalize it in the 1960s and 1970s. We know very little, however, about the practice or control of abortion while it was illegal in the United States.

This is the first study to address a crucial question in the history of reproduction: How did the state enforce the criminal abortion laws? I examine the methods of enforcement in Chicago from 1867, when Illinois made abortion illegal, to 1940, when changing conditions of abortion during the depression brought changes in the control of abortion. This study is based on research in legal records from the city of Chicago, Cook County, and Illinois and in the national medical literature. Coroners' inquests have been especially rich sources. The evidence shows continuity in the patterns of control followed by government officials in Chicago, and across the nation, for over half a century. In that period, in cases involving abortion, the state prosecuted chiefly abortionists, most often after a woman had died, and prosecutors relied for evidence on dying declarations collected from women near death due to their illegal abortions. Furthermore, the state focused on regulating the use of abortion by working-class women.

The history of abortion reveals the complexity of the medical profession's role in sexual regulation. Feminists, writing primarily in the 1970s, have tended to portray the medical profession as intent on controlling female sexuality. My analysis of the regulation of abortion shifts the focus away from the medical profession and to the state as the regulator of sexual and reproductive behavior. To obtain evidence against abortionists, the state needed to have physicians reporting abortions and collecting dying declarations from their patients, which many doctors were reluctant to do. Without doctors' cooperation, police and prosecutors could do little to enforce the criminal abortion laws. Illinois law did not require doctors to report evidence of abortions. But by threatening physicians with prosecution, officials successfully pulled doctors into a partnership with the state in the suppression of abortion. In cases of illegal abortion, doctors were caught in the middle between their responsibilities to their patients and the demands of government officials.... This essay analyzes the experience of ordinary people caught in criminal investigations, the routine procedures of the legal system, rather than analyzing the volume of cases that reached the courts or judicial rulings. In abortion cases, the investigative procedures themselves constituted a form of punishment and control.

Although women were not arrested, prosecuted, or incarcerated for having abortions, the state nonetheless punished working-class women for having illegal abortions through official investigations and public exposure of their abortions. Recognizing the impact of the criminal abortion laws on women requires looking closely at the details of women's experiences: especially the interactions between women and their doctors and between women and police and petty state officials. Our understanding of what punishment is needs to be refined and redefined, particularly in cases of women who violate sexual norms, to include more subtle methods of disciplining individuals. The penalties imposed on women for having illegal abortions were not fines or jail sentences, but humiliating interrogations about sexual matters by male officials – often conducted at women's deathbeds. During investigations of abortion, police, coroner's officers, and prosecutors followed standard procedures in order to achieve the larger end of putting abortionists out of business. No evidence suggests that officials consciously designed their investigative procedures to harass women, yet the procedures were punitive, and this punishment became a central aspect of the state's efforts to control abortion. For government officials, the procedures were routine; for women subjected to them, the procedures were frightening and shameful once-in-a-lifetime events. Moreover, media attention to abortion deaths warned all women that those who strayed from marriage and motherhood would suffer death and shameful publicity.

This essay also highlights the gendered character both of legally enforced standards of behavior and of punishment. The criminalization of abortion not only prohibited abortion but demanded conformity to gender norms, which required men and women to marry, women to bear children, and men to bear the financial responsibility of children. Although most women who had abortions were married, state officials focused on unwed women and their partners. Coroners' inquests into the abortion-related deaths of unwed women reveal the state's interest in forcing working-class men to marry the women they had impregnated. Historians of sexuality have given little attention to the regulation of male heterosexuality, concentrating instead on the sexual control of women and "deviants." Yet in the late nineteenth and early twentieth centuries, I was surprised to find, the state punished unmarried working-class men whose lovers died after an abortion. The sexual double standard certainly existed, but the state imposed penalties on men, in certain unusual situations, when they failed to carry out their paternal obligation to marry their pregnant lovers and head a "nuclear" family. Unmarried men implicated in abortion deaths were, like women, punished through embarrassing questions about their sexual behavior; in general, the state punished men in more conventionally recognized ways: arresting, jailing, and prosecuting them. . . .

Despite legal prohibitions, each year thousands of women around the country had abortions. In 1904 Dr. Charles Sumner Bacon estimated that "six to ten thousand abortions are induced in Chicago every year." Both midwives and physicians performed abortions in the early twentieth century, and many women induced their own abortions at home. At drugstores, women could buy abortificients and instruments, such as rubber catheters, to induce abortions. Most women survived their abortions, and most abortions remained hidden from state authorities. Yet, the number of deaths following illegal abortions was significant. In the late 1920s, a Children's Bureau study documented that at least 11 percent of deaths related to pregnancy and childbearing followed illegal abortion.[4]

Working-class women's poverty – in both wealth and health care – made it more likely that they, rather than middle-class women, would reach official attention for having abortions. All forty-four Cook County coroner's inquests that I have examined recorded investigations into the abortions and deaths of white, working-class women. Over half of the women were immigrants or daughters of immigrants. Working-class women may have had more abortions than did middle-class women. In addition, poor women, lacking funds, often used inexpensive, and often dangerous, self-induced measures and delayed calling in doctors if

they had complications. By the time poor women sought medical attention, they had often reached a critical stage and, as a result, had come
to the attention of officials. Affluent women avoided official investigations into their abortions because they had personal relations with private physicians, many of whom never collected dying statements,
destroyed such statements, or falsified death certificates. If necessary,
wealthier families might be able to pressure or pay physicians, coroners,
the police, and the press to keep quiet about a woman's abortion- related
death.[5]

I found only one case in which the Cook County coroner investigated
the abortion-related death of a black woman, in 1916, and, unfortunately, there is no record of the coroner's inquest into it. Despite a
tremendous increase in Chicago's black population after World War I,
I did not find any cases involving black women in the 1920s or 1930s.
The paucity of information on the abortion-related deaths of black
women may be an artifact of bias in the sources or may reflect the
relatively small size of Chicago's black population. Black women who
called in doctors or entered hospitals after their abortions would
presumably have been questioned as Petrovitis was. They might have
found it particularly upsetting to be questioned by white police officers
or coroner's staff. A black physician prosecuted for abortion complained
of racist treatment by the coroner's office; black women dying due
to abortions or their family members may have suffered similar
incidents.[6]

From the late nineteenth century through the 1930s, the state prosecuted abortionists primarily after a woman died. Popular tolerance of
abortion tempered enforcement of the laws. Prosecutors discovered
early the difficulty of winning convictions in criminal abortion cases.
Juries nullified the law and regularly acquitted abortionists. As a result,
prosecutors concentrated on cases where they had a "victim" – a woman
who had died at the hands of a criminal abortionist. In 1903 attorney H.
H. Hawkins reviewed Colorado's record and concluded, "No one is
prosecuted in Colorado for abortion except where death occurs. . . . the
law only applies to the man who is so unskilful as to kill his patient."
Thirty-seven out of the forty-three different abortion cases on which the
Supreme Court of Illinois ruled between 1870 and 1940 involved a
woman's death. Because prosecutors focused on abortionists responsible
for abortion-related deaths, they relied for evidence on dying declarations, such as those obtained from Petrovitis, and coroner's inquests. In
almost a third of the Illinois Supreme Court cases in which a woman had
died because of an abortion, the opinions commented on dying declarations.[7]

Counting convictions underestimates the state's commitment to enforcing the criminal abortion laws. Police arrests for abortion and coroner's inquests, however, indicate the state's interest in repressing abortion. Convictions were rare; police made dozens of arrests and the coroner's office averaged sixty inquests into abortion-related deaths each year. . . .

Abortion investigations began, as in the Petrovitis case, when physicians or hospital staff members noticed "suspicious" cases and reported them to the police or the Cook County coroner. In the first stage of an investigation, a woman was questioned by her doctor. She might be questioned again by police officers or special investigators sent from the coroner's office. Each interrogation was an attempt to obtain a legally valid dying declaration, in which the woman admitted her abortion and named her abortionist. A dying declaration not only led police to suspects; it also was crucial evidence that could be introduced at criminal trials. As one lawyer observed, it was almost "impossible" to obtain evidence of criminal abortion in any other way.[8]

The dying declaration was an unusual legal instrument that allowed the words of the dead to enter the courtroom. Legally, a dying declaration is an exception to the hearsay rule, which excludes the courtroom use of information that has been received secondhand. Common law allowed the admission of dying declarations as evidence in homicide cases, and states permitted this exception in abortion cases as well. Courts treated dying declarations as though given under oath based on the common law assumption that a dying person would not lie since she was, as the coroner put it during the inquest on Petrovitis, "about to leave the worlds – to meet her maker." The exception allowed prosecutors to present the dying declaration, in court, as the dead woman's own accusation of the person who had killed her.[9]

If the woman died, the abortion investigation proceeded to a second stage: an autopsy performed by coroner's physicians and an official coroner's inquest into the woman's death. During the inquest the coroner or his deputy questioned witnesses and attempted to collect the facts in the case. There the police for the first time presented the dying statements they had collected, other information uncovered during their investigation, or individuals possessing information. Family members, lovers, friends, midwives, physicians, and hospital staff all testified at the inquests. A coroner's jury then deliberated on the proceedings and decided the cause of death. Although the legal purpose of an inquest was simply to determine the cause of death, the coroner in fact wielded significant power. The coroner's inquest was a highly important stage in the legal process since it generally determined whether anyone would be criminally prosecuted. The jury decided the guilt or innocence of various people involved in a case, and if the jury determined that the woman's death resulted from "murder by abortion," it ordered the police to hold the suspected abortionist and accomplices. The suspects remained in jail or out on bail until the case was concluded. Once the coroner's jury made its determination, prosecutors brought the case before the grand jury, which then indicted the suspects. Both prosecutors and the grand jury tended to follow the findings of the coroner's jury; if the coroner's jury failed to accuse anyone of criminal abortion, prosecutors generally dropped the case. Abortion cases did not come to trial exclusively after inquests into abortion-related deaths; some abortionists were caught during raids, and sometimes women testified in court against them, but most prosecutions for criminal abortion followed the death or injury of a woman.

A visible and vocal minority of physicians actively assisted state officials in efforts to suppress abortion in Chicago. At various times, members of the Chicago Medical Society's criminal abortion committee worked to remove abortion advertising from the pages of local newspapers, assisted coroner's investigations, and joined efforts to investigate and control midwives in order to end abortion in their city. The AMA, headquartered in Chicago, collected information on abortionists and abortifacients and shared it with local and federal officials investigating violations of the criminal law.[10]

Not all physicians wanted to help prosecutors bring abortionists to trial, however. Publicly, the leaders of the medical profession opposed abortion; privately, many physicians sympathized with women's need for abortions, performed abortions, or referred patients to midwives or physicians who performed them. Dr. Rudolph Holmes discovered during his work on the criminal abortion committee that physicians often decline to testify against abortionists. He reported that "so-called reputable members of our Chicago Medical Society regularly appear in court to support the testimony of some notorious abortionist." Furthermore, he concluded, "the public does not want, the profession does not want, the women in particular do not want any aggressive campaign against the crime of abortion." Dr. Charles H. Parkes, chairman of the Chicago Medical Society's criminal abortion committee in 1912, confessed that state authorities believed the society's members to be "apathetic in the extreme" regarding abortion. Some members were abortionists.[11]

The illegality of abortion made caring for patients who had had abortions not only a medical challenge but also a legal peril. In abortion cases, physicians performed emergency curettements, repaired uterine tears and wounds, tried to stop hemorrhaging, and, most difficult in an age without antibiotics, fought infections. Once a woman had a widespread, septic infection (characterized by chills and fever), it was very likely that she would die. If a woman died despite a doctor's efforts, he became a likely suspect in the criminal abortion case. According to the New York attorney Almuth C. Vandiver, police arrested physicians "simply because they were the last physician attending the patient and they had not made their report to the coroner."[12]

The state could not investigate abortion cases without medical cooperation; state officials won doctors' help by threatening them. Physicians learned that if they failed to report criminal abortion cases, the investigative process could be turned against them. At a 1900 meeting of the Illinois State Medical Society, Dr. O. B. Will of Peoria warned his associates of the "responsibilities and dangers" associated with abortion by relating his own "very annoying experience" when a patient died because of an abortion. He was indicted as an accessory to murder in an abortion case for "keeping the circumstances quiet,... not securing a dying statement from the patient, and... not informing the coroner." Will declared that he was not required to notify the coroner and that the woman had refused to make a statement, but his story implied that cooperation with the authorities might help other doctors avoid similar notoriety. One doctor told his colleagues horror stories of Boston physicians who had been arrested, tried, and, though acquitted of abortion charges, nonetheless ousted by the Massachusetts Medical Society. Doctors who were associated with illegal abortion also risked losing their medical licenses. In Illinois a physician had to be convicted of abortion to lose his or her license, but some states revoked medical licenses without a trial. Physicians learned from tales like these that if they treated women for complications following abortions, they should report the cases to local officials or collect dying declarations themselves in order to avoid being arrested and prosecuted.[13] ...

A few New York physicians voiced the indignation that many doctors may have felt toward coroners and the treatment they received from them. Doctors who were the last attending physicians in abortion cases resented being pursued by the police and subjected to "disagreeable inquest[s]." New York physicians felt harassed by the city's coroners, who were, doctors complained, far too ready to arrest and investigate physicians in criminal abortion cases.[14]

One way to protect themselves from legal trouble and notoriety in abortion cases, physicians learned, was to secure dying declarations. In 1912 the chairman of the Chicago Medical Society's criminal abortion committee, Dr. Parkes, reminded the society that "it is extremely easy for anyone to become criminally involved when connected with these cases, unless properly protected." Parkes presented to the medical society a model dying declaration drafted by State's Attorney John Wayman that would be legally admissible as evidence, that would "stand the supreme court test." Wayman advised the doctors to ask the dying woman the following questions: "Q. Do you believe that you are about to die? . . . Q. Have you any hope of recovery? . . . Q. Do you understand these questions fully? . . . Q. Are you able to give a clear account of the causes of your illness?"[15]

The state's attorney also provided a standardized format for the dying woman's answer. She should answer, "I am Miss ———. Believing that I am about to die, and having no hope of recovery, I make the following statement, while of sound mind and in full possession of my faculties." To be considered valid in court, the statement had to establish that the woman believed she was near death. The woman was then expected to name her abortionist; to tell when, where, and how the abortion was done; and to name the man "responsible" for her pregnant "condition." Although most women who had abortions were married, the state's prosecutors focused on abortions by unwed women, and this formulaic dying declaration assumed that the dying woman would be unmarried.[16]

Physicians advised each other to deny medical care to a woman who had had an abortion until she made a statement. . . . If a woman refused to give information, the smart doctor, according to these advisers, would walk out and refuse to attend her. And some physicians, like Dr. Kahn in the Petrovitis case, threatened to do just that. In 1916 a Chicago fireman called in Dr. G. P. Miller to attend his wife who had been sick for three weeks following her abortion. Dr. Miller told her, "If I take this case . . . I want you to tell me the truth and who did it, who it was. Under the understanding that I was going to leave the house and have nothing to do with it, she told me the whole story." Physicians' refusals to treat abortion cases seem to have reached women's consciousness. In 1930 Mathilde Kleinschmidt, ill from her abortion, rejected her boyfriend's plan to call in a second doctor and insisted that he instead find the doctor who had performed the abortion. "Another doctor wont look at me," she explained. "He wont take the case."[17]

Fear of undeserved prosecution encouraged physicians to distrust their female patients. New York attorney Vandiver warned doctors, "Unscrupulous women and their accomplices have it within their power . . . to successfully blackmail the reputable practitioner, who omits the essential precautions for his protection." Dr. Henry Dawson Furniss told a story that encapsulated doctors' worst fears. He had "absolutely refused" to perform an abortion for a woman who later died from one. Under questioning, she got even with Furniss for spurning her plea by blaming him for her abortion.[18]

It seems that women rarely falsely accused physicians, and many, perhaps the majority, protected their abortionists by refusing to name them to doctors or policemen. The prosecuting attorney for St. Louis,

Ernest F. Oakley, marveled at the loyalty of women who refused to reveal their abortionists' names. Dying declarations, he thought, were obtained in only "four out of ten cases." One New York woman, who was hospitalized following her abortion, told the doctors who pressed her to name her abortionist, "She was the only one who would help me, and I won't tell on her."[19] Because the illegality of abortion compelled doctors to regard all miscarriages as suspect and to protect themselves against prosecution, women's health care suffered. Fearing prosecution, many physicians treated their female patients badly – rudely questioning them in attempts to gain dying declarations or delaying or refusing to provide needed medical care. . . .

While some frightened doctors threatened to deny medical care to women who had abortions and insisted that they make statements, others agreed with one physician who said that he refused "to act as a policeman" for the state. Dr. Parkes reported that Chicago officials "believe that the best hospitals now smother these cases and hinder in every way the work of investigation." Dr. William Robinson, a radical who advocated legalized abortion, scorned physicians who "badger[ed]" sick women to make dying statements. "The business of the doctor is to relieve pain, cure disease and save life," he declared, "not to act as a bloodhound [for] the state."[20] . . .

Making a patient's medical history public undermined the private and personal relationships physicians had with their patients. Some physicians expressed their intention of maintaining patients' confidentiality, regardless of the wishes of authorities. Dr. Louis Frank of Louisville, Kentucky, commented on the issue in 1904, "If I was called in I would not give testimony compromising a young lady, and I would not put it on record, no matter what the facts were, and I would not 'give away' a girl, but would attempt to protect her." Doctors Richard C. Norris and A. C. Morgan of Philadelphia strongly believed in the patient's right to confidentiality and proclaimed that medical ethics barred them from testifying against abortionists if such testimony violated their relationships with patients.[21]

The names of women who had had illegal abortions and the intimate details of their lives periodically hit the newspapers. Press coverage of abortion-related deaths warned all women of the dangers of abortion: death and publicity. Sometimes newspapers covered abortion stories on the front page and included photos; often abortion-related deaths and arrests of abortionists appeared in small announcements. The story of an unwed woman's seduction and abortion-related death made exciting copy and could dominate local newspapers for days. In 1916 Chicago and Denver newspapers published Ruth Merriweather's love letters to a Chicago medical student, who was on trial for his involvement in her abortion-related death. In 1918 the *Chicago Examiner* ran a series of "*tragedies*," excerpted from coroners' inquests, that told the stories of unwed women "*who were killed through illegal operations.*" The articles in this series and others like them, warned young women of the dangers of seduction and abortion and also warned rural fathers of the need to protect their daughters from the dangers of city life. The names and addresses of married women who had abortions often appeared in the press too, but their stories were not presented as seduction tales. Newspapers sometimes highlighted police officers' discovery of thousands of women's names in an abortionist's patient records. In doing so, they implicitly threatened women who had had abortions with the danger that they too could be named and exposed in the newspaper.[22]

Public exposure of a woman's abortion – through the press or gossip – served as social punishment of women who had abortions and members of their families. A Chicago police officer recalled that when he questioned Mary Shelley, she "remark[ed] that she didn't want the statement in the newspapers." Some women whose abortions had been reported in the local press lived to face the shame of public exposure. Doctors observed that even when a woman died after an abortion, families did not want authorities to investigate because they wanted "to shield her reputation." Some families invited state investigation of abortions and pursued prosecution, yet even they may have resented publicity about the case. One mother whose daughter had died as a result of an illegal abortion cried at a public hearing that her whole family had "keenly felt the disgrace" of the crime. When Frances Collins died, police visited "all houses on both sides" of her home as well as "some ladies" in her old neighborhood and questioned them in hopes of finding a "woman confidant." The police failed to find any information, but they had informed the woman's entire community of her death by abortion and displayed the state's interest in controlling abortion.[23]

To the women whose abortions attracted the attention of medical and legal authorities, the demands of physicians and police for dying statements felt punitive. One woman described her hospital experience after an abortion as "very humiliating. The doctors put me through a regular jail examination." In their efforts to obtain dying declarations, policemen and physicians, usually male, repeatedly questioned women about their private lives, their sexuality, and their abortions; they asked women when they last menstruated, when they went to the abortionist, and what he or she did. Were instruments introduced into "their privates"? If so, what did the instruments look like and how were they used? If the woman was unmarried, she was asked with whom she had been sexually intimate and when, precisely the information that she may have hoped to conceal by having an abortion. Furthermore, as in the Petrovitis case, the police routinely brought the suspected abortionist to the bedside of the dying woman for her to identify and accuse. Hundreds of women who had abortions may have been questioned annually by physicians, police, or coroner's officers without their names ever entering official records because they survived their abortions.[24] . . .

Criminal abortion investigations reveal the importance of marriage – and especially of the lack of it – in the eyes of state officials. When police collected dying statements, they routinely asked about the woman's marital status, and at inquests into the deaths of unmarried women, many of the coroner's questions focused on marital status. At inquests the coroner probed to discover whether the man had offered marriage. To a man, all claimed to have "promised to marry her." Perhaps men understood that this was the only way they could redeem themselves in the eyes of the law and the community. Yet there is evidence of genuine intention to marry. One man had bought a wedding ring; some even married after the abortion. In some cases, the woman wanted to delay marriage; in others, couples found marriage and children financially impossible. At the trial occasioned by the abortion-related death of his girl friend, William Cozzi testified "that he went to Dr. Rongetti to get rid of the baby because he could not afford it."[25]

Just as dying women endured intrusive questioning about their abortions, their unmarried lovers endured similar interrogations at inquests. For both unmarried women and men, the official prying into their private sexual lives, and their own mortification, served as punishment for their illicit sexual behavior. The coroner's questions to Marshall Hostetler about his sexual relationship with his sweetheart (who died in 1915) were not unusual at inquests into abortion deaths. The coroner asked Hostetler, "When did you become intimate with her? . . . have any relations with her? . . . When did that occur? . . . Had you been intimate with her before? . . . How many times? . . . Where did that occur?"[26]

During public investigations into abortion, men, too, tried to avoid answering questions about sex. Charles Morehouse, for example, readily answered numerous questions about his girl friend's abortion, how they borrowed money from an aunt, and how the family had tried to avoid an investigation. He also explained that the doctor had used "a spray." But when the coroner asked "Where?" Morehouse was silent. "A No response. Q What portion of the body? A Well, the privated parts."[27]

The "sweetheart of the dead girl" could be punished severely for having transgressed sexual norms. When an unwed woman died because of an abortion, her lover was automatically arrested, jailed, interrogated by the police and coroner, and sometimes prosecuted as an accessory to the crime. Bob Berry's experience in 1931 was typical. When Alma Bromps died, policemen arrived at Berry's door, arrested him, and jailed him. The next morning he identified the body of his girl friend and was questioned at the inquest into her death. He remained in jail for at least a week and ultimately became a witness for the state against the accused abortionist. Unmarried men involved in abortion deaths often spent at least one night in jail before the inquests. If they had no money to bail themselves out, they might spend several days or weeks, depending on the length of the inquest. Some spent months in jail waiting for their cases to come to trial. In 1917 Charles Morehouse spent four months in jail after the death of his girl friend. The state prosecuted Patrick O'Connell, a poor laborer, along with Dr. Adolph Buettner, for the abortion that led to Nellie Walsh's death. Although O'Connell was acquitted, it appears that he spent the nine months between Walsh's death and his criminal trial in the Cook County Jail. Other men were convicted and sentenced to prison for their part in an abortion.[28]

The actions of state officials toward unmarried men implicated in criminal abortion deaths reveal the state's stake in enforcing marriage in cases where an unwed woman became pregnant. The state punished young men for the moral offense of engaging in premarital intercourse and then failing to fulfill the implicit engagement by marrying the women they had made pregnant. Police routinely arrested and incarcerated unmarried men as accomplices in the crime of abortion, and the state's attorney sometimes prosecuted them. In contrast, husbands, who often had been just as involved as unmarried men in obtaining abortions, were very rarely arrested or prosecuted as accomplices when their wives died.[29] . . .

The official response to unmarried men in abortion cases, as in bastardy cases, warned other young men of the dangerous consequences of avoiding marriage and children when pregnancy occurred. The newspaper story of an abortion-related death often told of the arrest, imprisonment, and interrogation of the "sweetheart of the dead girl," and young men probably traded detailed information about the events that transpired during abortion investigations. Newspaper coverage of abortions warned women that they could die and men that they could be thrown in jail – some may have concluded that it was better to marry.[30]

Jilted women could exploit the state's readiness to hold unmarried men accountable in illegal abortions as a weapon to strike back at their lovers. Alice Grimes of southern Illinois actively encouraged official investigation into her abortion for this reason. As she was dying in 1896, Grimes told her mother that her boyfriend, James Dunn, "ought to suffer some" as she had. When Grimes learned that her uncle had had Dunn arrested, she told her brother she was "glad of it."[31]

From the late nineteenth century through the 1930s, the state concentrated on collecting dying declarations and on prosecuting abortionists when a woman had died, but the experiences of the 1930s changed the state's methods of abortion control. During the depression abortion increased just when advances in medicine were making it possible to save the lives of women who, in earlier decades, would have died from their abortion-related injuries and infections. The changes in the conditions and practice of abortion in the 1930s presaged changes in the investigation and control of abortion in the 1940s. Abortion control in the 1940s took two forms. First, hospitals took over much of the control of abortion through newly created therapeutic abortion committees; second, police and prosecutors stepped up raids on abortionists' offices. Rather than waiting for a death, the state's attorney's office sent police to raid the offices of suspected abortionists where they arrested abortionists and patients and collected medical instruments and patient records. In criminal trials of accused abortionists, the prosecution relied for evidence on testimony from women who had been patients of the abortionist, rather than on dying declarations. In the 1940s the system changed, but the process remained punitive for the women caught in it; criminal trials of abortionists required public exposure of women's sexual histories and abortions.[32]

The state's control of abortion was by no means entirely successful, but neither was it insignificant. Thousands of women regularly defied the law and had the abortions they needed. When questioned by doctors or police about their abortions, many defied their interrogators and refused to provide the information needed to prosecute abortionists. Yet the state punished women for having abortions, damaged the relationships between women and their doctors, and undermined women's health care. Officials focused on regulating the sexual behavior of working-class women and men, and especially the unmarried. Investigations and inquests into abortions forcefully reminded all involved not only of the illegality of abortion but also of the power of the state to intervene in the private lives of ordinary people in order to prevent and punish violations of sexual codes that demanded marriage and maternity. . . .

This study of the investigation of abortion in Chicago calls attention to the social punishment inherent in the state's routine processes of investigation and illuminates the ways in which punishment has been gendered. The state may not have prosecuted women for having abortions, but it did punish women through persistent questioning by doctors and police and through public exposure of their abortions. The harassment of sick or dying women in the name of criminal investigation continued until the decriminalization of abortion.[33]

At inquests into abortion deaths, the state reinforced the norms requiring men to marry the women they had made pregnant. Through arrests, incarceration, interrogation, and prosecution, unmarried women's lovers were punished for illegal abortions as well as for their illicit sexual behavior. The treatment of unmarried men in these cases reveals the implicit assumption of state authorities that the unwed women who had abortions had been forced to do so because their "sweethearts" had refused to marry. This underlying assumption ignored the evident agency of many women who sought abortions and delayed marriage. The punishment of unmarried men maintained age-old patriarchal standards that gave community support to fathers when they forced men to marry the women they had impregnated.

At a time when abortion is a political issue of national importance, the history of the enforcement of the criminal abortion laws should serve as a warning against recriminalizing abortion. If abortion is made illegal again, we can expect that the punitive procedures of the past will be revived. The antifeminist movement, which is pressuring the state to recriminalize abortion, will pressure the state to punish women if abortion is made illegal. We can expect that women will once again besiege doctors with requests for abortions and that the state will threaten to prosecute physicians who fail to report women who have, or perhaps even seek, abortions. As in the past, doctors are likely to be roped into assisting the state by interrogating and reporting women who have had abortions. Some women, like Carolina Petrovitis, will be injured or die from abortions induced by themselves or by inept practitioners. Many more may be interrogated, captured by police during raids of abortionists' offices, or publicly exposed. Today, as in the past, enforcement of any criminal abortion law will target the most powerless groups – poor and working-class women, women of color, and teen women – and their health care will be harmed the most. The history of illegal abortion is a history that should not be repeated.

Notes

1   Inquest on Carolina Petrovitis, March 21, 1916, case 234- 3-1916, Medical Records Department (Cook County Medical Exmainer's Office, Chicago, Ill.). For another example of a physican closely questioning a woman about an abortion, see Inquest on Matilda Olson, April 30, 1918, case 289-4-1918, ibid.

2   My summary of the history of abortion in the eighteenth and nineteenth centuries is based primarily on the pathbreaking study, James C. Mohr, *Abortion in America: The Origins and Evolution of National Policy* (New York, 1978). See also Linda Gordon, *Woman's Body, Woman's Right: A Social History of Birth Control in America* (New York, 1977), 49–61; Rosalind Pollack Petchesky, *Abortion and Woman's Choice: The State, Sexuality, and Reproductive Freedom* (New York, 1984), 67–100; Carroll Smith-Rosenberg, *Disorderly Conduct: Visions of Gender in Victorian America* (New York, 1985), 217–44;

Michael Grossberg, *Governing the Hearth: Law and the Family in Nineteenth-Century America* (Chapel Hill, 1985), 155–95; Carl N. Degler, *At Odds: Women and the Family in America from the Revolution to the Present* (New York, 1980); and Clifford Browder, *The Wickedest Woman in New York: Madame Restell, the Abortionist* (Hamden, 1988).

3 Mohr, *Abortion in America*, 205–6, 325.

4 For the estimate by Dr C. S. Bacon, see "Chicago Medical Society, Regular Meeting, held Nov. 23, 1904," *Journal of the American Medical Association,* Dec. 17, p. 1903, p. 1889.

5 On the number of working-class versus middle-class women having abortions, see Regine K. Stix and Dorothy G. Wiehl, "Abortion and the Public Health," *American Journal of Public Health,* 28 (May 1938), 624; and Paul H. Gebhard et al., *Pregnancy, Birth, and Abortion* (New York, 1958), 109–10, 120, 139. James Mohr, "Patterns of Abortion and the Response of American Physicians, 1790–1930," in *Women and Health in America,* ed. Judith Walzer Leavitt (Madison, 1984), 122.

6 I requested the inquest on Flossie Emerson, who died Feb. 28, 1916, but the Cook County Medical Examiner's Office has no record of her death. Emerson's abortion-related death was one of the cases for which Dr Anna B. Schultz-Knighten was prosecuted, *People v. Schultz-Knighten,* 277 Ill. 238 (1917). Dr Schultz-Knighten complained that the coroner's physician, Dr Springer, had "sneered" at her and called her a "nigger." Abstract of Record, *People v. Schultz-Knighten,* 277 Ill. 238 (1917), Case Files, Supreme Court of Illinois. Allan H. Spear, *Black Chicago: The Making of a Negro Ghetto* (Chicago, 1967), 140–46, 223.

7 "Symposium. Criminal Abortion. The Colorado Law on Abortion," *Journal of the American Medical Association,* April 18, 1903, p. 1099; James Foster Scott, "Criminal Abortion," *American Journal of Obstetrics and Diseases of Women and Children,* 33 (Jan. 1896), 77; Wilhelm Becker, "The Medical, Ethical, and Forensic Aspects of Fatal Criminal Abortion," *Wisconsin Medical Journal,* 7 (April 1909), 633.

8 William Durfor English, "Evidence – Dying Declaration – Preliminary Questions of Fact – Degree of Proof," *Boston University Law Review,* 15 (April 1935), 382.

9 Ibid., 381–82; Inquest on Petrovitis, case 234-3-1916, Medical Records Department.

10 Chicago Medical Society, Council Minutes, [Oct. 1905–July 1907], meetings of Oct. 9, 1906 and May 14, 1907, Chicago Medical Society Records (Archives and Manuscripts Department, Chicago Historical Society, Chicago, Ill.). Chicago Medical Society, Council Minutes, [Oct. 1911–June 1912], meeting of Jan. 9, 1912, pp. 51, 55–56.

11 R. W. Holmes, commenting on Walter B. Dorsett, "Criminal Abortion in Its Broadest Sense," *Journal of the American Medical Association,* Sept. 19, 1908, p. 960. Chicago Medical Society, Council Minutes, [Oct. 1911–June 1912], meeting of Jan. 9, 1912, pp. 53, 57, 59, Chicago Medical Society Records.

12 Almuth C. Vandiver, "The Legal Status of Criminal Abortion, with Especial Reference to the Duty and Protection of the Consultant," *American
Journal of Obstetrics and Diseases of Women and Children*, 61 (March 1910),
434–35, esp. 497.

13 O. B. Will, "The Medico-Legal Status of Abortion," *Illinois Medical Journal*,
2 (1900–1901), 506, 508; Edward W. Pinkham, "The Treatment of Septic
Abortion, with a Few Remarks on the Ethics of Criminal Abortion," *American Journal of Obstetrics and Diseases of Women and Children*, 61 (March
1910), 420.

14 Vandiver, "Legal Status of Criminal Abortion," 496–501, esp. 500; "Criminal Abortion from the Practitioner's Viewpoint," *American Journal of Obstetrics and Diseases of Women and Children*, 63 (June 1911), 1094–96.

15 Chicago Medical Society, Council Minutes, [Oct. 1911–June 1912], meeting of Jan. 9, 1912, pp. 53–54, 56–57, Chicago Medical Society Records.

16 Ibid., p. 57. For judicial discussions on the validity of dying declarations
and examples of dying declarations, see *Hagenow v. People*, 188 Ill. 545,
550–1, 553 (1901); *People v. Buettner*, 233 Ill. at 274–77; *People v. Cheney*,
368 Ill. 131, 132–35 (1938).

17 Inquest on Emily Projahn, Oct. 10, 1916, case 26-12-1916, Medical
Records Department.

18 Vandiver, "Legal Status of Criminal Abortion," 435. Dr Henry Dawson
Furniss commenting on "Criminal Abortion from the Practitioner's Viewpoint," 1096.

19 H. Wellington Yates and B. Connelly, "Treatment of Abortion," *American
Journal of Obstetrics and Gynecology*, 3 (Jan. 1922), 84–85. See also "Dying
Girl Runaway Hides Name of Slayer," *Chicago Examiner*, March 8, 1918,
Abortionists Files, Historical Health Fraud Collection; and "Slain Girl Dies
Hiding Her Tragedy from Kin," *Chicago Examiner*, March 9, 1918; Robin-
son, *Law against Abortion*, 106–7, 110; "Abortion 'Club' Exposed," *Birth
Control Review*, 4 (Nov. 1936), 5.

20 "Symposium. Criminal Abortion," 1099. See also Will, "Medico-Legal Status of Abortion," 508; and "Criminal Abortion from the Practitioner's Viewpoint," 1095–96. Chicago Medical Society, Council Minutes, [Oct. 1911–
June 1912], meeting of Jan. 9, 1912, p. 55, Chicago Medical Society Records.

21 Dr Louis Frank commenting on C. J. Aud, "In What Per Cent Is the Regular
Profession Responsible for Criminal Abortions, and What Is the Remedy?"
Kentucky Medical Journal, 2 (Sept. 1904), 100; "North Branch Philadelphia
County Medical Society. Regular Meeting, held April 14, 1904," *Journal of
the American Medical Association*, May 21, 1904, pp. 1375–76. Attorneys
disagreed about whether or not physicians should act as informers in abortion
cases. "Symposium. Criminal Abortion," 1097, 1098. Illinois did not privilege communications between doctors and patients.

22 "Girl's Letters Blame Dr Mason in Death Case," *Chicago Tribune*, April 9,
1916; Abortionists Files, historical Health Fraud Collection; "Voice from
Grave Calls to Dr Mason during Trial as His Financee's Betrayer," *Denver
[Colorado] Post*, April 5, 1916.

23 Inquest on Mary Shelley, Oct. 30, 1915, case 352–10-1915, Medical Records Department: "Chicago Medical Society," 1889. Mamie Ethel Crowell's family tried to prevent an investigation into her abortion by lying to physicians and the coroner. Inquest on Mamie Ethel Crowell, April 16, 1930, case 305-4-30, ibid.

24 Comments of "Esther E.," *Birth Control Review*, 4 (Sept. 1920), 15.

25 Inquest on Dimford, case 75-11-1915. Inquest on Kissell, case 300-8-1937. Inquest on Esther Stark, June 12, 1917, case 65- 6-1917. *People v. Carrico*, 310 Ill. 543, 547 (1924). For an example of a woman who did not want to marry, see Inquest on Mary Colbert, March 25, 1933, case 7-4-1933, Medical Records Department. *People v. Rongetti*, 344 Ill. 278, 284 (1931).

26 Inquest on Anna Johnson, May 27, 1915, case 77790, Medical Records Department.

27 Inquest on Matson, case 330-11-1917.

28 "Death Threat to Hostetler," *Chicago Tribune*, June 5, 1915. Abortionists Files, Historical Health Fraud Collection. The police and press often called the man in such a case "the sweetheart."

29 I know of only one case where the husband was charged. Bertis Dougherty pled guilty to abortion and testified as a state witness against the abortionist in *People v. Schneider*, 370 Ill. 612, 613–14 (1939).

30 On common perceptions of juvenile court proceedings regarding statutory rape, see Mary Ellen Odem, "Delinquent Daughters: the Sexual Regulation of Female Minors in the United States, 1880–1920" (PhD dissertation, University of California, Berkeley, 1989), 75–136.

31 Transcript of *Dunn v. People*, 172 Ill. 582 (1898), Case Files, vault no. 7876, Supreme Court of Illinois.

32 *People v. Martin*, 382 Ill. 192 (1943); *People v. Stanko*, 402 Ill. 558 (1949); *People v. Smuk*, 12 Ill. 2d. 360 (1957).

33 Jerome E. Bates and Edward Zawadzki, *Criminal Abortion: A Study in Medical Sociology* (Springfield, 1964), 61, 100, 103.

Documents

The first document, an article published in the American Medical Association journal in 1904, describes the dramatic appeal before the governor of Maryland on behalf of a convicted abortionist, a doctor of high esteem who, according to one supporter, "had fallen into an indiscretion." An unexpected appearance of the dead girl's mother completely altered the outcome of the pardon hearing. What do you think was so persuasive about the mother's comments? What role did shame play in the process? Where was it assumed that fault lay for the girl's "trouble"?

A Maryland Abortionist Gets No Pardon

Mention has been made of a petition to the governor for the pardon of Dr. George C. Worthington, a convicted abortionist now serving a ten years' sentence in the Maryland penitentiary for manslaughter by criminal mal-practice. On this petition were the names of state senators and represent-atives, a member or two of Congress, lawyers, merchants, clergymen, women and doctors. November 2, backing this appeal, a large delegation appeared before the governor at Annapolis. The spokesman, an ex-state senator, appeared in behalf of "the citizens of Baltimore and the state of Maryland." The object of the appeal, he said, had become a physical wreck since his incarceration; his financial condition was also a wreck; his wife and daughter were without means of support; a mother in her eighty-ninth year awaited him; the majesty of the law had been vindicated, and transgressors taught that they would be punished for their offenses; a multitude of people desired the pardon; the jury had unanimously signed a petition for his release; he would henceforth live beyond the confines of the state; while he may have done wrong, who shall cast the first stone? If the operation had been successful and shame had been saved the woman's family, nothing would have been said, etc. A state senator said that at least one-half of the members of the house of delegates and a majority of the members of the senate had signed the petition. A *physician* is reported to have stated to the governor "that he had practiced medicine eighteen years and could readily understand how Dr. Worthington had fallen into an *indiscretion*, and while the law had been violated, it would be well to remember that by his acts he had saved many a young woman from going forth marked with disgrace and shame." Silence ensued, broken only by a sob from near the door. This evidence of grief was supposed to come from some of Dr. Worthington's friends. "Is there anything further to be said?" asked the governor. There was silence for a few seconds when, in a half-hesitating way, the slight figure of a woman approached the governor, who turned and looked inquiringly. A convulsion of grief shook her from head to foot. It was but for an instant. Then, throwing her head erect, with both hands outstretched, she cried: "I am the mother of the dead girl!" A storm of pent-up grief burst forth while the members of the delegation stood aghast. Controlling herself as best she could, the woman continued: "I object to this pardon. I am a Christian woman. I have lived eighteen years

---

Taken from "A Maryland Abortionist Gets No Pardon," *Journal of the American Medical Association*, 43 (November 12, 1904), pp. 1475–76.

in my neighborhood and you may ask any of my neighbors concerning my respectability. I am not responsible for the death of my poor girl. I tried to rear her properly. She told me on her dying bed that Allgive was responsible for her condition and that Dr. George C. Worthington had performed the operation which later caused her death. I could tell you more that she said, but on account of this frightful crime I have keenly felt the disgrace which it has brought to me and my family, and on these grounds, lone mother that I am, I come here to protest in my humble way against granting a pardon to this man and to ask that he shall serve out his full time and receive full punishment for the crime he has committed." This unexpected appeal fell like a bolt out of the clear sky. Several minutes elapsed before the members of the delegation could collect themselves, and the governor showed plainly the effects of the incident. The governor was the first to speak, saying that the opinion was almost universal that the punishment meted out to the prisoner was not commensurate with the grave crime committed by him. He, therefore, declined to extend executive clemency. The members of the delegation then filed out in silence, while the woman took the governor's hand, exclaiming: "God bless you!"

Dying Declarations Obtained in Abortion Case as Condition to Rendering Aid

The second document is similarly taken from the *JAMA* in the first decade of the twentieth century and explores the conditions under which a dying declaration could be admissible as evidence. In the case cited here, how was the declaration extorted? What do you think would have been the emotional impact of these statements?

The Court of Criminal Appeals of Texas says, on the appeal of Jackson vs. State, that the Texas statute requires that a dying declaration, to be admissible in evidence, must be freely and voluntarily made. In this case it appeared that the girl on whom it was charged that a criminal abortion had been performed was suffering acutely, giving loud and vociferous exclamations of pain, and expressing the opinion that she was going to die. Under this condition of things, with her mind influenced in this way and by her pain, two physicians informed her that they would not do

---

Taken from "Dying Declarations Obtained in Abortion Case as Condition to Rendering Aid," *Journal of the American Medical Association*, 52 (April 10, 1909), p. 1204.

anything for her unless she told them about how her trouble came about and who performed the operation.

The testimony raised the issue that the dying declaration was not voluntary, but by overpersuasion, or duress, for that the evidence of the two physicians showed that they had declined to treat or relieve the declarant of what she thought was her dying condition, unless she gave the name of the party who had operated on her. This sufficiently presented the question, so as to require the court to submit the issue to the jury as to the condition of her mind at the time, and if they should find that she was under duress or overpersuasion, or not under a sense of impending death, then they should disregard her statement in arriving at a verdict.

In discussing parts of an instruction given to the jury, the court says that if the defendant appealing was guilty of a criminal abortion, there was no excuse for this, nor was there any justification; and certainly from no standpoint could there arise the question of "self-defense."

Comments of "Esther E."

The third document addresses the desperation felt by women burdened with unwanted pregnancies. Published in Margaret Sanger's *The Birth Control Review* in 1920, Esther E.'s story was meant to convince anti-birth control advocates of the necessity for legal birth control. In the details of her story we find out that women aborted their own fetuses and endured humiliating hospital interrogations when they needed medical attention afterwards.

Esther E. – Thirty years old – four living children – two miscarriages. Oldest living child 12 years old; she now is seven months pregnant.

She was waiting while Annie M. was telling her story.

"Nurse, have you a minute for me? Please do you know any where, where I can go and be told how to care for myself? I know I must have this baby as I am seven months gone. My husband has heart and kidney trouble and can only work about four days in the week. He does piece work and runs a machine and it is very hard for him. He made wages until taken sick, but now only makes $35.00 a week. As long as I could I did an occasional day's cleaning, but cannot do so any longer.

Excerpted from *The Birth Control Review*, 4 (September 1920), pp. 14–15.

"I would not have had this baby, but was afraid to try another abortion, (have induced two) and I was very ill the last time; and my hospital experience was very humiliating.

"The doctors put me through a regular jail examination. Had I been to a doctor, had he used instruments, had he given me a drug? He seemed determined to fasten the abortion on someone. But I could stick to my story as I had induced the abortion myself at a very great risk to my life, I was very ill and in the hospital for six weeks.

"I must say I received good care and much kindness from all but one thoughtless young nurse, who when I went to say good-bye to her, said, 'You will do that trick once too often, and I do not think any decent minded woman would do such a thing.'

"I only wish I could place her for six months in my place."

I think it would be a good idea to place some of these thoughtless anti-Birth Control people in the homes of these over-burdened mothers.

> "Good is best when soonest wrought,
> Lingered labors come to naught."

Good would be to save a mother as soon as we see the need. A worn out tired and sick mother is indeed a life come to naught.

Further Reading

Alexander, Ruth. The "Girl Problem": Female Sexual Delinquency in New York, 1900–1930. Ithaca, NY: Cornell University Press, 1996.

Brodie, Janet. Contraception and Abortion in Nineteenth-century America. Ithaca, NY: Cornell University Press, 1994.

Luker, Kristin. Abortion and the Politics of Motherhood. Berkeley: University of California Press, 1984.

Mohr, James C. Abortion in America: the Origins and Evolution of National Policy. New York: Oxford University Press, 1978.

Odem, Mary. Delinquent Daughters: Protecting and Policing Adolescent Female Sexuality in the United States, 1885–1920. Chapel Hill: University of North Carolina Press, 1995.

Petchesky, Rosalind Pollack. Abortion and Woman's Choice: the State, Sexuality and Reproductive Freedom, rev. edn. Boston: Northeastern University Press, 1997.

Reagan, Leslie J. When Abortion Was a Crime: Women, Medicine, and the Law, 1867–1973. Berkeley: University of California Press, 1997.

Solinger, Rickie. The Abortionist: a Woman against the Law. New York: Free Press, 1994.

10

Contraceptive Consumers

Introduction

Andrea Tone explores the relationship between marital sexuality, the technical illegality of birth control, and the burgeoning birth control industry in the 1930s. The illicit industry expanded despite restrictions invoked by the Comstock Act of 1873, which banned the circulation and sale of items used explicitly for birth control. Throughout the nineteenth century and into the twentieth, consumers regularly used condoms, douches, vaginal sponges, and cervical caps, among other contraceptive devices, available through mail-order houses and pharmacies. As long as the item under question was not marketed specifically for birth control, the government could not prosecute the manufacturer.

The culture of secrecy, fostered by birth control's illegality, blended with a more general Victorian reluctance to talk openly about birth control. By the 1930s, however, Margaret Sanger's successful efforts at making family planning a public health issue dramatically increased women's demands for safe methods of birth control. The industry responded; still somewhat hampered by governmental restrictions, manufacturers could nonetheless sell products if they avoided explicitly naming their particular use. As a result, euphemistic slogans peppered advertisements throughout the 1930s, selling women hygiene products for their "female constitution," for example, while insinuating that these same products could be used effectively for birth control. Often these products simply were not safe, and they certainly did not prevent conception. Selling to women in their homes or in spaces primarily devoted to women, such as department stores, was thought to prevent public exposure and potential embarassment. Thus the innovations of modern consumerism reinforced women's traditional responsibility for reproductive matters, including birth control.

Contraceptive Consumers: Gender and the Political Economy of Birth Control in the 1930s

Andrea Tone

In 1933, readers of *McCall's* probably noticed the following advertisement for Lysol feminine hygiene in the magazine's July issue:

> The most frequent eternal triangle:
>
> A HUSBAND . . . A WIFE . . . and her FEARS
> Fewer marriages would flounder around in a maze of misunderstanding and unhappiness if more wives knew and practiced regular marriage hygiene. Without it, some minor physical irregularity plants in a woman's mind the fear of a major crisis. Let so devastating a fear recur again and again, and the most gracious wife turns into a nerve-ridden, irritable travesty of herself.[1]

Hope for the vexed woman was at hand, however. In fact, it was as close as the neighborhood store. Women who invested their faith and dollars in Lysol, the ad promised, would find in its use the perfect panacea for their marital woes. Feminine hygiene would contribute to "a woman's sense of fastidiousness" while freeing her from habitual fears of pregnancy. Used regularly, Lysol would ensure "health and harmony... throughout her married life."[2]

The *McCall's* ad, one of hundreds of birth control ads published in women's magazines in the 1930s, reflects the rapid growth of the contraceptive industry in the United States during the Depression. Birth control has always been a matter of practical interest to women and men. By the early 1930s, despite long-standing legal restrictions and an overall decline in consumer purchasing power, it had also become a profitable industry. Capitalizing on Americans' desire to limit family size in an era

Excerpted from Andrea Tone, "Contraceptive Consumers: Gender and the Political Economy of Birth Control in the 1930s," *Journal of Social History*, 29 (March 1996), pp. 485–506.

of economic hardship, pharmaceutical firms, rubber manufacturers, mail-order houses, and fly-by-night peddlers launched a successful campaign to persuade women and men to eschew natural methods for commercial devices whose efficacy could be "scientifically proven." In 1938, with the industry's annual sales exceeding $250 million, *Fortune* pronounced birth control one of the most prosperous new businesses of the decade.[3] ...

Depression-era manufacturers were the first to create a mass market for contraceptives in the United States. Through successful advertising they heightened demand for commercial birth control while building a permanent consumer base that facilitated the industry's subsequent expansion. Significantly, this consumer constituency was almost exclusively female. Condoms, the most popular commercial contraceptive before the Depression, generated record sales in the 1930s. But it was profits from female contraceptives – sales of which outnumbered those of condoms five to one by the late 1930s – that fuelled the industry's prodigious growth.[4] Then, as now, women were the nation's leading contraceptive consumers.

An important feature distinguished the birth-control market of the 1930s from that of today, however: its illegality. Federal and state laws dating from the 1870s proscribed the inter-state distribution and sale of contraceptives. Although by the 1920s the scope of these restrictions had been modified by court interpretations permitting physicians to supply contraceptive information and devices in several states, the American Medical Association's ban on medically dispensed contraceptive advice remained intact. Neither legal restrictions nor medical disapproval thwarted the industry's ascent, however. Instead, they merely pushed the industry underground, beyond regulatory reach.[5]

Contraceptive manufacturers in the 1930s exploited this vacuum to their advantage, retailing devices that were often useless and/or dangerous in a manner that kept the birth-control business on the right side of the law. The industry thrived within a grey market characterized by the sale of contraceptives under legal euphemisms.[6] Manufacturers sold a wide array of items, including vaginal jellies, douche powders and liquids, suppositories, and foaming tablets as "feminine hygiene," an innocuous-sounding term coined by advertisers in the 1920s.[7] Publicly, manufacturers claimed that feminine hygiene products were sold solely to enhance vaginal cleanliness. Consumers, literally deconstructing advertising text, knew better. Obliquely encoded in feminine hygiene ads and product packaging were indicators of the product's *real* purpose; references to "protection," "security," or "dependability" earmarked purported contraceptive properties.[8]

Tragically, linguistic clues could not protect individuals from product adulteration or marketing fraud. Because neither the government nor the medical establishment condoned lay use of commercial contraceptives, consumers possessed no reliable information with which to evaluate the veracity of a product's claim. The bootleg status of the birth control racket left contraceptive consumers in a legal lurch. If an advertised product's implied claims to contraceptive attributes failed, they had no acceptable means of recourse.

Within this highly profitable and unfettered trade, women became the market's most reliable and, by extension, most exploited customers. The rise of the birth-control industry was an important episode in the advance of consumer society in inter-war America. Mass production, a predominantly urban population, and innovations in consumer credit supplied the structural underpinning for the expansion of the consumer economy. The advertising industry, manufacturers, retailers, and political leaders provided a concomitant cultural ethos that celebrated the emancipating properties of consumption; the power to purchase was lauded as a desirable, deserved, and quintessentially American freedom. Women became favored recipients of this self-congratulatory encomium. . . .

Depression-era manufacturers and retailers of birth control adopted the same consumption/liberation formula used to sell women lipstick, Hoover vacuum cleaners, and Chrysler cars to construct the first contraceptive mass market in the United States. Just as consumption was trumpeted as a characteristically female freedom, so, too, was reproduction portrayed as a distinctively female task. On this latter point, women needed little convincing. By virtue of biology, pregnancy was an exclusively female experience; by virtue of convention, raising children in 1930s was principally a female responsibility. Drawing upon and simultaneously reinforcing the prevailing gender system, the birth control industry reified the naturalness of women's twin roles as consumers and reproducers. Conjoining these functions, manufacturers and retailers urged women to use their purchasing "power" to assume full responsibility for pregnancy prevention. The industry's sales pitch struck a resonant chord with American women in the 1930s. At a time when the cost of raising children was rising and an unprecedented and increasing proportion of the laboring population was officially unemployed, controlling fertility assumed added urgency. With public birth control clinics few in number and privately prescribed diaphragms financially and medically out of reach to most women, access to easily acquired, affordable, and effective birth control became a widely shared goal. With advertisers' prodding, millions of women turned to the contraceptive market to achieve it.[9] . . .

When Congress enacted the Comstock Act in 1873, a new nadir in reproductive rights had arrived. The anti-obscenity law, the result of the relentless campaigning of its namesake, purity crusader Anthony Comstock, proscribed, among other things, the private or public dissemination of any

> book, pamphlet, paper, writing, advertisement, circular, print, picture, drawing, or other representation, figure, or image on or of paper or other material, or any cast, instrument, or other article of an immoral nature, or any drug or medicine, or any article whatever for the prevention of conception.[10]

Passed after minimal debate, the Comstock Act had long-term repercussions. Following Congress's lead, most states enacted so-called "mini" Comstock acts which criminalized the circulation of contraceptive devices and information within state lines.[11] Collectively, these restrictions demarcated the legal boundaries of permissable sexuality. Sexual intercourse rendered nonprocreative through the use of "unnatural" – that is, purchased – birth control was forbidden. Purity crusaders contended that if properly enforced, the Comstock and mini-Comstock acts would regulate birth control out of existence. Instead, they made birth control an increasingly dangerous, but no less popular, practice.[12]

By the time state and federal legislatures had begun to abandon their laissez-faire attitude toward birth control, a fledgling contraceptive industry had already surfaced in the United States. Indeed, the two developments were integrally yoked: the initiative to regulate contraceptives arose out of the realization that there was a growing number to regulate. The nineteenth century witnessed the emergence of a contraceptive trade that sold for profit goods that had traditionally been prepared within the home. Douching powders and astringents, dissolving suppositories, and vaginal pessaries had supplemented male withdrawal and abstinence as mainstays of birth-control practice in preindustrial America.[13] As the nineteenth century progressed, these conventional contraceptives became increasingly available from commercial vendors. Technologically upgraded versions of other standard contraceptives also entered the birth-control trade. . . . By the 1870s, condoms, douching syringes, douching solutions, vaginal sponges, and cervical caps could be purchased from mail-order houses, wholesale drug-supply houses, and pharmacies. Pessaries – traditionally used to support prolapsed uteruses but sold since the 1860s in closed-ring form as "womb veils" – could be obtained from sympathetic physicians. Thus when supporters of the Comstock Act decried the "nefarious and diabolical traffic" of "vile and immoral goods," they were identifying the inroads commercialized contraception had already made.[14]

After the Comstock restrictions were passed, birth control continued to be sold, marketed for its therapeutic or cosmetic, rather than its contraceptive, value. Significantly, however, commercial contraceptive use became more closely associated with economic privilege. The clandestine nature of the market prompted many reputable firms – especially rubber manufacturers – to cease production altogether. Those that remained charged exorbitant prices for what was now illegal merchandise. For many wage-earning and immigrant families, the high price of contraceptives made them unaffordable. In addition, the suppression of birth-control information reduced the availability of published material on commercial and noncommercial techniques, as descriptions previously featured openly in pamphlets, books, journals, broadsides, and newspaper medical columns became harder to find. In effect, contraceptive information, like contraceptives themselves, became a privileged luxury.[15]

Only in the 1930s were birth-control manufacturers able to create a mass market characterized by widespread access to commercial contraceptives. This market developed in response to a combination of important events. The birth-control movement of the 1910s and 1920s, spearheaded by Margaret Sanger, made birth control a household word (indeed, it was Sanger who introduced the term) and a topic of protracted debate and heated public discussion. Sanger insisted that women's sexual liberation and economic autonomy depended upon the availability of safe, inexpensive, and effective birth control. Sanger conducted speaking tours extolling the need for female contraception and published piercing indictments of "Comstockery" in her short-lived feminist newspaper *The Woman Rebel*, the *International Socialist Review*, and privately published pamphlets. In October 1916, she opened in Brooklyn the first birth-control clinic in the United States where she instructed neighbourhood women on contraceptive techniques. The clinic's closure and Sanger's subsequent jail sentence only increased her notority. Sanger was not alone in her efforts to legitimize contraception, of course. The birth control movement was a collective struggle waged by hundreds of individuals and organizations, including IWW locals, women's Socialist groups, independent birth control leagues, and the liberal-minded National Birth Control League.[16] But Sanger's single-minded devotion to the birth control cause and her casual and frequent defiance of the law captured the media spotlight. In the 1910s it was Sanger, more than anyone else, who pushed contraception into the public arena and who, quite unintentionally, set the stage for the commercial exploitation that followed. . . .

As the demand for birth control accelerated, the inability of existing institutions to satisfy it became apparent. By 1932, only 145 public clinics operated to service the contraceptive needs of the nation; twenty-seven states had no clinics at all. Each year in New York City, birth-control organizations received over 10,000 letters requesting contraceptive information; because of chronic understaffing, most went unanswered.[17] Many women, spurred on by public attention to birth control but unable to secure the assistance needed to make informed contraception choices, took contraception – and their lives – into their own hands. A Chicago physician noted in 1930 with alarm the growing number of doctors reporting the discovery of chewing gum, hair pins, needles, tallow candles, and pencils lodged in female patients' urinary bladders. The doctor blamed these desperate attempts to restrict fertility on the "wave of publicity concerning contraceptive methods that has spread over the country." Equally eager to control reproduction through self-administered means, other women turned to the burgeoning birth-control market to purchase what they believed were safe and reliable contraceptives.[18]

That there was a commercial market to turn to was the result of liberalized legal restrictions that encouraged manufacturers to enter the birth-control trade. The structure of the birth-control industry of the early 1930s was markedly different from that which preceded it only a few years earlier. From 1925 to 1928, Holland-Rantos had enjoyed a monopoly on the manufacture of diaphragms and contraceptive jellies in the United States; other manufacturers expressed little interest in producing articles that might invoke government prosecution and whose market was confined to a handful of non-profit clinics. A 1930 decision, *Youngs Rubber Corporation, Inc.*, v. *C.I. Lee & Co.*, *et al*, lifted legal impediments to market entry. The *Youngs* case, in which the makers of Trojan condoms successfully sued a rival company for trademark infringement, forced the court to decide whether the contraceptive business was legal, and thus legitimately entitled to trademark protection. The court ruled that in so far as birth control had "other lawful purposes" besides contraception, it could be legally advertised, distributed, and sold as a non-contraceptive device. The outcome of a dispute between rival condom manufacturers, the *Youngs* decision left its most critical mark on the female contraceptive market. Companies that had previously avoided the birth control business quickly grasped the commercial opportunities afforded by the court's ruling. Provided that no reference to a product's contraceptive features appeared in product advertising or on product packaging, female contraceptives could now be legally sold – not only to the small number of birth control clinics in states where physician-prescribed birth control was legal, but to the consuming public nation-wide. Manufacturers realized that the court's legal latitude would not affect the diaphragm market, monopolized, as it was, by the medical profession. Because diaphragms required a physician's fitting, the number of buyers, given financial and regional obstacles to this type of medical consultation, would remain proportionately small. Jellies, suppositories, and foaming tablets, on the other hand, possessed untapped mass-market potential. They could be used without prior medical screening. And because chemical compounds were cheaper to mass produce than rubber diaphragms, they could be sold at a price more women could afford.[19] ...

The contraceptive industry thrived in the 1930s precisely because, while capitalizing on public discussions of birth control to which the medical community contributed, it operated outside customary medical channels. Manufacturers supplied women with something that clinics and private physicians did not: birth control that was conveniently located, discretely obtained, and most importantly, affordably priced. While the going rate for a diaphragm and a companion tube of jelly ranged from four to six dollars, a dollar purchased a dozen suppositories, ten foaming tablets, or, most alluring of all, up to three douching units, depending on the brand. Contraceptive manufacturers pledged, furthermore, that customer satisfaction would not be sacrificed on the altar of frugality. They reassured buyers that bargain-priced contraceptives were just as reliable as other methods. Without lay guides to help them identify the disjunction between advertising hyperbole and reality, women could hardly be faulted for taking the cheaper path. By the late 1930s, purchases of diaphragms accounted for less than one percent of total contraceptive sales.[20]

Manufacturers' grandiose claims aside, not all contraceptives were created alike. The dangers and deficiencies of birth control products were well known in the health and hygiene community. Concerned pharmacists, physicians, and birth-control advocates routinely reviewed and condemned commercial preparations. Experts agreed, for instance, that vaginal suppositories, among the most frequently used contraceptives, were also among the least reliable. Suppositories typically consisted of boric acid and/or quinine, ingredients not recognized as effective spermicides. Melting point variability posed an added problem. Suppositories, usually based on cocoa butter or gelatin, were supposed to dissolve at room temperature. In practice, weather extremes and corresponding fluctuations in vaginal temperature made suppositories' diffusion, homogeneity, and contraceptive attributes unpredictable. The "protection" given by foaming tablets was no better. Comprising an effervescent, moisture-activated mixture such as tartaric acid and sodium bicarbonate (which, when triggered, produced a protective foam), tablets often remained inert until *after* male ejaculation.[21]

But critics reserved their harshest comments for the most popular, affordable, and least reliable contraceptive of the day, the antiseptic douche. Noting the method's alarming failure rate – reported at the time to be as high as seventy percent – they condemned the technique as mechanically unsound and pharmacologically ineffectual. For one thing, the method's technique weakened its potential for success: by the time the solution was introduced, seminal fluid that had already penetrated the cervix and surrounding tissues was difficult to reach and negate. In addition, the method's ineffectiveness was compounded by the benignity or toxicity of the solutions themselves. Scores of douching preparations, while advertised as modern medical miracles, contained nothing more than water, cosmetic plant extracts, and table salt. On the other hand, many others, including the most popular brand, Lysol disinfectant, contained cresol (a distillate of coal and wood) or mercury chloride, either of which, when used in too high a concentration, caused severe inflammation, burning, and even death. Advertising downplayed the importance of dilution by drawing attention to antiseptics' gentleness and versatility; single ads praising Lysol's safety on "delicate female tissues" also encouraged the money-wise consumer to use the antiseptic as a gargle, nasal spray, or household cleaner. By the same token, the makers of PX, a less-known brand, sold a liquid disinfectant that ads claimed could be used interchangeably for "successful womanhood" or athlete's foot.[22]

This strategy won sales, but it did so only by jeopardizing women's health. With even one-time douching a potentially deleterious act, women guided by the logical assumption that "more was better" strove to beat the pregnancy odds by increasing the frequency of their douching and the concentration of the solution used. In one case, a nineteen-year old married woman relied on regular douching with dissolved mercury chloride tablets for birth control. Eager to avoid pregnancy, she doubled the dose and douched "several times daily." Her determination landed her in a doctor's office where she was diagnosed with acute vaginal and cervical burns. In what must have seemed to her like a grave injustice, she also learned she was pregnant.[23]

Reports on douche-related deaths and injuries and the general ineffectiveness of popular commercial contraceptive were widely discussed among concerned constituents of the health community. Sadly, however, these findings failed to prod the medical establishment as a united profession to take a resolute stand against the contraceptive scandal. Nor, regrettably, did blistering indictments of manufacturing fraud trickle down to the lay press where they might have enabled women to make informed contraceptive choices. The numerous women's magazines that published feminine hygiene ads – from *McCall's* to *Screen*

Romances to the *Ladies' Home Journal* – were conspicuously silent about the safety and efficacy of the products they tacitly endorsed. The paucity of information impeded the development of informed consumerism. In advertising text and in many women's minds, the euphemism "feminine hygiene" continued to signify reliable contraception. For unscrupulous manufacturers eager to profit from this identification, feminine hygiene continued to be a convenient term invoked to sell products devoid of contraceptive value.

Manufacturers absolved themselves of responsibility by reminding critics that by the letter of the law, their products were not being sold as contraceptives. If women incurred injuries or became pregnant while using feminine hygiene for birth control, that was their fault, not manufacturers'. Thus contraceptive firms whose profits depended on consumers' loose and liberal deconstruction of advertising text duplicitously clung to a rigid, literalist construction of language when defending their own integrity. The Norwich Pharmacal Company, for example, manufacturers of Norforms, the most popular brand of vaginal suppositories in the country, deployed precisely such an argument to justify its advertising policy. Norform suppositories were advertised exclusively as feminine hygiene, a term that the company's vice-president Webster Stofer conceded had become synonymous with contraception in many women's minds. All the same, Stofer insisted, Norforms were not sold as birth control. Asked why the company did not then change its marketing slogan to avoid misunderstanding, Stofer expressed his regret that it was "too late" to advertise suppositories as anything else. "The term has become too closely associated with Norforms," Stofer contended. "And anyway, we have our own definition of it."[24]

Added to the growing list of groups unwilling to expose the hucksterism, of the birth-control bonanza was the federal government. Neither the Food and Drug Administration (FDA) nor the Federal Trade Commission (FTC) was in a strong position to rally to consumers' aid. The FDA, authorized to take action only against product mislabelling, was powerless to suppress birth-control manufacturers' rhetorically veiled claims. The FTC, in turn, regulated advertising, but only when one company's claims were so egregious as to constitute an unfair business practice. The subterfuge prevalent in all feminine hygiene marketing compaigns, as well as a unanimous desire on manufacturers' part to eschew protracted scrutiny, kept the FTC at bay. Sadly for the growing pool of female contraceptive consumers, without regulation and reliable standards for discriminating among products, the only way to discern a product's safety and efficacy was through trial and error.[25]

Clamoring for a larger share of the hygiene market, manufacturers did their utmost to ensure that their product would be one women would want to try. Aggressive advertising was instrumental to the industry's success. Appealing to women in the privacy of their homes, feminine-hygiene companies blanketed middle-class women's magazines in the 1930s with advertisements, many of full-page size. Targeting the magazines' predominantly married readership, advertisements were headlined by captions designed to inculcate and inflate apprehensions in readers' minds. Ads entitled "Calendar Fear," "Can a Married Woman Ever Feel Safe?," "Young Wives Are Often Secretly Terrified," and "The Fear That 'Blights' Romance and Ages Women Prematurely" relied on standard negative advertising techniques to heighten the stakes of pregnancy prevention.[26]

Ads conveyed the message that ineffective contraception led not only to unwanted pregnancies, but also to illness, despair, and marital discord. Married women who ignored modern contraceptive methods were courting life-long misery. "Almost before the honeymoon ends," one ad warned, "many a young bride is plagued by foreboding. She pictures the early departure of youth and charm . . . sacrificed on the altar of marriage responsibilities." Engulfed by fear, the newlywed's life only got worse – fear itself, women were told, engendered irreparable physical ailments. According to one douche advertisement, fear was a "dangerous toxin." "[It] dries up valuable secretions, increases the acidity of the stomach, and sometimes disturbs the bodily functions generally. So it is that FEAR greys the hair . . . etches lines in the face, and hastens the toll of old age."[27] . . .

Having divulged the ugly and myriad hazards of unwanted pregnancy while saddling women with the burden of its prevention, advertisements emphasized that peace of mind and marital happiness were conditions only the market could bestow. Readers of feminine hygiene ads, newly enlightened, returned to the world with the knowledge necessary to "remove many of their health anxieties, and give them that sense of well being, personal daintiness and mental poise so essential to wifely security." In the modern age, the personal tragedies accompanying a woman's existence were easily avoided. "Days of depressing anxiety, a wedded life in which happiness is marred by fear and uncertainty – these need be yours no longer," one douche ad reassured. In the imagined world of contraceptive advertising, feminine hygiene was the commodity no modern woman could afford to be without. Fortunately, none had to. The path to unbridled happiness was only a store away.[28]

As advertisements reminded prospective customers, however, not all feminine-hygiene products were the same. The contraceptive consumer had to be discriminating. Hoping both to increase general demand for hygiene products and to inculcate brand loyalty, manufacturers presented their product as the one most frequently endorsed for its efficacy and safety by medical professionals. Dispelling consumer doubts by invoking

the approval of the scientific community was not an advertising technique
unique to contraceptive merchandising – the same strategy was used in
the 1930s to sell women laxatives, breakfast cereal, and mouth wash.
What was exceptional about contraceptive advertising, however, was
that the experts endorsing feminine hygiene were not men. Rather, they
were female physicians whose innate understanding of the female condition permitted them to share their birth control expertise "woman to
woman."[29]

The Lehn and Fink corporation used this technique to make
Lysol disinfectant douche the leading feminine-hygiene product in the
country.[30] In a series of full-page advertisements entitled "Frank Talks by
Eminent Women Physicians," stern-looking European female gynecologists urged "smart-thinking" women to entrust their health only to doc-
tor-recommended Lysol disinfectant douches. "It amazes me," wrote Dr.
Madeleine Lion, "a widely recognized gynaecologist of Paris,"

> in these modern days, to hear women confess their carelessness, their lack
> of positive information, in the so vital matter of feminine hygiene. They
> take almost anybody's word ... a neighbor's, an afternoon bridge part-
> ner's ... for the correct technique ... Surely in this question of correct
> marraige hygiene, the modern woman should accept only the facts of
> scientific research and medical experience. The woman who does demand
> such facts uses "Lysol" faithfully in her ritual of personal antisepsis.[31]

... While insisting that women defer to medical opinion when choosing
birth control, contraceptive ads simultaneously celebrated the tremendous "power" women wielded in the consumer market. The two claims
were not antithetical; advertisements contended that women who
heeded physicians' advice and purchased "scientific" birth control
were intelligently harnessing the advances of modern medicine to promote their own liberation. Consistent with the consumer ethic of the
day, birth-control advertising successfully equated contraceptive consumption with female emancipation. An ad by the Zonite Products
Corporation claimed that birth control was not only a matter of prag-
matism, but also a "protest against those burdens of life which are
wholly woman's." When it came to as important an issue as birth
control, Zonite explained, the modern woman was not interested in
the "timid thoughts of a past generation;" her goal was "to find out
and be sure." It was no surprise, the company boasted, that Zonite
hygiene products were favored by "women of the independent, enlightened type all over the world."[32]

Contraceptive manufacturers' creation of a mass market in the 1930s
depended not only upon effective advertising, but also on the availability

of advertised goods. Prospective customers needed quick, convenient, and multiple access to contraceptives. Manufacturers made sure that they had it. Flooding a wide array of commercial outlets with their merchandise, companies guaranteed that contraceptives became a commodity within everyone's reach. Here, again, gender was the crucial variable, determining product availability and sales venue. Condoms were sold in pharmacies, but also in news stands, barber shops, cigar stores, and gas stations – locations where men were most likely to congregate. Women, on the other hand, were targeted in more conventional female settings: in stores and in the home.[33]

The department store became the leading distributor of female contraceptives in the 1930s. By the mid 1930s women could purchase feminine hygiene products at a number of national chains, including Woolworth, Kresge, McLellan, and W. T. Grant.[34] Already fashioned as a feminized space, department stores established sequestered "personal hygiene" departments where women could shop in a dignified and discreet manner for contraceptives and other products related to female reproduction such as sanitary napkins and tampons. Stores emphasized the exclusively female environment of the personal hygiene department as the department's finest feature. The self-contained department was not only separated from the rest of the store, where "uncontrollable factors ... might make for ... embarrassment," but it was staffed solely by saleswomen trained in the "delicate matter of giving confidential and intimate personal advice to their clients." As one store assured female readers in the local newspaper: "Our Personal Hygiene Department [has] Lady Attendants on Duty at all Times." Female clerks, furthermore, were instructed to respect the private nature of the department's transactions; sensitive, knowledgeable, and tactful, they were "understanding wom[en] with whom you may discuss your most personal and intimate problems."[35]

Contraceptive manufacturers actively promoted the creation of personal hygiene departments by emphasizing to store owners and managers the revenues their establishment would generate. Advertisements in retailing trade journals such as *Chain Store Age* recounted a plethora of feminine hygiene sales success stories; although the ads varied, their transcendent morale told the same good news: selling feminine hygiene guaranteed a higher volume of customers and sales. The Zonite Products Corporation warned retailers not to miss out on the hygiene bonanza. "Did you know that feminine hygiene sales are six times greater than combined dentifrice sales?" one Zonite ad queried. "You'll be amazed [at] the way your sales and profits ... will soar by simply establishing a feminine hygiene department. By this simple plan, many dealers have tripled volume almost overnight." Zonite offered free company consultations and sales training to encourage store managers to establish hygiene departments. Other firms with the same goal in mind sent complimentary counter displays, dispensing stands for "impulse sales and quick service," and window exhibits that could be strategically placed "where women predominate in numbers." An economic incentive undergirded the company's promotional activities. The establishment of hygiene departments firmly committed stores to the long-term retailing of feminine hygiene products, while the dignified decorum of departments lent an air of credibility and legitimacy to the products themselves.[36]

Manufacturers reasoned that many prospective female customers would not buy feminine hygiene in a store. Many did not live close enough to one, while others, notwithstanding the store's discretion, might remain uncomfortable with the public nature of the exchange. To eliminate regional and psychological obstacles to birth-control buying, companies sold feminine hygiene to women directly in their homes. Selling contraceptives by mail was one such method. Mail-order catalogues, including those distributed by Sears, Roebuck and Montgomery Ward, offered a full line of female contraceptives; each catalogue contained legally-censored ads supplied by manufacturers. As a reward for bulk sales, mail-order houses received a discount from the companies whose products they sold. Other manufacturers bypassed jobbers and encouraged women to send their orders directly to the company. To eliminate the possibility of embarrassment, ads typically promised that the order would be delivered in "plain wrapper."[37]

To create urban and working-class markets, dozens of firms hired door-to-door sales representatives to canvass urban districts. All representatives were women, a deliberate attempt on manufacturers' part to profit from the prudish marketing scheme that tried to convince women that, as one company put it, "There are some problems so intimate that it is embarrassing to talk them over with a doctor."[38] ...

Contraceptive companies' tactics paid off. By 1940, the size of the female contraceptive market was three times that of the 1935 market.[39] The industry's unabated growth continued despite important changes in legal interpretation and medical attitudes in the late 1930s that might have reduced the industry's hold over American women. In 1936, the Supreme Court's *One Package* decision allowed physicians in every state to send and receive contraceptive devices and information. The following year, the American Medical Association reversed its long-standing ban on contraception, endorsing the right of a physician to prescribe birth control. The court's decision and the AMA's liberalized policy did not foster the immediate medicalization of birth control, a process that might have encouraged women to turn to the medical profession instead of the market for contraception. Indeed, in the short term, these sweeping changes proved remarkably inconsequential to the state of the industry. Many Americans could not afford the luxury of a personal physician, and only a minority lived close enough to the 357 public birth-control clinics operating in 1937 to avail themselves of clinic services. But of even more significance than medical barriers was manufacturers' enticing sales message. Companies' pledges to supply birth control that was affordable, immediate, and discretely sold – either anonymously or in a completely feminized setting – continued to strike a responsive chord with American women. In addition, manufacturers promised what no lay guide could dispute: that what was bought from the market was as effective as doctor-prescribed methods. Out of pragmatic necessity and personal preference, most women worried about pregnancy prevention continued to obtain birth control from the contraceptive market.[40] . . .

In a 1936 letter to Harrison Reeves, a New York journalist studying the commercial aspects of contraception for the *American Mercury*, Margaret Sanger reflected on the state of the birth-control business in America. Sanger was no stranger to the commercial scene. Since the early 1930s she had instructed her secretary to clip all commercial advertisements for birth control for Sanger's personal review. Sanger corresponded frequently with manufacturers eager to obtain her endorsement of new products. From direct involvement in the daily operation of public clinics that she had founded, to the multiple tests on birth control products conducted at her request by doctors at the Birth Control Clinical Research Bureau, Sanger was keenly aware of the perils and pitfalls of commercial contraception.[41]

And yet, in what amounted to more than a loyal defense of her husband's business activities, Sanger refused to vilify manufacturers for the commercial hucksterism, fraud, and misinformation that so many of them had spawned. As she explained to Reeves, "I do not feel as many do about manufacturing concerns . . . They have not lagged behind like the medical profession but have gone ahead and answered [a] growing and urgent need."[42]

Sanger's observation, although anchored in what in hindsight appears to be misplaced charity, perspicaciously speaks to the expanding role of manufacturers in shaping contraceptive practices in the 1930s. The strictures and liberties of the law, the inertia of the medical profession, and the determination of American women to find affordable and effective female-controlled birth control, provided new economic opportunities that manufacturers eagerly seized. By the end of the 1930s, manufacturers had created a lively and vigorous market that could be easily accessed in stores, by mail, and within the home. Drawing on a gendered culture that designated consumption and reproduction female roles, manufacturers implored women to "purchase" their happiness

and security from the contraceptive market. Reinforcing Victorian sensibilities about female sexuality that self-servingly bolstered their marketing scheme, they feminized sites of birth-control buying. Instead of
visiting a male doctor or druggist, women were encouraged to acquire
birth control in sex-segregated departments staffed by "discreet" female
attendants, from visiting saleswomen, or through the mail upon the
advertised recommendation of female physicians "who know."

The escalation of industry profits followed closely on the heels of the
construction of the female contraceptive consumer; by World War II, not
only did sales of feminine hygiene products surpass those of condoms,
but more women depended on feminine hygiene for birth control than
on any other method. Tragically, the very legal climate that permitted
the birth control business to flourish in a bootleg state also encouraged it
to peddle inferior goods. For too many women, the freedom, pleasure,
and security pledged by contraceptive manufacturers amounted to nothing more than empty promises.

The commercialization of birth control in the 1930s illuminates the
important but overlooked role of industry in shaping birth-control developments in the United States. Historians have typically framed birth-
control history as a tale of doctors, lawmakers, and women's rights
activists. The events of the 1930s suggest that we need to recast this
story to include the agency of a new set of actors, birth-control manufacturers. The commercialization that manufacturers engendered at this
time left an indelible imprint on the lives of ordinary women and men. It
also revealed a world in which industry, gender, and reproduction were
frequently and intimately intertwined.

Notes

1   *McCall's* LX (July 1933): 85.
2   *McCall's* LX (July 1933): 85.
3   "The Accident of Birth," *Fortune* (February 1938): 84.
4   According to *Fortune*, sales from condoms accounted for $38 million of the
    industry's annual $250 million sales. See "The Accident of Birth," p. 84.
5   For a discussion of the relationship between the American Medical Associa-
    tion and the birth-control movement, see J. M. Ray and F. G. Gosling,
    "American Physicians and Birth Control, 1936–1947," *Journal of Social
    History* 18 (1985): 399–408.
6   I have elected to use the term "grey market" to describe the sale of goods
    that, as they were marketed, were strictly legal but which, had they been
    packaged and labelled to reflect their intended application and purpose,
    would not have been. I am grateful to Michael Fellman for suggesting the
    suitability of the term to this study.

7   As one advertising leaflet put it, "Feminine hygiene is the 'nice' term . . . invented for the care and cleanliness of the vaginal tract from its outer opening to the cervix." Quoted in Rachel Lynn Palmer and Sara K. Greenberg, *Facts and Frauds in Woman's Hygiene: A Medical Guide Against Misleading Claims and Dangerous Products* (New York, 1938), p. 18.

8   Elizabeth H. Garrett, "Birth Control's Business Baby," *New Republic* (17 January 1934): 270; Dorothy Dunbar Bromley, "Birth Control and the Depression," *Harper's* (October 1934): 563; "The Accident of Birth," pp. 110, 112.

9   A poll published in *Ladies' Home Journal* in 1938 found that 79% of American women surveyed favored birth control. The most frequent argument given in its favor was economic considerations. See Henry F. Pringle, "About Birth Control," *Ladies Home Journal* 55 (March 1938): 15.

10 *Acts and Resolutions of the United States of America Passed at the Third Session of the Forty-Second Congress* (Washington, DC, 1873), pp. 234–5.

11 Twenty-four states enacted similar laws banning the circulation of contraceptives and contraceptive knowledge.

12 For a general discussion of the impact of the Comstock Act, see James Reed, *From Private Vice to Public Virtue: The Birth Control Movement and American Society Since 1830* (New York, 1978), chapter 3.

13 Linda Gordon, *Woman's Body, Woman's Right: A Social History of Birth Control in America* (New York, 1976), pp. 48–49, 64–71; Reed, *From Private Vice to Public Virtue*, pp. 4–13; Norman Hines, *Medical History of Contraception* (Baltimore, 1936), chapter 11.

14 Michael A. LaSorte, "Nineteenth-Century Family Planning Practices," *The Journal of Psychohistory* 4 (Fall 1976): 175–176; Vern L. Bullough, "A Brief Note on Rubber Technology and Contraception: The Diaphragm and the Condom," *Technology and Culture* 22 (January 1981), 104, 107–111; Reed, *From Private Vice to Public Virtue*, pp. 15–17; Gordon, *Woman's Body, Woman's Right*, pp. 67–70.

15 Anthony Comstock, appointed US Post Office Inspector to enforce the Comstock Act, boasted that he had singlehandedly destroyed 160 tons of obscene literature between 1873 and 1915, bringing 3,760 "criminals" to "justice." See Margaret H. Sanger, "Comstockery in America," *International Socialist Review* XVI (July 1915): 46.

16 Gordon, *Woman's Body, Women's Right*, pp. 231–232; Reed, *From Private Vice to Public Virtue*, chapter 9, passim; David Kennedy, *Birth Control in America: the Career of Margaret Sanger* (New Haven, 1970), p. 71.

17 Bromley, "Birth Control and the Depression," p. 566; James Rorty, "What's Stopping Birth Control," *The New Republic* (February 3, 1932): 313.

18 Dorrin E. Rudnick, "A New Type of Foreign Body in the Urinary Bladder," *Journal of the American Medical Association* 94 (May 17, 1930): 1565.

19 "*Youngs Rubber Corporation, Inc., v. C. I. Lee & Co., et al,*" 45 *Federal Reporter*, 2nd Series 103; Morris L. Ernst, "How We Nullify," *The Nation* (January 27, 1932): 114: Garrett, "Birth Control's Business Baby," p. 270.

The effectiveness of contraceptive jellies when used alone was well documented. See "The Accident of Birth," p. 85.

20   Reed, *From Private Vice to Public Virtue* pp. 244–46; Ray and Gosling, "American Physicians and Birth Control, 1936–1947," passim; Riley and White, "The Use of Various Methods of Contraception," pp. 896–900. "The Accident of Birth," p. 84; "Feminine Hygiene Products Face a New Marketing Era," *The Drug and Cosmetic Industry* 37 (December 1935): 745: Harrison Reeves, "The Birth Control Industry," 155 *American Mercury* (November 1936): 287; "Birth Control Industry," *The Drug and Cosmetic Industry* 46 (January 1940): 58; "Building Acceptances for Feminine Hygiene Products," *Drug and Cosmetic Industry* 38 (February 1936): 177.

21   Robert L. Dickinson and Louise Stevens Bryant, *Control of Conception: An Illustrated Medical Manual* (Baltimore, 1931), pp. 78–80; Dorothy Dunbar Bromley, *Birth Control: Its Use and Misuse* (New York, 1934), pp. 99–100; Palmer and Greenberg, *Facts and Frauds in Woman's Hygiene*, pp. 242–250.

22   Dickinson and Bryant, *Control of Conception*, pp. 39–45, 69–74; Bromley, *Birth Control*, pp. 92–98; Palmer and Gréenberg, *Facts and Frauds in Woman's Hygiene*, pp. 12–15, 142–151; Lysol ad from pamphlet by Dr. Emil Klarmann, *Formula LF. A New Antiseptic and Germicide*, (Lehn & Fink Inc.) appended to letter from Lehn & Fink to Margaret Sanger, 24 November 1931, reel 29, Margaret Sanger Papers, Library of Congress; PX ad from Margaret Sanger Papers, Box 232, folder "Commercial Advertisements, 1932–34." Library of Congress.

23   "Effects of Corrosive Mercuric Chloride ('Bichloride') Douches," *Journal of the American Medical Association* 99 (6 August 1932): 497.

24   "The Accident of Birth," pp. 110–112.

25   Garrett, "Birth Control's Business Baby," pp. 270–1; "The Accident of Birth," pp. 110, 112; Bromley, "Birth Control and the Depression," p. 572; Reed, *From Private Vice to Public Virtue*, p. 114, Kennedy, *Birth Control in America*, p. 183; Palmer and Greenburg, *Facts and Frauds in Woman's Hygiene*, pp. 21–24.

26   For sample captions see Bromley, "Birth Control and the Depression," the advertisement captioned "The Fear That Blights Romance and Ages Women Prematurely" is from *McCalls* LX (October 1932): 102.

27   "The Incompatible Marriage: Is it a Case for Doctor or Lawyer?" *McCall's* LX (May 1933): 107; "The Fear that Blights Romance and Ages Women Prematurely" *McCall's* LX (October 1932): 102.

28   "The Incompatible Marriage: Is it a Case for Doctor or Lawyer?" *McCall's* LX (May 1933): 107; Garrett, "Birth Control's Business Baby," p. 271: J. Rorty, "What's Stopping Birth Control?" *New Republic* 65 (January 28, 1931): 292–4.

29   Mary P. Ryan, "Reproduction in America," *Journal of Interdisciplinary History* X (Autumn 1979): 330; Ray and Gosling, "Physicians and Birth Control," p. 405; Roland Marchand, *Advertising the American Dream: Making Way for Modernity, 1920–1940* (Berkeley, 1985), passim.

30   "The Accident of Birth," p. 112.

31 "The Serene Marriage...Should it be Jeopardized by Needless Fears?"
    McCall's LXV (December 1932): 87.
32 "Why Wasn't I Born a Man?" *McCall's* LX (May 1933): 93; "Marriage is
    No Gambling Matter: Better Find Out, Better Be Sure About It" *McCall's*
    LX (March 1933): 107.
33 Garrett, "Birth Control's Business Baby," p. 270; Reeves, "The Birth Con-
    trol Industry," pp. 286–7; Bromley, "Birth Control and the Depression," p.
    570; Anne Rapport, "The Legal Aspects of Marketing Feminine Hygiene
    Products," *The Drug and Cosmetic Industry* 38 (April 1936): 474; Hines,
    Medical History of Contraception, p. 202; "The Accident of Birth," p. 85.
34 "The Accident of Birth," p. 112.
35 "Feminine Hygiene in the Department Stores," *Drug and Cosmetic Industry*
    40 (April 1937): 482; "12 Ways to More Sales in Feminine Hygiene
    Products," *Chain Store Age* (June 1941): 54.
36 Zonite advertisements in *Chain Store Age* (January 1941): 5 and (March
    1941): 66; "12 Ways to More Sales in Feminine Hygiene Products," p. 19;
    "Feminine Hygiene Products Face a New Marketing Era," *Drug and Cos-
    metic Industry* 37 (December 1935): 745–747; H. C. Naylor, "Behind the
    Scenes Promotion Builds Feminine Hygiene Sales," *Chain Store Age*
    (March, 1941): passim.
37 Garrett, "Birth Control's Business Baby," p. 269; Reeves, "The Birth
    Control Industry," p. 287; Kennedy, *Birth Control in America*, p. 212.
38 Ad quoted in Palmer and Greenburg, *Facts and Frauds in Woman's Hygiene*,
    p. 12.
39 "Birth Control Industry," p. 58.
40 "The Accident of Birth," pp. 108–114; "Birth Control Industry," p. 58;
    According to Mary Ryan, before the Pill became widely available, only
    twenty percent of American women consulted physicians about birth con-
    trol. See Ryan, "Reproduction in American History," p. 330.
41 Sanger to Harrison Reeves, 16 June 1936, reel 29, Margaret Sanger Papers,
    Library of Congress. Sanger's careful monitoring of the commercial side of
    birth control is evidenced in reels 29 and 30 of the Margaret Sanger Papers,
    Library of Congress.
42 Sanger to Reeves, 16 June 1936, reel 29, Margaret Sanger Papers, Library
    of Congress.

Documents

Advertisements for Lysol

NUMBER FOUR IN A SERIES OF FRANK TALKS BY LEADING WOMEN PHYSICIANS

"The fear that blights romance and ages women prematurely"

●

"Even in the early days of medicine, a Russian Scientist, Pavlov by name, proved that FEAR is a dangerous toxin. He demonstrated that fright dries up valuable secretions, increases the acidity of the stomach, and sometimes disturbs the bodily functions generally.

"So it is that FEAR grays the hair... etches lines in the face, and hastens the toll of old age.

"Yet many women suffer needless fear ... fear from minor feminine ails and irregularities that might easily be prevented. Fear caused by lapses in normal feminine health which could be averted readily by proper feminine hygiene and antisepsis.

"Not only for general health, but for peace of mind and mental poise, every married woman should practice intimate feminine cleanliness. That is a safeguard to youth, charm . . . and, often, happiness.

"But care should be taken in choosing the right germicide for healthful marriage hygiene. It is not safe to accept the counsels of the tea-table, or the advice of a well-meaning, but uninformed relative or friend. Some antiseptics are too mild to be effective, decomposing in contact with organic matter. Others are caustic and harsh, irritating, and often injurious to sensitive tissue.

"The safe antiseptic is "Lysol" disinfectant. There is no doubt about "Lysol." It has been recommended for many years by the gynecologists of Vienna . . . where medical science is very exacting. It is the standard antiseptic used in the delicate ministrations of childbirth. "Lysol" is penetrating and destroys bacteria which other antiseptics fail to reach . . . yet it is healing and soothing to tender membranes. The comfort of this thorough and gentle antiseptic does much to banish those feminine apprehensions that so frequently blight beauty and destroy marital happiness."

(Signed)

DR. AUGUSTE POPPER

Photographed by
Man Ray in Vienna

Dr. Auguste Popper, Graduated in Vienna; formerly with the second university women's clinic of Vienna. At present clinical physician with the Vienna children's clinic of Professor Pirquet.

Have you a young married daughter or friend who should know these facts?

For your own guidance, as well as for the enlightenment of any girl or woman who is near and dear to you . . . may we send you a copy of our interesting brochure—"The Facts About Feminine Hygiene"? Written by a woman physician, it handles the vital subject of marriage hygiene with rare delicacy and charm. Merely mail the coupon, and your copy will be sent, postpaid, in plain wrapper.

Lysol
Disinfectant

LEHN & FINK, Inc., Bloomfield, N. J., *Dept. C-10*
Sole Distributors of "Lysol" disinfectant
Please send me free, postpaid, a copy of "The Facts About Feminine Hygiene".

Name

Street

City_____ State____
© 1932, L. & F., Inc.

"The Fear that Blights Romance and Ages Women Prematurely," *McCall's*, 60 (October 1932); "The Incompatible Marriage: Is It a Case for Doctor or Lawyer?" *McCall's*, 60 (May 1933).

The first documents are part of a series of advertisements for Lysol from *McCall's Magazine* in the early 1930s. Featuring prominent European female gynecologists, the ads employed many of the techniques designed to persuade female consumers: they warned of possible marriage failure caused by pregnancy fears, and they implied that women's ignorance could be abated if only they listened to trustworthy, female doctors. What are the code words for pregnancy and birth control used in the advertisements? How do the doctors in this ad series appeal to women's vulnerability and lack of medical knowledge?

NUMBER EIGHT IN A SERIES OF FRANK TALKS BY EMINENT WOMEN PHYSICIANS

"The Incompatible Marriaqe
IS IT A CASE FOR DOCTOR OR LAWYER?"

"A wife's ill-health ... due to neglect of sensible marriage hygiene ... is frequently a contributing cause of marital discord and estrangement.

"A great American jurist, who presides over one of your Domestic Relations Courts, recently declared that many marriage failures can be traced directly to disquieting wifely fears, destructive of mutual happiness. Doctors know, all too well, how true this is.

"Almost before the honeymoon ends, many a young bride is plagued by forebodings. She pictures the early departure of youth and charm . . . sacrificed on the altar of marriage responsibilities. This worry results in physical irregularities which often seem like the beginning of a crisis.

"Such apprehensions, recurring again and again, are capable of changing the most angelic nature, of making it nervous, suspicious, irritable.

"I leave it to you . . . is it easy for even the kindliest husband to live with a wife like that?

"The pity of it is that so many such women finally turn to a lawyer for sympathy and relief . . . when what they really need is the advice of a doctor. So simple a m. ~al suggestion as the right technique of marriage h;⠀ene would remove many of their health anxieties; and give them that sense of well-being, personal daintiness and mental poise so essential to wifely security.

"I wish I might be sure of imparting to the young married women who read this, some sense of the

Doctor Anne Marie Durand-Wever of Berlin, distinguished German gynecologist, graduate of the University of Munich, Bachelor of Science, University of Chicago. Founder and Head of Advisory Board for Married People, Charlottenburg, Berlin. Author of standard German works on problems of birth and sex.

comfort and freedom I have given to hundreds of patients by insisting upon their regular use of "Lysol". It is not enough for a wife to realize the need for *feminine antisepsis;* she should know the safe and effective antiseptic to use.

"Lysol" has that rare quality of penetrating into every crevice and furrow of the membranes, destroying germ-life even in the presence of organic matter. Yet "Lysol" is gentle and soothing; it will not sear or coarsen sensitive tissue. It is so safe and sure that physicians the world over use it to prevent infection in childbirth."

(Signed)

DR. ANNE MARIE DURAND-WEVER

Have you a young married daughter or friend who should know these facts?

For your own guidance, as well as for the enlightenment of any girl or woman who is near and dear to you . . . may we send you a copy of our interesting brochure—"Marriage Hygiene—The important part it plays in the ideal marriage"? Written by three distinguished women physicians, it handles the vital subject of marriage hygiene with rare delicacy. Merely mail the coupon, and your copy will be sent, postpaid, in plain wrapper.

LEHN & FINK, Inc., Bloomfield, N. J. *Dept. LH-5*
Sole Distributors of "Lysol" disinfectant
Please send me free, postpaid, a copy of your new booklet, "Marriage Hygiene", with articles by three internationally famous physicians.

Name_____

Street_____

City_____ State____

© Lehn & Fink, Inc., 1933

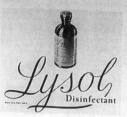

Lysol Disinfectant

Facts and Frauds in Women's Hygiene
Rachel Lynn Palmer and Sarah K. Greenberg

The second document is excerpted from a 1936 book, *Facts and Frauds in Women's Hygiene: a Medical Guide against Misleading Claims and Dangerous Products*. Written by two women, this guide exposes the dangerous and fraudulent claims of manufacturers hawking various products, such as disinfectant, as effective birth control methods. If some women knew of the potential hazards, why do you think they tried the products nonetheless? Can you think of any similar advertising dishonesty in today's world?

The Unnecessary Douche

"THE woman who has a proper regard for daintiness, cleanliness and general health should use the douche EVERY night – not merely at infrequent times." "The well-groomed woman of today has found feminine hygiene – the use of the feminine douche for personal cleanliness – an indispensable part of her toilette." "... a douche has a real place in the body-cleansing program of all fastidious women." So read the advertising leaflets of Mu-Col, Lorate, and Novo, respectively. They do their share to swell the chorus which is being raised by the manufacturers of douche powders, in the hope of persuading American women that they should douche as frequently as they wash their faces. That they have been at least partially successful is indicated by reports from doctors that douching has become very prevalent.

In the main, there are three parts to the manufacturers' theme song: a douche is necessary for cleanliness; a douche is necessary as a deodorant; a douche is an adequate contraceptive. All three of these contentions are absolutely wrong.

A douche does not make the genital tract cleaner. On the contrary, it may make it a great deal less clean than before the douche was taken. The normal vaginal secretion has natural powers of killing harmful bacteria. So effective are these powers that in the majority of women the cervix and upper half of the vagina are likely to be sterile. By washing away this normal vaginal secretion a woman is doing the opposite of

Excerpted from Rachel Lynn Palmer and Sarah K. Greenberg, *Facts and Frauds in Women's Hygiene: a Medical Guide against Misleading Claims and Dangerous Products* (New York: Garden City Publishing Co., Inc., 1936), pp. 128–31, 142–5.

achieving cleanliness in any real sense of the word. She is inviting the entrance of harmful germs, the action of which may cause a pus-laden discharge which is far from clean. The emphasis which the manufacturers of antiseptics and powders place on an "antiseptic" vagina is utterly absurd. It reveals woeful ignorance of what constitutes a healthy vagina or, more likely, deliberate intent to hoodwink potential customers. It is impossible, in the first place, to achieve an antiseptic condition of the vagina. If it were possible, it would be highly undesirable, for it would mean that the protective Döderlein bacilli would be killed.

That the douche is necessary as a deodorant is the second premise which the manufacturers are trying to establish. The Modess Company, makers of Novo, speak of the "need for a deodorizing douche." The Lorate Company expresses the same idea in a more roundabout way: "Modern styles, too, make feminine daintiness imperative. Soft, clinging garments only too readily allow unpleasant odors to reveal themselves." The douche powder manufacturers are evidently doing their best to capitalize on the "B.O." fear that has been built up in the mind of the public. As was pointed out in the previous chapter, the normal vaginal discharge is practically odorless. If there is an unpleasant odor, it comes from inadequate cleanliness of the external genital organs. No healthy woman who keeps herself and her underwear clean need have any fear about an unpleasant odor. To a woman who is really "fastidious" and "dainty" the highly perfumed quality of many of the douche powders would be absolutely repugnant.

What of the douche as a contraceptive? When used alone as a contraceptive measure, its record of failure has been as high as 70 percent. It is easy to understand why there has been such a high percentage of failures. Sometimes the spermatozoa are ejaculated directly into the cervix where no douche can reach them. Even if that has not occurred, a douche may be of no avail for a number of reasons. The sperm, which travel at the rate of about one-fourth of an inch a minute, may have made their way into the womb before a douche reaches them, unless the douche is taken immediately after ejaculation. Or they may have become imbedded in the cervical mucus, which is very tenacious and difficult to wash away. Still another possibility is that they may have lodged themselves in the depths of some of the innumerable vaginal folds, where again they are comparatively secure against any douche solution. . . .

Lysol and Zonite

. . . Just what is this Lysol, used by the Mrs. Robert Smiths of our country "as a means to intimate feminine daintiness and peace of mind"? It consists essentially of cresol, a distillate of wood and coal, which has been made soluble in water by treating it with soap. Cresol was discovered through the attempts of scientists to find a substance which would not be so poisonous as carbolic acid and yet as effective in killing germs. It is now recognized to be almost, if not equally, as dangerous as carbolic acid itself; swallowing Lysol has come to be a common – but extremely painful – means of committing suicide.

Lysol is "SAFE," says the Lehn and Fink Company, makers of this product. It takes more than the word "safe" in capital letters to refute the many cases, in medical literature, of injury and even death from Lysol. The United States Dispensatory reports the death of a woman from using Lysol in a vaginal douche. As long ago as 1911 Witthaus and Becker stated in *Medical Jurisprudence, Forensic Medicine and Toxicology* that they had collected the reports of eleven poisonings from uterine irrigations with Lysol. Five of the poisoned women died. In the *Journal of the American Medical Association* (June 29, 1935), Dr. Louis Pancaro tells of the death of a young woman who injected Lysol into her uterus in order to bring about an abortion. Within half an hour of doing so, the girl became delirious and unconscious, and died two days afterward without regaining consciousness. . . .

The mucous membranes of the vagina are considered so sensitive and easily injured that the Council on Pharmacy and Chemistry of the American Medical Association will not authorize the advertising of any antiseptic to the public for use on the genito-urinary tract. Yet Lehn and Fink, makers of Lysol, urge frequent vaginal douching with their caustic product.

What Do the American Women Think about Birth Control?

Henry F. Pringle

The third document is an article and survey concerning American women's attitudes toward birth control published in a 1938 issue of the *Ladies Home Journal*. Though it was still technically illegal for contraceptives and information about birth control to circulate through the mail, the survey indicates that, regardless of the law, American women favored birth control. Despite Margaret

Sanger's efforts to make birth control and its relation to female sexuality a topic of discussion, an overwhelming majority of these women (76 percent) said they favored birth control primarily for economic reasons; only I percent mentioned their own sexual pleasure as a factor in their decision. How does the article make it clear that this discussion was geared toward married women only? How might the article have been used to promote birth control?

No one in any part of the world today can be sure of what is ahead for tomorrow. But there are ways of putting an ear to the ground and listening. There are signs and there are portents. There are the facts of tomorrow, now taking shape – foretelling laws and customs, new ways of doing things and new discoveries. Tomorrow it will be in headlines; it will be news. Even now there is a pulse beat which you can hear, if you will listen very closely – throbbing, measured, rhythmic.

You can hear it in women's voices. . . .

What are they saying?

The women of America believe in birth control. They believe, just as firmly, in having children.

There is no contradiction in these two statements. The JOURNAL, in the second of its series of questions put to the women of the nation, asked, "Do you believe in birth control?"

The news is that a large majority of the women of America – 79 per cent – are openly, frankly and positively in favor of birth control. And it is their conviction that a subject which has been surrounded by silence should now be openly discussed and dealt with.

From farm and village and city and from every geographical section of the nation rose the affirmative chorus for birth control. It came from every age group.

The chorus varied little among married, widowed, divorced and single women. The churchgoers answered "yes" and so did the women who attend no church.

A majority among even the Catholic women – 51 per cent – declared their belief in some remedy for the problems which arise when children come too soon or too often, or into homes where poverty blocks their chance for health, happiness and life itself.

The women of America believe in having children. A ringing "no" was the answer to the JOURNAL's question, put only to the mothers, "Are you sorry you had children?" Only 2 per cent said "yes." And 69 per

Excerpted from Henry F. Pringle, "What Do the American Women Think about Birth Control?" *Ladies Home Journal*, 55 (March 1938), pp. 14–15, 94.

cent of the women with but a single child declared that they wanted at least one more. Nearly half of those with two children said they would like still another. More women said four children made up an ideal family than fixed on any smaller or larger number.

So the schools of the United States, however birth-control knowledge may be spread, are in no danger of depopulation, nor need the manufacturers of high chairs or nursing bottles prepare to shut down their plants.

Here are the answers of the women of America to the direct question, "Are you in favor of birth control?"

	YES	NO
National	79%	21%
Urban	81	19
Farmer	71	29
Small town	80	20
Protestant	84	16
Catholic	51	49
All others	89	11
Married women and widows	77	23
Divorced	91	9
Single	85	15
Income groups		
Over $1500 a year	85	15
Under $1500 a year	75	25
Age groups		
Under 30 years	88	12
30–45 years	80	20
Over 45 years	69	31

II

The women of America are consistent. Last month we heard them say that money was the chief cause of friction in marriage. Most of them now favor birth control on the ground that the average family income will not stand the strain of too rapid arrival of children.

It was, said the wife of a store owner in San Jose, California, "a crime to deprive children of the things they should have." Inadequate family finances, echoed a businessman's wife in Baltimore, "make for lack of attention to children."

The wife of a teacher in Racine, Wisconsin, voted affirmatively because birth control would "limit the number dependent on the state and city for relief." Perhaps she has seen the figures and is aware that families on the public pay rolls had 50 per cent more children than non-relief families. Data assembled by the Federal Emergency Relief Administration indicate that almost 250,000 children were born to relief families in 1933, and about the same number in 1934.

In the total figures, decreasing the number of the feeble-minded takes second place on the list of reasons given for approving of birth control.

Thus a sixty-year old widow in Charleston, West Virginia, stood for birth control so that "physically and mentally deficient people would not have children."

And a mechanic's wife in San Francisco said that knowledge of birth control might "stop degenerate people from having children."

Third in the arguments for birth control was the desire of American women to be healthy themselves, not to grow old prematurely under the burden of bearing child after child. This viewpoint was stated graphically, if inelegantly, by an Iowa farmer's wife.

"Us women ain't livestock," she told the JOURNAL's investigator. "We need a little time to do things and not always be havin' babies."

"What do you regard as the most important reason for favoring birth control?" was the specific question the interviewers put forth in order to learn why the women think as they do. The table below gives a startling picture of how closely similar are the views of all the women.

True, the ones with small incomes are slightly less worried about the birth of defectives, than the more prosperous women. It is true, also, that women who are still unmarried and who have not yet experienced the perplexities of running a home show less concern over the degree to which a large family can add to financial problems. The younger women, also, had apparently given less thought to maternal health than the women over forty-five....

An extraordinary fact brought out by the JOURNAL survey, in view of the controversy on this point, is that few or none of the women gave illegality as the basis of their opposition to birth control. The proportion was less than 1 per cent and therefore was not tabulated. Strictly speaking, it is *not* illegal in the United States for physicians to give birth-control information to preserve health. But confusion surrounds the whole subject. Recent court decisions have softened the restrictions of the old Federal law which forbade the mailing of contraceptives. The American Medical Association, in convention last June, affirmed the legal right of physicians to give advice.

"In all cases," stated a unanimously adopted report, "the legal justification is the medical need of the patient."

Few of the states, moreover, actually prohibit proper instruction by recognized clinics or by doctors. On the other hand, there are relatively few such clinics; about 350 for all the women of the country! The city

WHAT DO YOU REGARD AS THE MOST IMPORTANT REASON FOR FAVORING BIRTH CONTROL?

	Family Income	Birth of Defectives	Mother's Health	Happier Homes With No Undesired Children	Mother's Time	Spacing of Children	Happier Sex Relations	Better Parental Care
National	76%	24%	14%	3%	2%	2%	1%	1%
Urban	76	22	14	3	2	2	1	1
Farmer	74	29	13	3	2	2	—	1
Small town	77	30	14	4	1	1	—	1
Protestant	76	27	15	4	1	2	1	1
Catholic	83	17	11	2	1	—	—	2
All others	77	22	14	3	3	3	—	1
Over $1500 a year	76	25	16	4	2	2	1	1
Under $1500 a year	77	23	12	3	2	2	—	1
Under 30 years	77	22	12	3	2	2	—	1
30–45 years	75	25	14	4	2	2	1	1
Over 45 years	77	24	17	2	1	1	—	1
Married women and widows	77	23	15	3	2	2	1	1
Divorced	82	16	6	5	3	—	—	—
Single	73	29	14	3	2	2	—	1

Note: Where no figure is given the reason received less than 1 per cent.

woman can usually find one, but the farm woman may have none near. And the confusion which has for so long surrounded the legal status of birth control leads many a conservative physician to wash his hands of the whole subject. In some localities only married women with a certain number of children are served.

The Accident of Birth

In 1938 an undercover investigation by Fortune magazine discovered that the Dilex Institute of Feminine Hygiene sent out women sales representatives posing as nurses to sell the company's contraceptive kits. Available on the installment plan, each kit contained a "one-size-fits-all" diaphragm, contraceptive jelly, and a douching package. The company instructed the saleswomen to gain customers' confidence by appearing medically knowledgable, even though their only qualification for the job was previous sales experience. What features of this aggressive sales pitch might have been persuasive to potential buyers?

Good Morning. I am the Dilex Nurse, giving short talks on feminine hygiene. It will take only three minutes. Thank you – I will step in.

Undoubtedly you have heard of many different methods of feminine hygiene, but I have come to tell you of THE DILEX METHOD, which is so much more simple and absolutely sure and harmless, and which EVERY woman is so eager to learn about and have without delay.

At one time this was a very delicate subject to discuss, but today with all our modern ideas, we look at this vital subject as one of the most important of all time, and for that reason, we call to acquaint you with THIS GREAT SECRET, a most practical, convenient way.

The Dilex Method meets every protective and hygienic requirement. It is positive and safe and may be used with the utmost confidence. Each item has been given the most careful thought to fit the increasing strides in feminine hygiene...ABSOLUTE FEMININE PROTECTION is assured.

Excerpted from "The Accident of Birth," Fortune (February 1938), p. 114.

Further Reading

Chesler, Ellen. *Woman of Valor: Margaret Sanger and the Birth Control Movement in America*. New York: Simon & Schuster, 1992.

Gordon, Linda. *Woman's Body, Woman's Right: a Social History of Birth Control in America*. New York: Grossman, 1977.

Leavitt, Judith Walzer. *Brought to Bed: Childbearing in America, 1750–1950*. New York: Oxford University Press, 1986.

McCann, Carole R. *Birth Control Politics in the United States, 1916–1945*. Ithaca, NY: Cornell University Press, 1994.

Reed, James W. *The Birth Control Movement and American Society: from Private Vice to Public Virtue. With a New Preface on the Relationship between Historical Scholarship and Feminist Issues*. Princeton, NJ: Princeton University Press, 1984.

Rodrique, Jesse. "The black community and the birth control movement." In Carol Dubois and Vicki Ruiz (eds), *Unequal Sisters: a Multicultural Reader in US Women's History*. New York: Routledge, 1990.

Tone, Andrea (ed.), *Controlling Reproduction: an American History*. Wilmington, DE: Scholarly Resources, Inc., 1997.

Part IV
Modern America

11

Mixing Bodies and Cultures

Introduction

In the late nineteenth century, California and other states in the West enacted "antimiscegenation" laws, preventing marriages between white persons and any "Negro, Mulatto, or Mongolian." In this period negative attitudes toward sexual relations between Asians and whites joined similar hostilities toward such liaisons between whites and Indians and African Americans when exclusionary federal legislation encouraged the immigration of Chinese laboring men but severly restricted immigration for Chinese women. Images of menacing Asian men preying on innocent white women vied with notions of emasculated Asian men competing with white men for sexually alluring and pleasingly passive Asian women.

Set within the context of a more generalized anti-Asian hostility, the consternation of interracial sex and marriage has always included broader fears than prejudice alone might explain. Henry Yu's essay focuses on the particular obsession among American social scientists with sexual relations between whites and Asians. In the 1920s, many white social scientists worried about racial contamination and speculated that interracial sex and marriage would foster the blurring and eventual disappearance of racial boundaries. Emphasis was placed on racial difference. Whites and Asians were represented as so completely dissimilar that it became difficult for the public even to contemplate successful marriages between members of the two groups: what would couples possibly have in common? What would they see in each other?

By the 1950s, interracial marriage was seen differently; social scientists saw potential homogenization and erasure of difference as a way to alleviate racial problems in the United States. For at least some researchers, interracial sex and marriage grew desirable; the possibility of physical mixing became a bodily metaphor for the coveted cultural assimilation of the American "melting pot." The persistent consciousness of physical and cultural difference, enduring racism, and growing ethnic pride among Asian American groups, however, impeded such ethnic and racial "melting" and insured that Asian Americans would continue to be objectified and exoticized.

Mixing Bodies and Cultures: the Meaning of America's Fascination with Sex between "Orientals" and "Whites"

Henry Yu

On June 19, 1897, the Reverend Walter Ngon Fong, pastor of the Methodist Mission of San Jose and a recent graduate of Stanford University, was married. He and his bride, the new Mrs. Emma Fong, exchanged their vows in a small, quiet ceremony in Denver, Colorado.

Walter Fong had been an exceptional student at Stanford: he had served as the president of the Nestorian Debating Society and had consistently received high grades.[1] It was not, however, his academic achievements that had distinguished him. While studying in Palo Alto, Walter Fong had been the only Chinese student in the whole of Stanford University. After he graduated, his life continued to be marked by distinction. Fong became a lawyer in San Francisco and the head of the Chinese Revolutionary Party in the United States. Fong's professional status marked him as a rare, educated elite at a time when the majority of Chinese in America were merchants, laborers, or servants.[2] Fong's shining public status, however, was overshadowed by an even greater personal achievement. For a Chinese male in the United States in 1897, just being able to marry was a rare accomplishment. An

Excerpted from Henry Yu, "Mixing Bodies and Cultures: the Meaning of America's Fascination with Sex between 'Orientals' and 'Whites'," in Martha Hodes, ed., *Sex, Race, Love: Crossing Boundaries in North American History* (New York: New York University Press, 1999), pp. 44–63.

overwhelming percentage of the Chinese in America at the turn of the century were men – about 85,000 compared to a little more than 4,500 women. Labor migration had been the initial impetus for Chinese immigration to America in the 1860s and 1870s. The demographic pattern had been frozen by exclusionary federal legislation in the 1870s and 1880s, which had been explicitly designed to keep Chinese women out of the United States. American legislators believed that without Chinese women, Chinese men would be unable to establish families and therefore would never be allowed to settle in America.[3]

Yet there was even more that was exceptional about Walter Fong. Though he lived and worked in the Bay area, Fong had not been able to marry in his home state – California law prohibited him and his new bride from receiving a marriage license. The reason? Emma Fong was "white." In 1880 California's Civil Code had been amended to prohibit the issuance of any marriage license to a white person and a "Negro, Mulatto, or Mongolian." Most other states on the Pacific coast had also enacted "antimiscegenation" laws during this period. The Fongs were forced to travel to Colorado, one of the few western states without such laws, in order to sanction their union.[4]

Mrs. Emma Fong was herself an exceptional woman. Almost exactly twenty-five years after her wedding day, she related her autobiography in a series of articles in the *San Francisco Bulletin*. Entitled (in a manner recognizable to modern readers of tabloid magazines) "My Oriental Husbands – The story of a San Francisco girl, who married a Chinese graduate of Stanford University, and a year after his death became the wife of his lifelong friend, a Japanese instructor of the University of California, by Emma Fong Kuno," the story she told was amazing to the *Bulletin*'s readers, and more than a little controversial. She described the angry denunciations she had suffered, and the widespread condemnation of her spousal choices. Most of all, however, she detailed what it had been like to live with her two "Oriental" husbands: what the differences were between Chinese men and Japanese men, how they treated her, and how different they were, both from each other and from "white" Americans.[5]

The story of Walter Fong, his best friend, Professor Kuno, and their wife, Emma, is an interesting entrance into the social phenomena of interracial sex, love, and marriage between Asian Americans and "white" Americans in the twentieth century. The purpose of this essay, however, is not to explore the social dimensions of interracial sex and love. Such relations did occur, and with some frequency throughout the nineteenth and twentieth centuries. What is of much greater interest is just how interesting "white" Americans, and in particular "white" intellectuals, found such relationships.[6]

There was a peculiar fascination with sex between "Orientals" and "whites," particularly between "Oriental" men and "white" women, which was disproportionate to the small number of publicly reported cases. The marital history of Emma Fong Kuno is a perfect example. Her autobiographical story, which was published in installments to take maximum advantage of the anticipated readership, caused a great stir. The day after her series ended on June 14, 1922, the *Bulletin* published an editorial attack on intermarriage between races, and Emma Fong Kuno's text began its long life as a central piece in discussions about interracial love between "Orientals" and "whites." In 1924 the story became a key document in the massive Survey of Race Relations conducted by American social scientists on the West Coast. In 1946 her autobiography was reprinted by the Social Science Institute of Fisk University as part of a series of exemplary social documents concerning race relations and the social adjustment of "Orientals." This story, and a handful of other documented cases of intermarriage between Asian Americans and "white" Americans, became the focus for a fascination that American social science would have with sexual relations across racial boundaries.

The purpose of this essay is to explore the ways in which these social scientists defined and structured their interest in interracial sex – what it meant to them, how it fit into their conceptions of culture, race, and racial relations, how it reflected their ideological hopes and dreams for America. Beyond the individual examples of intermarriage between "Orientals" and "whites," which show little pattern except for a stubborn peculiarity unique to each case, I am much more interested in examining the scholarly fascination with sexual relations across racial boundaries. Social scientists thought that by examining an individual case of an "Oriental" man and a "white" American woman, they could learn something about race relations between "Orientals" and "whites" in general. This assumption led to an intense examination of individual cases of racial intermarriage, and attempts to find and gather as many of these cases for analysis as possible. This essay will focus on social scientists' interest in intermarriage in order to explore their theories about the importance of race and culture. A larger goal is to provide a historical context for scholarly interest in "intermarriage" and interracial sex. Recent studies of intermarriage have looked to the phenomenon as one fraught with great social meanings, just as have studies in the past. Perhaps outlining some of the reasons that intermarriage as a topic has historically been so hotly pursued will lead to more critical examinations of contemporary fascinations with interracial sex.

Throughout the twentieth century, intermarriage has been conceptualized in two ways: as the meeting point of different things, and as the ultimate erasure of the difference between things. Like a pendulum, the interest in intermarriage between "Orientals" and "whites" has swung from an emphasis in the 1920s upon exotic couples who were different from each other, to an obsession in the 1950s with homogenization and hybridization as a means of solving the problems of racial difference, and back and forth again in the last three decades between intermarriage as a sign of difference and interracial children as a sign of hybridization.

From the first large-scale appearance of Chinese in America in the 1850s, through the rise of Japanese immigration at the turn of the century, and up until the 1920s, the dominant public reaction of the American social body, and of the educated elite, was a fear and abhorrence of Asian immigrants. A few capitalists (such as Leland Stanford – whose money, much of it made through the labor of Chinese railroad workers, founded Stanford University) and missionaries welcomed Asian immigrants as malleable laborers or potential converts. However, anti-Asian activists succeeded in arousing a fear of an "Asiatic invasion" or a "yellow peril" overwhelming "white" workers and, potentially, American civilization itself. When Emma Fong Kuno's marital history was first published in 1922, the text and the subsequent attacks on it plugged into a larger context of debates over racial competition and fears about the long-term survival of the "white race." Racial death and the end of "white" supremacy and civilization were often prophesied. In the competition among the races, "whites" were warned to fear the alleged reproductive advantage of "Mongolians," who were believed to be more fertile, but intellectually and physically inferior. . . .

American social scientists, particularly those from the University of Chicago's department of sociology, extensively documented and explored cases of sexual contact between "Orientals" and "whites" during the twentieth century. In the 1920s sociologists from the University of Chicago, the University of Southern California, and the University of Washington made intermarriage between "Orientals" and "whites" one of the major aspects of their Survey of Race Relations on the West Coast. From the 1920s to the 1960s, a number of doctoral students in sociology at the University of Chicago, some of whom were Chinese American or Japanese American, continued to focus on intermarriage as one of the key aspects of race relations between "Orientals" and "whites" in America. The original theories produced during the 1920s continue to structure the ways in which race and culture are understood by social theorists to the present day.

During the Survey of Race Relations between 1924 and 1926, American social scientists and the missionary social reformers who gave them financial backing decided to study what they labeled the "Oriental problem" on the West Coast. Anti- Japanese agitation at the time, and anti-Chinese movements of the 1860s and 1870s, had rallied "white" Americans of the laboring classes against "Oriental" and "Asiatic" immigration, blaming Asian American workers for the difficult social and economic position of "white" workers. Anti-Asian legislation such as the federal Chinese Exclusion Act of 1882, California's Anti-Alien Land Acts of 1917 and 1923, and the federal National Origins Acts of 1924 discriminated racially against Chinese and Japanese immigrants and enjoyed widespread public support. Anti-Asian publications such as Valentine McClatchy's *Sacramento Bee* used the term "yellow peril" to describe the threat of Asian immigrant labor competing with "white" laborers migrating at the same time to the West Coast. A long history of lynching, violence, and rioting against Asians had provided a legacy of racial strife that social reformers and sociologists defined as the "Oriental problem" in America. One of the major interests of both the missionaries and the sociologists centered upon intermarriage between the "races."

In 1923 Robert Park, one of the leaders of the Chicago school of sociology, was enlisted by Protestant missionaries to direct an "objective" survey to study the "facts" of the "Oriental problem" on the West Coast. Park and his fellow sociologists believed that they could study an inflammatory issue such as the "yellow peril" with the detached air of a biologist studying a plant, maintaining critical distance from the conflicts surrounding the "Oriental problem" in America. It is no surprise that their attempts to maintain an "unbiased" and "uncontroversial" approach proved impossible, despite their rhetoric of "scientific objectivity." Even during the 1920s the claims of social science for "value-neutral" and "nonpartisan" research were a matter of bitter debate. The facade of "objectivity" proved the most difficult to maintain when the sociologists began to study the heated topic of interracial sex.

The intellectual interest of the sociologists and missionaries in the subject of intermarriage must be placed in the context of a wider curiosity about "miscegenation." Academic interest in the sexual relations of Chinese and Japanese American men with "white" women was inextricably tied to a widespread fear of the sexual behavior of "Oriental" men. No matter how enraged or emotional West Coast anti-Asian activists became over the issue of "Oriental" immigration in general, they became even more enraged with the subject of interracial sex – the idea of "mongrelization" and "dirty Orientals" lewdly fondling "white" women. The "yellow peril" rhetoric that infused pulp magazines and dime novels did not try to rationalize unfair labor competition or overly efficient farming practices; it dwelled instead upon "Oriental" men preying on helpless "white" women. Perhaps best realized in Sax

Rohmer's fictional character Fu Manchu, pulp magazines and novels depicted "Orientals" as scheming men with long fingernails, waiting in ambush to kidnap "white" women into sexual slavery.[7] Just as lurid were the denunciation of, and obsession with, "Oriental" women, as expressed through descriptions of them as "prostitutes" and "sex slaves."

The sexual threat of individual "Oriental" men and women stood for the larger threat of the "Oriental race." Would America be purely "white" in the future, or would the sexual threat of the "yellow peril" turn Americans into a "mongrel race"? Interracial sex was a taboo subject that seemingly everyone – "white" and "Oriental" – wanted to think about and read about, yet only pornographic novels or pulp fiction dared to explore. It is hard to recover just how hot a topic it was, how incensed people became about it, how fascinated and obsessed. Even in the sociologists' self-conscious attempts to write rhetorically neutral texts during the Survey of Race Relations, the wider context of prurient interest in interracial sex could not be ignored. Early on in the survey, the missionary J. Merle Davis, secretary of the Survey of Race Relations, asked Park to produce a sample questionnaire to pass around in an effort to drum up interest and financing for the survey. Park chose to give him an extensive document on "interracial marriage." Davis raved about the public response to the questionnaire:

> I have had fifty copies of this document mimeographed here in Seattle and am using them with people who are vitally interested. It is significant to note that *practically everyone is crazy to get a copy*, and it is plain that there is much more interest in this topic than appears on the surface.
>
> This document has already *revived the drooping interest* of some of our leaders here in Seattle, and will be useful with every group, as a concrete evidence of the spirit and method of approach to some of these difficult problems.
>
> You certainly made a happy choice in the subject of the first question-naire. *From the way folks act or react to it, one would be led to believe that most of these good people at one time or another had had serious thoughts about marrying a Chinese or Japanese.*[8]

Davis made hundreds of copies and sent them out in an effort to elicit donations for the survey. The missionaries did not pass on the opportunity to capitalize on interracial marriage as the technique to retool their flaccid fund-raising efforts. What was this amazing document that could revive "drooping interest" in the survey? What questions did it ask that would warrant such a response from inquiring minds up and down the Pacific coast? What did people want to know about interracial marriage and sex?

In fact, the questionnaire seems quite sedate, and never probed very deeply into the roots of sexual attraction between "races." But it is important to consider the different perspectives that anti-Asian activists brought to their readings of the questionnaire – they focused in on the provocative aspects of interracial sex:

> Of what height and coloring is the American woman married to an Oriental? Is it a type closely approximating that of the Oriental women? What kind of Oriental man does the American woman marry? Is he American in appearance? What seems to be the basis of the physical attraction? Are the American women who have married Orientals wholesome and conventional people? Do any of them belong to marked psychological types, the romantic, the neurotic, etc.?[9]

Anyone and everyone who ever wanted to know why "white" women would ever be attracted to "Oriental" men could identify with these questions. The "romantic" type and the "neurotic" type, who were being suggested as possible marriage partners, were obviously not the same as "wholesome and conventional people."

Park and the sociologists were also very interested in the class aspects of interracial marriage, asking whether the woman was of the same economic or social level as the man, and whether her status was raised or lowered by the union. Again, such an interest from the point of view of the sociologists was a neutral and seemingly dispassionate inquiry into the social and economic background of the lovers. Yet coupled with the question of whether the American woman was of a "conventional" and "wholesome" type, the inquiring mind of the reader could quickly tour the slums and ghettoes of urban America. Was she "white trash," or a prostitute perhaps? Was she somehow gaining status by marrying an "Oriental" of a better class when no "white" man would marry her?

These possibilities were hinted at by the line of questioning. The assumption that it would be an "Oriental" man marrying a "white" woman was telling, refracting the "yellow peril" fears that most "Orientals" in the United States were men who posed a sexual threat to "white" women, and that the few "Oriental" women were prostitutes believed unfit for marriage. While there were more Chinese American males in the United States in 1924 than there were females, the sex ratio of the Japanese was much more even; the basis for the questionnaire's assumption of a "white" woman marrying an "Oriental" man thus had as much to do with popular preconceptions of protecting "white" womanhood" as it did with demographics.

The interracial marriage questionnaire allowed for a wide range of interpretations that differed from the author's intended meanings. Robert

Park was purportedly interested in intermarriage for reasons having to do with social acceptance of the couple and their children. For instance, there were numerous questions about how other people regarded the marriage and its offspring, and family and community reactions were polled. Yet although the questionnaire was designed to elicit a history of people's attitudes about interracial marriage, the numerous fascinated readers could find their own interests within it. Those people obsessed with the question of interracial sexual relations could, for example, find hints of their own erotic fantasies in the text of the questionnaire.

Indeed, the interracial marriage document was deliberately provocative, and Park was aware of the potential ways in which it could be read. Having been a newspaper reporter and having been in charge of public relations at Booker T. Washington's Tuskegee Institute in Alabama, Park considered himself an expert on the range of receptions a text could invoke. Prior to writing the questionnaire, Park had responded coolly to Davis's request for a public relations release concerning the survey. Park believed that it was better to keep the survey's exact nature under wraps, so people could supply their own understandings of its purpose.[10] He believed in the technique of generating public interest through the hype of secrecy. Davis, however, convinced Park that there was a danger of anti-Asian agitators assuming that the survey would be pro-"Oriental," and thus refusing to cooperate. Instead of a press release, Park wrote the questionnaire.[11]

The questionnaire was a masterful text designed to arouse everyone's desire for more information about interracial marriage – it appealed to the sociologists' and missionaries' needs for enlightened knowledge at the same time that it stimulated the worst fears and obsessions of anti-Asians. The interest of Chinese and Japanese Americans was also piqued, and like nativists who could go on and on about the threat of "Oriental" men to "white" women, Chinese and Japanese Americans responded to the surveyors' questions about intermarriage with a clarity that revealed long reflection on the matter. . . .

Park was interested in intermarriage for two reasons. First, he understood intermarriage as the focal point of all race relations, the distillation and symbol of two different cultures coming into intimate contact. Whatever tensions there were between two groups' cultures and social attitudes, he believed the marriage between two individuals carrying those attitudes would certainly be the place to explore the dynamic of those tensions. The relationship between a man and a woman of two different "races" was the perfect experiment for discovering how different "cultures" and "races" could coexist. What changes in attitude were required? How was "race consciousness" overcome?

Park was not interested in whether the children of such "hybrid" relationships would be biologically inferior or superior – he was certain that such a question needed no answer except to discredit those who were claiming the genetic inferiority of such children. He was, however, interested in the children of intermarriages as "cultural" products, as the embodiment of two social groups in contact. Did either community ignore the children or ostracize them? Did either community cut off ties with the married couple? What about the families of the couple? These were the interesting questions for Park, and they tied into his second reason for research into intermarriage as the ultimate solution to the problem of "race prejudice." If physical differences such as skin color were the symbolic markers that allowed people to abstract their awareness of different "races," then physical "amalgamation" would eventually remove these racial markers.

This interest in intermarriage as a biological homogenizer was purely theoretical, and Park never advocated it as the ultimate solution. Indeed, his belief that "cultural assimilation" was the sufficient end of the "melting pot" did not result from personal fears of interracial marriage, but rather derived from his emphasis on the validity of "cultural assimilation" as a purely "social" phenomenon. The fact that the Japanese and Chinese in America were not permitted to intermarry with "whites" was disturbing to him not because "hybrid" children would never be produced, but because it indicated that the social interaction between the "races" was still not intimate enough. Assimilation in the cultural sense was obviously not taking place.

The emphasis that sociologists placed on intermarriage as a cultural phenomenon, and the consequent de-emphasis placed on its physical component, paralleled the missionaries' emphasis on conversion as a matter of faith. Protestant missionaries, in their desire to convert and Americanize "Orientals" and other people who were "racially" different from "Americans" (a term they used to mean "white"), came up with the idea of assimilation in a spiritual sense. As a matter of conscious faith and acts of piety, the missionaries' version of American assimilation had little to do with the physical body. Social scientists paralleled this separation of the physical body from the definition of assimilation by promoting the concept of "culture," which they defined as divorced from the biology of the body. Intermarriage, for Park and the sociologists, was more interesting as a social phenomenon than as a biological act. Indeed, if the concept of assimilation was to be a purely cultural interaction, then it was improper to discuss the body as anything except the site of cultural mixture.

The interest of American social science in sexual contact between "Orientals" and "whites" occupied a significant portion of the Survey of Race Relations research. In files coded "IM" for "intermarriage," documents touching on sex between "Oriental" and "white" Americans made up about ten percent of the four hundred or so life histories and interviews that the surveyors collected. The sociologists believed that their examination of sexual relations between individual "Orientals" and "whites" was of great consequence for the future of American society. Sex between individuals of different "races" would produce children who were both "American" and "Oriental" in culture, just as social contact in general between different "races" could lead to a society that was culturally "half-white" and "half-Oriental." Sexuality and sexual reproduction between individuals became the focal point for concerns about the metaphorical "reproduction" of the social body as a whole. Just as individual "Orientals" could stand as symbols for the larger threat of a "yellow peril" overtaking "white" civilization, sexual relations at the level of individual man and woman symbolized general social relations in American society. . . .

By the 1950s some Chicago sociologists studying the "Oriental problem" in America had become convinced that "social" or "cultural assimilation" between racial groups in the United States was not enough to eradicate racial prejudice. The writings of one social theorist, the Chinese American sociologist Rose Hum Lee, serve as an example of how an emphasis on the actual products of interracial sex, rather than the mere act, could shift the discourse on intermarriage from ideas about difference to hopes about the creation of sameness. Rose Hum Lee finished her doctorate at the University of Chicago in 1947, and by 1956 had achieved the height of a prolific career at Roosevelt University in Chicago by becoming the first woman, and the first Chinese American, to head a sociology department at an American university. [12]

Rose Hum Lee had begun her career emphasizing that cultural assimilation was enough to end racial prejudice, but by the end of the 1950s she had begun to despair of Park's emphasis upon culture. Lee's analysis contained one major difference from those of earlier sociologists. Robert Park's answers to the "Oriental problem" had emphasized that on a theoretical level, social assimilation was inevitable. Interracial relationships were merely singular instances of more general cultural interactions. Rose Hum Lee offered a more concrete prescription for the ultimate solution to America's "race" problems: the universal physical mixing of individuals. . . .

Rose Hum Lee's extolling of the need for biological race-mixing in order to remove all physical traces of difference was extreme even in the 1950s. This vision of the assimilation process went far beyond what might be termed the "culturalist" theories of the Survey of Race Relations sociologists. Physical differences, Park had said, had nothing to do with differences between the "races" except for the cultural consequences of seeing physical difference. It was self-consciousness caused by awareness of physical difference, not any physical difference in itself, that was at the root of racial awareness. Culture was a purely mental and social phenomenon. For Park, the ultimate "melting pot," which lay at the end of the assimilation cycle, was built purely out of shared memories and experiences – actual physical amalgamation was extraneous and unnecessary. Studying intermarriage and its importance to social relations, therefore, did not necessitate interest in the sexual act nor in its products. . . .

In many ways, Lee's move away from Park's emphasis on cultural assimilation toward a call for physical amalgamation signaled a fundamental weakness in the social scientists' model of culture in America. The existence of racial awareness and the consciousness of physical difference were of such permanence in American social life that racial boundaries were considered by Lee to be insurmountable through cultural means. Intermarriage, because it had been conceived as the meeting point between biological and cultural conceptions of racial contact, could embody a switch in emphasis from cultural to physical components.

Social scientists in the 1920s had defined intermarriage in such a way that it relied upon an awareness of differences in physical bodies, while seemingly emphasizing only the cultural aspects of the contact between those bodies. They seemed to erase the importance of the biological by focusing upon culture, but by choosing sexuality and sexual reproduction as the site of closest cultural contact, the sociologists placed an awareness of biology at the center of any definition of cultural difference. Sexual contact between two physical bodies did not necessarily result in the social institution of marriage, but the social scientists collapsed interracial sex and interracial marriage into the same category in order to emphasize the greater social meanings of sexual contact between individuals.

Rose Hum Lee, living in a body that would never be accepted as anything except different, could see no way out of America's racial dilemma short of racial homogenization. Rose Hum Lee saw herself as straddling the marginal space between an exotic "Orient" and a "white" America. Though born and raised in Butte, Montana, she never felt fully accepted, and played the role of a translator and interpreter of the Chinese experience to interested Americans. Rose Hum Lee was forced to exoticize herself and though she managed a successful academic career, her call for a time when "the cultural hybrid no longer poses a problem to himself and others" can be seen as referring as much to herself as it did to Chinese Americans in general.[13] To Lee, the "cultural hybrid" was not enough; only an actual "physical hybrid" would be free from racial discrimination. Rose Hum Lee saw "intermarriage" as the ultimate answer to the problem of racial prejudice and strife; interracial sex was the penultimate act that would produce the physically indistinguishable children of a "melting pot" America.

The meanings that "interracial sex" carried for American social thinkers seemed to go far beyond a prurient interest in sex across the color line. In the end, though, despite the multitude of meanings that interracial sex could convey, American social scientists and reformers could never escape the prurience of their own interest in the subject. They were fascinated by its connotations, and their obsession with exploring its hidden dimensions reflected a larger concern with its erotic and exotic potential. "Orientals" were the exotic "other" against which "white" Americans on the West Coast could measure themselves. "Orientals" were also an erotic fantasy, a mystery to be explored, the object of "white" men's loathing and "white" men's lust (and less apparent in images of popular culture, the object of "white" women's loathing and lust).

American sociologists' fascination with intermarriage between the "races" has always been more than social theory. The interest of social scientists in "interracial sex" inhabited the dark and liminal space connecting the sexuality of researchers and the social research they produced. The denial of such a connection has always been a precondition for the claims for validity of such social research, but it is a denial that speaks to the same tension between fascination and loathing that has marked the meanings of "miscegenation" in modern America. "White" social scientists consistently denied their personal fascination with exotic "Orientals." ...

The exoticization of "Orientals" was an act that always contained the possibility of smooth interchange between fear and lust. Loathed for being different, "Orientals" have always been desired at the same time for being different. If "Orientals" embodied the exotic, eroticization opened up the possibility of subsuming that difference within the sexual act. The tension still exists between a fascination with the exotic and a desire to unify America through similarity. Intermarriage remains the symbol for the meeting of difference and the ultimate disappearance of difference.

It is interesting to speculate about the possible reaction that Walter and Emma Fong's story might have generated if they had married in the 1990s rather than the 1890s. What would sociologists find fascinating about their history? Perhaps social scientific interest in Walter Fong would begin with his exceptional accomplishments; he was a perfect example of a "model minority." A highly educated, "overachieving" Asian American with a professional career, Walter Fong could serve as the poster boy for social scientific and political arguments that Asian Americans perform better than other minority groups in terms of education and income. The clincher would be his achievement of the ultimate symbol of acceptance into American society – his "white" wife. The perfect flourish to cap his achievements, the educated Emma Fong would represent acceptance and assimilation into "white" America.

The intimate connection between social acceptance and intermarriage might be best contained in a saying common in the 1970s that "sansei marry blondes." The notion that third-generation Japanese Americans were "marrying out" in significant numbers (backed by demographic reports of rates of exogamy among Japanese Americans that exceeded 50 percent) led to fears of "racial death," as well as hopes for the ultimate amalgamation of America. This time, the fears were articulated most vocally among Japanese Americans, who prophesied the eventual disappearance of their community.[14] For some community activists, intermarriage was the most extreme form of "selling out" to the American dream of assimilation and trying to "become white." For other Japanese Americans, intermarriage with "whites" was simply another indication that they had achieved acceptance and success in the larger American society.

There is a history to the idea that intermarriage between Asian Americans and "whites" is a meaningful symbol. It has represented the fulfillment of a certain "American dream," the "melting pot" process of turning difference into similarity. Among both "whites" and Asian Americans, intermarriage has appeared as both a sign of success in assimilation and a dangerous process of "race-mixing" and "cultural loss." Intermarriage was seen to represent both difference and the erasure of difference. Although Robert Park and his fellow social scientists insisted that culture was a mental phenomenon – a matter of consciousness divorced from physical attributes – the prime marker of cultural difference has almost always been the body. American sociologists, in fighting racial thinking based on theories of biological inferiority or superiority, argued for the concept of "culture," one of the most influential and important constellations of ideas in twentieth-century America. Theories about cultural assimilation triumphed both among social scientists and within popular thinking by the 1950s, succeeding in defining culture as absolutely nonbiological. Culture as a purely mental phenomenon, a result of consciousness and of acts caused by consciousness, was seen as the perfect road toward a homogenized melting pot.

The sociologists, however, could never break the connection between biological difference and their own awareness of cultural difference. They mapped different cultures onto different sets of bodies. This initial mapping worked because discrete sets of people who looked, for instance, "Oriental" did on the whole come from specific areas in Asia. In comparing Asian Americans to people who came from other places, "white" American social observers could homogenize the widely variant "cultural" practices of all "Orientals." They could then imagine that intermarriage would eventually erase the cultural differences between "Orientals" and "whites." Rose Hum Lee, however, recognized that it was not the existence of cultural difference that was the obstacle to social assimilation; racial thinking remained despite intimate social relations between the "races." Indeed, the erotic allure of social relations could be driven by the very awareness of racial difference that sociologists thought the sex act would erase.

An awareness of the physical markers of biology is still a part of American consciousness, and so there remains a masked connection between bodies and culture. It is only because of our fine-tuned awareness of bodily difference that our fascination with intercultural sex and marriage makes sense. As long as Americans connect cultural difference with physical difference, we shall equate the racial with the cultural, and we shall remain fascinated with the idea of sex across racial boundaries.

Notes

1　The story of Walter Fong and Emma Fong Kuno was originally published in the *San Francisco Bulletin*, May 24–June 14, 1922. Copies were collected by the Survey of Race Relations on the West Coast in 1923; Papers of the Survey of Race Relations, box 24, major document 53, Hoover Institution Archives, Stanford University. The story was reprinted in a Fisk University collection, *Social Science Source Documents No. 4: Orientals and Their Cultural Adjustment. Interviews, Life Histories and Social Adjustment Experiences of Chinese and Japanese of Varying Backgrounds and Length of Residence in the United States (Nashville: Social Science Institute, Fisk University, 1946).*

2　According to Judy Yung's work on US census manuscripts, about 7.5 percent of San Francisco Chinese men in 1900 were professionals; see Yung, *Unbound Feet: A Social History of Chinese Women in San Francisco* (Berkeley: University of California Press, 1995), 301.

3　Numbers from 1940 US census. See Yung, *Unbound Feet*, 303; and Sucheng Chan, "Exclusion of Chinese Women, 1870–1943," in *Entry Denied*, ed. Sucheng Chan (Philadelphia: Temple University Press, 1991), 95.

4　Yung, *Unbound Feet*, 29; Dick Megumi Ogumi, "Asians and California's Anti-Miscegenation Laws," in *Asian and Pacific American Experiences: Women's Perspectives*, ed. Nobuya Tsuchida (Minneapolis: Asian/Pacific American Learning Resource Center and General College, University of Minnesota, 1982), 6. By the 1920s, antimiscegenation laws forbidding marriage between "Orientals" and "whites" had been enacted in California,

Washington, Oregon, Nevada, Montana, and Idaho. California's law remained in effect until after World War II.

5   I use the term "Oriental" not because I condone its use as a name or marker, but because it reflects a specific historical usage and category. The current usage for people who can trace their heritage back to Asia or the Pacific Ocean is "Asian/Pacific Islanders," a label that encompasses Chinese, Japanese, Filipino, Korean, Samoan, Hawaiian, Vietnamese, Cambodian, Thai, Indonesian, and other such ancestry. The term "Asian American," which replaced "Oriental" in the 1970s, still works for many of the same people who were formerly known as "Orientals." I use the term "white" for the constellation of people who benefit by being defined as different from those Americans of "color." I have also initially highlighted the terms "race," "interracial," and "hybrid" as a way of demarcating them as terms dependent on definitions of racial difference in America.

6   Social scientists in the 1920s equated "white" with "American," and thus understood Emma Fong, born in Canada, as the "American" in an interracial relationship between an "American" and an "Oriental." She is an example of how easy it was for "white" immigrants to America, particularly from Canada or Great Britain, to assume and be given the identity of "American." For the wedding, see *San Francisco Chronicle*, June 20, 1897; *Denver Rocky Mountain News*, June 20, 1897.

7   Sax Rohmer was the pseudonym of Arthur Sarsfield Ward, who wrote a series of novels, beginning with *The Insidious Dr. Fu-Manchu* (New York: McKinlay, Stone, and McKenzie, 1913), involving the nefarious Fu Manchu, an evil "Oriental" genius out to conquer the world.

8   Davis to Park, Nov. 21, 1923, box 13, Park Correspondence, Papers of the Survey. Emphasis added.

9   Original of the full Intermarriage Document, box 6, Papers of the Survey. The questionnaire, which was only a portion of the larger document discussing "racial intermarriage," was reprinted in Emory Bogardus, *Introduction to Social Research* (Los Angeles: Sutton house, 1936).

10 Letters between Park and Davis, Dec. 1923, box 13, Park Correspondence.

11 There had been a debate among the survey organizers over the desirability of using the "red flag" of interracial sex to provoke interest; see letters between Davis and George Gleason, March 17, 20, 25, 1924, General Correspondence Folder, box 13, Papers of the Survey.

12 On Rose Hum Lee, see Biographical File, Roosevelt University Archives, Chicago; private letters and papers in the possession of her daughter, Elaine Lee; interviews by Henry Yu with her brother, Ralph Hum, Oct. 1992; and with a roommate at the University of Chicago, Beulah Ong Kwoh, Jan. 1992. Rose Hum Lee, "The Marginal Man: Re-evaluation and Indices of Measurement," *Journal of Human Relations* (1956): 27–28.

13 Lee, "The Marginal Man," 28.

14 For statistics, see Akemi Kikamura and Harry H. L. Kitano, "Interracial Marriage: A Picture of the Japanese Americans," *Journal of Social Issues* 29 (1973): 67–81.

Documents

The first document is a *San Francisco Chronicle* article reporting on the marriage of Walter Fong, a native of China, and Emma Ellen Howse, a white Canadian woman and graduate of Stanford University. The article appeared as a news story, rather than in the marriage section of the paper, perhaps because Fong and Howse had to travel out of state to marry legally. How do the descriptions of the bride and groom betray the newspaper's disposition toward interracial union?

A Stanford Girl Weds a Chinese

Romance of the University

The Groom a Graduate of the Institution
Miss Emma Howse and Walter Ngong Fong United at Denver

Special Dispatch to the "Chronicle."
DENVER (Col.), June 19. – Walter Ngong Fong, a native of Kwang Tung, China, aged 31, and Miss Emma Ellen Howse of Port Dalhousie, Ontario, both of Stanford University, California, were married by Rev. Dr. Cobern to-day at the residence of the minister. Fong recently graduated from the law course of the university and the bride is a student in the institution.

"It is not a runaway match," smilingly said Mrs. Fong when seen by a representative of the "Chronicle" at the Metropole Hotel this afternoon. "We met in the university, where we were students, and decided that we would get married. That is all there is of the story. We found that the laws of California do not permit the County Clerks to register the marriages which occur between persons born as we were, and Colorado was the nearest that extended privileges in the matter. We could have gone to Montana, but it was further away and we had a desire to see Denver, so we came here and had the ceremony performed."

Taken from "A Stanford Girl Weds a Chinese," *San Francisco Chronicle*, June 20, 1897, p. 20.

Mrs. Fong is a bright-looking little woman, with a snow-white complexion, while her husband is an unusually handsome-looking native of the Flowery Kingdom. He speaks English almost perfectly, and after taking a post graduate course at the university will settle down in San Francisco in the practice of the profession of law.

Walter Fong is a graduate in the history and law courses of Stanford University, finishing in the class of '96. He is also an alumnus of the University of the Pacific, from which institution he graduated in 1887 with the degree of bachelor of arts.

Fong earned his way, while a student, as an interpreter in the courts at San Jose and teacher in the Chinese Mission night school. The young Chinese is a professed convert to Christianity, and in San Jose was an active member of the First Methodist Church and a warm friend of the pastor, Rev. Dr. Cantone. He many years ago discarded queue and blouse and became a great favorite with all classes in San Jose, especially the Judges and lawyers, whose confidence he enjoyed as court interpreter.

Fong speaks English perfectly. He was known at the universities he attended as an advanced Chinese, with optimistic views regarding the early awakening and progress of his native land. A few months ago he was credited with being at the head of a powerful organization of educated Chinese in this country, whose object was the overthrow of the present dynasty and the transformation of the Chinese empire into a great Oriental republic.

The laws of California forbid the admission of a Chinese to the bar, except he be American born, but since his graduation from Stanford Fong has had an office in Chinatown where he is known as a legal adviser. He is connected with a well-known Stanford man who has been admitted to the bar and has offices up town.

Mrs. Fong is the daughter of a Mr. Horace, who conducts a billiard hall at Palo Alto. The young woman was for three years a special student in history at the university and was regarded as bright in her classes and quite attractive in her personality.

My Oriental Husbands

Mrs Emma Fong Kuno

This second document is an excerpt from a serialized article, "My Oriental Husbands," written by Mrs Emma Fong Kuno for the *San Francisco Bulletin*. After Mrs Kuno's first husband, Walter Fong, died from bubonic plague, she married one of his good friends, Yoshi Kuno, a Japanese man. Her story was newsworthy, not only because she was a white woman who married two Asian men, but also because the marriages were seemingly so successful and happy. Mrs Kuno addresses the issue of racial prejudice forthrightly, condemning the unreasonable negative public opinion she has endured. How does Mrs Kuno's explanation and justification of her marriage compare to the essay ("Why Japanese and Americans Should Not Intermarry") that appeared the day after her own article's last installment?

Chapter XVII

People frequently question whether I have made as much of my Oriental husbands as might have been possible with men of my own race.

I think that I have. While I have no doubt that I should have been content had an American husband come in the line of my life, yet, had I the decision to make over again I should do exactly as I have done. Speaking broadly, the joy and satisfaction that one gets out of life depends largely upon what he or she puts into it. My opportunity for service has been unique as I have been identified with two foreign peoples who have regarded me as one of themselves.

Mine has not been the isolated, shut-in life that some might imagine. On the contrary, I have had ample opportunity both for self-cultivation and self-expression. I have gone back to college from time to time and have succeeded in gaining three university degrees, two from Stanford and one from the University of California. I have also had leisure to write, and have had the satisfaction of seeing my articles published over a wide area from old Canton to London, England. My writings have appeared not only in various newspapers, but also in magazines, including so erudite a journal as the "Pedagogical Seminary." . . .

Excerpted from Mrs Emma Fong Kuno, "My Oriental Husbands," *San Francisco Bulletin*, June 13, 14, 1922.

Race prejudice is strong on the Pacific Coast, and some people have been unsparing in their condemnation of me for allying myself with the Orientals. I have had to face unkind remarks, snobbishness and cold familiarity, but these things have never affected my peace of mind.

I recall an instance in which this prejudice contributed indirectly to our making the acquaintance of one of our choicest friends. When Mr. Fong and I first came to Berkeley to look for a house we went into a real estate office on Shattuck avenue, where the supercilious clerk informed us, with an elevation of the eyebrows, that he wasn't renting houses that day. Nothing daunted, we turned up Center street and entered the office of Mr. Warren Cheney. That genial gentleman not only found for us just the sort of house we wanted, but walked all the way there and back with us for fear we might mistake our way. His conversation was both entertaining and instructive, and it gave us a good impression of Berkeley to find a real estate agent of such culture. Later, we learned that he was both a prominent author and one of Berkeley's most respected citizens. How we prized his friendship and how grateful we felt that the first agent had turned us away!

Chapter XVIII

In Berkeley, while the faculty and students at the University of California were free from prejudice, ours being a pioneer marriage of this kind, there was considerable undesirable publicity in the town. Women in their clubs and various chit-chat societies raked me over unmercifully. Occasionally some of their findings reached my ears, but I was too busy with things worth while to pause to inquire the names of the authors of these bursts of eloquence.

I should not speak of this but for the fact that a few weeks ago one of the pioneer women of Berkeley who has been much in the public eye and whose opinions have always carried considerable weight, upon seeing me pass the door, asked if I wouldn't come in and talk to her. I have known her by reputation and by sight for twenty years, but did not know that she was especially interested in me. Of recent years I have known her in a business way, and when we have met in the street she has generally stopped to pass the time of day and make inquiry regarding the well-being of my family.

On this particular day, after showing me to a seat, she declared to me that of all the women who had spoken bitterly of me she had been the most bitter; of all those who had criticized me, she had been the most active: that she had condemned me when I contracted the first marriage; and that she had anathematized me when I entered into the second.

Dumfounded I exclaimed: "You! Why you have always greeted me with a kind word and a smile."

"I couldn't help myself," she spluttered. "Every time I have looked into your face I have been disarmed. As I have observed you, year after year, I have found my position untenable."

There have been many American girls married to Orientals since I blazed the trail in 1897. Some of these have held up their heads, been proud of their husbands, and have won respect, while others have tried to conceal, from all but their immediate associates, the fact that the head of the house was an Oriental. They have never appeared in public with their husbands nor mentioned them to acquaintances except in a very general way.

I know of one such case here in Berkeley where both the Chinese husband and his beautiful young American wife were students at the University of California. In registering, she spelled the family name a little differently from what he did. Although they went to school at the same hour she never walked with him, neither did she recognize him on the campus. She made many friends among the women students, but she never dared invite any of them to her home, and she lived in mortal fear that some day they would find out that her husband was a Chinaman and banish her forever from their society. She didn't do very well in college and the joy gradually faded from her expressive blue eyes. I frequently talked to her about the falseness of her position, but she said that having started in that way she couldn't do otherwise.

For my own part, I feel that through my marriages I have been brought into contact with a type of people morally and intellectually superior to the average. Of one thing I am certain, and that is that at the present time I am receiving more than my share of invitations to social gatherings and to the homes of people of culture who are interested in my husband because of his broad scholarly attainments. Therefore, I consider that through my marriages to Orientals I have been helped up socially rather than dragged down.

Before concluding, however, I want to repeat that one shadow, a dark one, has been cast over my life by my Oriental alliances; that is, the loss of my citizenship. Whether technically Chinese, or technically Japanese, my heart has always been American, and never have I owed allegiance to any other flag than that of my own United States.

Why Japanese and Americans Should Not Intermarry

The inflammatory article appeared in the *San Francisco Bulletin* immediately following the conclusion of Mrs Emma Fong Kuno's autobiographical series. Why does the author insist that her successful marriage was exceptional? How might the author's fear of interracial marriage and hybridization potentially undermine readers' positive reactions to Mrs Fong Kuno's story?

The autobiographical story told by Mrs Emma F. Kuno, the last chapter of which appeared in The Bulletin yesterday, is an unusual human document. It is unusual because it tells of experiences so vastly different from the histories of many other white women that have been married to Asiatics that it can be regarded only as an exception to the general rule that such alliances commonly end in disappointment, disillusion and wreck.

That this educated woman of Anglo-Saxon stock became the wife first of a Chinese and later of a Japanese, and survives apparently without regret, may be due to the fact that both of her husbands came to this country in their youth, were educated here and were trained up with the ideas and ideals of the Occident; but there is another aspect of the case with which romantic maids that have a "universal outlook upon life and mankind" should be acquainted and not be permitted to forget. It has to do with the anthropological side of the subject and is of profounder significance than the romantic, the political or the economic. It is best expounded by Herbert Spencer in a letter he wrote thirty years ago to the Japanese statesman, Baron Kaneko Kentaro, in answer to a question as to whether it were advisable for the Japanese people to intermarry with Caucasians. Spencer's advice has been quoted several times in this country, but it is yet too little known and cannot be too often repeated. Spencer wrote:

> To your question respecting the intermarriage of foreigners and Japanese, my reply is that, as rationally answered, there is no difficulty at all. It should be positively forbidden. It is not at root a question of social philosophy. It is at root a question of biology. There is abundant proof, alike furnished by the intermarriages of human races and by the interbreeding of animals, that when the varieties mingled diverge beyond a certain slight degree THE RESULT IS INEVITABLY A BAD ONE in the long run. I have myself been in the habit of looking at the evidence bearing

Taken from "Why Japanese and Americans Should Not Intermarry," *San Francisco Bulletin*, June 15, 1922.

on this matter for many years, and my conviction is based on numerous facts derived from numerous sources.

When there is an interbreeding of the different varieties of sheep, widely unlike, the result, especially in the second generation, is a bad one – there arise an incalculable mixture of traits and what may be called a chaotic constitution. And the same thing happens among human beings – the Eurasians in India, the halfbreeds in America, show this. The physiological basis of this experience appears to be that any one variety of creature in course of many generations acquires a certain constitutional adaptation to its particular form of life, and every other variety similarly acquires its own special adaptation. The consequence is that, if you mix the constitutions of two widely divergent varieties which have severally become adapted to widely divergent modes of life, you get a constitution which is adapted to the mode of life of neither – a constitution which will not work properly, because it is not fitted for any set of conditions whatever. By all means, therefore, peremptorily interdict marriages of Japanese with foreigners.

I have for the reasons indicated entirely approved of the regulations which have been established in America for restraining the Chinese Immigration, and had I the power I would restrict them to the smallest possible amount, my reasons for this decision being that one of two things must happen. If the Chinese are allowed to settle extensively in America, they must either, if they remain unmixed, form a subject race standing in the position, if not of slaves, yet of a class approaching to slaves; or if they mix they must form a bad hybrid. In either case, supposing the immigration to be large, immense social mischief must arise, and eventually social disorganization. The same thing will happen if there should be any considerable mixture of European or American races with the Japanese.

If intermarriage of Orientals and Caucasians is bad for the former, it necessarily must be bad for the Caucasians in spite of the experience and testimony of the author of "My Oriental Husbands." And when the subject of Japanese immigration is discussed by our Legislators, they would do well to remember the serious fact that there is a more important feature of the matter to be considered than the purely economic; for two peoples do not live together or side by side without hybridization.

Intermarriage: Standpoint and Tentative Questionnaire – Confidential

In 1923, Robert Park, one of the leading researchers of the Chicago school of sociology, devised a sample questionnaire exploring interracial marriage, which he hoped would boost interest in the larger Survey of Race Relations that American social scientists were conducting. What are some of the implicit notions regarding sexual attraction between "oriental" and "whites" embedded in these questions? What other problems did Park highlight as potential concerns for interracial couples? How do you think Mrs Emma Fong Kuno's articles explicitly addressed these prejudices?

IV Questionnaire

The following questions are not set down so that they may be answered, but merely that they may suggest some of the aspects under which interracial marriage may be considered. It is probable that in the course of investigation and further study certain other aspects of intermarriage will prove to be more important than those set down here.

A   On interracial marriages

1   Of what height and coloring is the American woman married to an Oriental?
   a   Is it a type closely approximating that of the Oriental woman?
2   What kind of Oriental man does the American woman marry?
   a   Is he American in appearance?
   b   What would seem to be the basis of the physical attraction?
3   Are the American women who have married Orientals wholesome and conventional people?
   a   Do any of them belong to marked pathological types, the romantic, the neurotic, etc.?
   b   In case they are women of a marked type, did the isolation caused by their marriage, which placed them outside of the usual kind of

---

Taken from "Intermarriage: Standpoint and Tentative Questionnaire – Confidential," Original of the full Intermarriage Document, Box 6, Papers of the Survey of Race Relations, Hoover Institution Archives, Stanford University, pp. 6–9.

social competition, make life easier and more satisfactory to them?

4 Are the Oriental men who have married American women of a gay and open disposition, or are they steady and reserved?

5 In the cases where an American woman has married an Oriental man, did she belong by birth and circumstance to relatively the same economic and social class as he, and was her status raised or lowered by her marriage?

   a How did her family react to the news that she was going to marry the Oriental?

     Did their feelings alter with time?

     Did they talk about it with their friends?

   b How do her brothers and the men of her acquaintance regard her?

     Do her women friends think her marriage is unfortunate or romantic?

   c How large is the circle of her acquaintance?

     Is it smaller than it was before her marriage?

     In case it is smaller has this affected her happiness? How does she show it? Pride, defensive self-sufficiency?

     Does her circle of acquaintance include both Americans and Orientals?

     Are her friends and acquaintances people of the same class and cultural background as her own?

6 What kind of social life does the Oriental have who is married to an American woman?

   a How is the Oriental affected in his business relations with Americans who know of his marriage?

   b Do his countrymen consider that he has raised or lowered his status by marrying an American woman?

   c Do they ask him to their homes as readily as they otherwise would?

     Do they ask his wife?

     Do they treat him with any reserve or suspicion?

   d Does the Oriental bring his Oriental friends to his home? Does he bring his American friends? To what extent do the friends of the husband and wife mix?

7 In general, do these couples regard their marriage as successful?

   a Are there any cases in which Orientals are said to have gone insane because of the conflicts that arose out of their loneliness, home-sickness, and their relations with American women, which were a result of their enforced isolation in the American community?

b   In case the Oriental marries an American woman, is his family life stabilized by this same isolation?

c   If the marriage seems to be a happy and successful one, on what elements in the personalities of the husband and wife, and what elements in their situation does this success depend?

B   *On the child of mixed parentage*

1   Could any of these children pass for Americans?

a   If not, what physical characteristics do they possess that are a result of their Asiatic blood?

2   Do these children do well in school?

a   Do they have any bad traits that either Oriental or white children do not have to the same extent?

b   Do they often get into trouble?

c   What occupations do they engage in upon leaving school?

3   In how many different kinds of communities has the child of mixed blood lived, and how did these different experiences affect him?

a   Has he lived for the most part in –

a   An American community?

b   An Oriental community?

c   A mixed community?

b   Were his playmates and friends, children of white, Oriental or mixed blood?

c   Is there any disposition on the part of the child of mixed blood to hold aloof from the children of both racial groups? In case this tendency exists, does it manifest itself more strikingly when the child's family lives in –

a   An American community?

b   An Oriental community?

c   A mixed community?

4   What mental conflicts does the child of mixed parentage have?

a   What is the attitude of the child toward its parents?

5   How is the child of mixed parentage accepted in the American group?

a   Is he treated as any other child would be by the members of his mother's family? Is the child of unusual intelligence and charm accepted without any perceptible reservations by its American kin?

In case the child of mixed parentage does not feel that he is wholly acceptable to the white American group, how early and under what circumstances did he become aware of this? Playing with the neighborhood children, school, dances, teasing?

6 How is the child of mixed parentage accepted in the Oriental group?
   a Is he taught Chinese or Japanese, or do his parents want him to be as American as possible?
   b To what extent does he seek acquaintances and friends among his father's friends? On what kinds of occasions is he likely to meet them?

7 Are there any special friendships, or gangs, or clubs, among young people of mixed blood?
   a Does the child of mixed Oriental and American parentage ever marry other children of mixed blood parentage, e.g., the Indian half-breed?
   b Does he ever intermarry with other peoples of sallow or swarthy complexion, e.g., the Spaniard, Portuguese, Armenian, or Syrian or with any of the other Mediterranean peoples?
   c Is there any difference in the behavior of the sexes in this respect?
   d Does the man of mixed blood ever prefer not to marry at all, in order to evade the fixing of his status by attaching himself definitely through marriage to either racial group?

Further Reading

Almaguer, Tomás. *Racial Fault Lines: the Historical Origins of White Supremacy in California.* Berkeley: University of California Press, 1994.

Fong, Colleen, and Judy Yung. "In search of the right spouse: interracial marriage among Chinese and Japanese Americans." *Amerasia Journal,* 21 (1995/6), 77–98.

Pascoe, Peggy. "Miscegenation law, court cases, and ideologies of 'race' in 20th century America." *Journal of American History,* 83 (June 1996), 44–70.

Spickard, Paul. *Mixed Blood: Intermarriage and Ethnic Identity in Twentieth-century America.* Madison: University of Wisconsin Press, 1989.

Takaki, Ronald. *Strangers from a Different Shore.* New York: Penguin, 1989.

Wu, William. *The Yellow Peril: Chinese Americans in American Fiction, 1850–1940.* Hamden, CT: Archon Books, 1982.

Yung, Judy. *Unbound Feet: a Social History of Chinese Women in San Francisco.* Berkeley: University of California Press, 1995.

12

The Sexualized Woman

Introduction

If nineteenth-century intimate friendships with women cannot be categorized definitively as lesbian, by the twentieth century there is no mistaking lesbian relationships and lesbian identity. Everyone from medical doctors to psychologists, news reporters, and lesbians themselves became increasingly conscious that women loved other women romantically and, more important, that women were sexually involved with other women. The opinions expressed about the meaning and intent of lesbian relationships varied greatly, but most public commentators defined lesbians as sexual deviants. As Donna Penn shows in her essay, in the post-war era, expert opinion conspired with popular culture in fashioning the sexualized, aggressive lesbian, allied with the prostitute as a symbol of the "fallen woman." Prostitutes and lesbians became symbols of decay and unbridled lust, two kinds of women against which the "normal," heterosexual woman could define herself.

As mainstream America "discovered" lesbians, so too did lesbians discover themselves and assume greater prominence. Though some lesbians internalized the negative ideas advanced by popular culture, others enthusiastically embraced the notion of the sexualized woman. In the reality of bar life and in the fictionalized world of pulp novels, lesbians made their presence known in ways that included public expressions of sexuality.

The Sexualized Woman: the Lesbian, the Prostitute, and the Containment of Female Sexuality in Postwar America

Donna Penn

The 1962 production of *Walk on the Wild Side* centers on Jo [Barbara Stanwyck], Dove [Laurence Harvey], and Hallie [Capucine], characters in a love triangle in depression-era New Orleans. Dove Linkhorn finds Hallie Gerard, the woman who left him three years earlier, living with Jo Courtney in the building that houses Jo's business establishment – a brothel and bar where the women in Jo's employ wait for their customers. What emerges is the story of Jo's possessive obsession for Hallie – her mean-spirited, overbearing, domineering, authoritarian expressions of jealous rage. Jo, who seems to live twenty-four hours a day in a highly tailored suit, the uniform of the "masculine" woman, carries on a "maternal" relationship with the young sculptress, who might otherwise be a "normal" woman. Instead, Hallie's potential is dwarfed by the power of Jo's possessiveness, leaving "hooking" as her only form of sexual expression. In the end, this story of lesbian love, right down to the quintessential lesbian nickname "Jo," employs the plot formula used in many stories of the fallen woman. Jo, while attempting to shoot Dove, accidentally kills Hallie. Tried for murder and for her illicit business activities, she is imprisoned, while Dove may finally secure peace.

This film must be understood as part of a national crusade to make lesbianism visible to an otherwise unsuspecting public. Partly in response to fears of sexual chaos and partly in response to the increasing public visibility of lesbian subcultures, by the second half of the twentieth century, "experts" and disseminators of expert opinion demonized the lesbian in order to position her, along with the prostitute, as the essence of female sexual degeneracy. Cultural critics and various professionals intensified an assault on those with "lesbian tendencies or inclinations" as sexually deviant and depraved women. Lurid and sensationalistic accounts of those who strayed from monogamous,

Excerpted from Donna Penn, "The Sexualized Woman: the Lesbian, the Prostitute, and the Containment of Female Sexuality in Postwar America," in Joanne Meyerowitz, ed., *Not June Cleaver: Women and Gender in Postwar America, 1945–1960* (Philadelphia: Temple University Press, 1994), pp. 358–81.

heterosexual bliss filled the cultural landscape. In their efforts to make absolutely clear to an otherwise ignorant public what dangers lurked in the shadows, the purveyors of the dominant discourse painted a sinister association between the lesbian and the prostitute as sisters of the sexual underworld. In this way, they linked two haunting images of fallen womanhood.

Earlier in the century, the most prevalent culturally constructed image of lesbianism was rarely linked to prostitution. Instead, expert observers often associated lesbians and "mannish women" with unmarried career women, social reformers, and feminists. By the 1920s, all these women were vilified for their gender transgression. In this earlier version of the "lesbian threat," white middle-class lesbians, and unmarried women generally, threatened "race suicide" by rejecting or otherwise compromising their proper and "natural" social role to bear and rear children. These prewar New Women were castigated primarily as asexual gender traitors.[1]

In the postwar era, the "lesbian threat" took on more ominous meanings. Lesbians were portrayed not only as gender transgressors but also as sexual demons. The rather tame cultural response to Katherine B. Davis's study of 1929, which found a significant proportion of homosexual experiences among the 2,200 women surveyed, contrasts sharply with the uproar that accompanied the publication of Alfred Kinsey's studies two decades later.[2] These differing cultural responses bespeak the very different cultural climates into which these two studies were received and thereby underscore the sometimes subtle but nevertheless significant shift in thinking about the lesbian from the prewar asexual career woman to, like the prostitute generally, a postwar sexual devil.

Walk on the Wild Side therefore gave expression, through the medium of film, to an increasingly prevalent view that fused the lesbian with the prostitute as symbols of female sexual desire, female sexual excess, uncontained female sexuality, and therefore female sexual deviance and danger. The subject of this essay is the degree to which and purpose for which these two powerful images of fallen womanhood came to be associated during the postwar years. I examine the ways in which public discussions and portrayals of deviant female sexuality captured in this association served to establish the boundaries of culturally sanctioned female heterosexuality. These two examples of deviant female sexual behavior were constructed to define, bind, and contain the so-called norm. Prescriptions for the "normal" were defined in strict inverse relationship to that which was deviant. Whereas the prostitute had historically served as the symbol of female wantonness and degeneracy, during the postwar years the lesbian, in the popular culture, joined her in filling that role. As such, this association helped make publicly visible those who formerly went undetected and thereby helped define the parameters of the normal and acceptable.

The Sexualized Lesbian

...The broader cultural context within which to place the specific experience of those defined by the postwar culture as sexual deviants is provided by Elaine Tyler May in her study documenting the fears of sexual chaos that preoccupied the American imagination during the Cold War years. May suggests that "it was not just nuclear energy that had to be contained, but the social and sexual fallout of the atomic age itself...the nation had to be on moral alert."[3] As May has shown, this anxiety informed not only prescriptions for private behavior but preoccupations about the destiny of the nation. The program for moral readiness focused on a domestic ideology that sought to contain female sexuality in the home, within marriage, and attended by motherhood. This formula, according to May's reading of the experts, promised to save the nation and the American family from foreign and domestic threats. In its most blatant form, it made the future of the American way of life dependent on the containment of female sexuality within certain culturally determined bounds. In so doing, deviant female sexuality achieved an unprecedented place and face in the American imagination, for it served to define not only the parameters of prescribed gender and sexual behavior but also the fate of the nation. In this context, we can make meaning of the cultural preoccupation with the lesbian and the prostitute as the symbols of moral decay associated with uncontained female sexuality.

My focus on sexual deviance challenges a dominant approach in lesbian historiography. Much of the scholarship in this emerging field has dissociated lesbians from deviant sexual styles and emphasized, instead, the romantic love shared by some women. This analytical approach has been most successful as a strategy for resurrecting lesbians (and those claimed as such by historians) from the dustbins of history.[4] Nevertheless, this strategy suffers on two counts. First, it utilizes a definition of "lesbian" so broad that it potentially includes many who did not experience their lives from a deviant subject position during historical moments when it was nearly impossible to construct a life including same-sex desire and escape this taint. Consequently, historians claim as "lesbian" women who did not necessarily, during their lifetimes, suffer the specific cruelties and marginalization reserved for sexually deviant women. Furthermore, an essentialist view of women as nurturant and romantic, rather than fueled by "lust and desire, seduction and fulfillment,"[5] combined with the methodological difficulty in documenting genital contact in the historical source material, has led some historians to employ a definition of lesbian that, in effect, desexualizes these subjects. As a result, the centrality of lesbian sexual desire in our working understanding of the lesbian is at best obfuscated and at worst rendered invisible.

It is in the context of these concerns that I restore sexual agency, sexual desire, sexual adventure, sexual fulfillment, and sexual deviance to my examination of the dominant cultural understanding and subcultural experience of lesbianism during the postwar era. This "sexualized" approach is particularly relevant when exploring the postwar decades because expert observers and popular culture attempted to link the lesbian with the prostitute as the essence of female sexual degeneracy in the period. Yet, although we may be tempted to credit or fault the authorities with responsibility for creating this new sexualized image of the lesbian, they did so in the context of a flourishing lesbian subculture that was, in fact, fueled by subversive models of lesbian/female sexual desire. Therefore, I am suggesting that the experts *discovered* the centrality of lesbian sexuality and lesbian desire prevailing in the lesbian world, rather than created it. What they did do, however, was to draw together these two symbols of the sexualized female, publicize their deviance, and thereby develop the boundaries and terms for proper female heterosexuality. Certainly, both lesbians and prostitutes have been assigned to the category of deviance since the late nineteenth century. What was new in the postwar era was the extent to which experts exposed and publicized this connection and the uses to which it was put.

Therefore, as sexual outlaws and symbols of fallen womanhood, lesbians and prostitutes share a history. The history of lesbianism must therefore be explored in the context of deviant sexual behavior. As sexually defined women, Joan Nestle suggests, "both dykes and whores ... have an historical heritage of redefining the concept of womanhood."[6] Furthermore, both the lesbian and the prostitute have found themselves subject to the control of the state and other authorities. Gayle Rubin stresses that although it may disturb many lesbians who come out of a lesbian-feminist or radical lesbian tradition, as far as the state, the public, and legal and medical experts are concerned, the lesbian has "shared many of the sociological features and suffered from many of the same social penalties as have gay men, sadomasochists, transvestites, and prostitutes."[7] ...

Early Examples of the Lesbian–Prostitute Connection

In the nineteenth century, some European observers associated both the lesbian and the prostitute with physical degeneracy. According to the historian Sander Gilman, a standard gynecological text published in 1877 associated the "over development of the clitoris" with those "excesses" that "are called 'lesbian love.'"[8] A Russian physician, Pauline Tarnowsky, in a work published in 1893, also claimed that one could read deviance on the body. Her work examined the physical changes in appearance from which the prostitute allegedly suffered as she aged. Tarnowsky concluded that as she aged, the prostitute appeared more and more mannish, characterized by "strong jaws and cheek-bones, and their masculine aspect... hidden by adipose tissue, emerge, salient angles stand out, and the face grows virile, uglier than a man's; wrinkles deepen into the likeness of scars, and the countenance, once attractive, exhibits the full degenerate type which early grace had con-cealed."[9] Thus, according to Gilman, "the link is between two... models of sexual deviancy, the prostitute and the lesbian. Both are seen as possessing physical signs that set them apart from the normal."[10]

American social scientists, adapting this work to less rigidly heredit-arian models of degeneracy, conducted extensive studies at the turn of the century that linked the lesbian, the prostitute, and female criminal offenders generally. Their chief area of concern was to establish the environmental and social influences contributing to the formation of the "criminal type," rather than strictly biological explanations for devi-ant behaviors. These issues and debates formed the heart of American criminological inquiry from its inception, but they did not extend widely in the popular imagination until after World War II.

Although various early references testify to or at least suggest a con-nection between the prostitute and the lesbian, in the American context the full power of this linkage was reserved for the post-World War II decades. During the war, psychiatric authority on the homosexual ques-tion expanded by virtue of wartime opportunities for these professionals to advise the military on procedures for diagnosis, hospitalization, sur-veillance, interrogation, and discharge. After the war, the psychiatric world was in a position to consolidate its power as an agent of cultural authority. At the same time, the criminal justice system marshaled its powers to respond to the believed menace of the "sexual psychopath" who roamed American streets threatening innocents and time-honored sexual morality, and law enforcement agencies were mandated to cleanse the streets of vice and immorality.[11] Various experts attacked a deviant sexual underworld, including an emerging lesbian subculture that prom-ised to challenge and perhaps disrupt the efforts of those who sought to contain female libidinous excess. Whereas earlier efforts, particularly those of American social scientists, sought to explain with compassion the social circumstances that might lead *individuals* down the wrong path, some postwar authorities saw in these deviant populations quasi-organized *communities* whose existence threatened the social order. In a Cold War atmosphere infused with fears of external threats to national security, psychiatric personnel, with the full backing of institutional and professional authority only recently acquired during the war, as well as legal authorities and their popular supporters, mobilized their ranks in order to deploy their collective forces in the name of containing a moral menace that no longer threatened as individuals but now constituted a social group.

The Postwar Era: The Sexual Demonization of the Lesbian

This belief that homosexuals, like prostitutes, now constituted an expanding, quasi-organized sexual underworld was not merely a homophobic phantasmagoria but was a reflection of real social and cultural shifts taking place as a consequence of the war. The scholarship in the field of gay and lesbian history singles out World War II as something of a "national coming out" experience: Many gay men and lesbians took advantage of wartime social dislocation and employment opportunities to leave their families of origin and pursue the ever-increasing possibilities for establishing a gay way of life in many of the nation's urban centers. For women, fashioning a lesbian way of life generally required economic independence from men, a situation increasingly possible in the wartime and postwar cities. . . .

Social commentators, equally aware of the expanding possibilities for those with "lesbian tendencies," now vigorously lamented the deplorable lack of information on the lesbian. They commented often on the wealth of material available on the male homosexual, the cumulative effect of which, they believed, was the achievement of real understanding of that "problem." But there were few studies and therefore little expert knowledge about the lesbian, thereby leaving that problem culturally invisible. Those who speculated on the reason for this difference generally concurred that fewer lesbians sought psychiatric or related therapeutic intervention than male homosexuals, thereby limiting the pool of available cases for investigation. They agreed that lesbians less often faced criminal or civil prosecution, the sentences for which generally included some sessions on the couch. As for those who might voluntarily seek therapy to remedy their condition, many fewer lesbians than male homosexuals availed themselves of the opportunity, indicating, at best, a better adjustment to their neurotic and pathological condition. At worst, the fewer numbers of female homosexuals seeking cure indicated and reflected the rather large cultural space available for them to go undetected. A leading psychoanalyst, Clara Thompson, wrote in 1949:

Until recent times there was a much stronger taboo on obvious non-marital heterosexual situations. Two overt homosexual women may live together in complete intimacy in many communities without social disapproval if they do not flaunt their inversion by, for example, the assumption of masculine dress or mannerisms on the part of one. Sometimes even if they go to this extreme they are thought peculiar rather than taboo. On the other hand, two men attempting the same thing are likely to encounter marked hostility.[12]

Experts grew increasingly dissatisfied with the broad range of affectional expressions permitted two women that enabled many inverted and deviant women to live together unsuspected – a luxury rarely afforded two men. These purveyors of the dominant discourse now took it upon themselves to make the lesbian visible and narrow the cultural space previously available that allowed them to go unnoticed, thereby delimiting if not establishing the boundaries of deviant female sexuality.

In their efforts to make the lesbian visible to the unsuspecting public, an image emerged that characterized the lesbian as a promiscuous, oversexed, conquering, aggressive dyke who exercised masculine prerogatives in the sexual arena. Whereas earlier images, especially those of the middle class, centered on companionable relationships between two "ladies" who controlled their sexual appetites and lived quiet lives together, this new image sexualized the lesbian and saw the jealous rage as the cornerstone of the lesbian relationship. Particularly when describing those of the working classes, the image of the lesbian took on a dark and sinister quality. The very essence of the lesbian, like the prostitute, was an expression of uncontained female sexuality – in this case, a sexuality that in no way required the participation of men or held the promise of marriage.

Therefore, a somewhat repressed deviant sexuality, as seen in the film character Jo, was rivaled in the popular imagination by another expression of lesbian love prevalent at the time, namely, the aggressive, promiscuous dyke who, according to one touted as knowledgeable on the subject, "will bust a gut for a toss in the hay."[13] Another claimed that she came "to know homosexual women, but they exhibited such elemental passion, brutality, sensuality, that, notwithstanding all my yearning for 'homosexual' love, I remained unresponsive."[14] In these cases, a sexualized and necessarily demonized image of lesbians was broadcast and disseminated into the popular culture of the post-war era. Lesbians were increasingly described and publicized as a predatory lot whose lives were based on sexual conquest and the determined pursuit of sexual gratification, which ultimately, they could not achieve anyway, since, according to the experts, lesbians engaged primarily in mere mutual masturbation, which in itself was an indication of immature if not deviant female sexuality. Frank Caprio, a psychoanalyst whose area of expertise during these years was female homosexuality and sexual variance generally, went so far as to suggest that female promiscuity, masturbation in marriage, and "unconventional sex practices" such as cunnilingus, fellatio, and anal penetration were themselves indicative of latent homosexuality.[15]

Yet active, rather than latent, female homosexuality was the area of chief concern in the immediate postwar years. Estelle Freedman describes the national hysteria concerning the perceived epidemic of sexual psychopathology during this period. Medical experts, social hygiene reformers, and law enforcement officials sought to squelch the new moral menace to youth and women.[16] Lesbians, although less often the subject of widespread public concern, did achieve a place on the rostrum of sexual deviants who threatened public decency. In 1947, Dr. Carleton Simon, criminologist for the International Association of Chiefs of Police, addressed members of the association at its annual convention on the subject of "Homosexualists and Sex Crimes" in which he asserted:

> Psychopathic women homosexualists – commonly called Lesbians, also Sapphists... are fickle minded and always eager to add to their list of conquests. They seek new acquaintances, not solely as passive victims but also as active participants.... They are... extremely jealous of the object of their lust.... Usually large cities attract them, where the selective field is more expanded and where, if necessary, they can cover up their predilections.... Though the victim of acquired sexual obsession, they may have lofty ideals and many marry and find eventually a normal sex adjustment.[17]

Simon's depiction of sexual wantonness, reflecting the achievement of popular dissemination of expert ideas, helped expose the "truth" about lesbians to an otherwise ignorant public. Literature on prison conditions similarly painted a portrait of the aggressive predatory lesbian who, in this instance, had a captive audience in the inmate population.... In all these cases, the "true" lesbian was identified by her insatiable need for sexual conquest, which made her a threat to the social order as well as to the containment of female sexuality within the home and marriage.

Despite, or perhaps because of, a rhetoric in which deviant women might disguise themselves under the cloak of asexuality, many postwar experts and their popularizers sought to give these women a face and a name that the public could recognize for the neurotic, pathological, faulty adjustment that the experts believed it to be, thereby further narrowing the terms of and space for appropriate female sexuality. Thus the lesbian, now sexualized, joined the prostitute to form the boundaries of a circular model of deviance that contained culturally sanctioned female sexuality. As fallen women by virtue of their demonized sexuality, the association between the lesbian and the prostitute further elaborated the contours of female sexual deviance and served as a warning of what might befall those who would dare to stray from the increasingly restricted "straight and narrow" sexual ideology of these years. . . .

The Lesbian–Prostitute Connection: Evidence of the Link

In Polly Adler's 1953 autobiographical memoirs of life as a New York madam, she recounts that "inevitably I had a few Lesbians, some of them troublemakers, some very peaceful souls. It has often been said that a prostitute becomes so tired of being mauled by men that she turns to a woman for tenderness. Maybe so. I have no figures on the incidence of female homosexuality, but it's my observation that it occurs in every walk of life."[18] The tone of nonchalance with which she reports this phenomenon bespeaks an increasingly accepted view in which the lesbian and the prostitute, whether distinct individuals or one and the same, shared a cultural space as sexually defined women, thereby placing them at the margins of respectability. Whereas the prevailing image of the lesbian for the prewar generation was generally one of lifelong companions of the middle class or mannish upper-class women like Radclyffe Hall's protagonist in *The Well of Loneliness*, this image of genteel unmarried women altered during the postwar years. The lesbian was now, like the prostitute, a sexual demon. If she repressed her inverted desires, she was likely to suffer frigidity in sexual relations with her husband, which, in this Kinseyan era of devotion to sexual satisfaction, spelled certain disaster. Consequently, heterosexual marriage was generally not recommended as appropriate treatment for curing homosexuality. It would likely fail the individual and make a mockery of the heterosexual union.

As suggested earlier, a primary strategy employed for exposing the lesbian was to identify her as a sexual degenerate and to link her with the prostitute as the essence of female sexual deviance and danger. The image of these two sexual demons and efforts to portray the degree to which they supposedly overlapped is most sensationally summed up in a 1965 *Life* magazine photoessay, titled "Lesbians Try to Peddle Each Other." The author suggested that "telling the players without a program can be all but impossible in Times Square. The four people in the three pictures at left all are women. Two are drug addicts, and one is a pusher. Two are prostitutes, the other two are pimps. All are Lesbians.

They are among hundreds of perverts, prostitutes, and addicts drawn to the Times Square area by each other and by the easy marks they can prey on." The text that accompanied the photos told a sordid tale of perverted sexuality, drug addiction, and crime that served to reenforce the public's view of the sexual psychopathology that afflicted those who strayed from rigid prescriptions for female sexuality.[19]. . . .

Popular efforts to develop and disseminate this image of the "butch-as-pimp-for-her-fem-junkie-whore" served to dispel further the previously prevailing image of the lesbian as a middle-class social activist and, instead, call attention to the lives of true depravity that those of her ilk fashioned for themselves.

The connection increasingly disseminated into the popular culture between these two examples of female sexual degeneracy was also explored by experts, among whom Frank Caprio is perhaps the most notable. His work during this period commented extensively on his many adventures in Europe and elsewhere where he encountered many lesbians among brothel workers. . . .

He found that "the prevalence of lesbianism in brothels throughout the world has convinced me that prostitution, as a behavior deviation, attracts to a large extent women who have a very strong latent homosexual component. Through prostitution, these women eventually overcome their homosexual repressions."[20] Thus, what Caprio offered was a pseudo-psychoanalytic explanation for the lesbian as prostitute and the prostitute as lesbian – the repressed lesbian fled from her fears of homosexuality into a life of heterosexual excess in which, because of her true homosexual desires, she failed to find sexual satisfaction, which in turn led her to find fulfillment in the arms of another of her sex. The prevailing image in this and other accounts of its kind is of sexual activity run amok.

For many psychologists and their popularizers, these two examples of sexually deviant females not only represented two sorts of maladjusted women but often were one and the same. When speaking of lesbians, Carleton Simon reminded his audience that "a great many are predatory prostitutes to obtain their living and to enable them to carry on their licentious practices without financial worry."[21] Whether true or not, accurate or contrived, the significance of these portrayals lies in their power to fuse the lesbian and the prostitute as individuals and social categories that represented uncontained and therefore deviant female sexuality.

Portrayals that fused the lesbian and the prostitute also served a larger purpose: to ensure national security through domestic tranquility and sexual containment. A major strategy in this effort was the national campaign to squelch what was perceived to be an epidemic of sexual offenders. Although largely concerned with the perpetrators of violent crimes motivated by a sexual "abnormality," public attention extended to the nuisance offender as well. Members of the sexual underworld became prime targets of state-sanctioned harassment. Homosexuals and prostitutes represented moral decay associated with sexual excess that had to be eradicated or, at the least, driven further underground. Legislative committees rewrote statutes dealing with the disposition and treatment of sex offenders that now made efforts to view these criminals as psychologically impaired individuals in need of treatment, rather than mere criminals deserving incarceration. And psychiatrists jockeyed for position as this new approach promised them a central role in rehabilitative treatment centers as well as in advising members of the criminal justice community on the proper adjudication of such cases.[22]

Vice-control units of local police departments, in association with liquor licensing boards, private reform groups like the American Society for Social Hygiene, and public health officials routinely executed round-ups of those involved in "immoral" social and sexual activities. Law enforcement officials made efforts to clean lesbians and prostitutes, whose public presence disturbed moral decency, off the city's streets. Sex deviants and sex workers of various shades found themselves the targets of a law enforcement crusade during the 1950s and 1960s that was conducting a kind of urban renewal of the social landscape to clean the cities of "degenerates" and "deviants." The hooker, the whore, the B-girl,[23] the call girl, the expense-account girl, and the homosexual all became victims of police raids, harassment, and arrests. In Boston, for example, a spate of newspaper articles during this period document police activities designed to harass and arrest individuals associated with sexual deviance and shut down establishments that catered to them. Stories abound of "girls" picked up on morals charges and of bars and clubs under investigation by the Alcohol and Beverage Control Commission for alleged illicit activities. Names of individuals held by the police for idle and disorderly conduct were routinely printed in the newspapers.

The relationship between the lesbian and the prostitute, whether discovered or created, conceptual or actual, was by this period real. Although members of both groups worked, played, and lived in all parts of the metropolitan area, at least one spatially defined area was generally designated as the locus of the sexual underworld. In many cities, the very same territory identified as the red-light district, in which prostitutes conducted their business, also contained or was adjacent to neighborhoods that housed many of the city's sites of gay nightlife. For example, during much of this postwar, pre-gay liberation period, many of Boston's lesbian bars, gay male bars, and those that served both segments of the "twilight world" were to be found in and around the streets of the city's red-light and porn district, locally referred to as the "Combat Zone." The clusters of streets today known as Bay Village and the downtown shopping district were once the home of the majority of lesbian bars, which shared the territory with sex workers and other institutions of the sex industry. These sexually marginalized and stigmatized populations not only shared a sinful pathology in the expert and popular imagination but shared an urban geography as well. The very real spatial proximity of these two segments of the sexual under-world underscores the degree to which they shared the role of sexual and social blight on the urban landscape.

The Centrality of Sexuality in the Lesbian World

Lesbians themselves struggled with the newly publicized strictures of the culture in an effort to make sense of their lives. In 1947 Jane Mac-Kinnon, a self-proclaimed lesbian, published a piece in the *American Journal of Psychiatry*. Despite her plea for understanding, MacKinnon seemed to accept the prevailing cultural views, and her article fanned the flames that portrayed the lesbian as one guided by an insatiable hunger. In her taxonomy of lesbianism, Types I and II were the aggressive sorts whose relationships with their partners could "be likened to that of a mother with a helpless child.... They cannot be satisfied unless they dominate.... Education, breeding, all those things do not prevent the homosexual from drawing.... a woman into her orbit of dominance if she possibly can. Her need for relief from sexual tension...is too great."[24] ...

Other lesbians engaged to varying extents in the transformation of dominant cultural messages concerning them. While some lesbians lived discreetly in the suburbs and elsewhere, many were constructing a more aggressive challenge to the dominant discourse. By and large, lesbians who participated in the vibrant bar culture of the pre-Stonewall years, who found community in that setting, interpreted their lives in ways that bore resemblance to the dictates of normal female sexuality but funda-mentally challenged it in that they were, by all accounts, deviant and homosexual. Aware of some of the basic recipes for deviance being articulated by the experts, they made efforts to employ and apply those "scientific facts" to themselves before eventually abandoning them as false. As one woman explains:

> To realize...you were...sick.... We used to think that. Well, we were told that. You know, the guys would say, "Gee, I wasn't a mama's boy. I wonder how I ever became gay because I had a good relationship with my

father? Maybe there's something wrong with me. I'm not the right kind of a queer like I'm supposed to be. I'm supposed to be a mama's boy and I wasn't." Or maybe, "She was attacked by men when she was young and that's why she's gay." [We heard] all these kinds of things and [we'd] think, "Gee, that never happened to me. How did I ever become gay?" You tr[ied] to figure out how you became gay because according to all the information out there something awful should have happened to you to make you that way. So you kept saying, "So what is it? What happened? Why am I gay?"[25]

...Lesbians themselves subverted the dominant discourse to make meanings more consistent with their own feelings and experiences. It is in this context that the social organization of the butch and femme becomes an important area for analysis. The butch–femme experience both resembled dominant cultural prescriptions for culturally sanctioned sexuality and fundamentally challenged and altered those terms. That the butch was supposed to be the aggressor in sexual contacts and the femme was the "passive" one appears, on the surface, to resemble the format for postwar heterosexual relations. And yet, as Elizabeth Lapovsky Kennedy and Madeline Davis's work on Buffalo indicates, butches and femmes quite radically renegotiated the terms of the dominant discourse while retaining a model that superficially approximated it. . . .

Butch–femme did not merely describe and govern a set of *private* sexual relations or rituals but, perhaps most significantly, represented a defiant *public* challenge to the dominant code. As Nestle suggests, by appearing together in public, butch and femme couples achieved a "style of self-presentation that made erotic competence a political statement in the 1950s."[26] She explains:

Does the longevity of butch–femme self-expression reflect the pernicious strength of heterosexual gender polarization – or is it, as I would argue, a lesbian-specific way of deconstructing gender that radically reclaims women's *erotic* energy? . . . [L]esbian life in America . . . was organized around a highly developed sense of sexual ceremony and dialogue. Indeed, because of the surrounding oppression, ritual and code were often all we had to make public erotic connections. Dress, stance, gestures, even jewelry and hair styles had to carry the weight of sexual communications. The pinky ring flashing in a subway car, the DA haircut combed more severely in front of a mirror always made me catch my breath, symbolizing as they did a butch woman announcing her erotic competence. A language of courtship and seduction was carefully crafted to allow for expression of both lust and love in the face of severe social repression.[27]

During a historical moment when women's fulfillment was to be accomplished within marriage, home, and motherhood, these women, both by choosing other women as sexual partners and by daring to explore their sexual desires and longings, aggressively and publicly carved out an alternative meaning from the dominant code. They demonstrated that uncontained female sexuality and female sexual autonomy were their right and privilege.

This defiantly public sexual presence was largely organized around the lesbian bar, which was the site of community formation during a period in which few other social or political organizations catered to the sexual deviant. As such, lesbian bars served various purposes. They were where lesbians found others like themselves with whom to interrupt the sense of isolation that frequently accompanied gay life in this period. Perhaps more important, they were where lesbians found sexual adventure. Lesbians who went to the bars uniformly admit that possible arrest was a risk they were willing to take for the opportunity to participate in a social life rich with sexual possibilities. Stories lesbians tell about their evening adventures at lesbian and gay bars are filled with a tone of anticipation that clearly betrays lesbian sexual desire. The thrill of going to a bar was fueled by desire. . . .

Similarly, lesbian pulp fiction of the era provided messages about the gay life and lesbian desire that were an alternative to the prescriptions proliferating in the dominant culture. For those fortunate enough to pluck the novels of Ann Bannon, Claire Morgan, Valerie Taylor, and Paula Christian off the dime-store racks, tales of lesbian struggle and fulfillment entered their consciousness and validated their experience, thereby challenging the expert and popular diagnoses of sexual deviancy and perverted desire. The first paragraph of Valerie Taylor's *Return to Lesbos* suggests the excitement and anxiety connected to sexual longing that the lesbian found in the bar:

> Karla's place was jumping. Frances Ollenfield stood at the edge of the sidewalk and watched the blue door swinging open and shut behind the couples: two girls in bermudas and knee socks, two slim boys moving gracefully in unison, more girls. Smoke and voices and juke music drifted out. Frances shivered a little, although it was a June evening in Chicago.
>
> She hadn't been in a gay bar for a year. She had promised never to visit one again. But her need was too strong. She took a deep breath and walked down the three stone steps, feeling her mouth go dry and her heart begin to hammer with excitement. The blue paint was flaking off the door and the gold scroll letters had faded. It's been a while, Frances thought.[28]

This passage, which opens the final volume in the Erika Frohmann series, is describing a sexual adventure as much as a visit to a gay bar. Frances "shivered" despite the summer heat because "her need was too strong." This "need" that made her "mouth go dry" was to be engaging in lesbian sexual activity, not merely having a cocktail. When Taylor writes that for Frances, "it's been a while," the reader would have to go to great lengths to miss the point. We all know, truly, what "it's been a while" since.

During a period in which a national crusade was on to contain female sexuality within the home and marriage, women daring to desire was a bold act. That the form this desire took was same sex was a dangerous act. That they actively, passionately, and relatively publicly pursued their desire was a revolutionary act. ...

Notes

1 For a discussion of this earlier meaning and application of the "lesbian threat," see Christina Simmons, "Companionate Marriage and the Lesbian Threat," *Frontiers*, Fall 1979, 54–59.
2 Katharine B. Davis, *Factors in the Sex Life of 2200 Women* (New York: Harper & Row, 1929); Alfred Kinsey et al., *Sexual Behavior in the Human Female* (Philadelphia: W. B. Saunders, 1953).
3 Elaine Tyler May, *Homeward Bound: American Families in the Cold War Era* (New York: Basic Books, 1988), 93–94.
4 See, especially, Blanche W. Cook, "Historical Denial of Lesbianism," *Radical History Review*, Spring/Summer 1979, 60–65.
5 Joan Nestle, *A Restricted Country* (Ithaca, NY: Firebrand Books, 1987), 10.
6 Ibid., 161.
7 Gayle Rubin, "Thinking Sex: Notes for a Radical Theory of the Politics of Sexuality," in *Pleasure and Danger: Exploring Female Sexuality*, ed. Carole Vance (Boston: Routledge and Kegan Paul, 1984), 308.
8 Sander Gilman, *Difference and Pathology: Stereotypes of Sexuality, Race and Madness* (Ithaca, NY: Cornell University Press, 1985), 89.
9 Ibid., 96.
10 Ibid., 98.
11 Estelle B. Freedman, " 'Uncontrolled Desires': The Response to the Sexual Psychopath, 1920–1960," *Journal of American History*, June 1987, 83–106.
12 Clara Thompson, "Changing Concepts of Homosexuality in Psychoanalysis," in *A Study of Interpersonal Relations*, ed. Patrick Mullahy (New York: Hermitage Press, 1949), reprinted in *The Homosexuals: As Seen by Themselves and Thirty Authorities*, ed. A. M. Krich (New York: Citadel, 1954), 255.
13 As quoted in George Henry, *All the Sexes* (New York: Rinehart, 1955), 293.
14 Anonymous, "To What Sex Do I Really Belong?" in Iwan Bloch, *Sexual Life of Our Time* (1900), reprinted in Krich, *The Homosexuals*, 12.

15 Frank Caprio, *Female Homosexuality: A Psychodynamic Study of Lesbianism* (New York: Citadel, 1954), 303–307.

16 See Freedman, " 'Uncontrolled Desires'."

17 Carleton Simon, "Homosexualists and Sex Crimes," speech to International Association of Chiefs of Police, September 1947, Massachusetts Society for Social Hygiene Papers 6, 57, Radcliffe College Schlesinger Library.

18 Polly Adler, *A House Is Not a Home* (New York: Rinehart, 1953), 110.

19 J. Mills, "Lesbians Try to Peddle Each Other," *Life*, December 3, 1965, 98–99.

20 Frank Caprio, *Variations in Sexual Behavior* (New York: Citadel, 1955), 183–184.

21 Simon, "Homosexualists and Sex Crimes," 57.

22 On the consolidation of psychiatric authority, see Seymour Halleck, "American Psychiatry and the Criminal: A Historical Review," *American Journal of Psychiatry*, March 1965, i–xxi.

23 "B-girls" were members of the sex industry along with prostitutes, strippers, call girls, etc. Their particular job involved "enticing" men in bars, especially "strip joints," to purchase more and more drinks, for which they received a percentage, or commission of sorts.

24 Jane MacKinnon, "I Am a Homosexual Woman," in Krich, *The Homosexuals*, 5.

25 Interview with "Mary," conducted by author, January 7, 1990.

26 Nestle, *A Restricted Country*, 104.

27 Joan Nestle, *The Persistent Desire: A Femme–Butch Reader* (Boston: Alyson, 1992), 14–15; italics added.

28 Valerie Taylor, *Return to Lesbos* (Tallahassee: Naiad Press, 1982), 7. Originally published in 1963.

Documents

In this 1955 study, Dr Frank Caprio explicitly links the threat of lesbianism to women's growing economic, social, and political independence throughout the twentieth century. Though he alleges a number of psychological problems associated with lesbianism, he nonetheless argues that it is a social issue. What specific factors contribute to the "psychic masculinization" of modern women, according to Caprio? How does he characterize lesbians?

Variations in Sexual Behavior: a Psychodynamic Study of Deviations in Various Expressions of Sexual Behavior

Frank Caprio

Female homosexuality is becoming an increasingly important problem. It is believed by some that women are becoming rapidly defeminized as a result of their overt desire for emancipation, and that this "psychic masculinization" of modern woman contributes to frigidity. Many contend that women are modifying their position in the world; that in innumerable ways their status has changed legally, economically, politically and socially during the past century. The process is still going on and we should not be surprised if it spreads to the sexual sphere.

Some sexologists fear that this defeminization trend may seriously affect the sexual happiness of modern women. They claim it will more than likely influence the susceptibility of many to a homosexual way of thinking and living.

The masculinity complex found in many women as a result of defeminization trends in modern society should be dealt with if it is responsible for the development of homosexual patterns of behavior. Dr. William G. Niederland claims that women who have a masculinity complex should be made aware that, if unchecked, it can lead to serious difficulties. Lesbianism, he says, is only one of several consequences. Such women can, through psychoanalysis, voluntarily renounce the desire for masculinity, reverting to their original role of woman.

Many women turn to female homosexuality because they are either sex-starved, rejected by men, or unable to achieve sex satisfaction with the opposite sex. Thus they experience greater stimulation from intimacies with their own sex.

While some women prefer homosexuality, others seek the help of a psychiatrist. Such women feel a sincere anguish because of their inability to enjoy a normal sexual relationship and deeply desire marriage and family life. . . .

Excerpted from Frank Caprio, *Variations in Sexual Behavior: a Psychodynamic Study of Deviations in Various Expressions of Sexual Behavior* (New York: The Citadel Press, 1955), pp. 160–65

Between 1952 and 1953 I completed a trip around the world for the purpose of accumulating scientific information in connection with the prevalence and practices of lesbianism. Much of my information was obtained from personal interviews, in some instances with the assistance of an interpreter.

Upon my return to this country, many of my professional colleagues were kind enough to discuss their own clinical experiences and observations with me. The following represent some of the more important conclusions drawn from the study.

Female homosexuality is as old as the human race. It constitutes a problem of universal significance. It has existed in every period of civilization, among every people. It is widespread and the methods of gratification are multiple. Many prostitutes, strangely enough, are lesbians.

Many crimes committed by women show, upon investigation, that they were either confirmed lesbians who killed through jealousy or were latent homosexuals with a strong, aggressive, masculine drive. Some lesbians manifest pronounced sadistic and psychopathic trends. Kleptomaniac tendencies, for example, are not uncommon among lesbians.

Lesbianism is environmentally determined. The concept of a "third sex," as we previously stated, is a myth and totally lacking in scientific basis.

Female homosexuality at best is a form of cooperative, or mutual, masturbation – a symptomatic expression of a neurotic personality; a disturbance in the infantile psychosexual development; a regression to narcissism; a manifestation of an emotional maladjustment usually influenced by such factors as a girl identifying herself with her father or brother. Other contributory factors are instability of the parents, unpleasant sexual experiences in childhood or adolescence, feelings of inferiority, loneliness, fear of marriage, personality deficiencies and exposure to the advances of an older lesbian.

Many lesbians are compulsive obsessional neurotics.

There are no complete males or complete females, rather relative degrees of masculinity and femininity.

Strong moral restrictions and strict religious censorship can interfere with normal psychosexual development.

Guilt, often unconscious, manifests itself in self-induced masochism (suicide, alcoholism, drug addiction, psychopathic or criminal behavior, prostitution and dissipation). Guilt associated with homosexual indulgences is influenced by religious and social taboos.

Artists, dancers, musicians, writers and actresses, because of their accelerated mode of living, Bohemian morals and neurotic temperaments have a predisposition to bisexual gratifications.

The vast majority of lesbians are emotionally unstable and neurotic. Many are disturbed over the realization that psychiatrists regard them as "sick individuals" badly in need of treatment.

We know, however, that their neurosis can be traced to various environmental traumatic influences during childhood and adolescence (broken homes, sexually maladjusted parents, a sadistic attitude toward the opposite sex, death of a parent, predisposition to masculinity and precocious sexuality). We know too that pronounced ambivalent feelings toward one or both parents are common to the majority of lesbians.

Lesbianism, in many instances, is traceable to the fixation of the libido upon a parent. Hence psychoanalysts regard it as an arrested development of the libido because it never reached the stage of sexual maturity.

While the fixation of the lesbian's libido to her father (Electra complex theory) is a plausible one, the causes of lesbianism are multiple and complex and cannot be explained by a single theory. Those homosexual experiences which are transitory in nature are usually brought about through circumstances and unforeseen situations. They occur among all classes of people. Lesbians are found among the elite as well as the poorer class. Not all lesbians, however, hate men or find their bodies repulsive. Many are bisexual, craving new sensations.

Because of their socially disapproved *modus vivendi*, female inverts suffer from a pervading sense of loneliness and as a consequence are unhappy. I personally am convinced that lesbians would not be healthy persons even if they lived in a society where sexuality with their own sex was socially acceptable. There is seldom any permanence to a lesbian alliance. Lesbians become dissatisfied, jealous and change partners frequently. They usually recognize each other by various revealing traits. Mannish lesbians, as a rule, prefer women partners who are feminine in nature. They establish husband–wife relationships, and assume the male role. I have observed in my psychoanalytic study of lesbians that unconsciously under the disguise of the husband–wife relationship, they act out the child–mother relationship.

Many overt lesbians deny experiencing a sense of guilt although they complain of numerous ailments for which they seek medical aid. They are depressed, suffer from headaches, fatigue, insomnia or digestive disturbances. Others have pains around the heart, fainting spells and dizziness. Failing to appreciate the role which anxiety and guilt, associated with their sexual inversion, play in the development of their symptom-complaints, they consult a physician. Occasionally homosexual experiences may result in the precipitation of a psychosis.

Alcohol which tends to release one's inhibitions is frequently responsible for homosexual seductions. The latent homosexual component is more apt to come to the surface under the influence of alcohol.

Some women enter into a homosexual affair as a result of curiosity or sex experimentation.

An experienced lesbian in seducing an innocent young girl may seriously affect her normal sexual development. In this respect lesbians are essentially sick individuals.

I Am a Homosexual Woman

Jane McKinnon

Jane McKinnon's autobiographical essay, written in 1954, included in an anthology of mostly medical authorities, suggests the internalization of negative cultural attitudes toward lesbians that posited them as a deviation from the heterosexual norm. Her understanding of her predicament expresses ambivalence about the reasons for her homosexuality as well as its adverse effects on her happiness. In what ways does her attitude toward homosexuality support the prevailing medical opinion that lesbians were socially and psychologically depraved?

Representing as it does an entirely different way of thinking and living, it is odd how easy it is to conceal homosexual tendencies. This holds particularly true where women are concerned because a masculine woman attracts less attention than an effeminate man. In many cases, she is respected and admired for her manly qualities. As a woman who is at the same time a homosexual and a member in good standing in her community and profession, I can vouch for the truth of this.

No doubt one reason for the ease with which we can conceal our attitude is that so few people are at all conscious of our existence. Homosexuality in men has been studied so fully that the general public is more aware of their problem. . . .

What is it like to be this way?

You are always lonely. It makes no difference how many friends you have or how nice they are. Between you and other women friends is a wall which they can not see, but which is terribly apparent to you. This wall represents the difference in the workings of your minds.

Excerpted from Jane McKinnon, "I Am a Homosexual Woman," in A. M. Krich, ed., *The Homosexuals: as Seen by Themselves and Thirty Authorities* (New York: The Citadel Press, 1954), pp. 3–10.

Between you and men friends is another difficult misunderstanding. Very few men desire platonic friendships, the only kind of which you are capable so far as they are concerned. The endless bitter disagreements with them cause many of us to renounce their companionship entirely. Very few men understand the need we have for their friendship and the aversion we feel for sexual love. Unable to find love or its most acceptable substitute friendship, we frequently become psychiatric cases. You can not keep a healthy state of mind if you are very lonely.

The inability to present an honest face to those you know eventually develops a certain deviousness which is injurious to whatever basic character you may possess. Always pretending to be something you are not, moral laws lose their significance. What *is* right and wrong for you when your every effort is toward establishing a relationship with another which is completely right to you, but appallingly wrong to others?

How do homosexuals feel about one another?

One of the saddest facts in this entire picture is that we seldom like one another. On the surface this appears ridiculous, but there are good reasons for it. In order to make it more clear, let me describe the general categories into which we fall.

There are certain things which are characteristic of each type. However, it is important to remember that merely because a woman may have some of the following characteristics, she is by no means to be considered a homosexual or even one who has such tendencies. This is because the intelligent homosexual always adopts the manners and customs of the group to which she belongs. Physical build plays a large part in determining what type you are.

Type I is a large person, that is, tall although not necessarily heavy. She is successful in the business world. She is intelligent and uses her manly qualities to advance her in her work. Her clothes are good, she frequently wears tailored suits and dresses and does not care for fussy hair styles or frills of any kind. She is not drawn to another like herself because she is the aggressive sort whose efficiency and capability make her desire a partner who would be emotionally dependent on her. In many cases her behavior with her friend can be likened to that of a mother with a helpless child.

Type II is small, feminine in appearance. She can be just as aggressive as the woman described above and, although the two types do mix, the relationship is not entirely satisfactory to either. This is because both would want to dominate.

Types I and II have certain things in common. They are both completely homosexual in their desires. They are always the active, aggressive partner. They can not be satisfied unless they dominate, that is, assume the role of the man. That they associate at all is usually due to the inability to find another partner.

There is another more delicate factor to be mentioned. What we are considering here is something so intimate that few people have any idea of the contradictory elements present. To a homosexual there is something incongruous, embarrassing, about making love to another like herself. The entire basis of the friendship is the pretense that one of the women is a man. It is uncomfortable to have in the back of your mind the idea that your associate feels just as you do instead of as a woman would. It is so much a business arrangement that it seems rather indecent.

Type III is not a real homosexual, but has strong tendencies that way. This type of girl is a natural object for the attentions of the types described above. No homosexual woman would force her attentions upon another who was completely unwilling.

This third type is almost without exception a weak individual. She may have some strong characteristics but her craving for sexual gratification is so great that she will accept it from the homosexual woman if there is no man to satisfy her.

The fact that many of these women would be heterosexual if we let them alone is no deterrent to us if they appear at all amenable to our suggestions. Education, breeding, all those things do not prevent the homosexual from drawing such a woman into her orbit of dominance if she possibly can. Her need for relief from sexual tension and loneliness is too great. Yet, so weak are most women who yield to an aggressive homosexual, that this situation often becomes a tormenting one for the latter. This is because the weaker individual can not break off the relationship nor can she reconcile her conscience to it. Unlike the complete invert, she often feels it is wrong but can neither accept it nor end it. . . .

Type IV hardly deserves mention. They are those who capitalize on the curiosity of people who are willing to pay to see something disgusting. I refer, of course, to those whose activities in night clubs in the larger cities attract many people looking for a thrill. The entire matter is much too personal to be exploited in such a way. The behavior of commercial inverts does much to color the public's ideas of us.

What happened to me? Why do I have to be this way?

No doubt every homosexual has pondered these questions, searching for an answer that will bring her peace of mind. Realization of the tendency comes slowly. It is not a question of waking up some morning and thinking: "Why, I'm a homosexual." I was nineteen before I ever heard the word, a sophomore in college at the time. The way in which it was mentioned in a conversation made me wonder if that was what was wrong with me. A quick look at the dictionary told me immediately that not only was I a homosexual, but that I was a most unpleasant individual, a person whom anyone decent would avoid like the plague. The next impressions I received of myself through reading were equally terrifying. I had heard of degenerates, but never realized that many would think me one if they knew a little more about me. Puzzled, bewildered, I could find nowhere a single kind word being said. Most of the writers of the books could not seem to understand that a homosexual is not a *term*, but a *person*. She has feelings just as anyone else. She has an additional burden – the necessity of being quiet about her troubles, the inability to tell her friends anything about herself. What is her position? She must occasionally be present when her friends talk about her and those like her in the most unpleasant terms you can conceive. Yet her friends and her employer, not knowing, like her a lot. If she were to say – and it is often a temptation – "I am a homosexual," the repercussions would be all that anyone could imagine. . . .

What can be done to correct our situation?

Hardly anything has appeared in print which would warn parents of such tendencies in their children. Almost without exception, they ignore any warnings which appear in puberty. Instead, like venereal disease and other hush-hush subjects, publications that deal with this problem are often banned. Therefore, many are almost completely unaware of its existence.

The rapidly developing science of psychiatry, by bringing this out into the light, could help us by making available more facts of why we are as we are. Some of us torment ourselves with the idea that we are "evil." We are not degenerates, yet many refer to us in such terms. We are considered a sort of sex criminal. Not only should people realize that there are lots of us, but they should have their attitudes toward us changed. Then the parent, instead of being horrified, will be able to help his child to adjust to a rather hard world.

Self-examination is not enough to resolve the confusion in our minds, a confusion arising from our idea of ourselves *vs.* the idea voiced by the heterosexual person. The best way to keep us from compensating our loneliness and sense of inadequacy at the expense of weaker individuals is to provide us with knowledge about our place in the order of things. There will be fewer homosexual women in mental hospitals and psychiatric offices if we are recognized as human beings instead of as material for a chapter in a book on abnormal psychology.

The Detective

James Mills

This excerpt from a photo essay appeared in *Life* magazine in 1965. The article focused on the activities of George Barrett, a New York detective renowned for his anti-vice activities among those he called "germs," "degenerates, perverts and lawbreakers" in New York. Lesbians and prostitutes are conflated in the pictures and captions. How does this lumping implicate lesbians in the alleged disintegration of morality in urban America?

I'm obsessed," he says, "with the idea that I've *got* to win, and these animals can smell it. No one's going to mess with me and win because I've been around, I've been up against the bad guys. These animals on Broadway? I'll eat them up. I've got the tools and I know how to use them. If I can't get the best of the guy with punches, I'll kick him, and if he's a better kicker than I am, I'll go with the stick or the jack, and if I have to, I'll use my gun."

To some people George Barrett is precisely what's wrong with law enforcement. To others he is all that can save it.

In late evening darkness he stands on New York City's West 52nd Street, the 16th Precinct's northern border, and looks south into the flashing neon fireball of Times Square. This is Broadway, the Great White Way, the fabled street of dreams. Barrett calls it the sewer. Down it flows the worst America has to offer in the way of degenerates, perverts and lawbreakers – to Barrett, "germs."...

On Broadway, between 43rd and 45th streets, the male prostitutes line up like whores in Hamburg – baby-faced youngsters and broad-belted, black-booted toughs, any type the trade demands. Around the corner in the alleylike darkness of 43rd Street, homosexual exhibitionists skip between Broadway and Eighth Avenue, shouting affectionate female curses at each other. On 42nd Street, beneath brilliant white marquees touting movies called *Orgy at Lil's Place*, *The Dirty Girls*, and *Rape*, flow streams of degenerates of all varieties. And everywhere, up and down the precinct, are the junkies, the pill addicts and the pushers....

George Barrett works in the busiest precinct in New York – and one of the meanest. More crimes are committed in it than in any other precinct

Excerpted from James Mills, "The Detective," *Life* (December 3, 1965), pp. 90–9.

in the city. In this photographic essay some of the 16th Precinct's law-breakers are seen actually at work.

Telling the players without a program can be all but impossible in Times Square. The four people in the three pictures at left [not reproduced here] are all women. Two are drug addicts, and one is a pusher. Two are prostitutes, the other two are pimps. All are Lesbians.

They are among hundreds of perverts, prostitutes and addicts drawn to the Times Square area by each other and by the easy marks they can prey on. "They have to come here," says Barrett. "It's the only place in the world they can find this much action."

Many came first as runaways from home. Some started on drugs in other neighborhoods and gravitated naturally to Times Square. The police are often urged to clear them out, but they find it nearly impossible to do so. "To clean up Times Square," says Barrett, "you would have to lock up crowds of people every night, and keep doing it for months and months until they just decided to go somewhere else. And then as soon as you relaxed, they'd start coming back."

Figure 1   Not all the prostitutes around Times Square are women. Some are men posing as women, like the wigged individual above propositioning a John, a man looking for a prostitute (his face has been retouched). Though this impersonator is breaking the law by dressing as a woman (he was arrested several days after this picture was taken), the male homosexuals in Figure 2 are relatively safe from arrest.

Figure 2 Though some of these young men wear female wigs, earrings and women's slacks, they avoid arrest by not wearing dresses. They have spotted the photographer and strike poses.

Figure 3   Five minutes after giving her a shot of heroin, a Lesbian dressed as a man leads her pony-tailed girlfriend around the corner to meet two other Lesbians.

Beebo Brinker

Ann Bannon

This excerpt from Ann Bannon's legendary *Beebo Brinker* epitomizes the lesbian pulp fiction genre of the 1950s and 1960s. Unlike lesbian novels written earlier in the century, Bannon's series did not deny lesbian sex or cloak it in euphemisms, nor were her characters filled with self-hate, depression, and loneliness. In this scene set in New York's Greenwich Village, the protagonist, Beebo, has her first sexual experience with a woman. How would you characterize Bannon's portrayal of love between women?

But now it seemed incredible that this exquisite stranger should reach out for her from the middle of nowhere. "Paula," she said, "I think we're both just lonely. I think it would be best if I go. You don't want to wake up tomorrow and hate yourself." She was still hedging about the ultimate test with a girl.

"I *was* lonely. I will be again if you go."

"Maybe you'd be better off lonely than sorry."

"Beebo, do I have to beg you?" Paula pleaded, her voice coming up stronger with her emotion.

Beebo reached for her in one instinctive motion, suddenly very warm inside her jacket. "No, Paula, you don't have to beg me to do anything. Just ask me."

"I did. And you didn't want to stay."

"I didn't want to scare you. I didn't understand."

"I thought it was Mona. She can make herself so – so tempting."

"I can't even remember what she looks like."

"Aren't you in love with her?"

Beebo's hands, with a will of their own, closed around Paula's warm slim arms. "I met her last week for the first time. You can't be in love with someone you just met."

"You can't?" Paula demurred cautiously, looking down at her big pajamas.

"I never was," Beebo said, feeling sweat break out on her forehead. She pulled gently on Paula and was almost dismayed when Paula moved

Excerpted from Ann Bannon, *Beebo Brinker* (Tallahassee, FL: The Naiad Press, Inc., 1986; first published 1962), pp. 79–83.

docilely toward her. Beebo became feverishly aware that the plaid pajamas did not conceal all of Paula Ash. The sweeping curve of her breasts
held the cotton tops out far enough to brush Beebo's chest with a feather
touch. Beebo felt it through the layers of her clothes with a tremor so
hard and real it tumbled eighteen years of daydreams out of her head.

She held Paula at arm's length a moment, looking at this lovely little
redheaded princess with a mixture of misgivings and want too powerful
to pretend away. Paula took her hands and held them with quivering
strength, returning Beebo's gaze. Beebo saw her own doubts reflected in
Paula's eyes. But she saw desire there, too; desire so big that it had to be
brave: it hadn't any place to hide.

Paula kissed Beebo's hands with a quick press of her mouth that
electrified Beebo. She stood there while Paula kissed them over and
over again and a passionate frenzy mounted in them both. Paula's lips,
at first so chaste, almost reverent, warmed against Beebo's palms . . . and
then her kitten-tongue slipped between Beebo's fingers and over the
backs of her broad hands until those hands trembled perceptibly and
Paula stopped, clutching them to her face.

Beebo reclaimed them, but only to caress Paula's face, bringing it
close to her and seeing it with amazement.

"I never guessed I'd feel love for the first time through my hands," she
murmured. "Paula, Paula, I would have done this all wrong if you hadn't
had the guts to start it for me. I would have manhandled you, I –"

Paula stilled her with a finger over Beebo's mouth. "Don't talk now,"
she said.

And Beebo, who had never done more than dream before, slipped her
arms around Paula and pulled her tight. It was a marvel the way their
bodies fitted together; the way Paula's head tipped back naturally at so
beckoning an angle, and rested on Beebo's arm; the way her eyes closed
and her lips parted and her hair scattered like garnet petals around her
flower-face.

Beebo kissed her mouth and kissed her mouth again, holding her
against the wall with the pressure of her body. Paula submitted with a
sort of wistful abandonment. Everywhere Beebo touched this sweet girl,
she found thrilling surprises. And Paula, coming to life beneath Beebo's
searching hands, found them with her.

It was no news to Beebo that she was tall and strong and male-inclined.
But her voluptuous reaction to Paula shocked her speechless. Paula began
to undress her and Beebo felt herself half-fainting backwards on the sofa
into a whirlpool of sensual delight. The merest touch, the merest flutter of
a finger, and Beebo went under, hearing her own moans like the whistle of
a distant wind. Paula had only to undo a belt buckle or pull off a shoe, and
Beebo responded with a beautiful helpless fury of desire.

It was no longer a question of proceeding with caution, of "learning how." The whole night passed like an ecstatic dream, punctuated with a few dead-asleep time-outs, when they were both too exhausted to move, even to make themselves comfortable.

Beebo had only a vague idea of what she was doing, beyond the overwhelming fact that she was making ardent love to Paula. She seemed to have no mind at all, nor need of one. She was aware only that Paula was beautiful, she was gay, she was warmly loving, and she was there in Beebo's arms: fragrant and soft and auburn-topped as a bouquet of tiger lilies.

Beebo couldn't let her go. And when fatigue forced her to stop she would pull Paula close and stroke her, her heavy breath stirring Paula's glowing hair, and think about all the girls she had wanted and been denied. She was making up, this night, for every last one of them.

Paula whispered, "Do you still believe you can't love someone you just met?"

"I don't know what I believe any more."

And Paula said, "I love you, Beebo. Do you believe that?"

Beebo lifted Paula's fine face and covered it with kisses while Paula kept repeating, "I love you, I love you," until the words – the unadorned words – brought Beebo crashing to a climax, rolling over on Paula, embracing her with those long strong legs.

Further Reading

Faderman, Lillian. *Odd Girls and Twilight Lovers: a History of Lesbian Life in Twentieth-century America.* New York: Penguin, 1991.

Freedman, Estelle. "The prison lesbian: race, class, and the construction of the aggressive female homosexual, 1915–1965." *Feminist Studies* (Summer 1996), 397–423.

Kennedy, Elizabeth Lapovsky, and Madelaine Davis. *Boots of Leather, Slippers of Gold: the History of a Lesbian Community.* New York: Routledge, 1993.

Nestle, Joan. *A Persistent Desire: a Femme–Butch Reader.* Boston: Alyson Press, 1992.

Newton, Esther. "The mythic mannish lesbian: Radclyffe Hall and the new woman." In Martin Bauml Duberman et al. (eds), *Hidden from History: Reclaiming the Gay and Lesbian Past.* New York: New American Library, 1989, pp. 281–93.

Vicinus, Martha. " 'They wonder to which sex I belong': the historical roots of the modern lesbian identity." *Feminist Studies*, 18 (Fall 1992), 467–98.

Walters, Suzanna Danuta. "From here to queer: radical feminism, postmodernism, and the lesbian menace (or, why can't a woman be more like a fag?)." *Signs: Journal of Women in Culture and Society* (Summer 1996), 830–69.

13

The Population Bomb and the Sexual Revolution

Introduction

In the 1950s and 1960s, pregnancy rates for both black and white teenage girls skyrocketed. Dismayed by the growing number of unmarried teens having babies, social commentators and policy makers alike tackled this "social problem" in radically different ways, according to the race of the girls in question. Black, unmarried, and pregnant girls were imagined to be part of a larger population explosion crisis and contributors to the rapid decline of the cities, economic decay, and racial tension. For social commentators their pregnancies stemmed from their uncontrollable sexuality. America's perceived urban crisis became in part a sexual problem, one blamed on young black women. For white girls, the problem of teen pregnancy was interpreted in less threatening ways. White, unmarried girls were not seen as contributing to a population crisis; critics instead focused on loose sexual morals that allowed these innocent girls to be lured into sexual relationships which ultimately led to their pregnancies.

Policy makers cast the solutions as well as the problems in racialized terms. Programs were designed to teach black girls how to be effective mothers, based on a model of white marriage and motherhood. Overcoming widespread reservations about dispensing birth control to teens, social service agencies, law makers, and schools acceded to offer black girls birth control pills to control future pregnancies. By contrast, authorities did not distribute contraceptives to white teens with similar alacrity because they construed such action as encouraging female sexuality and independence. Sexual and immoral, black girls clearly needed the cure of birth control; white girls, represented as pure and innocent despite their pregnancies, required redirection from this sordid behavior toward more wholesome activities. Only reluctantly was white female sexuality acknowledged.

The Population Bomb and the Sexual Revolution: Toward Choice

Rickie Solinger

> " 'While the rich in America do whatever it is they do, the poor are begetting children,' says former Assistant Secretary of Labor Daniel Moynihan."
>
> *The New Republic*
> September 25, 1965

In the 1950s the treatment of unwed mothers was not, in general, the subject of public debate, even while the subjects of female premarital sexuality and childbearing, black and white, were of increasing public concern. Public debate was very narrow or absent in part because the vulnerability of unmarried sexually active girls and women was not in doubt; the vulnerability of single *pregnant* females was particularly enforceable. Since the family, service providers, policy makers, and the public could count on this vulnerability as they demanded and arranged for unwed mothers to be sequestered, or ignored, or punished, by race, single pregnant girls and women did not emerge as a population – or populations – of dangerous aggressors against society between 1945 and 1965.

By the early 1960s, however, public discourse about both black and white nonmarital sexuality and maternity had shifted. It now used a new language that denied the vulnerability of unmarried, sexually active females and transformed these girls and women – both those who were

Excerpted from Rickie Solinger, "The Population Bomb and the Sexual Revolution: Toward Choice," in *Wake up Little Susie: Single Pregnancy and Race before Roe v. Wade* (New York: Routledge, 1992), pp. 205–32. Reproduced by permission of Taylor & Francis, Inc./Routledge, Inc., http://www.routledge-ny.com.

pregnant and those who might become pregnant – into aggressors against a vulnerable society. By 1965, the end point of this study, the white unwed mother had been changed in the public consciousness from a species of mental patient into a sexual revolutionary. The black unwed mother was still portrayed as a participant in an aberrant culture of sexuality and as the taxpayers' nemesis. But at the highest levels of policy discussion, she was increasingly cast as the triggering device affixed to the Population Bomb, USA.

The "sexual revolution" and the "population bomb" were racially specific metaphors of destruction. Their widespread use after 1960 reflected, in part, the hopelessness with which influential segments of society regarded their own capacity to control nonmarital female sexuality and its consequences. The two separate and contemporaneous metaphors also reflected common feelings about the need to fashion explicitly race-specific defenses, even in the face of an overwhelming task. Since the "revolution" and the "bomb" were identified with female sexual behavior, the metaphors also suggested public perception of a terrible new capacity embodied by unmarried girls and women. By virtue of these tropes, unwed mothers, along with all unmarried sexually active females, were assigned apocalyptic importance. . . .

Black Unwed Mothers and The Population Bomb

Between 1945 and 1960, public efforts to respond to black illegitimacy took one of three forms, all of which were *ex post facto*. First, various states legislated punitive sanctions against poor women who had illegitimate children. Second, public agencies simply ignored the black unwed mother and her child, or the welfare system grudgingly supported them in the "culture of poverty." Third, the child welfare apparatus in some localities tried to promote a willingness among black unwed mothers to put their illegitimate children up for adoption and tried to develop placements for these babies. None of these efforts influenced the rate of illegitimate pregnancy among black women, although all of them directly or indirectly aimed to demonstrate that unsanctioned sexuality and illegitimate pregnancy carried harsh consequences for black women in the United States.[1] . . .

When oral contraceptives became available in 1960, policy makers, service providers, and concerned citizens had an entirely new option: to support preventative rather than punitive strategies to reduce the black fertility rate. At this point, an array of supporters of pregnancy prevention who usually expressed their project in terms of population control began to present their cases publicly. Population control strategies had the disadvantage of seeming to sanction illicit female sexuality, but the distinct advantage of curtailing fertility *a priori*. William A. Ryan, a representative to the Michigan State House, expressed the dilemma facing a politician: "My bills [prohibiting welfare workers from initiating birth control discussions with clients] are an attempt to draw the line between two dangers... excessive illegitimacy at public expense on the one hand, and the idea that the State sanctions sexual promiscuity by providing birth control information to unmarried women on the other."[2]

Increasingly in the early 1960s, politicians and their constituents came to two conclusions; first, that black unmarried women typically have sexual relations, and secondly, that the financial and demographic burdens of illegitimacy were more onerous for society to bear than the moral strain. Illinois State Senator Morgan Findlay, who had opposed a bill to provide birth control to poor unwed women in 1963, said two years later, when he changed sides, "I felt it boiled down to the lesser of two evils, the so-called evil of bringing unwanted children into the world and increasing the public payrolls, or the evil of giving contraceptives to unmarried people." Findlay chose to support birth control for poor, unmarried girls and women because, he said, it was "good for the entire population of the State of Illinois," a decision one national television commentator called "a triumph of pocketbook over principle" that was occurring "almost everywhere" in the United States by 1965.[3]

During the early 1960s, state after state and then the federal government selected oral contraceptives as the method of choice for addressing unacceptably high rates of black illegitimacy. This development represented an instance of remarkably rapid consensus building among groups with distinct views of black illegitimacy. In June 1965, United States Senator Ernest Gruening, chairman of the Senate Subcommittee on Foreign Aid Expenditures of the Committee on Government Operations, opened hearings on S. 1676, which called for offices, staff, and programs in the Department of State and the Department of Health, Education and Welfare to deal with population problems abroad and in the United States. Senator Gruening called hundreds of expert witnesses to offer their perspectives on the nature of the population crisis. The thousands of pages of testimony from these hearings, and the appended magazine and journal articles, books, conference proceedings, radio and television transcripts, newspaper editorials, and political speeches constitute a rich record of the range of thinking of many who could claim membership in the contraceptive alliance.

The most voluble members of this coalition were politicians, demographers, agronomists, and civic leaders concerned about the population bomb. These participants were convinced of the volatile, inexorable relationship between "overpopulation" in the US black community and social chaos. Joining this group were others with at least five different agendas, but all shared the vision that supplying contraceptives to unwed black women was a solution to "overpopulation."

Philip Hauser, a former assistant director of the United States Census Bureau and a prominent demographer from the University of Chicago, dramatically framed his concern about the consequences of postwar fertility rates in terms that set the tone of the hearings. Overpopulation of the cities will, Hauser asserted, "worsen the United States unemployment problem, greatly increase the magnitude of juvenile delinquency, exacerbate already dangerous race tensions . . . greatly increase traffic accidents and fatalities, augment urban congestion and further subvert the traditional American governmental system."[4]

The Gruening hearings began the summer of the uprising in the Watts section of Los Angeles, and many witnesses made the direct connection between black illegitimacy rates and, as James V. Bennett, the former director of the Federal Bureau of Prisons, testified, "the almost insuperable problem of law enforcement in such overpopulated areas as Los Angeles' Watts, New York's Harlem, or Philadelphia's ghettos." Bennett added, "We know that these areas generate severe tensions because of the constantly expanding population, pressure which the law, as it is now organized, cannot cope with."[5] By the mid-1960s, the fertility of black women, especially the unmarried, was constructed as an explosive issue, profoundly threatening to the fabric of American life. For many, it was now immaterial whether black women had too many babies because of their biological or their cultural propensities; the point was that they must be stopped.[6] . . .

Another pair of members of the contraceptive alliance were the tax resisters, those who resented the financial burden associated with illegitimacy and the ADC program, and those who minded most being taxed to support the sin of illegitimacy. Demonstrating the logic of the first group, *The New York Times* explained, "Nationally the illegitimacy rate has tripled since 1940, and the children's aid program, heavily burdened by unwed mothers, has grown to four million cases, costing $1.5 billion. In 1955 there were $639 million [sic]. In short, there is a tax savings in birth control."[7] . . .

President Lyndon Johnson promoted birth control as cost-effective, as well, when he addressed the twentieth anniversary celebration of the United Nations in San Francisco, three days after the Gruening hearings began. At a time when presidential pronouncements on population issues and fertility were rare and very carefully phrased and noted, Johnson recommended, "Let us act on the fact that less than five dollars invested in population control is worth $100 invested in economic growth."[8] These cost-accounting arguments extended the grounds for accusing poor unwed mothers, often black, of consumer violations: an

unmarried girl or woman who failed to buy into the contraceptive
bargain was forcing society to pay full price for an unwanted item.[9]

Most of the advocates of a federal population control policy were convinced that contraceptives could reduce the birth rate of poor minorities
and thus promote the health, safety, and prosperity of American society.
Still, there was a distinct group appearing before the Gruening subcommittee who wanted contraceptives to be available to poor and black
women because the women themselves might want them and because
social justice demanded that if more affluent white women had access to
birth control, all women should. Often, however, this "rights" position
was quickly confounded by the issue of "duty." Michigan Representative John Conyers, the only black among sixty witnesses to appear in the
first round of hearings, for example, cited the influential observations of
the National Academy of Sciences in their report, *The Growth of US
Population*: "The freedom to limit family size to the number of children
wanted when they are wanted is, in our view, a basic human right. The
evidence cited in this report shows clearly that most Americans of high
income and better education exercise this right, as a matter of course,
but that many of the poor and uneducated are in effect deprived of the
right."[10] Having established the "right" of black women to access,
Conyers went on to associate his support of contraceptives for black
women with the argument that fewer black babies would "stabilize and
improve the Negro family structure," a structure severely compromised
by "the tragedy of unwanted children." Thus, the interest in social
justice and the rights of black women to have protected sex lives was
eclipsed by the notion that these females had the duty to use birth
control if the black community were to be saved from the "disintegrating
effects of too many children" and the country as a whole were to be
saved from the effects of the population bomb....

It is, of course, noteworthy that black women did not have a voice in
the public discussion of these issues in the mid-1960s. The discussants,
almost exclusively white and male, had and took a great deal of latitude
in constructing the importance of birth control for black women. Black
women made an appearance at the Gruening hearings exclusively in the
descriptions of policy makers – descriptions that stressed how their
helplessness and ignorance fueled the population bomb. Senator Joseph
Tydings offered a typical assessment: "It is absolutely incredible the
number of adult women on welfare rolls who, by reason of their background and their complete lack of parental supervision, their complete
lack of education, have had illegitimate children and yet do not really
...know about the birds and the bees."[11]

It is likewise meaningful to link the advent of oral contraceptives and
the IUD as policy options to the emergence of the "population bomb" as

a compelling description of the demographics of the ghetto. The point is, for black women the early history of the new contraceptive technology was controlled not by a value-free technological development, or by a discourse of women's rights, but by public discussion that blamed black women for the problems of their community and demands that these women accept measures to halt "excess reproduction." The new reproductive technologies were not publicly sanctioned or offered to black women in a user-friendly mode. The rhetoric promoting their efficacy often had more in common with public justifications of sterilization of black women than it did with discussion of reproductive rights.[12]

As the contraceptive alliance gathered influential proponents in the early 1960s, those who did not join failed, more and more often, to control or even influence policy outcomes. The nonjoiners, like the joiners, represented a variety of perspectives. Prominent and persistent among them were public officials who felt strongly that unmarried mothers, especially teenagers, should not be engaging in sexual relations and should, therefore, not be provided with birth control. Some who took this exclusionary position were Catholics opposed to all contraception. Others were traditionalists upset that governmental bodies were facilitating nonmarital coitus. Some who may have been associated with either or both of these two groups were moralists disgusted by the notion of sex on the loose and by the distribution of birth control materials that could exacerbate the spread of rampant sexuality. Richard B. Nowakowski, a Milwaukee alderman, expressed outrage that federal money had been committed to support five birth control clinics in his city: "We will have 'sexmobiles' moving around the streets passing out birth control to whomever wants it – just like popcorn wagons."[13] In the early 1960s, the contraceptive coalition had to beat back these groups of nonjoiners to establish the eligibility of unwed mothers. The coalition succeeded in this effort in part by invoking the population bomb in the media, in the Gruening hearings, and in other legislative proceedings as an artifact of black illegitimacy rates. By the mid-1960s, the positions of the antis were no longer competitive.

Despite some thirteenth-hour attempts on the federal level to exclude unwed mothers from contraceptive services, the trend was otherwise. The Webster School, a model, federally funded facility for unwed mothers in Washington, DC, was prohibited by the District's board of education from discussing family planning and the use of contraceptives in the classroom. But by the mid-1960s, the DC Department of Public Health was able to provide birth control materials to the school's students, almost all of whom were black, at the six week postpartum examination. Only girls fifteen and younger needed their parents' approval.[14] . . .

By the early 1960s, birth control was perceived as the prime effective deterrent against the causes of social chaos, including the cause most frequently identified in the 1950s, juvenile delinquency, and the more recently named cause, illegitimacy, leading to overpopulation and poverty. Whereas in the 1950s, boys, as juvenile delinquents, were most often perceived as threatening to the social fabric, now girls, specifically unwed mothers, became not simply breeders of unwanted babies, but bearers of social pathology and of social breakdown. In this period, for the first time, young black girls were identified as a target population for programs and services designed to curtail antisocial, destructive behavior.

"Comprehensive Programs" for Black Unwed Mothers

At this point, the designers of such programs and services became innovators. None of the postwar approaches to black unwed mothers – benign neglect, punitive, or benevolent reform – commanded credibility at the federal level by the early 1960s since black illegitimacy rates remained at unacceptably high levels. Ignoring black unwed mothers and their babies did not lower illegitimacy rates or social costs. Nor did punishing them, nor developing casework treatment for black mothers and adoption placements for their babies.

The innovation consisted of a two-pronged attack. In cities across the country, black unwed mothers were presented with the technological solution of birth control pills combined with the vocational solution of community-based "comprehensive" programs against illegitimacy and its destructive social consequences. The new approach situated pathology primarily in the outcome rather than the cause of unwed sexuality. Concerning black women, the social potency of illicit sexuality and conception was in the fact of more illegitimate children to challenge the social fabric. Consistent with this view, public health experts in New York "urged that large-scale rehabilitation programs be undertaken for unmarried mothers [in order to] break the cycle of the out of wedlock child turned into a delinquent who will repeat the parental pattern."[15] The innovation thus did conform to traditional ideas about biological transmission of the taint of illegitimacy, with experts predicting that the sins of the mothers would be replicated.

The technology of birth control could effectively abort the biological consequences of illegitimate sex and thus the transmission of a delinquent culture. In addition, for the first time, social programs aimed to penetrate this culture, through the experiences of black girls and women, and remake both black culture and its female members in a whiter image. This was an interesting departure from the project of benevolent reformers who aimed to elevate the dignity and the opportunities of black unwed mothers by assigning them the neuroses associated with white unwed mothers. Now that blacks were specifically targeted for social programs, rather than construct them as being as disturbed as white unwed mothers were, the intention was to improve them so they could meet the healthy behavior standard of white culture. Project directors in the early 1960s freely acknowledged that black unwed mothers were different from whites. They believed, however, that their projects must eradicate that difference, in the name of deterrence. The Webster School Project in Washington, DC, which quickly became a model for nearly forty similar projects serving about eight thousand unwed mothers across the country,[16] took what its directors and evaluator called a "middle class approach" to its black clients. The Webster School offered a "behavior modification" program designed "to rehabilitate school-age girls to acceptable social standards," and specifically to "middle class behavior," including the ability to plan for the future and to embrace norms regarding "sexual discipline." The staff also promoted the idea that its students should abdicate the mother role so as to be students and normative adolescents. This last premise endeared the Webster School program to the Children's Bureau's professionals who funded the project and who continued to prefer the position that unwed mothers were not-mothers. But it also put this school and its imitators in a paradoxical relation to another central thrust of programs for black unwed mothers – that the curriculum should be created "in the interests of establishing stable family life values" among black unwed mothers.[17] While recognizing a need to improve the environment of this population, many claimed that a higher purpose still was to "motivate [the girls] to want and appreciate the values of a stable and orderly family life,"[18] and to "accept the family pattern of the prevailing culture: marriage."[19] In attempting to remake black unwed mothers and their culture, the experts often drew on two of the most common strategies of white unwed mothers – relinquishment and marriage – strategies that were often unavailable or unacceptable to black girls and women. . . .

A program in Cleveland required all of its participants to join a therapy group, beginning in 1962. The group was led by a white male psychiatrist because the program director "thought that a male psychiatrist would be better than a female because of the characteristically matriarchal families [of the girls]."[20] Another worker in a model program for black unwed mothers in Cleveland diagnosed her clients in the quasi-psychological terms provided by Leontine Young, the prominent social worker who, herself, dismissed blacks as outside the bounds of her categories because of endemic family and community disorganization.

The Cleveland worker intrepidly defined the girls in her program as "passive dependents," unable "to see cause and effect" (in the sense that "they failed to see the connection between the sex act and childbirth") and "out of control." This woman, a "specialist" in working with unwed teen mothers, did not see the contradiction between this diagnosis and her determination that, in her own role toward the mothers, she must be "rather active, outgoing, and accepting to convey to the women that I was really interested in them and that I was not there to make judgments." In fact, demonstrating how thoroughly the white "experts" were indoctrinated by the social work literature and little else, she justified her diagnosis of "dependency" on the grounds that many of the girls and women in her program "desire to give their babies to their mothers or women custodians who serve as substitute mothers." Again, following the prescription of Leontine Young and others, prescriptions specifically devised to treat whites, this young woman aimed to wean her clients from dependence on their mothers and other female relatives, inserting herself, instead, as "substitute mother." In this role, she would develop "a trusting relationship with them, setting a good many limits and expectations and helping them to live up to them."[21]

The phenomenon of nonmarital conception consistently stimulated program designers to construct their target population as deficient in the qualities of an ideal type and to mount training programs to redress the deficiency. As white unwed mothers were schooled in maternity homes to assume the grooming and comportment of middle-class femininity and gentility, blacks were trained to be more like whites. As white unwed mothers were pressured to give up their babies so they could sustain the image of normative young womanhood, blacks, many hoped, would advance to the practice of relinquishing their illegitimate babies in a future time, when black culture had been successfully penetrated and rearranged to resemble white culture....

The efforts to reach and educate black unwed mothers became, by 1964, one of many similar thrusts in the name of the Great Society. The Children's Bureau launched a "massive frontal attack" against the social problems resulting from black illegitimacy[22] and oversaw, during the early 1960s, what one high-level employee called "the quiet revolution [in services to black unmarried mothers] which we have developed." He went on, "We cannot keep up with the mail we are receiving as community after community is changing its position in providing services...for this group of girls."[23] In the late 1950s only one or two "comprehensive programs" for black unwed mothers existed in the entire country; by the mid-1960s there were more than forty, including at least one program in most major cities. More were in the planning stages.[24] The director of the Erie County, New York, Anti-Poverty Action Committee described local efforts targeting unwed mothers as a "preventative device in the War on Poverty."[25]

As a metaphor providing direction to public policy in the early 1960s, the "population bomb" expressed white fear of the physical and fiscal dangers embodied by blacks in the United States. Most specifically, the bodies of black single mothers became a key symbol of destructiveness. "Unacceptable" rates of black illegitimacy became a powerfully convincing explanation for unacceptable welfare expenditures, unacceptable demographic changes in the big cities of the United States, unacceptable levels of juvenile delinquency and poverty.

The population bomb metaphor structured solutions as well. As the bomb squad dismantles and defuses the bomb, so public policies aimed to address the phenomenon of black illegitimacy. Through exclusion from public grants, through sterilization, through public pressure to use oral contraceptives, black females had constraints put on the explosive potential of their fertility. In a secondary effort, black unwed mothers were trained in "sexual discipline" and other alleged middle-class values so as to extinguish the behaviors threatening to detonate the population bomb.

The Sexual Revolution

Ironically, the sexual discipline of white middle-class single girls and women, so urgently invoked to subdue blacks, was itself a seriously threatened construct by the early 1960s. At that time, academics and the media prepared a salacious feast on the tasty subject of white female sexuality, or the "sexual revolution," and invited the public to sample such morsels as the Radcliffe senior who explained that "Stealing food from the dormitory refrigerator . . . would be more condemned around here than fornicating on the livingroom couch."[26] As the public became fascinated with the sex lives of female college students-as-sex-revolutionaries, white unwed mothers were increasingly considered a subset of a much larger, nearly normative group – white sexually active young women – rather than the discrete, anormative phenomenon they had represented in the 1940s and 1950s. As such, white single pregnant girls and women were less frequently described as neurotic, as pathological, or as in the prewar decades, fallen women.

In the 1940s and 1950s, the white unwed mother was diagnosed as psychologically disordered first because she was pregnant without a husband. Her mental problems were allegedly the product of her parents' neuroses. In distinction, the young woman who had sex, even if she became pregnant, in the early 1960s, was often characterized as rebellious without a husband, not sick. Her behavior was conditioned by peers and social pressures, not parents; her participation in intercourse was decidedly sexual. Before the 1960s, experts counseled that the unwed mother must be constrained, retrained, institutionalized. She was a dependent, a victim, a daughter. By the early 1960s, experts increasingly viewed these girls as beyond the bounds of institutions. Not victims, they were agents of social change. Not daughters, they were "college girls," or "career girls."[27] They were independent, sexualized, and at large. The earlier crop of unwed mothers was, by definition, "not-mothers"; for the later group, even this hard-and-fast certainty was softening.

The shifting of the public image and treatment of white unwed mothers reflected a pervasive shift in the view of the relationship between behavior and the social context in which it occurred. The postwar view of white unwed mothers as mental patients was part of a general belief that nonconformists were aberrant in an otherwise well-functioning society. In fact, the exceptional nature of individual and family pathology that experts associated with the root of unwed motherhood, constituted proof that, as a rule, postwar family life in the United States was healthy. . . .

On the one hand, these experts and many others placed a degree of responsibility on "society," thus defining unwed mothers as passive victims of social forces, hardly the stuff of sexual revolutionaries. On the other hand, if "society," not the individual, were the agent responsible for both constructing and destroying social-sexual values and behavior, then young women themselves became, in an interesting sense, free agents able to pursue sexual experimentation, able even to become pregnant without blame. Indeed, one investigator of the attitudes of single pregnant girls noted at this time, "Contemporary unwed mothers, however their feelings may be described, do not seem to feel very guilty."[28]

In a new twist, white unwed mothers were absolved in one sense, but nailed nonetheless. The new charge recognized that society created the context for sexuality, but girls and women who moved freely in that context were at fault. A medical columnist for *Look* expressed his feelings about single pregnant women this way, "Women have more freedom now – are sexual, supposed to experiment but...I can't help wishing women had somehow managed to make better use of the emancipation they worked so hard to achieve."[29]

The white unwed mother could be blamed now as an abuser of her free agency, of her emancipation in the context of the so-called sexual revolution. A typical assessment claimed that "The [sexual] revolution...has primarily to do with women, and middle class women in particular. They are the ones who have finally come to embrace ways of thinking and behaving that have long been customary for others."[30] An account of the sexual revolution in *Time* placed the typical unwed mother on campus, participating in typical sexual behavior:

> Many girls are still sincere and even lyrical about saving themselves for marriage, but it is becoming a lot harder to hold the line. There is strong pressure not only from the boys but from other girls, many of whom consider a virgin downright square. The loss of virginity, even resulting in pregnancy, is simply no longer considered an American Tragedy.[31]

Newsweek placed all sexually active coeds similarly and suggested they were influential pioneers:

> "We've discarded the idea that the loss of virginity is related to moral degeneracy," a husky Ohio State senior explained. . . . The quest of sex on the campus is not just academic. Ultimately, the new morality will have a meaning for American society as a whole: today's campus code may be tomorrow's national morality.[32]

What is extraordinary about this reconstruction and repositioning of the white unwed mother is that contemporary experts now associated her directly with normal-middle class females in a startling break from expert opinion in the immediate past, which strictly isolated the white unwed mother from middle-class standards, values, and behavior.

In the recent past, the white-middle-class-unwed-mother-as-mental-patient had reassured the middle-class public that illegitimate pregnancy marginalized a female. At the same time, that construct threatened the same public by suggesting the vulnerability of families and daughters to the neuroses of the era. After 1960, the white unwed mother as participant in the middle-class sexual revolution remained paradoxically comforting and threatening to the middle-class public, but for new reasons. As a typical single female, she was "safe" because she was "one of our own," a girl with a lot to lose, a girl society was motivated to protect. In 1961, a play about the dilemma of the white unwed mother, produced under the auspices of the Family Service Association of America and presented across the country for professional, charitable, and student audiences, characterized the unwed mother this way:

> Carol Vaughn is attractive, wholesome, and competent. Having grown up in a relatively large community in the Midwest as the daughter of respectable middle-class parents, she fits very well the description of "the girl next door." Liked both at home and at college, she is to all appearances well adjusted to society and her group.[33]

At the same time, the same girl was threatening as a sexual revolutionary. Young women assuming sex lives and becoming pregnant were rendering the familiar middle-class daughter unrecognizable and dangerous. In this vein, society was less motivated to protect her than it was to protect itself from the wages of the sexual revolution. The prime concern, in either case, was not demographic or economic. The concern was, most often, for the health of traditional gender relations and generational relations *within the nuclear family* in the face of the sexualized single girl. As a leading family expert observed in 1960, "The basic reason that societies control sex behavior at all levels is not fear of pregnancy but experience with the intensity and uncontrollability of sex and the resultant social disorganization when social sanctions are not imposed."[34]

Given these views of sex, pregnancy, and the single girl, how were contraceptives viewed in relation to white illegitimate pregnancy after 1960? This was a confusing question for many professionals who had so recently equated nonmarital female sexuality and pregnancy with severe maladjustment. Now these same professionals had the option of prescribing pills to prevent illegitimate pregnancy while facilitating nonmarital sex. One doctor in a university town explained his rationale for routinely prescribing pills to coeds: "It is not that I will feel personally responsible if she gets pregnant. It is that I have it in my power to prevent that eventuality. If you had seen as much grief as I have, you wouldn't hesitate to exercise that power."[35] For this physician, contraceptives did not raise questions of sexual morality or unwanted babies, or social costs, but of emotional stress from which the girls themselves deserved protection. While engaging in a practice that promoted the "sexual revolution" of college girls, this doctor and many others responded to patients as if they were daughters, thus paternalistically deflecting focus from the sex itself and from the potential illegitimate babies, who, in any case, could quickly be taken off the hands of college girls. A New York gynecologist genially described the levels of deception he was willing to countenance in his office. He said that "a fourth of the young ladies who come to him for [contraception] don't have marriage immediately in mind, but he keeps up the pretense; they get embarrassed if you tell them you know. They like to think of us as kindly old idiots."[36]

A Boston doctor explained why he and his colleagues dispensed contraceptives to all who requested them: "I don't know a doctor who demands a marriage license before giving contraceptive advice or prescriptions. The law says 'health reasons' and leaves the interpretation up to our discretion. We proceed on the basis that unmarried women need contraceptive methods for their own and for society's health."[37] Society's health in this view was not so much threatened by the birth of fatherless babies, expensive to taxpayers, as by the birth of independent, sexualized, unmarried females. Doctors dispensing contraceptives to this population often took the position that in the current sexualized environment, since girls couldn't be stopped from having intercourse, the pills could allow them to mask their sex lives. Contraceptives could create a population of sexually active unmarried females who did not get pregnant, a population whose sexuality, therefore, would not be revealed by pregnancy and could only be confirmed by a doctor for sure.

In this sense, oral contraceptives simultaneously provided the last chance to obfuscate the active sex lives of unmarried girls and women and the first opportunity for the sexual freedom that allegedly followed from the freedom from fear of pregnancy. The pill thus became a "declaration of independence"[38] for unmarried females because it held the promise of protecting and liberating them at the same time. As Andrew Hacker observed at the time, "A device like the pill does away with obsessive and irrational feelings about sex and can serve to reduce the illegitimacy rate – which has been rising alarmingly in recent years."[39]

Dismantling the Psychological Explanation

The unmarried girl who became pregnant after 1960 thus became in a sense a fallen revolutionary: she was "liberated" but "unprotected." Her pregnancy became a technical failure, that is, a failure to utilize technology, or a technological breakdown. As such, it was not impossible to blame a pregnancy on neuroses, but somewhat more difficult than in the heyday of the ubiquitous diagnoses. After 1960, it became increasingly problematic to view such a pervasive experience as individually aberrant, particularly when sociologists and service providers had become willing to reconnect individual behavior, including white illegitimate pregnancy, to its social context. One of the most powerful blows against individual explanations of single pregnancy was the notion that white, female, premarital sexual activity in the United States was an expression of the new, postwar poverty of American culture. In this view, the culture had become bereft of values, with sex preoccupation filling the vacuum.[40] Experts found that many girls engaging in illicit sex felt they had "nothing to lose,"[41] or were experiencing "existential loneliness,"[42] a condition connoting the meaninglessness or normlessness of life. A Radcliffe student claimed that for her generation, sex was "the only way to get close to someone."[43] A political scientist observed, "If Freud was influential a generation go, today's intellectual rationale [for premarital sex] is to be found in existentialism."[44] A three-part article in *Better Homes and Gardens* in this era called "America's Moral Crisis" claimed that female "promiscuity" was "the unhappiness disease." Sexually active girls did not like sex, but "had fled to the vaunted refuge of sex freedom as an escape from reality's problems, just as others like them fled to heroin or marijuana."[45] In this formulation, nonmarital female sexuality was as unnatural and unhealthy as it had been for the postwar psychologists. The difference was that it now resulted from and expressed negative social conditions, not individual and family pathologies. In a related finding, female premarital sex was often associated with an increasing tendency to embrace a "fun morality" that defined "sex as play," an idea very disturbing "even among liberals."[46]

At a time when very conservative estimates counted 300,000 unwed mothers yearly, the "mental patient" explanation for single pregnancy became impractical, if not unbelievable.[47] The annual numbers of illegitimately pregnant teenagers in particular in the mid-1960s would have suggested a critical mass of "illness" that was untenable. For one thing, the constant focus on middle-class female nonmarital sex, in conjunction with these numbers, created the choice of accepting vast numbers of "our daughters" as neurotic or simply giving up the label. Indeed, Rose Bernstein observed, "The extension of unmarried motherhood into our upper and educated classes in sizeable numbers [renders] our former stereotypes less tenable . . . when the phenomenon has invaded our own social class – when the unwed mother must be classified to include the nice girl next door, the college graduate, the physician's or pastor's daughter."[48] . . .

The combination of new social analyses, steadily increasing numbers, and uncooperative unwed mothers caused some commentators to reconsider the bases for the psychological explanations of single pregnancy. Rose Bernstein, in her influential article "Are We Still Stereotyping the Unwed Mother?", suggested that behavior considered evidence of the pathology of unwed mothers "may be appropriate responses to an anxiety-producing situation."[49] Clark Vincent asked his colleagues to consider whether unwed mothers were sick or, like many married mothers, simply sick of unwanted pregnancies.[50] The new question was, to whom should white unwed mothers most aptly be compared. Typically, white unwed mothers had been compared with unmarried white virgins, to demonstrate the psychological or personality differences between these groups.[51] By the early 1960s, some students of illegitimacy began to consider the situation of white unwed mothers alongside of the situation of married mothers, of married women unhappily pregnant, and most often, alongside other sexually active but not pregnant white unmarried girls and women.[52] This last comparison often suggested that unwed mothers were simply unluckier but no less rational than "thousands of other women and girls who by their own admission, engage in illegal coition . . . [without] bearing children."[53] . . .

The Bomb and the Revolution Subdue Unwed Mothers

The population bomb and the sexual revolution apparently helped the American public to comprehend disturbing new evidence of female sexuality and fertility, and guided some policy makers' and professionals' attempts to deal with increasing rates of illegitimacy. But the racially specific approaches toward sexually active females and unmarried mothers that these constructs reflected did not have an impact on rates of single pregnancy.

In the early 1960s, Children's Bureau staff recognized how little had been accomplished in the areas of controlling illegitimacy and serving the illegitimately pregnant girl or woman, despite decades of trying. The Bureau's Committee on Services to Unmarried Mothers acknowledged, "It is obvious that the problems of illegitimacy are not yielding to approaches developed so far."[54] The old institutional methods were becoming dysfunctional or were under attack. Local welfare programs assisting poor unwed mothers used disproportionate resources to determine eligibility and punish clients or would-be clients. Maternity homes were losing their traditional client base and were being forced to reconsider their mission or close. The new, often government-sponsored, comprehensive programs for unwed mothers in urban settings were experimental, small, underfunded, and understaffed, as well as ideologically problematic. This lack of institutional coherence and vision reflected the public response to a social problem that had outgrown established strategies but had not gained additional public sympathy or support. Even the new government-supported birth control programs were not demonstrating a capacity to prevent a significant number of unwanted illicit pregnancies in any large population.[55] At this time, 67 percent of all unwed mothers experiencing a first illegitimate birth were teenagers, the population most excluded from contraceptive services by state laws, despite some liberalizing tendencies in the early 1960s.[56] The reigning metaphors suggested an intense lack of public sympathy for sexually active unmarried females. These metaphors undermined the possibility for female- or mother-centered support for unwed mothers.

Nonetheless, ideas for addressing the increasing rates of illegitimacy and the problems of single pregnant girls and women were not in short supply in the early and middle 1960s, although institutional support for most strategies was not forthcoming. When the Children's Bureau undertook to ask state Welfare Departments what services should be offered to unwed mothers in 1962, one state responded,

There is a serious need for the development under public auspices on a
statewide basis of a service geared specifically to helping unmarried
mothers whether they plan to give up their children, are receiving assistance, or are just floundering around without any counsel or direction. . . .
Funds are not available to develop such a service, employ staff, or meet any
individual costs.[57]

Yet at the same time, the Children's Bureau itself continued to present
and analyze the state of services to this population almost solely in terms
of the adoption scene for white illegitimate babies.[58] In the Cook County
Hospital in Chicago where 40 percent of the live births were illegitimate,
the hospital administration decided to abandon its practice of automatically referring unmarried mothers to its social service department
because of lack of staff and funds, despite the recognition that these
girls and women required social services.[59] Similarly in West Virginia,
after an agency for unwed mothers received a "tremendous response" to
an outreach campaign, it decided to curtail all efforts to attract new
clients because of lack of "facilities and funds."[60] Mary Verner of the
Salvation Army suggested that racial stereotyping of unwed mothers
remained the biggest obstacle to service delivery when she wrote, "We
must not expect our clients to fit the mold of the agency. Instead, we
must attempt to change the pattern of our programs to meet the needs of
those seeking help."[61]

In 1965, fertile unmarried females, black and white, remained a highly
vulnerable population. The fact that the "sexual revolution" and the
"population bomb" metaphors were so widely accepted suggests some
answers to why the needs of these girls and women continued to be
addressed in such a meager and often punitive fashion. The population
bomb precisely captured – and also structured – the white public's
postwar fears about social instability, economic insecurity, gender insubordination, and black challenges to race hierarchy in the United States.
The builders of the population bomb metaphor instructed the white
public that the black illegitimacy rate was a profound domestic threat
in all these areas because the babies themselves had the potential to
fundamentally change American society for the worse. The women
producing these babies were of interest to the population controllers of
the early and mid-1960s as excessive reproducers. The population bomb
suggested simply that the reproduction should be halted, one way or
another. Beyond that, the population bomb metaphor offered little to the
black unwed mother or to a public considering the relationship between
female sexuality and fertility and other social issues.

The sexual revolution, on the other hand, expressed the discovery in
the United States, in the twentieth century, of white female sexuality,

and to some degree, the public's acceptance of it, via the alleged behavior of middle-class coeds. The association of white unwed mothers with this relatively privileged population undermined the possibility of a sense of social responsibility for the more typical white unwed mother who had few resources,[62] who was not a revolutionary, fallen or otherwise. The public focus on female sexuality as "revolutionary" curtailed discussion of what remained the same for sexually active unmarried girls in a male-dominated society. The public focus on sex in relation to the lives of unmarried girls and women, and in relation to social change, could cancel out the dangers of revolution by sustaining these subjects as titillating and harmless.

Yet both the bomb and the revolution also cast unmarried females, black and white, as aggressors against American society and diminished an appreciation of their true vulnerability, particularly when they became unwed mothers. By constructing unwed mothers as aggressors, the public was justified in meting out punishment, scorn, and disrespect, in racially specific ways.

Finally, the history of the racially specific treatment of unwed mothers after World War II, captured and apotheosized by the prevailing metaphors of the early and mid-1960s, added new grounds for racial separation, racial alienation, and intra-gender hostility between black and white women. This history suggests why the contemporary politics of female fertility continues to be rent by race.

The treatment of unwed mothers in the postwar era demonstrates how female sexuality and fertility and the unwed mother herself have been used in our recent past as proving grounds for theories of race, gender, motherhood, and social stability. In the postwar era, the unwed mother supplied babies to childless couples, took the blame for rising tax bills, symbolized the wages of gender insubordination, was cast as the source of all problems in the black community, was described and treated as mentally ill, frigid, wantonly sexual, and as a typical American girl. The variety of roles unwed mothers were assigned and constrained to fill in our recent past indicates the consistent vulnerability of sexually active, especially pregnant, girls and women without male protection. The variety of roles also illuminates the shifting requirements of a society that depends upon sustaining gender, class, and racial inequality under changing historical conditions.

Throughout the Gruening hearings in the mid-1960s, many testifiers cited a powerful argument to justify federal support of contraceptives: widespread access to contraceptives was the most effective deterrent to widespread abortion.[63] Walter Tobriner, the president of the Board of Commissioners of the District of Columbia, called abortion rates "higher than a healthy society can tolerate";[64] Senator Gruening, himself, referred to abortion as a "desperate act"; and Alan Guttmacher labeled abortion in America as a "serious disease." Guttmacher, president of Planned Parenthood, elaborated, "I feel that the only way to eliminate this hideous problem [of abortion] is by making effective contraceptives available to everyone who needs it and who desires it. . . . If we could have effective, simple methods [of contraception] . . . we could cut down this one million [abortions a year] figure to probably a few hundred thousand."[65] The abortion issue, statistically associated with whites, made a frequent, although race-neutral appearance at the hearings. For the antiabortionists, contraceptives constituted a deterrence weapon, a traditionally appealing concept to defense-minded Americans.

By the mid and late 1960s, however, many experts acknowledged that contraception alone was not functioning well enough as a deterrent either to illegitimate pregnancy or to abortion.[66] Consequently, many policy makers again made a choice, determining that the population bomb and the sexual revolution held more serious repercussions for society than the legalization of abortion. Abortion became an acceptable way to meet an old goal, that is, containing the social consequences of illicit female sexuality and fertility.

The legalization of abortion was a feminist victory; this study, however, offers one explanation of why the time was right in the late 1960s and early 1970s for feminists and other prochoice proponents to prevail. It suggests that the treatment of unwed mothers between 1945 and 1965 was conditioned by a stubbornly persistent public attitude that the unprotected pregnant female is a social resource of sorts. The multiple uses of unwed mothers described here suggests why a pregnant woman's prerogatives have been so hard to establish and sustain.[67]

Notes

1 See *Illegitimacy and Its Impact on the ADC Program*, Bureau of Public Assistance, Social Security Administration, Department of Labor (Washington, DC: Government Printing Office, 1960), pp. 5–6; and Phillips Cutright, "Illegitimacy in the United States: 1920–1968," in Charles F. Westoff and Robert Parke, Jr, eds. *Demographic and Social Aspects of Population Growth* (Washington, DC: Commission on Population Growth and the American Future), p. 384.

2 *Detroit News*, April 8, 1965.

3 US Congress, Senate, Committee on Government Operations, Subcommittee on Foreign Aid Expenditures; *Population Crisis: Hearings on S. 1676, A Bill to Reorganize the Department of State and the Department of Health, Education and Welfare*, August 31, September 8, 15, 22, 1965, part 3-B (89th Cong., 1st sess. [Washington, DC: Government Printing Office, 1966]), pp. 1974–86.

4   Ibid., part 3-A, pp. 1540–1.

5   Ibid., p. 1414.

6   Ibid., pp. 1153–70.

7   *New York Times*, March 28, 1965.

8   Population Crisis, p. 1662.

9   See John R. Birmingham to Ernest Gruening, Ibid., part 4, p. 2042, and "Economic Impact – Birth Control Seen as an Investment Tool," *Washington Post*, September 19, 1965.

10 *Population Crisis*, part 2-A, pp. 796–7.

11 Ibid., part 1, p. 361.

12 See Rickie Solinger, *Wake up Little Susie: Single Pregnancy and Race before Roe V. Wade*, 2nd edn (New York: Routledge, 2000).

13 *New York Times*, March 28, 1965.

14 Elizabeth Herzog to Lester Kirkendall, March 29, 1967, Box 1169, File 7–4–3–1, Record Group 102, National Archives (hereafter cited as N.A.).

15 *New York Times*, November 2, 1960.

16 Philip Holman to Dorothea Andrews, October 25, 1967, Box 1169, File 7–4–0, Record Group 102, N.A.

17 P. Frederick DelliQuardri to Mary Switzer, December 17, 1968, Box 1169, File 7-4-3-1-4, Record Group 102, N.A.

18 Jean Pakter, M.D., et al, "Out-of-Wedlock Births in New York City: II – Medical Aspects," *American Journal of Public Health* 51 (June 1961): 862.

19 William Rashbaum, M.D., "Use of Social Services by Unmarried Mothers," *Children* 10 (January–February 1963): 16.

20 Mary Verner, "Effective Techniques of Communication with and Rehabilitation of Hard-to-Reach Out-of-Wedlock Families," paper presented at the National Conference on Social Welfare, 1963.

21 Sarah J. Short, "Effective Techniques of Communication with and Rehabilitation of 'Hard to Reach' Out of Wedlock Families," paper presented at the National Conference on Social Welfare, 1963.

22 National Association on Services to Unmarried Parents Papers, NASUP Newsletter 4 (September 1964), Social Welfare History Archives, University of Minnesota (hereafter cited as SWHA).

23 Charles Gershenson to the Secretary, December 17, 1968, Box 1169, File 7-4-3-1-4, Record Group 102, N.A.

24 Katherine B. Oettinger to Marion Obenhaus, June 8, 1967, Box 1169, File 7-4-0-7, Record Group 102, N.A. Also see "Comprehensive Programs for School-Age Pregnant Girls, 1968," Box 1169, File 7-4-3-1-4, and Charles Gershenson to Regional Child Welfare Representatives, August 16, 1968, Box 1169, File 7-4-3-1-4, Record Group 102, N.A.

25 C. A. Peters to Elizabeth Herzog, August 16, 1965, Box 1039, File 7-4-3-1-1, Record Group 102, N.A.

26 "The Morals Revolution on the US Campus," *Newsweek*, April 6, 1964, p. 52.

27 See Helen Gurley Brown, *Sex and the Single Girl* (New York: Bernard Geis, 1962).

28 Deborah Shapiro, "Social Distance and Illegitimacy: A Comparative Study of Attitudes and Values," D.S.W. dissertation, Columbia University, 1966, p. 129.

29 Virgil G. Damon, M.D., and Isabelle Taves, "My Daughter Is in Trouble," *Look*, August 8, 1962, p. 26.

30 Andrew Hacker, "The Pill and Morality," *New York Times Magazine*, November 21, 1965, p. 140.

31 "The Second Sexual Revolution," *Time*, January 24, 1964, p. 57.

32 "The Morals Revolution," *Newsweek*, p. 52.

33 Barbara Kay Davidson, *The Sweet Potato Vine* (New York: Family Service Association of America, 1961).

34 Thomas S. Poffenberger, "Individual Choice in Adolescent Premarital Sex Behavior," *Marriage and Family Living* 22 (November 1960): 327.

35 Hacker, "The Pill," p. 32.

36 Gloria Steinem, "The Moral Disarmament of Betty Coed," *Esquire*, September, 1962, pp. 153–4.

37 Ibid., p. 153.

38 "The Morals Revolution," p. 54.

39 Hacker, "The Pill," p. 140.

40 Thomas S. Poffenberger, "The Control of Adolescent Premarital Coitus: An Attempt at Clarification of the Problem," *Marriage and Family Living* 24 (August 1962): 258.

41 Helen H. Perlman, "Unmarried Mothers, Immorality and the ADC Program," paper presented at the Annual Conference of the Florence Crittenton Association of America, Cleveland, Ohio, 1963.

42 Hacker, "The Pill," p. 139.

43 "The Morals Revolution," p. 56.

44 Hacker, "The Pill," p. 139.

45 Howard Whitman, "The Slavery of Sex Freedom," *Better Homes and Gardens*, June 1957, pp. 172, 218.

46 Nelson Foote, "Sex As Play," in Jerome Himmelhoch and Sylvia Fleis Fava, eds., *Sexual Behavior in American Society* (New York: W. W. Norton, 1955), pp. 237–43.

47 Ira Reiss, "The Sexual Renaissance: A Summary and Analysis," *Journal of Social Issues* 22 (April 1966): 127.

48 Rose Bernstein, "Are We Still Stereotyping the Unmarried Mother?", *Social Work* 5 (July 1960): 108.

49 Bernstein, p. 110.

50 Clark Vincent, "Illegitimacy and Value Dilemmas," Christian Century, June 19, 1963, (Glencoe, IL: The Free Press, 1961). p. 804.

51 See, for example, Clark Vincent, *Unmarried Mothers*.

52 Robert Bell, "Parent-Child Conflict in Sexual Values," *Journal of Social Issues* 22 (April 1966): 34–44. See also Gertrude Barker, "Self-Esteem of the Unwed Mother," Ed.D. dissertation, Boston University, 1967.

53 Perlman, "Unmarried Mothers," p. 9.

54 Ursula Gallagher to Mrs. Oettinger, October 27, 1961, Box 893, File 7-4-3-1, Record Group 102, N.A.

55 See Cutright, "Illegitimacy in the United States 1920–1968," p. 426.

56 Phillips Cutright, "Illegitimacy: Myths, Causes and Cures," *Family Planning Perspectives* 3 (January 1971): 46.

57 US Congress, House of Representatives, *Hearings Before the Subcommittee of the Committee on Appropriations,* (87th Congress, 1st sess. [Washington, DC: Government Printing Office, 1962]), p. 750.

58 Ibid., "Report on the Problem of Unwed Mothers Supplied by Dr. Katherine Bain, Deputy Chief, Children's Bureau," pp. 747–51.

59 Ursula Gallagher, Field Report, Chicago, 1959, Box 894, File 7-4-3-1-1, Record Group 102, N.A.

60 Dorothy Allen to Kate Helms, April 5, 1962, Box 893, File 7-4-3-0, Record Group 102, N.A.

61 Mary E. Verner, "Administrative Concepts in Comprehensive Services for Unmarried Parents," in *Unmarried Parenthood: Clues to Agency and Community Action* (New York: National Council on Illegitimacy, 1967), p. 46.

62 According to Cutright, about 60 percent of white unwed mothers were poor.

63 This argument was often made in the postwar era. See, for example, Mary Calderone, ed., *Abortion in the United States* (New York: Harper and Brothers, 1958), chapter 8.

64 *Population Crisis*, part 2-B, p. 1060.

65 Ibid, p. 975.

66 See Cutright, "Illegitimacy, Myths, Causes and Cures."

67 Ibid., p. 45.

Documents

In this exposé written for *Better Homes and Gardens* in 1957, the author presents statistics about teen pregnancy designed to shock readers into realizing the depth of moral depravity into which the nation had fallen since the Second World War. Not only does "sex freedom" lead to unhappy relationships and unwanted pregnancies, according to this author, it produces unfulfilling future marriages because young women never recover from psychological trauma induced by sex before marriage. According to the author, why are so many young women having premarital sex? Is it due to individual psychological problems, or does it stem from bigger flaws in the social fabric?

The Slavery of Sex Freedom: America's Moral Crisis

Howard Whitman

A college girl in a class in Human Behavior in a fine Pennsylvania college stood up to answer a professor's question on the role of sexuality in life. "Sex is like raw meat," she said. "When you're hungry you take it."

A shocking answer?

Or are we shockproof after an era in which sex freedom has been touted as the great emancipator of a constricted mankind and morality has been seen as a confining dungeon? For 12 years, since the close of World War II, we have seen a campaign of "liberation." Men, women, and adolescents, too, were to be freed of the inhibitions of an outmoded morality. Human emotions, gagged into neurosis and on the verge of psychological suffocation, were to have air. And instead of gloom and shadows there would be light – from the sun of science by day, and by night from the stars of statistics. And so, stone by stone, the confining dungeon has been reduced.

We look around now. And we wonder.

Was that a dungeon we tore down? Or was it the house we live in?

Illegitimate births have reached an all-time high. The US Public Health Service reports the latest annual total at 176,600, an increase of 36 percent in 6 years. The mothers of 40 percent of illegitimate babies are teen-agers....

If sex freedom alone has been the goal in the postwar era it certainly has been achieved. It has come to pass with flying colors. We have accomplished what Sociologist Pitirim Sorokin, of Harvard, calls a "sex revolution." We have gone further. Dr. Goodrich Schauffler, of Portland, Oregon, reported to a Congress on Obstetrics and Gynecology that America has arrived at "sex hysteria."

Is this what we were promised? Or did the liberators tempt us with something beyond sex freedom? We were to find, once the dungeon walls were down, a new freedom of the human spirit, an emotional contentment that would be like honey to the wormwood of frustration. We were to be

Excerpted from Howard Whitman, "The Slavery of Sex Freedom: America's Moral Crisis," *Better Homes and Gardens* (June 1957), pp. 59, 172, 218–21.

expressively and creatively free – and then just watch those troublesome neuroses disappear!

This is what we were *promised*. What we actually found I saw etched upon the faces of a dozen girls, sitting in a somber circle at a social service agency in New York. Each was soon to have a baby. None was married. I had been invited to speak to them on the nature of love. I did, but what I learned from them seemed more revealing than any knowledge I imparted in the course of my talk to them.

"I don't think love had anything to do with it," said one girl of 19, speaking of the experience which brought her here. "I hardly knew the boy, and I've never even seen him since."

Another girl remarked, "It seemed all right at the time. All I really wanted was to be popular and have some dates. I guess the boys expect that sort of thing. That's what the other girls said, and, anyway, I sure wasn't the only one!" . . .

Hence the two-word definition: "unhappiness disease." And the comment of one of the clinic staff: "As the girls became happier, they ceased being promiscuous."

Repeated studies have confirmed the San Francisco findings, as do the daily experiences of psychiatrists in treating individuals with sex problems. Illicit sex experience is not a goal in itself. It is a symptom of unhappiness, in which the most frequent underlying, and often hidden, motives are:

1. *The need for acceptance.* An individual feels insufficiently loved, or admired, by others – or insufficiently attractive to others – and seeks reinforcement of his ego in being "sexually accepted."

2. *Rebellion.* Sex activity is seen as a form of "getting even" – sometimes for parental harshness, or, in married individuals, as a way of striking back at an unloving or rejecting mate.

3. *Lack of confidence.* This may be a male's lack of confidence in his maleness (which he must prove to himself over and over again through "sex conquest") or a woman's doubts that her physical response is complete and "normal."

Does sex freedom heal these sores of unhappiness? If it did there might, psychologically at least, be a case for it; it would be therapy. But during the very era when sex freedom has been hailed as a way out of emotional turmoil – a relief from the "frustration" of morality – individuals who have tried it have figured prominently in the swelling psychiatric case load.

They have craved acceptance. What they have found is the remorseful realization that in illicit sex relations they have been "used," not accepted. Perhaps a psychiatrist helps them realize that true acceptance comes first in a meaningful interpersonal relationship, in love, in marriage – then in a sex relationship which does honor, not dishonor, to the partner.

They have rebelled. But whom have they hurt? As they gain insight and learn the psychological mechanism of *sado-masochism*, they see that sex rebellion hurts not only the harsh parent, the rejecting mate, or society at large – but themselves as well. They are the *sadist* in inflicting pain on others, the *masochist* in inflicting pain on themselves. Sex dereliction will not make the parent less harsh, the mate more loving. In effective therapy, such individuals learn the art of constructive rebellion: making the situation better, not making it worse.

They have sought confidence. For the male it may take hours of patient counseling to make him see that true maleness is developed in the inner personality; it has nothing to do with sexual "conquest." Over a hundred years ago, Dr. Jules Guyot compared the promiscuous male to "the wretched fiddler who demands another violin, hoping that a new instrument will yield the melody he knows not how to play." And the female, in psychiatric therapy, frequently discovers that her own emotional attitudes toward sex are the primary cause of incomplete responses. An illicit relationship, where emotional attitudes are further distorted by guilt and shame, can only make matters worse.

Thus, far from being a way out of problems, sex freedom has simply sunk unhappy individuals deeper into the mire. . . .

The 12 years since World War II, with their heady philosophies of sex freedom, have not yielded true freedom, far from it. They have, instead, acquainted us with a new form of slavery: enslavement to neurosis, to maladjustment, and futility.

Where, then, is freedom found? Where it always has been; it has not strayed. True sexual realization – the human maximum in gratification of the flesh and the spirit, too – stems from the full, unfettered, and unashamed relationship of marriage: two individuals growing through loyalty and love into "one flesh."

And so we look around now. And we wonder about that moral structure which we saw dismantled stone by stone. Was it a dungeon? Or the house we live in?

And our children's house.

Are We Still Stereotyping the Unmarried Mother?
Rose Bernstein

This 1960 article, published in a specialized social work journal, questions the assumption that unmarried women must have unresolved emotional and psychological conflicts, which explain their desire for pregnancy. The author, Rose Bernstein, suggests the implausability of such an interpretation now that so many "nice" middle-class teens are getting pregnant. She raises the question of blame; is it fair to tolerate extramarital sex silently yet condemn the young woman who gets pregnant? Bernstein exhorts social workers to examine their own biases. How might social workers' prejudices have encouraged young mothers to give up their babies for adoption?

The theory of out-of-wedlock pregnancy currently accepted among social workers and members of other helping disciplines is that it is symptomatic and purposeful, an attempt by the personality to ease an unresolved conflict. The extent to which we are committed to this point of view can be seen in some typical excerpts from the literature.

> The caseworker should recognize that pregnancy for the unmarried woman is a symptom of underlying emotional difficulty. [She] is a person who solves her emotional problems through acting out, as exemplified by the pregnancy.

> We recognize unmarried motherhood as a symptom of a more pervading personality difficulty.

> Her illegitimate pregnancy is the result of an attempt to solve certain emotional conflict....

> [The unmarried mother]...has failed to attain a mature pattern of adaptation to the demands of her social reality.

> ...everything points to the purposeful nature of the act. Although a girl would...not plan consciously...to bear an out-of-wedlock child, she does act in such a way that this becomes the almost inevitable result.

Excerpted from Rose Bernstein, "Are We Still Stereotyping the Unmarried Mother?" *Social Work* (July 1960), pp. 22–8.

The popular magazine articles have been echoing this point of view.

In many situations it is a useful approach. The results of treatment are often dramatic and gratifying when a girl is able to make use of help in understanding and dealing with some of the underlying problems related to her out-of-wedlock pregnancy. However, in contacts with residents in a maternity home, and particularly in reviewing material for a study, one becomes concerned about the limited applicability of this theory in a number of cases. One has the impression that in some situations factors other than, or in addition to, underlying emotional pathology have been of greater significance; that emphasis on a single point of view has prevented us from seeing other essential aspects of the experience and, correspondingly, has resulted in a limited treatment offering. This has seemed a good time, therefore, to re-examine the theory and look at other hypotheses which might be applicable in our work with unmarried mothers.

Social Mores

By and large, unmarried motherhood in our society is looked on as the violation of a cultural norm. It should therefore be possible to isolate and identify the norm in question. But this is not easy. For one thing, it is not clear whether the offended norm is the taboo against extramarital relations or against bearing a child out of wedlock. We point to the symptomatic nature of the pregnancy ("there are no accidental conceptions"), but in speaking of prevention we are unable to clarify what we are trying to prevent – unsanctioned sex experience or out-of-wedlock pregnancy. . . .

Our society has been undergoing a change in its sexual behavior. The relaxation of taboos which usually accompanies the upheavals of war has been accelerated in the last two generations by the development of a widely publicized psychology. Permissiveness, self-expression, sexual adjustment, and freedom from inhibition have become in some quarters the marks of the well-adjusted American. The idea of extramarital sex experience is accepted among many college students; among some groups its practice is almost a social *sine qua non*. . . .

The extension of unmarried motherhood into our upper and educated classes in sizable numbers further confounds us by rendering our former stereotypes less tenable. Immigration, low mentality, and hypersexuality can no longer be comfortably applied when the phenomenon has invaded our own social class – when the unwed mother must be classified to include the nice girl next door, the college graduate, the physician's or pastor's daughter. In casting about for an appropriate explanation for her predicament we find it more comfortable to see the out-of-wedlock mother as a girl whose difficulty stems from underlying, pre-existing personality problems. We are forced into the position of interpreting the situation primarily in terms of individual pathology, failing to recognize the full extent to which the symptom may be culture-bound. We do, when pressed, acknowledge the possible influence of cultural factors, but in the main we do not tend to incorporate these elements significantly into our thinking.

There are no ready answers to this perplexing question, but as social workers we cannot adequately deal with the problem of the unmarried mother unless we see it within the framework of our conflicting mores. We must make room in our thinking for factors in the social scene – not only as they contribute to unwed motherhood, but also as they color the girl's reaction to her out-of-wedlock status in pregnancy.

It is understandable that we should incline toward a theory of underlying pathology as the cause of unmarried motherhood. Frequently, when we see the illegimately pregnant girl, she presents a picture of severe disturbance. Guilt, panic, suspicion, and denial are not uncommon reactions. More often than not she will give a history of deprivation in primary relationships. However, if we are to assess correctly the sources and appropriateness of these reactions, we must take into consideration the circumstances under which we are seeing them. . . .

Pregnancy and Motherhood

It is generally accepted that the experience of pregnancy can contain elements of crisis even for the married woman. "So-called 'normal pregnant women' might be highly abnormal, and even if they are not, they are anxious to a degree beyond that of the so-called 'normal nonpregnant female.'" "Particularly during the first pregnancy women are apt to suffer terrifying dreams and phantasies of giving birth to a dead or misshapen child." With the additional pressures to which the unmarried pregnant woman is subjected, we should not be surprised to see an intensification of the reactions which in her married counterpart we are prone to accept with tolerant indulgence. In themselves they are not necessarily signs of severe pathology. By the same token, the "normal deviations" of adolescence should figure prominently in our assessment of the meaning of out-of-wedlock pregnancy in the teen-ager. . . .

For most unmarried mothers this is a first experience in motherhood and as such it may be an important influence in the image a girl establishes of herself as a mother-person. Part of our goal should be to help her emerge from it with as positive an image of herself as a mother as her personality and circumstances will permit. To do this we need to be ready, at appropriate points, to de-emphasize the unmarried, socially deviant aspect of her experience and accentuate its normal motherhood components. In fact we may well ask ourselves whether, in failing to exploit the full possibilities of motherhood for the unmarried mother, we may not be encouraging the blocking out of large areas of affect in her experience in maternity, whether she is surrendering her baby or keeping it. . . .

If we see illegitimate pregnancy primarily as a symptom of underlying emotional pathology, we are likely to interpret much of an unmarried mother's behavior in similar terms. We will be on the alert for signs of pathology and will undoubtedly find them; one wonders whether we may not sometimes even be guilty of promoting the "self-fulfilling prophecy." In trying to assess the nature and degree of disturbance, no matter how skillfully we proceed we may turn valid exploration into inappropriate probing, and find ourselves contributing to the very disturbance we are trying to diagnose. . . .

Technically we may claim that our underlying point of view does not influence us and that each girl is allowed to make her own decision regarding her baby. And technically this is probably correct in most cases. But the subtle communication of our essential attitude cannot be denied – as observed by one girl who felt she was being pressured into surrendering her baby: "It's not what Mrs. K says exactly, it's just that her face lights up when I talk about adoption the way it doesn't when I talk about keeping Beth."

Population Crisis: Hearings before the Subcommittee on Foreign Aid Expenditures of the Committee on Government Operations

In this excerpt from the 1965 Gruening hearings on the population crisis, Philip M. Hauser, a professor of sociology at the University of Chicago and director of the Population Research and Training Center, outlined the social issues he saw as endemic to the country's increasing population, including juvenile delinquency, chronic unemployment, and racial tensions. For Hauser, "continued indifference" and the refusal to consider contraception programs as a solution to these problems were no longer options. But these sexual

Excerpted from "Population Crisis: Hearings before the Subcommittee on Foreign Aid Expenditures of the Committee on Government Operations" United States Senate Eighty-ninth Congress First Session on S. 1676, a Bill to Reorganize the Department of State and the Department of Health, Education, and Welfare August 31; September 8, 15, and 22, 1965. Part 3–A, pp. 1540–2.

solutions were hardly colorblind. In what ways does Hauser implicate blacks as the major cause of the population crisis and its attendant social ills? How do segments of the African American population figure as particular objects for social engineering?

The United States

Accelerating population growth is also generating major problems for the United States.

Our postwar boom in babies is exacting a high price from the American people – as measured in human as well as financial costs. The baby boom will from now on worsen the US unemployment problem, greatly increase the magnitude of juvenile delinquency, exacerbate already dangerous race tensions, inundate the secondary schools and colleges, greatly increase traffic accidents and fatalities, augment urban congestion and further subvert the traditional American governmental system.

Needless to say high fertility is by no means the only factor accounting for these difficult problems. But it is a major factor in making them worse. This is well illustrated by the way in which the baby boom is now contributing to high employment. Our postwar babies who reached flood stage after demobilization in 1946, are reaching labor force age in the sixties. The number of new workers under 25 years of age entering the labor force, averaging 600,000 per year during the sixties, is three times the number of new workers who entered the labor force between 1955 and 1960. The bulge in new entrant workers, coming at a time when we are experiencing a high level of chronic unemployment and increasing automation, may constitute the gravest challenge our economy has ever faced in peacetime. If the volume of unemployment mounts as our postwar offspring begin to reach 18 in 1964, it may be anticipated that unemployment compensation and relief costs will mount; and that the Government will be obliged to experiment with various types of programs to effect decreases in unemployment. Under such circumstances, it may also be anticipated that consumer demand will slough off in many areas – the teenage market, the marriage market and other markets oriented to the marriage market including consumer durables; and that general consumer demand may decline as the public interprets mounting unemployment as indicating an uncertain economic outlook. We have yet to demonstrate that we can generate new jobs as fast as we did babies after the war.

Similarly although the high birth rate is not responsible for juvenile delinquency it will greatly increase the volume of juvenile delinquency during the sixties. Persons 15 to 19 years of age, who account for most juvenile delinquency, will increase by 44 percent during the decade. This means that even if juvenile delinquency rates remain the same, the number of delinquents of this age will increase by 44 percent at a time when the social order is already sorely troubled by its present magnitude.

High fertility does not directly produce internal migration, but it does accelerate imbalance between population and resources in the relatively underdeveloped areas of the country and, therefore, stimulates increases in migratory streams. There can be no doubt that high fertility has increased the volume of internal migration from the South to the North and West including the flow of Negroes.

Moreover, the high fertility of the Negro, at levels little below that of India, is a major deterrent to his economic and social advance. The large numbers of children born to low income Negro families cannot hope to achieve the level of education and skill prerequisite to the Negro's climbing the economic and social ladder. Continued frustration in their efforts to achieve higher living levels and broader social acceptance, it may be expected, will worsen present already serious race tensions....

The Dilemma

We are forced to live with and in some manner to deal with the population problems that we have inherited from the past. For example, under the pressures generated by our postwar resurgence in population growth, we have expanded our elementary school plant, and we are faced with doing the same during this decade with our secondary school and college plants. But despite our efforts, we are experiencing depreciation in the quality of our education. As our postwar babies reach labor force age during the sixties, we shall pay a high price in striving to provide jobs or support of some kind for our tidal wave of new workers.

It is easier to ignore the tasks that aim at preventing the population problems of the future. In consequence, we are expending huge resources for treating the deleterious consequences of past rapid population growth while, in the main, we continue to do little or nothing about the present excessive growth which will produce even more acute problems in the future. For example, as a nation we are just beginning to consider whether we should assist the underprivileged who desire such assistance to control their fertility – both within the United States itself and abroad.

In this situation lies the population dilemma – the choice of unsatisfactory alternatives. It is to be found in the necessity to choose between continued indifference to the implications for the future of present population growth and the acceptance of the consequences of such indifference. To formulate appropriate population policy and take necessary action requires changes in established attitudes and behavior which meet with resistance – more from some quarters than from others. But to take the easy way out at the present time is to compound the difficulties of the future. To avoid the ounce of prevention in the present will, in the future, require many pounds of cure.

What is to be done to control runaway population growth? There are only two ways to dampen world population increase. One is to increase the death rate and the other is to decrease the birth rate. There are no nations or cultures in the world prepared to accept an increase in mortality as a way of controlling population growth. In consequence, only the control of fertility remains as a way to check population increase.

In the Western World both death and birth controls are widely accepted. In general, western countries, to resolve problems arising from too rapid population growth, need only do a little more of what they are already doing. In the Western World, it is primarily the poor and the uneducated who do not yet control their fertility.

In the underdeveloped areas the problem is much more difficult. First, the mass populations in these areas do not yet have the motivation and incentive to control the size of their families. Second, forms of family planning do not yet include methods acceptable, feasible and efficacious enough to meet the needs of the economically underdeveloped areas. Certain it is that efforts to increase family planning even in countries with policies of population control like India and Pakistan have not yet met with widespread notable success.

Further Reading

Asbell, Bernard. *The Pill: a Biography of the Drug that Changed the World*. New York: Random House, 1995.

Bailey, Beth L. *Sex in the Heartland*. Cambridge, MA: Harvard University Press, 1999.

Breines, Wini. *Young, White, and Miserable: Growing up Female in the Fifties*. Boston: Beacon Press, 1992.

Coontz, Stephanie. *The Way We Never Were: American Families and the Nostalgia Trap*. New York: Basic Books, 1992.

Gordon, Linda. *Pitied but Not Entitled: Single Mothers and the History of Welfare, 1890–1935*. New York: Free Press, 1994.

Luker, Kristen. *Dubious Conceptions: the Politics of Teenage Pregnancy*. Cambridge, MA: Harvard University Press, 1996.

Roberts, Dorothy. *Killing the Black Body: Race, Reproduction, and the Meaning of Liberty*. New York: Pantheon Books, 1997.

Rosen, Ruth. *The World Split Open: How the Modern Women's Movement Changed America*. New York: Viking, 2000.

Solinger, Rickie. *Wake up Little Susie: Single Pregnancy and Race before Roe v. Wade*, 2nd edn. New York: Routledge, 2000.

Watkins, Elizabeth Siegel. *On the Pill: a Social History of Oral Contraceptives, 1950–1970*. Baltimore: Johns Hopkins University Press, 1998.

14

Sex Change and the Popular Press

Introduction

Discussions of sexuality and gender are usually based on common understandings of "man" and "woman." Though most people take their gender and their sex for granted, these categories come into explicit question for people who identify as transgendered. Joanne Meyerowitz explores the evolution of transsexualism in the twentieth century. Advances in medical technology made it possible for patients to receive hormones and undergo sex reassignment surgery in this country by the 1950s. These advances, however, did not create transsexual patients. Before the term "transsexual" existed, readers of popular magazines sought out stories of such surgeries in Europe in the early twentieth century, and they avidly pursued any leads that would help them alter their physical bodies to align with their perception of themselves.

Christine Jorgensen's famous sex-change opened a floodgate. Like-minded people saw themselves in her public struggle. For the first time, sex-reassignment surgery seemed available not only for those who may have been born with ambiguous genitalia and sought surgical correction – the intersexed – but for the anatomically "normal" as well. Jorgensen's biography, constructed by the press as well as herself, became a model for other transsexuals seeking to follow in her medical footsteps. The transsexual desire to transform physically was hardly new, but the popular media, obsessed with Jorgensen's sensational metamorphosis, helped to fuel the requests for surgery and hormones and mark a new era in sexual history.

Sex Change and the Popular Press: Historical Notes on Transsexuality in the United States, 1930–1955

Joanne Meyerowitz

On 1 December 1952, the New York *Daily News* announced the "sex change" surgery of Christine Jorgensen. The front-page headline read "Ex-GI Becomes Blonde Beauty: Operations Transform Bronx Youth," and the story told how Jorgensen had traveled to Denmark for "a rare and complicated treatment." The initial scoop soon escalated into an international media frenzy. Reporters cast Jorgensen, who was young and beautiful, as a starlet on the rise, and within two weeks had sent out fifty thousand words on her through the news wire services.[1] In the winter of 1953, Jorgensen returned to the United States and surrendered to her celebrity. That spring, she embarked on a show business career that kept her name on marquees and her body in spotlights for the rest of the decade.

The press coverage accorded to Jorgensen triggered an avalanche of publicity about sex change through surgery and hormones, but she was not the first transsexual, nor was her story the first media attention to sex change. Stories of "sex reversals," "sex changes," and "sexual metamorphoses" had appeared in American newspapers and magazines since the 1930s. These stories differed from the more frequent reports of "passing," in which a person known previously as one sex was discovered living as the other. Rather, these were sensationalized stories of bodily change that, in the decades before Jorgensen's fame, introduced American readers to the concept of sex transformation.

In this article, I place Christine Jorgensen in broader historical context. I focus on the European origins of medicalized sex change in the early twentieth century, on specific examples of American media coverage of sex changes in the 1930s and 1940s, and on the responses of people whom we might now label transsexuals. Although the stories in the American press conflated a European version of sex change surgery for "transvestites" with the more widely known surgeries for intersexed

Excerpted from Joanne Meyerowitz, "Sex Change and the Popular Press: Historical Notes on Transsexuality in the United States, 1930–1955," *GLQ: a Journal of Lesbian and Gay Studies, the Transgender Issue* (1998), pp. 159–88.

conditions, they allowed some nonintersexed readers to envision sex change as a real possibility for themselves.[2] I then turn to the media blitz on Jorgensen to position it as a culminating episode in which the unprecedented scope of publicity expanded the process by which some readers identified new options for themselves in the popular culture.

The emphasis on popular culture and on transsexuals themselves revises the limited scholarly literature on the history of transsexuality, an abbreviated rendition of which might read as follows: in the late nineteenth century, sexologists placed cross-gender identification in the same categories of "inversion" that included homosexuality. In the early twentieth century, as homosexuality increasingly referred to same-sex object choice, sexologists Magnus Hirschfeld and Havelock Ellis defined "transvestism" or "eonism" as an independent category that included cross-gender identification as well as cross-dressing. But transsexualism as a separate sexological classification depended on medical technology such as synthetic hormones and plastic surgery that enabled sex change treatment. In the most recent historical account, transsexuals "appeared on the medical and social landscape of the West" only in the late 1940s and early 1950s when doctors David Cauldwell and Harry Benjamin first coined and publicized the English term *transsexual* and when Jorgensen entered the public domain.[3]

In this article, I suggest that a transsexual identity of sorts emerged well before the sexological category of transsexualism. I do not refer here to the sense of being the other sex or in the wrong body, which existed in various forms in earlier centuries and other cultures. I refer specifically to modern transsexuality as defined through requests for bodily transformation via surgery and hormones. Especially in gay and lesbian studies, historians have begun to explore how, when, and in what forms specific sexualized identities appeared in the modern era. These identities are "neither innate nor *simply* acquired," as Teresa de Lauretis has written, "but dynamically (re)structured by forms of fantasy both private and public, conscious and unconscious, which are culturally available and historically specific."[4] Recent works in cultural studies explore the processes by which readers engage actively with mass culture to inform and transform their fantasies and practices of everyday life. In the history of transsexuality, marginalized subjects used available cultural forms to construct and reconfigure their own identities. From the 1930s through the 1950s, certain readers appropriated public stories of sex change and included the quest for surgical and hormonal transformation as a central component of their senses of self. Through reading, some transgendered individuals – self-identified in the terms available in their day as eonists, transvestites, homosexuals, inverts, and hermaphrodites – came to a new sense of who they were and what they might become.

BC (Before Christine)

The concept of medicalized sex change did not depend on the invention of synthetic hormones or the development of sophisticated plastic surgery techniques. Surgical attempts at changing sex first won publicity in the early 1910s when Eugen Steinach, a physiologist in Vienna, attracted international acclaim for his "transplantation" experiments on rats and guinea pigs. . . .

By the early twentieth century, a few records of surgery for human "inverts" refer simply to removal of body parts such as testicles, uteri, and breasts, a form of intervention that did not require advanced medical technology. In 1902, for example, twenty-eight-year-old New Yorker Earl Lind, a self-proclaimed invert, androgyne, homosexual, and fairy, convinced a doctor to castrate him. He pursued the castration ostensibly to reduce his sexual "obsession" and as a cure for the frequent nocturnal emissions he saw as ruinous to his health. But he also acknowledged that he saw himself as a woman, preferred "to possess one less mark of the male," and hoped castration would eliminate his facial hair, which he considered his "most detested and most troublesome badge of masculinity."[5] Alberta Lucille Hart, a medical doctor in Oregon, also pursued surgery as an expression of gender identity. In 1917, Hart persuaded psychiatrist J. Allen Gilbert to recommend hysterectomy. . . . After surgery, haircut, and change of attire, Alan Lucill Hart "started as a male with a new hold on life" and had a successful career as a radiologist and novelist.[6] . . .

By the 1920s, Germany stood at the forefront of the human sex change experiments, with Magnus Hirschfeld's Institute for Sexual Science in Berlin at center stage. Hirschfeld encountered female-to-male "transvestites" who requested mastectomy and preparations for beard growth and males-to-females who sought castration, elimination of facial hair, and "apparatus for making the breasts bigger."[7] For Hirschfeld, hermaphrodites, androgynes, homosexuals, and transvestites constituted distinct types of sexual "intermediates," natural variations that all likely had inborn, organic bases. He considered transvestism "a harmless inclination" and advocated the social acceptance of transvestites.[8] He listened seriously to the desire to change sex expressed by some of the subjects he studied, and he began to recommend surgery. In 1931, German physician Felix Abraham, who worked at the Institute, published the first scientific report on modern transsexual surgery, an article on the male-to-female genital transformation (*Genitalumwandlung*) of two "homosexual transvestites."[9] The illustrated account of surgery included castration, amputation of the penis, and creation of an artificial vagina. Abraham believed that countless other patients wanted similar operations.

Word of the sex change experiments in Germany reached a wider public in the early 1930s when the press reported on one of Hirschfeld's patients, Danish artist Einar Wegener, who became Lili Elbe.... The story broke in Danish and German newspapers and soon thereafter appeared in book form in both Danish and German. (In the book version, the pseudonymous Dr. Hardenfeld provides a thinly veiled cover for Magnus Hirschfeld.)[10] ...

While few Americans, it seems, traveled to Europe for sex changes, more began to learn through the mass media of new possibilities for medical intervention. By the 1930s, stories of sex changes began to appear in English. In 1933, Dutton published the first English translation of the Lili Elbe story, *Man into Woman: An Authentic Record of a Change of Sex*. The book presented its subject as an occasional cross-dresser whose female personality had come to predominate. More dubiously, it also depicted her as a hermaphrodite with "stunted and withered ovaries" as well as testicles.[11] The book included an introduction by British sexologist Norman Haire, who informed readers of Steinach's transplantation experiments on animals but considered it "unwise to carry out, even at the patient's own request, such operations" as those performed on Elbe.[12]

After the publication of *Man into Woman*, a few American magazines reported on Lili Elbe. These accounts downplayed Elbe's transvestism and emphasized her alleged (and extremely unlikely) hermaphroditism. In December 1933, *Sexology*, a popular magazine on the science of sex, related the case in "A Man Becomes a Woman." The article distinguished Elbe from the "purely mental" inverts whose "disorder of the mind" stemmed from unhappy childhoods. The distinction lay in "the surprising discovery" that Elbe's "body contained female organs." According to *Sexology*, Elbe's physical condition presented specialists with "the opportunity" for changing sex previously "taken only with animal subjects." The article admitted that it was "hard to explain the case" but suggested that further investigation might bring "more relief" to "the 'borderline' cases where the apparent sex and the inclinations seem to be in sharp conflict."[13]

Another account, "When Science Changed a Man into a Woman!" associated Elbe with other alleged intersex cases. As the subtitle proclaimed, "The Cases of Two Girls Who Are Being Transformed into Two Boys Parallel the Extraordinary Drama of the Danish Painter Who Became a Beauty." The article presented Claire Schreckengost of rural Pennsylvania and Alice Henriette Acces of France as intersexed, with "organs of both sexes." Both had undergone transformative surgery to correct what the article presented as mistakes of nature. In Elbe's case, the article noted, she and the scientists she consulted "became convinced that Nature had intended him to be a woman but, in some wretched way, had bungled her handiwork." With typical reticence, the report refrained from mentioning genitalia or reproductive organs. It did not specify what any of the surgeries involved; it related only that one of Schreckengost's operations was "of the ductless gland type." In the case of Acces, the article suggested that surgery had resulted because Acces "was found to be adhering not at all to her girlish role."[14]

These and other stories of sex changes attempted to lure American readers with shocking accounts of unusual behavior, rare biological problems, and astonishing surgical solutions. Such stories often appeared on the margins of the mainstream press, in sensational magazines, tabloid newspapers, or publications like *Sexology* that presented the science of sex to a popular audience. They covered cases of cross-gender behavior, intersexuality, homosexuality, and transvestism, sometimes without distinguishing among them, and frequently depicted them all as interrelated pathologies in need of medical cure. They occasionally mentioned "sex reversals" of the "purely psychical" kind but presented them as homosexuality that did not qualify for surgery.[15] Sometimes they reported metamorphoses wherein a woman or man, perhaps with a glandular disturbance, underwent spontaneous changes in bodily sex and gendered behavior during late adolescence or adulthood. (A typical headline read, "Boy Prisoner Slowly Changing into a Girl.")[16] More generally, though, the articles mentioned surgery but failed to specify what it entailed. They depicted sex change surgery as unveiling a true but hidden physiological sex and thus tied the change to a biological mooring that justified surgical intervention. These stories often reinforced stereotypes of gender and sexuality by locating the sources of gendered and erotic behavior in the sex of the physical body. In this binarist vision of sex, science could and should correct nature's tragic "rare blunders," creating an unambiguous male or female sex from a condition of ambiguity.[17]

In the second half of the 1930s, these features appeared in widely reported accounts of European women athletes who became men. In 1935, twenty-three-year-old Belgian cycling champion Elvira de Bruyne changed sex and began to live as Willy. About a year later, British shot-put and javelin champion Mary Edith Louise Weston underwent two operations and adopted the name Mark, and Czechoslovakian runner Zdenka Koubkova became Zdenek Koubkov through what one report termed "a delicate surgical operation." ....

Were Koubkov and the others intersexed or what we would now consider transsexual? One quasi-scientific 1938 pamphlet, *Women Who*

Become Men, suggested that "women-athletes" were "changing their sex" through transplants of testicular tissue, but, it claimed, "the press is too delicate to give us exact information."[18] *Sexology*, however, reported the various stories of sex changes as accounts of intersex and "arrested development"[19] ...

The publicity accorded to sex change surgery caught the attention of individuals who identified possibilities in it for themselves. *Sexology* published several letters from readers in search of information. In 1934, one letter writer explained: "I have a peculiar complex – I believe it is called 'Eonism.' That is, I desire to dress as a woman. . . . The fact is I have an even stronger desire, and that is – I wish I were a woman. . . . I am interested in the Steinach operation in regard to change of sex. I would like more information."[20] In 1937, a "Miss E. T." asked: "Is it possible through a surgical operation, or several operations, to change a female into a male? I have read something – not very informative – about such things having been done. . . . Could you give me any idea of the method, and also of the cost?"[21] In "They Want to Change Sexes" (1937), *Sexology* acknowledged that press reports on European athletes had "stirred" some of its readers, who now asked "whether it is possible, and if so, how and where."[22] The magazine summarized a handful of letters (both male-to-female and female-to-male). The fragmentary presentation of the letters makes it impossible to know to what extent readers used the popular narratives to plot stories about themselves, but one letter suggests some readers might have fitted the stories of intersexuality to their own wants. A woman who described herself as "nothing feminine" but "apparently of [the female] sex" asked: "If it were true that I have both male and female organs of reproduction, would it not be advisable to undergo what operations are necessary to become the male I wish to be? Can you refer me to a competent surgeon who would be interested in my case?"[23]

The magazine did not offer the information that letter writers sought and tried instead to discourage them. In response to one male-to-female inquiry, the editor acknowledged that the letter writer could have "the operation of complete castration" and thereafter live as a woman but warned that surgery would create a "completely sexless creature."[24] The editor stated bluntly to a female-to-male correspondent, "There is no operation whereby a *normal female* can be changed to a normal male, or a normal male into normal female. The operations you have read of were performed on 'hermaphrodites.' "[25] Through the 1940s *Sexology* continued to advise such readers, whom it sometimes called "inverts" or "homosexuals," that doctors performed such surgery for cases of intersexuality only. Nevertheless, it continued to run stories about men who became women and women who became men, and letter writers continued to ask for sex change operations.

Such surgery was not available in the United States. Take the case of Daniel Bass (a pseudonym), born in 1904. Bass knew from an early age of his desire to be a woman. A voracious reader of scientific and popular literature, he understood the possibilities for medical intervention and went in search of what he called "feminizing operations." In Chicago in the 1930s and 1940s, he consulted at least eight doctors, mainly psychiatrists, none of whom would help. He wrote: "I cannot understand why they make no honest effort to help me whereas in literature I see that so many patients have been helped directly. . . . Doctors have given me to understand that such desires as I have are real and basic and that I can not get away from them. Yet, when I ask them to help me realize my desires, they refuse to do so."[26] By the mid-1940s, he had given up temporarily on the quest for surgery to pursue female hormones and self-feminization, which he hoped to accomplish by binding his testicles into his abdomen, where he thought they might atrophy. He did not yet have the word *transsexual*, but neither did he see himself as intersexed or homosexual. He labeled himself a "true invert": "I am a woman in every way with the exception of the body."[27]

Bass identified the dilemma faced by mid-twentieth-century Americans who hoped to change sex. On one side, the press published a stream of sensational stories that hinted at new surgical options for sex transformation. On the other, American doctors refused to offer or recommend treatment unless the patient could lay convincing claim to an intersexed condition. Some American doctors, especially psychiatrists, expressed a chilling hostility to their nonintersexed transgendered patients. Two psychiatrists in Chicago considered one patient's request for surgery as an example of "his senseless, silly and asinine statements commensurate with mental deficiency."[28] Caught in the middle, self-identified inverts such as Daniel Bass were increasingly eager to pursue new medical possibilities but increasingly frustrated and depressed by the resistance they encountered. As Bass put it: "I constantly think of suicide as the only way out."[29] But each new piece of publicity offered another shred of hope.

And the publicity continued. In July 1941, newspapers featured the story of Barbara Richards, who had petitioned the Superior Court of California in order to change her name from Edward and assume the legal status of woman. Reporters pursued the story avidly, presenting it, as did Richards herself, as a case of spontaneous sexual metamorphosis. Richards, then twenty-nine, told the court in Los Angeles that two years prior she had "realized that some vital physiological change was taking place." She noted changes in her beard growth, voice, skin, and figure.

Adhering to prevalent gender stereotype, she also related that she had become "increasingly fond of cooking and housework."[30] In her petition to the court, she described herself as a hermaphrodite whose female characteristics had become predominant, a story strikingly similar to Lili Elbe's. In one later account, though, Richards granted that a medical specialist had found no "organic evidence" of an intersexed condition.[31] Endocrinologist Marcus Graham, who presented her case at a medical conference, attributed the change to hormonal imbalance resulting from childhood illness.[32]

The story remained in the public eye for several months, introduced with such startling headlines as "Prank by Mother Nature Turns Los Angeles Salesman into Woman" and "My Husband is a Woman."[33] Richards and her wife, Lorraine Wilcox Richards, explained to a curious public Barbara's childhood, their courtship and marriage, and the details of the sexual metamorphosis. While Richards portrayed herself as a victim of changes beyond her control, she conceded that she was "thrilled at being a woman." Echoing Lili Elbe, she invoked the imprimatur of nature: "I know now that nature intended me for a girl."[34] As the story unfolded, though, new details suggested that active human intervention might have played a larger role than the stories of passive metamorphosis implied. In October, a newspaper reported that Richards was taking "feminine hormone injections" to "stabilize her condition."[35] In January 1942, another account suggested that Richards anticipated "plastic operations" to make the "outer body conform to . . . inner necessities."[36] (Later, out of the public view, Lorraine Wilcox Richards also changed sex, female-to-male, through surgery and hormones, and the couple remained together as Barbara and Lauren Wilcox.)[37]

As before, the news reports caught the attention of people who hoped to transform their own sexes. Daniel Bass followed the Richards coverage, searching for details that might explain what exactly had transpired. "In July, 1941," he wrote, "the newspapers had a write up about a man turning into a woman through some freak of nature. . . . I am very much frantic over the fact that I have not been able to get the necessary information on this case."[38] Another person wrote directly to Richards, "How did hair disappear from face, and breast grown, this I would really like to have done, and be same as you."[39] Dr. David O. Cauldwell, *Sexology*'s question-and-answer department editor, also noted the response to cases such as Richards's. The occasional "legal alteration," he wrote, "leads to brass check proclamations on a wholesale scale that an individual has been medically metamorphosed from one sex into another." Such reports, he claimed, "make a target of my mailbox. . . . One question predominates. . . . 'Where can I get this done?' "[40]

Faced with such requests, Cauldwell began to publish more widely on the subject of altering sex. In a 1949 *Sexology* article, he chose the phrase "psychopathia transexualis" (playing on Krafft-Ebing's famous nineteenth-century treatise, *Psychopathia Sexualis*) to describe the case of "Earl," who asked Cauldwell "to find a surgeon" who would remove breasts and ovaries, "close the vagina," and construct "an artificial penis."[41] Cauldwell acknowledged that a surgeon could perform such operations, but he refused to endorse them, stating that the artificial penis would have "no material use" and "no more sexual feeling than a fingernail." Furthermore, he considered it "criminal" for a doctor to remove healthy glands and tissues (278).

What distinguished this article from earlier ones was the definition of "psychopathia transexualis" as an independent sexological category. Cauldwell dissociated this request for surgery from cases of intersexuality and glandular disorder. To Cauldwell, a psychiatrist, transsexuals were "products, largely of unfavorable childhood environment" (280). And although Earl was sexually drawn to women, the article also distinguished transsexuals from homosexuals. The caption to an accompanying surreal illustration (of a double-headed man/woman binding his/her breasts) read, "Many individuals have an irresistible desire to have their sex changed surgically. . . . These persons are not necessarily homosexuals" (274). Cauldwell elaborated in a 1950 pamphlet, *Questions and Answers on the Sex Life and Sexual Problems of Trans-Sexuals*. The pamphlet's subheading summarized the key points: "Trans-sexuals are individuals who are physically of one sex and apparently psychologically of the opposite sex. Trans-sexuals include heterosexuals, homosexuals, bisexuals and others. A large element of transvestites have trans-sexual leanings." In this way, Cauldwell separated gender, described as psychological sex, from biological sex and sexuality. Cross-gender identification and the request for surgery were not necessarily linked either to intersexed conditions or to same-sex desire. . . .

AD (After Denmark)

In 1952 and 1953, the coverage of Christine Jorgensen far exceeded any previous reporting on sex changes. Jorgensen rose to the rank of celebrity in the mainstream press as well as in tabloid, pulp, and countercultural publications. Aside from their more extensive dissemination, though, the initial stories on Jorgensen generally replicated the key features found in earlier accounts of sex change. They announced a startling bodily change, referred to surgery but usually failed to specify what it encompassed, and attempted to tie the change of sex to an intersexed condition. Reporters consulted American doctors, most of whom assumed that Jorgensen was a pseudohermaphrodite with internal female gonads but external male characteristics. For one Associated Press story, "Thousands Do Not Know True Sex," a reporter went to the American Medical Association convention and interviewed doctors, who immediately associated sex change surgery with such intersexed conditions.[42] In other reports, journalists found doctors who reported cases of pseudohermaphroditism that they considered similar to Jorgensen's. Urologist Elmer Hess of Erie, Pennsylvania, told of "Hundreds of Boy–Girl Operations."[43] Another doctor claimed to have "performed five operations similar to" Jorgensen's, cases in which "the actual sex had been disguised and was simply released."[44] *Time* magazine soon assessed these reports as the "expert opinion" of doctors who "pooh-poohed the story as anything new . . . far from a medical rarity . . . [with] similar cases in hospitals all over the US right now."[45]

Nonetheless, there was from the beginning a hint that the Jorgensen story might be different. In the first week of publicity, G. B. Lal, the science editor of *American Weekly* (a nationally distributed Sunday newspaper supplement), suggested that Jorgensen "was physically speaking, adequately a male, yet somehow felt the urge to be a woman." Such a situation "would call for drastic alterations – such as no doctor would perform in this country." Lal then referred to endocrinologist Harry Benjamin and cases of "transvestism" but immediately retreated to a discussion of intersexed conditions. "We may assume," Lal wrote, "still without knowing the facts, that Jorgensen was a case of sex confusion – what is known as pseudo-hermaphroditism, in which one's inborn real sex is hidden."[46] As in earlier cases, the muddled reporting attracted transgendered readers who wondered about the journalists' claims. In early December, shortly after the story broke, Louise Lawrence, a full-time male-to-female cross-dresser in San Francisco, wrote to Benjamin: "This case, I think, has received more publicity even than Barbara [Richards Wilcox]'s ten years ago." She could not, though, "make any concrete decision regarding it because there have actually been no absolute facts given." Still, she wondered why Jorgensen would have traveled to Denmark for "a case of hermaphroditism" that "could be handled in this country very easily. . . . From the papers, it seems that such cases are being handled all over the country."[47]

As the publicity continued, the press began to publish new details that gradually undermined the initial reports. In mid-February, *American Weekly* orchestrated Jorgensen's return to New York to coincide with the publication of its exclusive five-part series, Jorgensen's "The Story of My Life," "the only authorized and complete account of the most dramatic transformation of modern times."[48] The series adopted a first-person confessional formula that personalized the coverage and invited readers to sympathize with Jorgensen's ordeal. As *American Weekly* later reported, it saw the story "not as a sensationalized bit of erotica, but as the courageous fight of a desperately unhappy person with the fortitude to overcome a seemingly hopeless obstacle."[49] With the help of a veteran reporter, Jorgensen emphasized the "feminine qualities" she had manifested as the lonely boy George, including a teenage romantic attraction to a male friend.[50] To explain her problem, Jorgensen did not adopt the metaphor, common by the 1960s, of a woman "trapped" in a male body.[51] Instead, she referred to herself as "lost between sexes," a phrase that implied a physical condition as much as a psychological one.[52] As in earlier stories of sex change, she presented her problem as a biological disturbance, in this case a "glandular imbalance," and as a spiritual longing to become "the woman [she] felt sure Nature had intended."[53] But Jorgensen veered away from earlier accounts when she described her doctors, her diagnosis, and what her treatment entailed. In Denmark, endocrinologist Christian Hamburger (a student of Steinach) had agreed to treat her free of charge. Hamburger had reassured her that she was not, as she feared, a homosexual but rather had a "condition called transvestism" and might have female "body chemistry" and female "body cells."[54] Over the course of two years, she had undergone hormone treatments, psychiatric examination, "removal of sex glands," and plastic surgery.[55]

Before and after the series, entrepreneurial journalists realized that Jorgensen attracted readers. She caught the public imagination in part because her story embodied tensions central to the postwar culture. In the atomic age, Jorgensen's surgery posed the question of whether science had indeed triumphed over nature. In an era of overt cultural contests over changing gender roles, the press stories on Jorgensen enabled a public reinscription of what counted as masculine and what counted as feminine. At the same time, though, they also incited the fantasy of boundary transgression, with convincing evidence of how a person might present a masculine persona on one day and a feminine one on another.[56] As homosexuality became increasingly visible and as homophobic reaction intensified, Jorgensen brought the issue into the mainstream news with the confession of her preoperative longing for a male friend. But she also confounded the category as she distinguished a depathologized version of cross-gender identification (in which she loved a man because she understood herself as a heterosexual woman) from a still-pathologized version of same-sex desire. And all along, she demonstrated an affinity for the media that kept her in the public eye. She reinforced her popularity by adopting a feminine style that played on the postwar cult of "blond bombshell" glamor. At least one author has speculated that Jorgensen, despite her expressed surprise, leaked her

own story to the press.[57] Whether she did or not, she eventually courted
the attention to boost her career on the stage.

The unremitting interest allowed a public hashing out of what Jorgensen represented, especially after the *American Weekly* series provided a
more detailed account. Journalists soon began to question Jorgensen's
status as "100 per cent woman."[58] By mid-March, they asserted that
Jorgensen was "neither hermaphroditic nor pseudo-hermaphroditic":
she had "no vestiges of female organs or female reproductive glands."[59]
Following these leads, the *New York Post* ran a six part exposé, "The
Truth about Christine Jorgensen," that was reprinted in other cities.
Based on interviews with Danish doctors, reporter Alvin Davis claimed
that Jorgensen was "physically . . . a normal male" before her treatment,
and now a castrated male, with no added female organs.[60] (Jorgensen
did not undergo vaginoplasty until 1954.) Davis classified Jorgensen as a
transvestite, hinted at homosexuality, and referred to her disrespectfully
with male pronouns. He contrasted American doctors' outrage at what
they saw as mutilating surgery with Danish doctors' advocacy of the
operations. In the wake of the exposé, *Time* declared, "Jorgensen was no
girl at all, only an altered male," and *Newsweek* followed suit.[61] In the
mainstream American press, an intersexed person had a legitimate claim
to female status, but a male-to-female "transvestite," even surgically and
hormonally altered, apparently did not. Jorgensen's doctors in Denmark
seemed to confirm the exposé in the *Journal of the American Medical
Association*, in which they described Jorgensen's case as one of "genuine
transvestism."[62] Pulp magazine sensation followed. *Modern Romances*,
for example, ran "Christine Jorgensen: Is She *Still* a Man?" Another
pulp called the case "Sex-Change Fraud."[63]

Not surprisingly, these reports upset Jorgensen. She had not represented herself as a pseudohermaphrodite, although she clearly preferred
organic explanations that presented her problem as a biological disorder,
often described as a hormonal imbalance. She followed her Danish
doctors who, in accord with Hirschfeld and others, saw cross-gender
identification not as psychopathology but as a somatic condition. Her
emphasis on biological causes helped cleanse her cross-gender identification of the taint of sin or weakness and underscored how deeply she
felt the need for surgery. Mostly, though, she bridled at the insinuation
that she "had perpetrated a hoax" when calling herself a woman, and she
resented the disrespectful tone and "pseudo-scientific commentary" of
some of the reports.[64] Ultimately, the stories did little to damage her
popularity. Shortly after the exposés, a crowd of "more than 2000" met
her at the Los Angeles airport.[65] Journalists continued to follow her
every move – her nightclub tour, her interview with Alfred Kinsey, her
romances with men. While occasional reports portrayed her as an oddity

or a joke, in general the press continued to treat her as a woman and a star.[66] . . .

From the beginning, the Jorgensen story had tremendous impact on its readers. Letter writers flooded Jorgensen with requests for advice. In her 1967 autobiography, Jorgensen referred to "some twenty thousand letters" in the first few months of publicity. Because of her celebrity, letters addressed simply to "Christine Jorgensen, United States of America" reached their destination.[67] Some letters came from admirers or critics, but a "briefcase full" came from people who identified with Jorgensen and expressed "a seemingly genuine desire for alteration of sex."[68] In Denmark, Christian Hamburger also reported hundreds of letters requesting surgery. In less than a year after Jorgensen entered the public domain, Hamburger received "765 letters from 465 patients who appear to have a genuine desire for alteration of sex."[69] Of the 465 letter writers, 180 wrote from the United States. Within the United States, other doctors reported themselves "besieged by would-be castrates pleading for the Danish 'cure.' "[70]

As in the 1930s and 1940s, some readers of the popular press saw themselves in the stories about sex change. With Jorgensen, though, the sheer magnitude of coverage, depth of detail, and public accounting of what the surgery entailed provided a more highly informative how-to story. An unprecedented number of readers identified with Jorgensen, who in turn used her access to the media to encourage them. "The letters that say 'Your story is my story; please help,'" she wrote, "make me willing to bare the secrets of my confused childhood and youth in the hope that they will bring courage, as well as understanding, to others."[71] The exposés that provided the diagnosis of transvestism also helped transgendered readers who were not visibly intersexed to find their own stories within Jorgensen's. In various cities, some of these readers paid homage by collecting press clippings about Jorgensen. Louise Lawrence, for example, compiled a carefully constructed Jorgensen scrapbook, now housed in the archives of the Kinsey Institute. These clipping collections, several of which still exist today, offer tangible testimony to Jorgensen's popularity and the impact of the press on isolated readers.

For some such readers, Jorgensen stood jointly as revelation, role model, and public defender of the cause. One MTF remembered her overwhelming sense of "being a freak." Before reading about Jorgensen, she had understood herself variously (and uncomfortably) as "effeminate, homosexual, a transvestite, a narcissist, a masturbator, . . . a would-be castrate, a potential suicide, and a paranoid." Then:

The Jorgensen case appeared in all the newspapers and changed my life. . . . Suddenly, like a revelation, I knew WHO and WHAT I was – and something COULD BE DONE ABOUT IT! Christ only knows how much time I spent poring over every last item about Christine I could lay my hands on. Not Christ but Christ-ine, I thought, was my Saviour! Now everything about me made perfect sense, I knew what had to be done, and I had some real HOPE of being able to live a normal life *as a woman*! Talk about your shock of recognition! Man, this was IT![72]

For others, the "shock of recognition" provoked more ambivalent feelings. Daniel Bass, who had resigned himself to his inversion, focused on one sentence in one of the stories in the *Chicago Sun-Times*: "They may have the physical form of one sex and think, act and feel like the opposite." "This seems to describe me to the dot," he wrote. He recognized Jorgensen immediately as "a normal man" not a pseudoherm-aphrodite and tortured himself with the thought that he could not gain access to the surgery she had managed to obtain.[73] "When I read about Christine's case," he wrote, "I got terribly upset. I was really very frantic."[74] On the East Coast, Gerard Farber (a pseudonym) had a similar reaction: "Life . . . was bearable, at least it was until the Jorgensen story came out. From then on, I have suffered, because *her* life parallels mine so closely! It is *me* twenty years younger. . . . Her story is my story. . . . I need help, I need relief and I need it soon."[75] On the West Coast, Barbara and Lauren Wilcox were interested in Jorgensen "from the point of view of, 'when and where will the operation be made available to Barbara.' "[76]

In the wake of the Jorgensen story, FTMs were only a small minority of the letter writers seeking surgery. Of the 180 Americans who asked Christian Hamburger about sex change surgery, only thirty-nine sought female-to-male operations. Commentators of the era believed that MTFs far outnumbered FTMs.[77] The lesser response of FTMs might have reflected economic and technological inequities. Those who lived and worked as women were less likely to have the economic means to finance medical intervention, and FTMs in general were less likely to pursue a surgical solution that still could not produce a functioning penis. As Hamburger acknowledged, the media probably had some influence as well.[78] The publicity accorded to Jorgensen helped mark transsexuality as a male-to-female phenomenon, a distinct reversal from the 1930s when stories of female-to-male sex changes predominated in the popular press. In the 1950s, FTMs did not identify automatically with reports of male-to-female surgery. "Joe," for example, did not seek surgery until an MTF acquaintance gave him his "first hint that the sex change possible for males might also have its counterpart for the female."[79] Some FTMs, though, did see themselves immediately in Jorgensen's story. In a later account, Mario Martino described his reaction at the age of fifteen when he first read press accounts on Jorgensen: "Over and over I read the news stories I'd secreted in my room. . . . At last I had hope. *There were people like me.*"[80]

The publicity showered on Jorgensen did not bring direct relief to those who identified with her. Overwhelmed with sex change requests, Danish officials forbade operations for foreigners. Jorgensen and Hamburger began to refer correspondents to endocrinologist Harry Benjamin, who offered paternalist sympathy, hormone treatment, and the diagnosis "transsexual" but not surgery. Benjamin helped a few male-to-female patients arrange operations through urologist Elmer Belt in Los Angeles for a brief period in the 1950s and sent others to Holland and Mexico for surgery. But many avowed transsexuals, especially poorer ones, had no access to surgery. Some "agonize," Benjamin wrote, "between hopefulness and frustration."[81] In this situation, a couple of Benjamin's patients reached the point of desperation and successfully cut off their own testicles, thereby also removing the alleged legal obstacle to additional surgery in the United States.[82] FTMs, for whom surgery was never deemed illegal, seem to have had even fewer surgical options.[83]

Not until the 1960s did American surgeons begin to engage publicly in sex reassignment surgery. Nonetheless, the ground had shifted for transsexuals by the mid-1950s. The mass media reported frequently on sex change surgery. The popular press now acknowledged the European version of sex change surgery for "transvestites," not for intersexed conditions. American doctors began to adopt the new term *transsexual* and to enter into heated debates about the merits of surgical intervention. An American scientific literature on transsexuality, which did not exist before the 1950s, now engaged the older European literature that originated in Germany. Harry Benjamin assumed his role as public spokesperson for transsexuals, and increasing numbers of patients found their way to hormone treatments under his care.

Just as important, Benjamin began to introduce his male-to-female patients to one another. By mid-decade, a small group visited and corresponded with each other, shared information on doctors, traveled together for surgery, compared surgical results, and occasionally lived together. Molly Anderson (a pseudonym) explained: "It makes a cruel problem easier to bear."[84] By 1955, Anderson was corresponding with at least six other MTFs. After her surgery in Holland, she moved from New York to Los Angeles and lived in the Barbizon, a hotel for women, where another postoperative transsexual, also a patient of Benjamin's, already resided. Later, she lived in Phoenix, San Francisco, and Seattle with

SEX CHANGE AND THE POPULAR PRESS

another transsexual friend, who came along when she went to visit her brother and sister for the first time after her surgery. Anderson also maintained a friendship with Louise Lawrence. For at least a few MTFs, then, the Jorgensen story inaugurated a chain of events that began to end their isolation. Transsexual advocacy organizations did not emerge until the 1960s, but in the meantime MTFs had begun to establish social networks that could offer emotional support and foster a sense of community.

These early episodes help complicate our understanding of the history of transsexuality. They move us beyond a history of sexologists, endocrinologists, and surgeons and toward a history of mass media and of transsexuals themselves. In the popular culture and in responses to it, we find early articulations of transsexual identity in the United States. Sensational stories in the popular press opened possibilities for persons who already had various forms of cross-gender identification. The popular tales of sex change attracted certain readers who recognized themselves in and refashioned themselves through the stories they read. In the ongoing process of constructing their own identities, they drew on the popular culture to forge new understandings of what they might become. For some, the various stories might have provided a language – about hermaphroditism, pseudohermaphroditism, spontaneous metamorphosis, hormonal imbalance, or transvestite leanings – that could be used to explain an otherwise inexplicable drive for change of sex. They did not yet have the label *transsexual*, but in the press they found exemplars, however pathologized and sensationalized, who seemed to embody what they knew they wanted for themselves.

This early history helps place the Christine Jorgensen media blitz in historical context. The extent of publicity, the range of the stories, and the depth of detail exceeded earlier accounts, but in some ways the Jorgensen episode replicated on an exponentially magnified scale the earlier process in which some transgendered subjects saw themselves in sensational stories of sex change. In her autobiography, Jorgensen explained her own response to reading a book about hormones. "Throughout the narrative," she wrote, "there was woven a tiny thread of recognition pulled from my own private theories."[85] In turn, Jorgensen provided more than a "thread of recognition" to others who came after her. And because she remained a public figure until her death in 1989, she had an impact on successive generations, especially of MTFs.

What does this history tell us more generally about modern sexual identification? As in recent works in the history of sexuality, it suggests the importance of mass media and reading in the construction and articulation of identities. While the popular press often homogenizes

American culture and pathologizes those on its margins, it might also contribute to what Jennifer Terry has called, in another context, "the conditions whereby marginal subjects apprehend possibilities for expression and self-representation."[86] Readers who had a sense, however vague, of cross-gender identification seem to have read the stories of sex change with a different eye. By our standards today, the stories often adopted stereotypes of gender and sometimes expressed unveiled hostility toward homosexuals and transvestites. Surely these features influenced the responses of readers. Nonetheless, for some, the stories in the press also served as a crucial resource that allowed them to reassess their own senses of self. The mass media were not, of course, the only such resources. By the 1960s, we find direct evidence that some transsexuals learned about sex change surgery in subcultural networks of cross-dressers, butch lesbians, female impersonators, and gay male prostitutes. But earlier in the century, well before American doctors adopted the term *transsexual*, the mass media seem to have played a crucial role in disseminating the concept of surgically altered sex.

Notes

1 "Christine and the News," *Newsweek*, 15 December 1952, 64.
2 I use the term *intersex* as it is generally used today to refer to conditions of sexual ambiguity of the gonads, reproductive system, and/or genitalia. *Intersex* encompasses the older categories of hermaphroditism, in which an individual has gonads of both sexes, and pseudohermaphroditism, in which the gonads of one sex coexist with various forms of genital ambiguity. In using the word *transvestite*, I am adopting the term chosen by European sexologists, especially Magnus Hirschfeld, who recommended sex change surgery for some people with cross-gender identification. Through the mid-twentieth century the term appeared frequently in medical and popular literature to describe nonintersexed people who expressed desires for sex change. I do not intend to suggest that these "transvestites" were only cross-dressers lacking an authentic identification with the so-called other sex. My point is that cross-gender identification and the desire for bodily alteration through hormones and surgery predate the English term *transsexual*.
3 Bernice L. Hausman, *Changing Sex: Transsexualism, Technology, and the Idea of Gender* (Durham, N.C.: Duke University Press, 1995), 119. See also Vern L. Bullough and Bonnie Bullough, *Cross Dressing, Sex, and Gender* (Philadelphia: University of Pennsylvania Press, 1993), chap. 11, and Gordene Olga MacKenzie, *Transgender Nation* (Bowling Green, Ohio: Bowling Green State University Popular Press, 1994), chap. 2. Hausman, the Bulloughs, and MacKenzie all follow this general chronology. They acknowledge individual examples of earlier surgery but neglect the more complicated history of sex change before 1949.

4 Teresa de Lauretis, *The Practice of Love: Lesbian Sexuality and Perverse Desire* (Bloomington: Indiana University Press, 1994), xix.

5 Earl Lind, *Autobiography of an Androgyne* (New York: Medico-Legal Journal, 1918), 196. A note on pronouns: I use masculine pronouns when someone self-presented as male; I use feminine pronouns when someone self-presented as female. In quotations, I have not altered the pronouns used in the original texts.

6 J. Allen Gilbert, "Homo-Sexuality and Its Treatment," *Journal of Nervous and Mental Disease* 52 (October 1920): 297–322, quotation on 321. In Gilbert's article, Hart is referred to as "H." Jonathan Katz's sleuthing uncovered Hart's identity. See Jonathan Katz, ed., *Gay American History: Lesbians and Gay Men in the USA* (New York: Avon, 1976), 419.

7 *Sexual Anomalies and Perversions: a Summary of the Work of the Late Dr Magnus Hirschfeld, Compiled as a Humble Memorial by His Pupils* (London: Francis Aldor, 1944), 179, 218.

8 Magnus Hirschfeld, *Transvestites: The Erotic Drive to Cross Dress* (New York: Prometheus Books, 1991 [1910]), 235.

9 Felix Abraham, "Genitalumwandlung an zwei männlichen Transvestiten," *Zeitschrift für Sexualwissenschaft und Sexualpolitik* 18 (10 September 1931): 223–26, quotation on 223.

10 See Preben Hertoft and Teit Ritzau, *Paradiset er ikke til salg: Trangen til at vaere begge koen* (Paradise is not for sale: the desire to be both sexes) (Denmark: Lindhart og Ringhof, 1984), 82–83.

11 Niels Hoyer, ed., *Man into Woman: An Authentic Record of a Change of Sex* (New York: Dutton, 1933), 178. The claim to hermaphroditism is hard to believe. By the late 1930s, the reigning expert in the field, Hugh Hampton Young, found only twenty medically confirmed cases of hermaphroditism; not one of them had, as the story of Lili Elbe suggested, two ovaries in the pelvis and two testes in the scrotum. See Hugh Hampton Young, *Genital Abnormalities, Hermaphroditism and Related Adrenal Diseases* (Baltimore: Williams and Wilkins, 1937), 200–201.

12 Ibid., xi–xii.

13 "A Man Becomes a Woman," *Sexology*, December 1933, 250–54, quotations on 252, 253–54.

14 "When Science Changed a Man into a Woman!" n.d. [ca. 1934], "Order Book" scrapbook, box 1/1 scrapbooks, Virginia Prince Collection, Special Collections, Oviatt Library, California State University at Northridge, Northridge, Calif. (CSUN), n.p.

15 "Man in Woman's Body," *Your Body*, September 1937, 12–15, quotation on 15.

16 "Boy Prisoner Slowly Changing into a Girl," n.d. [ca. 1936], "Order Book" serapbook, box 1/1 scrapbooks, Virginia Prince Collection, CSUN, n.p.

17 "When Science Changed a Man into a Woman!" 2.

18 Joseph McCabe, *Women Who Become Men: The Development of Unusual Variations, Including Hermaphrodites, Pseudo-Hermaphrodites, and Virgin Birth* (Girard, Kans.: Haldeman-Julius Publications, 1938), 29.

19 "Women into Men by Surgery?" *Sexology*, August 1936, 774–75, quotation on 775.
20 "Dissatisfaction with Sex," *Sexology*, August 1934, 810.
21 "Changing Sex," *Sexology*, December 1937, 265.
22 "They Want to Change Sexes," *Sexology*, September 1937, 32–35, quotation on 32.
23 Ibid.
24 "Dissatisfaction with Sex," 810.
25 "Changing Sex," 265.
26 Daniel Bass [pseud.], "Case History," n.d., TV-BNJ notebook, Harry Benjamin Collection, KI, 7, 9.
27 Daniel Bass [pseud.], letter to Alfred C. Kinsey, 2 November 1945, in ibid.
28 D. M. Olkon and Irene Case Sherman, "Eonism with Added Outstanding Psychopathic Features," *Journal of Nervous and Mental Disease* 99 (January–June 1944): 159–67, quotation on 166.
29 Daniel Bass [pseud.], letter to Alfred C. Kinsey, 20 October 1945, TV-BNJ notebook, Harry Benjamin Collection, KI.
30 "'Man' Asks Legal Right to Assume Woman Status," *Los Angeles Examiner*, 3 July 1941, TV Barbara Richards envelope, no. 82, diary room, KI.
31 Barbara Ann Richards, as told to Bart Lytton, "Nature Betrayed My Body," *Sensation*, November 1941, box 1/4 clippings, Virginia Prince Collection, CSUN, 88.
32 "Young Bride Won't Leave Mate Who's Victim of Sex Change," *Oakland Tribune*, 4 July 1941, "Photo and Return" scrapbook, Louise Lawrence Collection, KI.
33 "Prank by Mother Nature Turns Los Angeles Salesman into Woman," *Los Angeles Times*, 3 July 1941, TV Barbara Richards envelope, no. 82, diary room, KI; Lorraine Wilcox Richards, "My Husband is a Woman," n.d. [ca. 1941], blue notebook, box 1/1 scrapbooks, Virginia Prince Collection, CSUN, n.p.
34 Richards, "Nature Betrayed My Body," 88.
35 "Edward Changes Name to Barbara," *Los Angeles Herald Express*, 10 October 1941, TV Barbara Richards envelope, no. 82, diary room, KI.
36 Myron Weiss, "The Husband Who Changed into a Woman," *Spot*, January 1942, in ibid.
37 On Lauren Wilcox, see Louise Lawrence autobiography, large box, Louise Lawrence Collection, KI, 71–72; Louise Lawrence diary, 28 May, 2 June, 28 June 1944 in ibid.; Louise Lawrence, letter to Alfred C. Kinsey, 21 September 1950, folder: Alfred C. Kinsey, in ibid. See also Karl M. Bowman and Bernice Engle, "Medicolegal Aspects of Transvestism," *American Journal of Psychiatry* 113 (January 1957): 587.
38 Daniel Bass [pseud.], letter to Alfred C. Kinsey, 13 February 1948, TV-BNJ notebook, Harry Benjamin Collection, KI.
39 "A.O.," letter to Barbara Richards, 30 May 1942, TV Barbara Richards envelope, no. 82, diary room, KI.

40 David O. Cauldwell, *Questions and Answers on the Sex Life and Sexual Problems of Trans-Sexuals* (Girard, Kans.: Haldeman-Julius Publications, 1950), 5–6.
41 David O. Cauldwell, "Psychopathia Transexualis," *Sexology*, December 1949, 276, 278.
42 Alton Blakeslee, "Thousands Do Not Know True Sex," New York *Daily News*, 7 December 1952, C6.
43 Jack Geiger, "Sex Surgery Specialist Reports Hundreds of Boy-Girl Operations," n.d. [ca. 2 December 1952], Christine Jorgensen scrapbook, Louise Lawrence Collection, KI, n.p.
44 "Doctor Tells of Five Sex Operations," New York *Daily News*, 18 December 1952, C4.
45 "The Great Transformation," *Time*, 15 December 1952, 59.
46 G.B. Lal, "MD's and Public to Eagerly Follow Christine's Life," *New York Journal-American*, 7 December 1952, 18L.
47 Louise Lawrence, letter to Harry Benjamin, 9 December 1952, TRNSV notebook, Louise Lawrence Collection, KI.
48 Christine Jorgensen, "The Story of My Life," *American Weekly*, pt. 1, 15 February 1953, 5.
49 "How AW Got and Prepared Christine Story," *Editor and Publisher*, 28 March 1953, 62.
50 Jorgensen, "Story of My Life," pt. 1, 9.
51 The concept of a woman "trapped" in a male body is a modernized version of the older "female soul in a male body," which homosexual emancipationist Karl Ulrichs employed in the nineteenth century. Ulrichs used this phrase to describe homosexuality, which he associated with gender inversion, and in the popular culture the phrase continued to connote homosexuality into the mid-twentieth century. See Gert Hekma, " 'A Female Soul in a Male Body': Sexual Inversion as Gender Inversion in Nineteenth-Century Sexology," in *Third Sex, Third Gender: Beyond Sexual Dimorphism in Culture and History*, ed. Gilbert Herdt (New York: Zone Books, 1996), 213–39.
52 Christine Jorgensen, "The Story of My Life," *American Weekly*, pt. 2, 22 February 1953, 4.
53 Ibid., 6; Christine Jorgensen, "The Story of My Life," *American Weekly*, pt. 4, 8 March 1953, 8.
54 Jorgensen, "Story of My Life," pt. 4, 8.
55 Ibid., 9.
56 Susan Stryker, "Transsexuality: The Postmodern Body and as Technology,"*Exposure: The Journal of the Society for Photographic Education* 30 (1995): 38–50.
57 Dallas Denny, "Black Telephones, White Refrigerators: Rethinking Christine Jorgensen," unpublished essay, 1995, 12–13.
58 "Christine Discounted as 100 Pct. Woman by Her Copenhagen Doctor," *San Francisco Call-Bulletin*, 18 February 1953, Christine Jorgensen scrapbook, Louise Lawrence Collection, KI.
59 "AMA Studies Christine – Some US Doctors Say She's Not a Woman Still," *San Francisco Chronicle*, 11 March 1953, Christine Jorgensen scrapbook, Louise Lawrence Collection, KI.

60   Alvin Davis, "The Truth about 'Christine' Jorgensen," *New York Post*, pt. 1, 6 April 1953.

61   "The Case of Christine," *Time*, 20 April 1953, 82; "Boy or Girl?" *Newsweek*, 4 May 1953, 91.

62   Christian Hamburger, Georg Stürup, and E. Dahl-Iversen, "Transvestism: Hormonal, Psychiatric, and Surgical Treatment," *Journal of the American Medical Association* 152 (May 1953): 391–96, quotation on 396.

63   Robert King, "Christine Jorgensen: Is She *Still* a Man?" *Modern Romances*, August 1953, ONE/IGLA, file: Christine Jorgensen; "Sex-Change Fraud," *Exclusive*, February 1955, vertical file: Christine Jorgensen, KI.

64   Christine Jorgensen, *Christine Jorgensen: A Personal Autobiography* (New York: Paul S. Eriksson, 1967), 207, 209.

65   "2000 in L.A. Greet Christine," *Los Angeles Herald and Express*, 7 May 1953, Christine Jorgensen scrapbook, Louise Lawrence Collection, KI.

66   For a different interpretation of the media's treatment of Jorgensen, see David Harley Serlin, "Christine Jorgensen and the Cold War Closet," *Radical History Review* 62 (spring 1995): 137–65.

67   Jorgensen, *Christine Jorgensen*, 189.

68   Ibid., 217.

69   Christian Hamburger, "The Desire for Change of Sex as Shown by Personal Letters from 465 Men and Women," *Acta Endocrinologica* 14 (1953): 361–76, quotation on 363.

70   Davis, "The Truth about 'Christine' Jorgensen," pt. 4, 9 April 1953.

71   Jorgensen, "Story of My Life," pt. 1, 7.

72   R. E. L. Masters, *Sex-Driven People: An Autobiographical Approach to the Problem of the Sex-Dominated Personality* (Los Angeles: Sherbourne, 1966), 229–32.

73   Daniel Bass [pseud.], letter to Alfred C. Kinsey, 8 December 1952, correspondence file: Daniel Bass, KI.

74   Daniel Bass [pseud.], letter to Harry Benjamin, 2 July 1954, TV-BNJ notebook, Harry Benjamin Collection, KI.

75   Gerard Farber [pseud.], letter probably to Harry Benjamin [ca. March 1954], TV-BNJ2 notebook, Harry Benjamin Collection, KI.

76   Louise Lawrence, letter to Harry Benjamin, 6 April 1953, TRNSV notebook, Louise Lawrence Collection, KI.

77   On ratios of MTFs and FTMs, see Ira B. Pauly, "Male Psychosexual Inversion: Transsexualism," *Archives of General Psychiatry* 13 (August 1965): 179. The ratios offered by various doctors in the 1950s and early 1960s ranged from 6:1 to 2:1. They generally reflect the numbers of MTFs and FTMs that doctors encountered in their practices. In general, the published ratios have declined over time, and some today now posit an equal number of FTMs and MTFs. In the 1950s, though, MTFs clearly predominated in the doctors' estimates, and some mid-century sexologists considered transvestism and transsexualism, like fetishism, largely, if not wholly, "male" conditions. Did a smaller proportion of transgendered FTMs go to doctors for surgical intervention? (Mid-century newspaper reports suggest that more FTM cross dre-

ssers lived full-time as men without benefit of surgery or hormones.) Among the broader population of transgendered people, were there in fact more MTFs than FTMs? If so, why? These larger questions remain unanswered.

78   Hamburger, "The Desire for Change of Sex," 364.
79   Harry Benjamin, *The Transsexual Phenomenon* (New York: Julian Press, 1996), 245–46.
80   Mario Martino, with Harriet, *Emergence: A Transsexual Autobiography* (New York: Crown, 1977), 40.
81   Harry Benjamin, "Transvestism and Transsexualism," *International Journal of Sexology* 7 (August 1953): 13.
82   The accounts of surgery are drawn from the collected correspondence in the Harry Benjamin Collection, KI.
83   Pauly, "Male Psychosexual Inversion," 179.
84   Molly Anderson [pseud.], letter to Harry Benjamin, 3 January 1955, TV-BNJ3 note-book, Harry Benjamin Collection, KI.
85   Jorgensen, *Christine Jorgensen*, 79.
86   Jennifer Terry, "Theorizing Deviant Historiography," *Differences: A Journal of Feminist Cultural Studies* 3 (summer 1991): 55–73, quotation on 56.

Documents

In the 1930s, the popular press featured several stories of European women athletes who became men. Zdenka Koubkova, a Czechoslovakian runner, achieved particular prominence when she came to New York. In this 1936 magazine article, how does she describe her transition? According to the article, what does it take to be a man? How might her story have made other readers more optimistic about the possibility of sex change surgery?

Girl Changes into Man

Zdenka Koubkova, the world-famous Czechoslovakian woman athlete, has been operated upon and transformed into a man. The athlete who was once Miss Koubkova is now Mr Koubek.

She – or rather he – is now definitely a man, a young man – for he is only twenty-one – and a handsome one at that. He wears a well-cut suit, white shirt and blue necktie. He works in the same office, at the same job he had previously done as a woman.

Taken from, "Girl Changes into Man," *Your Body* (June 1936), pp. 616–18.

Prague knows Koubek nowadays as a very elegant young gentleman, with broad shoulders, a narrow waist. His soft, wavy blonde hair, beautifully groomed and parted excites admiration wherever he goes.

Koubkova, the woman, held the world record for the 80 and 800 metres. She won the 800 metres at the White City, London, in 1934, knocking six seconds off the record with the time of 2 minutes 12-4/10 seconds. She also held several Czech women's records. But Koubek, the man, has now a new career to make in competition with men.

"I have been a man for a few days," he confided to a *Pearson's Weekly* representative in Prague, "but I never thought it would be so difficult to become one.

"I have given all the dresses I wore as a girl to my sister, but as she is not as broad-shouldered as I am, she will have to alter the clothes to suit her requirements."

Here is the rest of the strange story in Mr Koubek's own words:

"On the other hand, I have had to order several men's suits, hats and other male wear, which was a very troublesome business. I never knew that men's suits cost so much, or that they were so much dearer than women's costumes.

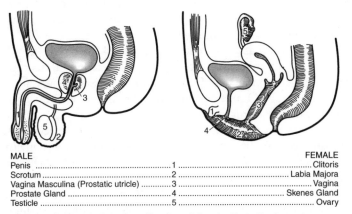

MALE		FEMALE
Penis	1	Clitoris
Scrotum	2	Labia Majora
Vagina Masculina (Prostatic utricle)	3	Vagina
Prostate Gland	4	Skenes Gland
Testicle	5	Ovary

Corresponding parts in the male and female genital organs. Under-development or over-development of some of these parts may make a member of one sex resemble the opposite sex.

"As the official process of becoming a man is a very complicated one, I had to get a permit from the authorities in Prague to have my certificate altered. I engaged a lawyer and gave him my medical certificate to prove I had really become a man.

"Before this could be done, a death certificate had to be issued to me declaring that my life as a *girl* had come to an end. Then I was handed a new birth certificate recording my entrance into the world as a male – at the age of twenty-one!

"My operation was quite simple and did not hurt me at all. There is still a minor one to be performed on me, and when that is over the process will be at an end.

"Now I feel myself positively and completely a man. I first began feeling this strange new sensation last spring. I immediately stopped my training as a girl athlete.

"I have set up various records as a woman athlete. They will remain as athletic records established by a woman until some other girl who can beat them comes along.

"But I shall not discontinue sport for good. I intend to keep it up as a man.

"My record in the 800 metres running championship has remained unbeaten. One day, however, I hope to be able to set up a world record for men over the same distance. But I should like to indulge in other masculine sports as well, and to start my career as a male footballer next spring.

"I am of an age that makes me liable to military service to my country, and very soon I shall be conscripted. I hope they will not make an exception in my case, as I see no reason why I should not serve as a soldier. I can easily picture myself in military tunic, and exercising in the courtyard of the barracks with my hair close-cropped.

"I have often been asked recently," concluded Mr Koubek, "whether I ever thought of marriage. The question is rather a delicate one. Besides, I am so young that I do not think it is necessary for me to answer it just yet, but I may confidently say that later on I may seriously consider the matter of marriage."

Those are Mr Koubek's own words. His appearance, speech, gestures, and attitude towards life are now those of a virile young man. Indeed, he seems more masculine than many a person of his own age who was born a man and has always been accustomed to men's ways.

Anybody coming face to face with Mr Koubek instinctively feels and reacts to the mysterious change that has been wrought in him. It is plainly visible in his face, his every movement. What is more, he is proud of being a man.

Psychopathia Transexualis

Dr D. O. Cauldwell

Dr Cauldwell, staff writer for the popular magazine *Sexology*, presents an ambivalent portrayal of a patient, "Earl." Though Cauldwell's article alerts readers to the possibility of female-to-male transsexual surgery, it simultaneously punctures illusions some readers might harbor about the ease of such procedures. Reading between the lines, what characteristics would Dr Cauldwell expect among candidates for transsexual surgery? How does this article reveal that by mid-century sex change operations were no longer confined exclusively to those born in an intersexed condition?

One of the most unusual sexual deviations is PSYCHOPATHIA TRANSEXUALIS – a pathologic-morbid desire to be a full member of the opposite sex. This desire is so powerful that the individual insists on – often impossible – elaborate surgery that would turn him into a complete woman, or her into a biologically perfect male. Our distinguished author gives us a most interesting case review under his personal observation. The condition, incidentally, is not at all rare. Thousands of cases exist.

Among both sexes are individuals who wish to be members of the sex to which they do not properly belong. Their condition usually arises from a poor hereditary background and a highly unfavorable childhood environment. Proportionately there are more individuals in this category among the well-to-do than among the poor. Poverty and its attendant necessities serve, to an extent, as deterrents. ...

When an individual who is unfavorably affected psychologically determines to live and appear as a member of the sex to which he or she does not belong, such an individual is what may be called a *psychopathic transsexual*. This means, simply, that one is mentally unhealthy and because of this the person desires to live as a member of the opposite sex. ...

Case History – Subject's Background

The subject of this study was born a normal female into a well-known and fairly well-to-do family. On the maternal side there was a physician

Excerpted from Dr. D.O. Cauldwell, "Psychopathia Transexualis," *Sexology* (December 1949), pp. 274–80.

whose son became a lawyer and succeeded in his aspirations to hold political office. The paternal grandfather was prominent in politics and civic affairs. The father was a spoiled son, petted and spoiled by his mother and sisters. He was frequently put in jail for drunkenness and his family were in the habit of sending his wife (the subject's mother) to retrieve him from the clutches of a courtesan in a brothel.

There were two brothers older than the subject. One, the eldest by 13 years, evidently had survived the environment and was on his way up in the world when the subject was born. The other, about 10 years old when the subject was born, was feeble minded, never learned to talk, and while in his 20's was committed to a state institution.

The subject, as a small girl, was impressed with the adulation with which the men of the family were showered. She herself was not, however, neglected. *Frequently she was dressed as a boy.* One of her fondest memories is a picture of herself in boy's attire and smoking a pipe. The picture was made when she was five years old. She was told often what a cute child she was and emphasis was placed on her cuteness as a "boy."

At no time did the subject desire to be a female. Though taught differently, she grew up thinking of herself as a boy. Early she began playing the role of a male on every occasion possible. When she was 18 she discarded feminine attire entirely. She determined that she would live as a male and that nothing could stop her.

Through having written numerous booklets on sexological and related subjects, I have built a large list of correspondents. I first knew of the subject of this study through a letter. After that there was a considerable correspondence. Eventually the subject wrote that she intended to visit relatives near my home and asked if she might see me. I extended an invitation – my wife acquiescing – to visit my home. In doing so I made it clear that my time was devoted entirely to writing and research in science and that I was not now engaged in active medical practice.

I shall call the subject Earl.... During Earl's brief stay with us we agreed that we had never had a more inoffensive guest in our home. She wore levis and regular men's shirts while at home but changed to feminine attire without prompting when we went for drives or away from home. She appeared to be more puzzled than determined to live as a male. She admitted one homosexual "crush." The relationship was one of heart rather than one of sexual indulgence, although she claimed to have had sexual satisfaction through various intimate bodily caresses, regular lip-kissing, and similar caresses. She assured me that no caresses of any kind had been bestowed lower than the breasts. Her friend had professed sexual satisfaction. The relationship was broken up, evidently by the other girl's family and circumstances pertaining to her own family.

Earl's paternal family had contributed to her upkeep and schooling. There was an aged grandmother and there were two aunts – one a maiden, the other a widow.

During her first visit Earl expressed the desire to undergo surgery which would, she hoped, bring about sex transmutation, thus making her a full male.

In cases of doubtful sex – usually cases of pseudo-hermaphroditism – surgical sex transmutation has often occurred. Actually, surgical measures have succeeded by establishing a nearer approach to the sexual integration of the individuals involved. . . .

Earl Determines to Be a Male

Earl was desperate to become a male. I listened as she calmly explained that she wanted me to find a surgeon who would remove her breasts, her ovaries, and close the vagina and then create for her an artificial penis. She would then take male hormones and that she thought would, with masculine attire and occupation, solve her problem. I was amazed at such utter simplicity.

I explained that what she desired was impossible. A surgeon can castrate a woman, of course, and can readily remove her breasts. A cosmetic penis for cosmetic effect only, has been created by successive grafts of bone, skin, etc. But it is of no material use on a female and has no more sexual feeling than a fingernail.[*] BUT – it would be criminal for any surgeon to mutilate a pair of healthy breasts and it would be just as criminal for a surgeon to castrate a woman with no disease of the ovaries or related glands and without a condition wherein castration might be beneficial.

Earl was dissatisfied with my explanation. Why was it criminal if she wanted it done? And why shouldn't a surgeon do anything to one who wanted it done? How unreasonable! Earl also wanted to know if I didn't believe what I advocated in my writings: that an individual has a right to live his or her sex life as he or she chooses provided that in doing so no innocent party is involved. A surgeon evidently did not appear as an innocent individual in her mind.

---

[*]An artifical penis that is biologically effective can be built. *Sexology* has reported a number of such cases. These cases, however, were all male ones. During the war a number of soldiers were mutilated by gun shot, mines, etc., which deprived them, in some cases, completely of their penis. By plastic surgery an artifical organ was then built up on the remaining stump. Such organs, strangely enough, permit the subject to have gratifying marital union and offspring – *Editor*.

Because Earl was of legal age, and the further fact that I felt her confidence should be fully kept, I had not communicated with any members of her family. Indeed, there had been no occasion for me to do so.

Just as I was beginning to learn that in my broad and tolerant consideration of people and of the sexual nature of the human being, I had overlooked the psychopathic traits in Earl, her brother and aunt called. We found them to be well integrated people and of the highest moral and social fiber. Earl's mother, not having heard from her for many days, had phoned that she might possibly be with us. (She had known of Earl's previous visit.)

By now we were beginning to learn something of the real Earl. We knew that her ambitions were to live parasitically. *She would not work.* She believed her grandmother and aunts were fabulously wealthy (which they were not) and that, without earning money herself, she could worm it out of them just as she had long wormed it out of them through deception. . . .

A Summary of Facts

Earl's relatives began learning of her activities during recent months through various sources. Earl had been asked to withdraw from college on account of suspected homosexual activities. A woman who thinks of herself as a physical and psychological male is capable of only pseudo-homosexual activities with either sex. (With males she still would be a sexological female and with females she also would be an imagined or fantasied psychological male.)

There had been but one homosexual affair according to Earl's statements. According to other authentic information, there had been a number of them. In some instances Earl had been, no doubt, the seducer and in others there had been mutuality and hence, no seduction.

She believed that she had a perfect right to go out just as any young male and court a female and, just as young males sometimes seduce young females, she thought that it was within her right to do the same thing.

Against her family Earl had death-wishes. They did not, she contended, know how to use or to enjoy money. She – Earl, did.

She resented being referred to as "her and she." She had been immensely happy when, in a restaurant (in male attire of terrible taste), she had been referred to, or addressed, as "Sir."

If doctors would not do exactly as Earl wanted them to, or could not, then she would continue as she had done and bind her breasts as tightly downward as possible, dress as a male and live as much the role of a male as possible. She already was pleased that she could use men's rest rooms. Frequently she had been referred to as "Sonny." She had shaved in an effort to grow a beard. She kept on her guard in her effort to affect a masculine voice. (It never sounded in the least masculine.) She delighted in ultra-loud (and severely tawdry) socks and ties. The men's shoes she wore were far too large for her and made walking difficult. Her hair was a conventional masculine trim. She was narcissistic and reveled in just seeing and feeling herself (as much when alone as otherwise) in the role of a male. She admired herself probably as much as the original Narcissus.

The expression of death wishes annoyed my wife. We had to do something with our guest. Fortunately we were able to turn her over to her brother and within two or three days he passed her on to her grandmother and aunts. They gave her all of the encouragement possible and bought her a complete feminine wardrobe. She would not don or touch a garment.

Unable to cope with a personality such as Earl's her family gave her a ticket to a city where she assured them she would get a job. They gave her enough cash for an intelligent person to get along on until more can be earned. They did not, any more than I, expect that Earl would get a job or work. They felt as I feel that she would soon run afoul of the law and that the State would find it necessary to make some legal disposition of the case.

That there are better integrated transexuals we are well aware. There are case histories of outstanding social, civic and other leaders who were transexuals. In Arkansas a comparatively few years ago a Dr Brown lived and practiced until in the 60's and was regarded as a male and a highly competent physician. She lived with a sister. In her final illness physicians who treated her discovered her true sex.

In my files I have numerous case histories of males who have lost their genitals through accident and who have become well-integrated transexuals living useful lives and helping, rather than hindering, society. I have other case histories of females who, usually because of an endocrine disturbance or an adrenal tumor, or ovarian disease, have felt that their masculine characteristics were a hindrance to them in careers as females. They have succeeded as well-integrated individuals, living as transexuals. These transexuals are, however, transexuals by affectation only. Evidently, they are all, in their sexual activities, purely autosexual.

Dr Hirschfeld's Pronouncement

In "Sexual History of the World War," by Dr Magnus Hirschfeld, a case is reported of a young woman who sought to enlist in the German Army of the first world war. She made several unsuccessful attempts. Eventually she was examined by Dr Hirschfeld who pronounced her "a psychological male." She was thereupon accepted and became an excellent fighter, serving as a male soldier.

The psychopathic characteristic is manifested not, as may be thought, in actual homosexuality or transvestism, nor yet in the adoption of a male role and career, but in such practices as seduction, parasitism, violation of the social codes in numerous ways, frequently kleptomania and actual thievery, pathological lying, and other criminal and unsocial tendencies. (The adoption of a female role and career applies in the case of actual males.)

Although heredity has a part in producing individuals who may have psychopathic tendencies, such pitiful cases as that described herein are products, largely, of unfavorable childhood environment and overindulgent parents and other near relatives.

Some of the individuals involved, as was the subject of this study, are amenable through a few organizations now in existence. A large enough number of suitable organizations might succeed in rehabilitating the majority of individuals of both sexes falling into the category of *psychopathia transexualis*.

Progress is being made. Within a quarter of a century social education may serve as a preventive in all but a few cases and social organizations may be able to rehabilitate the few who fall by the wayside.

New Sex Switches: Behind the Sensational Headlines Loom Unpleasant Medical Facts

This sensational article from the mid-1950s about "sex changelings" assures readers that sex change operations are primarily for those born with anomalous genitalia as opposed to transvestites "whose trouble is psychological." At the same time it suggests the influence of Christine Jorgensen's famous transition on men seeking surgery, and it even goes so far as to imply that sex change could spontaneously occur to unsuspecting "normal" people.

Next to the recurrent hydrogen bomb headlines, reports of sex changes are becoming the most persistently startling world news. Latest US case in point is Charles – Charlotte McLeod. But similar stories crop up elsewhere: In Teheran, surgeons help a 16-year-old girl turn into a

Excerpted from "New Sex Switches: Behind the Sensational Headlines Loom Unpleasant Medical Facts," *People Today* (May 5, 1954), pp. 15–17.

soldier of the Shah. In London, a dashing fighter pilot and father re-adjusts to life as a sophisticated lady. In Naples, 13-year-old Adrianna becomes Andrew.

What are the facts behind these tales? How can a man turn into a woman, and to whom does this happen? PEOPLE TODAY herewith presents the latest authentic information about these secrecy-shrouded phenomena.

News reports generally avoid medical details and precise classification of sex changelings, but each case falls into one of the following groups.

Most Sex Changelings Keep It Quiet

True hermaphrodites. Normally, sex glands turn male or female early in the life of the embryo. But sometimes there's a mixup; the child develops some of the genital organs of both sexes. Before treatment, doctors weigh which sex predominates as well as the patient's upbringing. Then hormone doses and surgery make as good a man or woman as possible. (Two Turkish sisters, both borderline cases physically, were about to be operated on to make them more male when doctors found feminine mental traits predominated. Treatment therefore accentuated the feminine.)

Pseudohermaphrodites. In some cases, sex glands may be properly male or female but the genital organs are so deformed that a boy is mistaken for a girl. An operation can make him more manly. But should the switch seem too difficult psychologically, surgeons try to fashion the best woman possible under the circumstances. In other cases, a disease of the adrenal glands causes excess output of male hormones in girls. This fosters male characteristics (deep voice, beard, etc.). Cortisone treatment may help.

> Most drastic new sex change: Car racer and RAF pilot Bob Cowell, 36. After 10-year marriage (and 2 daughters) he developed female characteristics. Doctors say "Roberta" now is a woman.

Transvestites. These are physically normal men and women whose trouble is psychological: an obscure but difficult-to-resist urge to dress in clothes of the opposite sex. It is more common in men than women. Transvestism, many psychiatrists believe, may be an unwholesome extension of "dressing-up" games of childhood, spurred by latent homosexuality. Like many mental disturbances, transvestism sometimes may be cured. Since Christine's case, some men keep asking doctors to make them women. Such tampering is forbidden by law everywhere in the US.

I Want to Become a Woman

In response to a letter writer who sought a surgical transformation from male to female, the editor of *Sexology* declared in no uncertain terms that such an operation was impossible and that the writer should discuss his problem with his parents and seek psychological help. How does the author of the letter try to convince the editor that he deserves to be turned into a woman? From his perspective, what makes him a good candidate for sex reassignment surgery?

Editor, SEXOLOGY:

I am 18 years old. I want to become a woman – that is my greatest desire. In the past three years my body has changed considerably. I had much body hair; now I have very little. I have a well-shaped body and small shoulders.

I cannot tell my mother and stepfather that I want to be a woman. I cannot consult a doctor because he would tell my parents, and then I would never find happiness. I want to be like Christine Jorgensen and Roberta Cowell (recent publicized cases of "sex change" operations). But must I wait the rest of my life to be happy? I do not want to wait until I am thirty or forty to become a woman. I can now do – and love to do – everything a woman can do – cook, sew, iron. I made some of my school shirts.

My feelings toward men become stronger every day. I walk and talk like a woman. I have stopped going out with girls. Information will be appreciated.

Mr B. D. A., Louisiana

Answer:

The sex of a human being cannot be changed. Your condition is a mental, not a physical one. You need competent medical advice and treatment. There is a chance that, at your age, you may find a way to achieve personality adjustment and happiness. Your sex cannot be changed.

In the cases referred to by you, there was in one instance evidently a *pseudohermaphroditic* condition. The surgeons sought to make whatever

---

Taken from a Letter to the Editor, *Sexology* (April 1956), pp. 594–5.

corrections it was possible to make. But the sex of the person was not changed. The person using the title "Miss," and permitted to pass as a female is only a male deprived of the male genital organ and the testicles. The individual is in no sense a woman, but simply a castrated male, in a medical sense.

Confide in your parents. Show them this letter and explain what you wrote us. Then discuss your problem with a doctor.

– *Editor*

Further Reading

Bornstein, Kate. *Gender Outlaw: Men, Women, and the Rest of Us*. New York: Routledge, 1993.

Califia, Pat. *Sex Changes: the Politics of Transgenderism*. San Francisco: Cleis Press, 1997.

Epstein, Julia, and Kristina Straub (eds). *Body Guards: the Cultural Politics of Gender Ambiguity*. New York: Routledge, 1993.

Halberstam, Judith. *Female Masculinity*. Durham, NC: Duke University Press, 1998.

Harley Serlin, David. "Christine Jorgensen and the Cold War closet." *Radical History Review*, 62 (1995), 136–65.

Hausman, Bernice. *Changing Sex: Transsexualism, Technology, and the Idea of Gender*. Durham, NC: Duke University Press, 1995.

Kessler, Suzanne J. *Lessons from the Intersexed*. New Brunswick, NJ: Rutgers University Press, 1990.

Prosser, Jay. *Second Skins: the Body Narratives of Transsexuality*. New York: Columbia University Press, 1998.

Stryker, Susan (ed.), *GLQ: a Journal of Lesbian and Gay Studies. The Transgender Issue*. Durham, NC : Duke University Press, 1998.

Index

abortion committees, therapeutic 241
abortions 6, 111, 154, 360–1
  criminalization of 229
  state and 227–49
Abraham, Felix 379–80
abuse, physical *see* violence
abuse, sexual
  hysteria and 176–7, 178, 179
  toward Native American women 55–6
  see also rape
Adair, James 59–60
Adams, John Quincy 120
Adler, Herman 184
Adler, Polly 319
adoption 344, 359, 371
adultery
  between white women and black
    men 145–68
  English and Native American perspectives
    on 60
advertisements: feminine hygiene 250,
    251–2, 258–9, 260–1, 262–3, 269–73
aggression, male 171, 174–5, 176–7
  hysteria and 180–2
  self-mutilation and 195
American Medical Association
    (AMA) 229, 234, 245
  and birth control 252, 263, 278
Anderson, Molly 391–2
animals *see* bestiality
appearance: Native American women
    50–2, 70–1
Arnold, Ervin 218–19, 220, 221
Asians: interracial marriages 283–309
assaults *see* abuse; violence
athletes: sex changes 381–2

B-girls 321, 326 n
Bannon, Ann: *Beebo Brinker* 339–41
Barrett, George 334–5
bars, lesbian 324–5
Bartram, William 51–2, 57
Bass, Daniel 383, 384, 390
beauty: of Native American women 50–2
Benjamin, Harry 378, 391
Bernard, John 58
Bernstein, Rose 357, 368–71
bestiality: in early New England 13–16,
    19–44
biological differences: race 293–5, 296–7
birth control 6–7, 374
  attitudes of American women to 274–8
  black unwed mothers 344–52, 359
  black women on welfare 6–7
  Noyes on 111–12
  unwed mothers 342–3
  see also contraceptives; male continence
birth control clinics 255–6, 278, 348
birth control movement 255
black fertility rates 373
black men: sex with white women 145–68
black women
  abortions 232
  birth control 6–7
  unwed mothers 342–3, 344–52, 359
blackface: Onderdonk trial 116, 120,
    130–1, 143–4
Boston 321–2
boundaries
  female heterosexual 312–13
  homosexual 198–221
  social 2–3
Bourne divorce case 145–68

Bradford, William 21
  on bestiality 35–7
bundling: New Hampshire 72–87
butch–femme 323
Byrd, William 49–50, 52, 53, 54, 56

Canup, John 16
Caprio, Frank 318, 320, 326–30
Carden, Maren Lockwood 103–4
Carolinas 68–9
Castiglioni, Luigi 51
categories, sexual 2
Catholics 4
Cauldwell, David O. 378, 384–5, 401–5
celibacy: Oneida community 101
Charcot, Jean-Martin 172–3
Chauncey, George Jr 198–216
Chicago 229, 232, 234
child-killing 111
children
  Anglo-Indian 58–9, 68–9
  of interracial marriages 292, 293, 308–9
  of unwed mothers 344
  of white women and black men 147,
    148–9, 151–2, 155, 161–3, 164–5,
    166–7, 168
  see also juvenile delinquency
children's aid programs 346
Children's Bureau 351, 358–9
Chinese: interracial marriages 283–303,
    306–9
class, social
  homosexuality and 207
  interracial marriage and 290
  lesbians and 317
  unmarried motherhood and 369
  see also middle; working
Cohen, Patricia Cline 116–34
coitus reservatus see male continence
college girls: sexual revolution 352, 353,
    354, 355, 360, 365, 369
colonists: sexual relationships with Native
    American women 45–71
color issue
  Native Americans 50–1
  see also black; white
Comstock Act (1873) 6, 250, 254
Comstock, Anthony 254, 266 n
condoms 6, 252, 262
consumerism: contraceptives and 250–79
contraceptives 6–7, 360–1
  consumerism and 250–79
  white unwed mothers and 355–6
  see also specific methods, e.g. condoms
Conyers, John 347
Cook County 229, 232
courts, law
  bestiality and sodomy in early New
    England 13–44
  dying declarations 233–4

courtship behaviour: New Hampshire
    72–87
Crawley, David 56
crime
  bestiality and sodomy as 13–44
  black illegitimacy and 346
  lesbians and 320–1, 334–5, 338
  by women 315–16, 328
criticism, mutual: Oneida community 102,
    105
cultures
  colonists and Native Americans 45, 47,
    50, 58–60
  ideas of sex 7
  interracial marriages and 283–309
  lesbian 322–5
  white, for black unwed mothers 350

Dale, Sir Thomas 64
Danforth, Samuel 19
Davenport, John 22
Davis, Alvin 388
Davis, J. Merle 289, 291
Davis, Katherine B. 312
Davis, Madeline 323
deaths
  abortion 231–2
  see also dying declarations
de Kock, Paul (Thompson) 129–30
de Lauretis, Teresa 378
demons, sexual: lesbians as 312, 316–19
department stores: feminine hygiene
    250–1, 262–3, 265
deviance 2–3
  bestiality and sodomy in early New
    England 13–44
  lesbianism and prostitution as 310–41
diaphragms: birth control 256–7
diplomacy: Native American 54
Diron D'Artaguiette, Bernard 50–1, 53
diseases, sexually transmitted: colonists and
    Native Americans 46–7, 48, 55
divorce
  adultery between white women and black
    men 145–68
  "common law" 81
doctors see medical profession
documents see source documents
double sexual standards 8 n, 231
  in early New England 28, 30
douches: birth control 258, 269–73
dress: modesty and 87–8
Dutton, Julia M. 185
dying declarations 227–45, 247–8

"Earl": sex change 401–5
Easton, Abel 101
Eaton, Theophilus 17
education: population crisis and 373
Elbe, Lili 380

Electra complex theory   329
Elliott, Bernard   59
Ellis, Havelock   101, 378
Emerson, L. E.   187 n
   case of Miss A.   189–96
   hysteria cases   175–87
engagements, marriage: New
      Hampshire   78–9
entertainment: New Hampshire   79, 80
eonism   378
   see also transvestism
Episcopalian Church, American
   homosexual identities and
      boundaries   198–9, 206–10, 214
   Onderdonk trial   119, 121, 131–2
eroticism: race and   295, 297
eugenics   94
evangelism: Onderdonk trial and   118
exchange culture: Native American   53, 54
exoticism: race and   295

faggots   198
fairies   198, 201–2, 213
family planning   see birth control
Farber, Gerard   390
Federal Trade Commission (FTC)   259
femininity: stereotypes of   120
Findlay, Morgan   345
foaming tablets: birth control   257
Fogarty, Robert   104
Fong, Emma   see Kuno
Fong, Walter   284–5, 295–6, 299–300, 302
Food and Drug Administration (FDA)   259
forts: Native American women in   54–5,
      70–1
Foster, Lawrence   93–115
Foucault, Michel   5, 212
France: bestiality   31
Frank, Louis   237
free love
   Noyes on   109–10
   Oneida community   93–108
Freedman, Estelle   318
Freemasonry   82, 83
Freud, Sigmund   172, 173, 178
frolics: New Hampshire   75, 79
Furniss, Henry Dawson   236

gaze, male: at Native American women   51–2
gender
   abortion and   231
   contraception and   253
   Onderdonk trial and   116, 118, 119–20,
      125
   religious groups and   132
   transsexualism and   376–409
   see also men; women
gender roles: homosexual   198, 201–3,
      204–5, 213–14
Germany: sex change   379–80

Gilbert, J. Allen   379
Gilman, Sander   314–15
girling: in New Hampshire   72–87
Godbeer, Richard   19, 45–64
government   see state
Graham, Marcus   384
Granger, Thomas: bestiality   21, 36
Green, Arthur   206, 207
Greenberg, Sarah K.   271–3
grey markets: birth control   252–3
Gruening, Ernest   345, 360–1
Gruening hearings   345–7, 360–1, 371–4
guilt: lesbians   329
Guttmacher, Alan   361
Guyot, Jules   367

Hacker, Andrew   356
Haire, Norman   380
Hall, Radclyffe: Well of Loneliness, The   319
Hamburger, Christian   387, 389, 390, 391
harassment, sexual: Onderdonk trial
      116–44
Hauser, Philip M.   346, 371–4
health
   birth control douches   258–9
   lesbians   329
   see also diseases
hermaphroditism   378, 382, 392
   defined   407
   see also pseudohermaphroditism
Hess, Elmer   386
heterosexuality
   boundaries of female   312–13
   regulation of male   231
   withdrawal from   176, 179–80, 182–3
Higginson, Francis   18
Himes, Norman   101
Hirschfeld, Magnus   378, 379, 393 n,
      405–6
history: sex and sexuality   1–2
Hoadly, Charles J.: on bestiality   37–44
Hodes, Martha   145–64
hog reeve, office of   79
Hogg, Thomas: bestiality   22, 42–4
Holmes, Rudolph   234
homes: feminine hygiene sales   263
homogenization, race   284, 287, 297
homosexuality   5, 378, 387
   identities and boundaries   198–221
   invention of   210–11
   medical model of   211–13, 224–6
   two stereotypes of   221–3
   see also lesbians; sodomy
homosociality
   boundaries with homosexuality   200,
      207, 208–9, 214
   defined   215 n
Hoyer, Niels: Man into Woman   380
Hudson, E. M.   211–12, 217–18, 219, 220,
      221

Hunter, Robert Jr 51, 54–5, 70–1
husbands, homosexual 198, 202, 213
hybridization 287
hygiene: Native American women 50–1
hygiene, feminine: contraception and 250–73
hypersexuality 171, 173–4, 187
hysteria 171–96

identities
    cross-gender 376–409
    homosexual 5, 198–226
ignorance, sexual 183–4
Illinois 229
Indians see Native Americans
infanticide 154
intersexuality 5, 377–8, 380–1, 382
    defined 393 n
inverts 201, 211, 212, 378
    surgery for 379

Jackson, Andrew 120
James, William 96
Japanese 296
    interracial marriages 304–5
Jefferson, Thomas 3–4
Jews 4
Johnson, Lyndon 346
Jorgensen, Christine 376, 377, 392, 406
    sex change 385–91
juvenile delinquency 352, 372–3

Kennedy, Elizabeth Lapovsky 323
Kent, Samuel 206–10, 219
Kentaro, Kaneko 304
Kinsey, Alfred 107n, 312, 388
Koubkova, Zdenka: sex change 398–400
Krafft-Ebing, Richard von 190, 221, 385
Kuno, Emma Fong 283, 285–6, 287, 295–6, 299–300, 304
    marriages 301–3
Kuno, Yoshi 285, 301

labor force: population and 372
Lal, G. B. 386
language and discourse: of sex 4–5
Lawrence, Louise 386, 389, 392
laws and legislation 5–6
    birth control 252, 256, 263–4, 278
    sexual crime 321
Lawson, John 46–7, 53, 54, 55, 58, 68–9
Leclerc, George Louis 3–4
Lee, Rose Hum 293–5, 297
lesbians 225
    attitudes to 310–41
    characteristics 331–2
libido: lesbians 329
Lind, Earl 379

literature, English
    influence in New Hampshire 80
    see also pulp fiction
loneliness: of lesbians 330–1
love, romantic
    of lesbians 313–14
    see also free love
Lunbeck, Elizabeth 171–89

McCabe, Joseph: Women Who Become Men 381–2
McClatchy, Valentine 288
McKinnon, Jane 330–3
magazines, women's: birth control 258–9, 260
mail: feminine hygiene sales 263, 265
male continence 93, 99–102
    Noyes on 110–14
Malthus, Thomas 111, 112
markers, sexual 2
marriage
    abortions and 239–40
    Anglo-Indian 47–50, 56–60, 64–8
    black unwed mothers 350
    complex 93, 94, 97, 102–3, 105
    discouragement of 112
    interracial 283–309
    Noyes on 109–10
Martino, Mario 391
Maryland 246–7
masculinity: stereotypes of 120
masculinization, psychic: of women 327
masochism 195
    and lesbians 328
masturbation
    early New England 17
    by lesbians 328
    Oneida community 101
    self-mutilation and 189, 191, 194
Mather, Cotton 23, 26–7
May, Elaine Tyler 313
media see magazines; press
medical model: homosexuality 211–13, 224–6
medical profession
    abortions and 227–49
    birth control 258–9, 261, 263–4
men
    abortions and 231, 239–40, 241–2
    bestiality and sodomy 13–44
    European, sexual relationships with Native American women 45–71
    homosexual identities and boundaries 198–226
    lesbians and 331
    stereotypes of masculinity 120
    see also black
menstruation
    ignorance of 183
    self-mutilation and 191, 192, 194

Meyerowitz, Joanne   376–98
middle-class behavior: for black unwed
   mothers   350
middle classes
   female non-marital sex   357
   lesbians   317, 319
   unwed mothers   353–5, 369
migration, internal   373
Miller, G. P.   236
Mills, James   334–8
missionaries
   Native Americans and   55
   religious conversion   292
morality
   enforcement of codes   82–3
   lesbians   331
   sexual freedom and   365–7
Mormons   4, 132
mothers
   teenage   358, 364–7, 370
   unwed, race and   342–64
   unwed, stereotyping of   368–71
   see also pregnancies
Murrin, John   13–35

Nairne, Thomas   53
Native American women: sexual
   relationships with European men
   45–71
Native Americans   3
   and bestiality   24–5
Navy, US: homosexual identities and
   boundaries   198–221
Nestle, Joan   314, 323
Netherlands: bestiality   15–16
neurosis: lesbians   328–9
New England
   bestiality and sodomy in early   13–44
   women as easily beguiled   3
   see also New Hampshire
New Hampshire: girling in   72–90
New Haven   37–44
New York   334–8
Newport, Rhode Island: homosexuality
   in   196–221
newspapers   see press
Niederland, William G.   327
Nowakowski, Richard B.   348
Noyes, John Humphrey
   Berean, The   98–9
   free love   93–115
   life of   96–8
   on male continence   110–14
   religious beliefs   97–9
Noyes, Pierrepont   101, 105
Noyes, Theodore   101
nymphomania   225

Oakley, Ernest P.   237
Oaks, Robert F.   16

obesity   194–5
objectivity: of social science   288
officials, colonial: sexual abuse of Native
   American women and   55–6
Onderdonk, Benjamin T.: trial of   116–44
Onderdonk, Henry   120–1
Oneida community   132
   features of members   103–5
   sexuality in   93–115
Orientals
   interracial marriages   283–309
   in pulp fiction   288–9
Osborne, Nathaniel   59
Owen, Robert Dale   111–12
Oxford Movement   119, 121

pain: self-mutilation and   193–4
Palmer, Rachel Lynn   269–73
pamphlets: Onderdonk trial   119, 126, 128
Pancaro, Louis   273
Park, Robert   288
   interracial marriage questionnaire
   289–91, 306–9
Parkes, Charles H.   234, 235–6, 237
passing   377
passivity, female   174–5
patriarchy: divorce and   151–2, 156, 161–2
Penn, Donna   310–26
Perry, James De Wolfe   219
pessaries: birth control   254
pills, birth control   6, 344, 349, 356
Plymouth colony   35–7
Pocahontas: marriage to Rolfe   48–9, 64–8
pogues   201–2, 204, 213
police
   lesbians and   334–5
   sexual crime   321
political economy: contraception and   250–
   79
population bomb: sexual revolution
   and   342–74
poverty   352
   abortions and   231–2
power, male: over women   128–9, 132
pregnancies
   ignorance of   183
   premarital in New England   72, 74, 78–9
   teen   364–7
press
   abortions   230, 237–8, 240
   birth control   258–9
   Onderdonk trial   117–18, 118–19, 126,
   128
   Oneida community   95
   transsexualism in   376–409
   see also magazines
Pringle, Henry F.   274–8
programs, comprehensive: for black unwed
   mothers   349–52, 358
prostitutes   310

lesbians and 314–16, 319–22
  military 222–3
  Native American women 46
pseudohermaphroditism 386, 392, 403, 409
  defined 407
psychiatry
  homosexuality 315–16
  hysteria 171–97
  sexual crime 321
pulp fiction
  lesbian 310, 324–5, 339–40
  Orientals in 288–9
punishment
  of abortions 230–1, 238, 239–40, 241–2
  of bestiality and sodomy in early New England 13–44
Puritans: susceptibility of women 3
purity: women as forces for 3

queers 198, 201–3, 204, 212
questionnaire: interracial marriage 289–91, 306–9

race 3–4
  birth control and 6–7
  interracial marriages 283–309
  interracial sex 145–68
  Onderdonk trial and 116, 120, 130–1
  unwed mothers and 342–64
race suicide 6
rape
  by black men 155–6
  Native Americans and 3, 60
Reagan, Leslie 227–45
red-light districts 321–2
Reeves, Harrison 264
Reis, Elizabeth 1–9
religion 4
  see also Episcopalian church; missionaries
relinquishment: for black unwed mothers 350, 351
reverse discourse 212
Richards, Barbara 383–4
Richards, Lorraine 384
Richmond, James 122, 124, 126–7, 129, 141–2
rights: to birth control 347
Robinson, William 237
Rohmer, Sax 288–9, 298n
Rolfe, John: marriage to Pocahontas 48–9, 64–8
Roosevelt, Franklin D. 200, 217, 218, 220, 221
Rubin, Gayle 314
Rudderow, Jane 123
  and Onderdonk trial 134–42
Ryan, William A. 345

sadism 195

sado-masochism 367
sailors: homosexual identities and boundaries 198–221
Salem witchcraft trials 26, 29
sales representatives, female
  birth control kits 278–9
  feminine hygiene 263, 265
Sanger, Abner: diary 72–85
Sanger, Margaret 248, 250, 255, 264, 274
satyriasis 225
seduction
  abortions and 237–8
  notion of 171, 172–3, 174–5, 176, 180, 182, 185
  self-mutilation 189–96
sex and sexuality
  attitudes to 3
  boundaries 2–3
  changing history of 1–2
  government policies 5–7
  language and discourse of 4–5
  race and 3–4
  see also specific terms, e.g. homosexuality
Sexology 380, 381, 382, 384, 385, 401, 408
sexual revolution: population bomb and 342–75
Shakers 97–8, 100, 112, 132
Simon, Carleton 318, 320
slaves, black male: adultery with white women 145–68
social meetings: New Hampshire 79, 80
social scientists
  homosexuality 315–16
  interracial marriages 285–97
social workers: stereotyping of unwed mothers 368–71
sodomy: in early New England 13–19, 30–1
soldiers
  homosexuality and 222–3
  Native American women and 54–5, 70–1
Solinger, Rickie 342–64
source documents 8
  abortion 245–9
  adultery between white women and black men 164–8
  bestiality in early New England 35–44
  contraception 269–79
  courtship behavior in New Hampshire 85–90
  free love 108–15
  homosexual identities and boundaries 216–26
  hysteria 189–96
  interracial marriages 299–309
  Onderdonk trial 134–44
  population bomb and sexual revolution 364–74

source documents (*cont.*)
  sexual relationships of European men with Native American women 64–71
  sexualized women 326–41
  transsexualism 398–409
Southard, Elmer 184–5, 186
space: lesbians and prostitutes 321–2
"Spectator": Onderdonk trial 128
Spencer, George: bestiality 21–2, 37–42
Spencer, Herbert 304–5
spiritualism 97–8
Stabler, Lois K. 72–85
standards, double *see* double
Stanford, Leland 287
state
  abortions and 227–49
  sexual abuse of Native Americans and 55–6
  sexuality and 5–7
"staying with": in New Hampshire 72–85
Steinach, Eugen 379, 380
sterilization 6
Stevenson, Edward 215n, 221–3
Stiles, Henry 74
  bundling 85–7
stirpiculture 94
Stofer, Webster 259
subjectivity, sexual 173
suppositories, vaginal 257, 259
Sweden: bestiality 15, 16

Tarnowsky, Pauline 315
tax: birth control and 346
Taylor, Valerie: *Return to Lesbos* 324–5
teenage mothers 358, 364–7, 370
Terry, Jennifer 393
Thomas, Robert David 103
Thompson, Clara 316–17
Thompson, George (Paul de Kock) 129–30
Thompson, Roger 16
Tobriner, Walter 360
Tone, Andrea 250–68
trade: homosexual 198, 203–4, 213
traders
  Anglo-Indian 59
  sexual relationships with Native American women 45, 46–7, 55–8, 68–9
trading girls: Native American 54
transsexualism 5
  popular press and 376–409
transvestism 378, 379, 385, 388, 389, 391, 392
  defined 393 n, 407–8
truth: hysteria and 178
two-way artists 201–2
Tydings, Joseph 347

Ulrich, Laurel Thatcher 3, 72–85
underdeveloped areas: birth control in 374

unemployment 372
unhappiness: unwed female sexuality and 356–7, 366–7
urban geography: lesbians and prostitutes 321–2

Vincent, Clark 357
violence
  by black men 158–9, 161
  divorce and 145, 150–1, 156–7, 157–8, 165, 166
  homosexuality and 205
  lack of towards black adulterers 159–61
  racial 288
voyeurism: of travelers 51–2

Walk on the Wild Side (film) 311, 312
Ward, Edward: *Female Policy Detected* 80, 89–90
Wayman, John 235–6
Webster School project 348, 350
white women
  adultery with black men 145–68
  sexual revolution and 352–7
  unwed mothers 342, 344, 357
Whitman, Howard 365–7
whore curtains 82–3
Wilcox, Barbara and Lauren 390
Willis, Nathaniel P. 127, 129
Winthrop, John 17, 20–1, 29
witchcraft 15–16
  in early New England 13, 25–6, 27–8, 29
women
  abortions 227–49
  bestiality and 15, 30
  as contraceptive consumers 250–79
  crimes committed by 328
  as forces of purity 3
  hysteria 171–97
  inconstancy of 89–90
  in Oneida community 101
  psychic masculinization of 327
  sexualized 310–41
  stereotypes of femininity 120
  susceptibility of 3
  Victorian 4
  witchcraft 13, 25–6, 29–30
  see also black women; lesbians; mothers; Native American; white women
working class
  abortions 229, 230, 231–2, 241
  feminine hygiene sales 263
  lesbians 317
  regulation of male heterosexuality 231
Worthington, George C. 246–7

yellow peril 288–9, 290
Young, Leontine 350, 351
Yu, Henry 283–98